Also by John K. Roth

AFTER-WORDS: Post-Holocaust Struggles with Forgiveness, Reconciliation, Justice (*edited with David Patterson*)

AMERICAN DIVERSITY, AMERICAN IDENTITY (*ed.*)

THE AMERICAN DREAM (*with Robert H. Fossum*)

AMERICAN DREAMS: Meditations on Life in the United States

AMERICAN DREAMS AND HOLOCAUST QUESTIONS

AMERICAN GROUND: Vistas, Visions & Revisions (*edited with Robert H. Fossum*)

THE AMERICAN RELIGIOUS EXPERIENCE: The Roots, Trends and the Future of American Theology (*with Frederick Sontag*)

APPROACHES TO AUSCHWITZ: The Holocaust and Its Legacy (*with Richard L. Rubenstein*)

A CONSUMING FIRE: Encounters with Elie Wiesel and the Holocaust

THE DEATH OF GOD MOVEMENT AND THE HOLOCAUST: Radical Theology Encounters the Shoah (*edited with Stephen R. Haynes*)

THE DEFENSE OF GOD (*edited with Frederick Sontag*)

DIFFERENT VOICES: Women and the Holocaust (*edited with Carol Rittner*)

ENCYCLOPEDIA OF SOCIAL ISSUES (*ed.*)

ETHICS AFTER THE HOLOCAUST: Perspectives, Critiques, and Responses (*ed.*)

ETHICS: An Annotated Bibliography

ETHICS: Ready Reference (*ed.*)

FIRE IN THE ASHES: God, Evil, and the Holocaust (*edited with David Patterson*)

FREEDOM AND THE MORAL LIFE: The Ethics of William James

FROM THE UNTHINKABLE TO THE UNAVOIDABLE: American Christian and Jewish Scholars Encounter the Holocaust (*edited with Carol Rittner*)

GENOCIDE IN RWANDA: Complicity of the Churches? (*edited with Carol Rittner and Wendy Whitworth*)

GOD AND AMERICA'S FUTURE (*with Frederick Sontag*)

"GOOD NEWS" AFTER AUSCHWITZ? Christian Faith within a Post-Holocaust World (*edited with Carol Rittner*)

GRAY ZONES: Ambiguity and Compromise in the Holocaust and Its Aftermath (*edited with Jonathan Petropoulos*)

HOLOCAUST: Religious and Philosophical Implications (*edited with Michael Berenbaum*)

THE HOLOCAUST CHRONICLE (*with Marilyn Harran et*

HOLOCAUST POLITICS

INSPIRING TEACHING (*ed.*)

D1251495

MEMORY OFFENDED: The Auschwitz Convent Controversy (*edited with Carol Rittner*)

IDEOLOGY AND AMERICAN EXPERIENCE: Essays on Theory and Practice in the United States (*edited with Robert C. Whittemore*)

THE MORAL EQUIVALENT OF WAR AND OTHER ESSAYS (*ed.*)

THE MORAL PHILOSOPHY OF WILLIAM JAMES (*ed.*)

POPE PIUS XII AND THE HOLOCAUST (*edited with Carol Rittner*)

THE PHILOSOPHY OF JOSIAH ROYCE (*ed.*)

PRIVATE NEEDS, PUBLIC SELVES: Talk about Religion in America

THE POLITICS OF LATIN AMERICAN LIBERATION THEOLOGY: The Challenge to U.S. Public Policy (*edited with Richard L. Rubenstein*)

PROBLEMS OF THE PHILOSOPHY OF RELIGION

THE QUESTIONS OF PHILOSOPHY (*with Frederick Sontag*)

REMEMBERING FOR THE FUTURE: The Holocaust in an Age of Genocide (*edited with Elisabeth Maxwell*)

RIGHTS, JUSTICE, AND COMMUNITY (*edited with Creighton Peden*)

WILL GENOCIDE EVER END? (*edited with Carol Rittner and James M. Smith*)

WORLD PHILOSOPHERS AND THEIR WORKS (*ed.*)

Genocide and Human Rights

A Philosophical Guide

Edited by

John K. Roth

First published in 2005 by
PALGRAVE MACMILLAN
Houndmills, Basingstoke, Hampshire RG21 6XS and
175 Fifth Avenue, New York, N.Y. 10010
Companies and representatives throughout the world.

PALGRAVE MACMILLAN is the global academic imprint of the Palgrave
Macmillan division of St. Martin's Press, LLC and of Palgrave Macmillan Ltd.
Macmillan® is a registered trademark in the United States, United Kingdom
and other countries. Palgrave is a registered trademark in the European
Union and other countries.

ISBN-13: 978–1–4039–3547–2 hardback
ISBN-10: 1–4039–3547–5 hardback
ISBN-13: 978–1–4039–3548–9 paperback
ISBN-10: 1–4039–3548–3 paperback

This book is printed on paper suitable for recycling and made from fully
managed and sustained forest sources.

A catalogue record for this book is available from the British Library.

Library of Congress Cataloging-in-Publication Data

Genocide and human rights : a philosophical guide / edited and introduced
by John K. Roth.
p. cm.
Includes bibliographical references and index.
ISBN 1–4039–3547–5 (cloth) — ISBN 1–4039–3548–3 (paper)
1. Genocide – Philosophy. 2. Human rights – Philosophy. 3. Philosophy –
Social aspects. I. Roth, John K.
HV6322.7.G453 2005
179.7—dc22   2005046340

10 9 8 7 6 5 4 3 2 1
14 13 12 11 10 09 08 07 06 05

Transferred to digital printing in 2006

To Carol Rittner, William S. Levine, and in memory of Ina Levine

> *Then God said, "Let there be light"; and there was light.*
> *And God saw that the light was good ...*
>
> Genesis 1:3–4

What have you done?
Listen; your brother's blood is crying out to me from the ground!
Genesis 4:10

Contents

List of Contributors

Robert Bernasconi is the Moss Professor of Philosophy at the University of Memphis. He is the author of two books on Martin Heidegger, *Heidegger in Question: The Art of Existing* and *The Question of Language in Heidegger's History of Being*, and numerous articles on various aspects of continental philosophy, social and political philosophy, and race theory. With Simon Critchley, he co-edited *Rereading Levinas* and *The Cambridge Companion to Levinas*. He also co-edited *The Idea of Race* with Tommy Lott. In addition, Bernasconi edits a reprint series with Thoemmes Press, which contains books on race from the eighteenth and nineteenth centuries.

Claudia Card is the Emma Goldman Professor of Philosophy at the University of Wisconsin, where she has teaching affiliations with Jewish Studies, Women's Studies, and Environmental Studies. She is the author of *The Atrocity Paradigm: A Theory of Evil; The Unnatural Lottery: Character and Moral Luck*; and *Lesbian Choices*. Card is also the editor of *The Cambridge Companion to Beauvoir; On Feminist Ethics and Politics; Adventures in Lesbian Philosophy*; and *Feminist Ethics*. During 2002–07, she is a Senior Fellow at the Institute for Research in the Humanities at the University of Wisconsin, where she is writing a book on responding to atrocities.

Stephen T. Davis is the Russell K. Pitzer Professor of Philosophy at Claremont McKenna College, where he has taught since 1970 and frequently chaired the Department of Philosophy and Religious Studies. He is the author of many articles on the philosophy of religion and has written or edited thirteen books, including: *Risen Indeed: Making Sense of the Resurrection; God, Reason, and Theistic Proofs*; and *Encountering Evil: Live Options in Theodicy*.

Emmanuel C. Eze is Associate Professor of Philosophy at DePaul University, where he teaches critical race theory and modern African and European philosophy. He is the author of *Achieving Our Humanity: The Idea of the Postracial Future* and the editor of several other volumes, including: *Race and the Enlightenment: A Reader* and *Postcolonial African Philosophy: A Critical Reader*. His scholarly articles have appeared in journals such as the *Journal of the History of Ideas, Soundings*, and *Philosophia Africana*.

Raimond Gaita is Professor of Moral Philosophy at King's College London, University of London, and Professor of Philosophy at Australian Catholic University. His main research interests and publications have been in moral philosophy, political philosophy, the philosophy of psychology, and on the nature and place of reason. Gaita's most important books include: *Good and*

Evil: An Absolute Conception and *A Common Humanity: Thinking about Love and Truth and Justice.*

Norman Geras is Professor Emeritus in the Department of Government at the University of Manchester, England. His research interests include Marxism, the moral philosophy of socialism, normative political theory, aspects of so-called anti-foundationalist thought, the Holocaust, and crimes against humanity. He is the author of many articles, and his books include *Marx and Human Nature: Refutation of a Legend; Solidarity in the Conversation of Humankind: The Ungroundable Liberalism of Richard Rorty*; and *The Contract of Mutual Indifference: Political Philosophy after the Holocaust.*

Roger S. Gottlieb is Professor of Philosophy at Worcester Polytechnic Institute. The author or editor of twelve books, his most recent works include *Joining Hands: Politics and Religion Together for Social Change; A Spirituality of Resistance: Finding a Peaceful Heart and Protecting the Earth; This Sacred Earth: Religion, Nature, Environment*; and *Liberating Faith: Religious Voices for Justice, Peace, and Ecological Wisdom.* He is "Reading Spirit" columnist for *Tikkun* magazine and book review editor for *Social Theory and Practice* and *Capitalism, Nature, Socialism: A Journal of Socialist Ecology.*

Leonard Grob, co-founder of the biennial Pastora Goldner Holocaust Symposium, is Professor of Philosophy and coordinator of philosophical studies at Fairleigh Dickinson University, where he has also directed the university's Core Curriculum Program. His publications include numerous articles on the philosophy of dialogue and the thought of Martin Buber and Emmanuel Levinas. Grob is the co-editor of *Education for Peace: Testimonies from World Religions* and *Women's and Men's Liberation: Testimonies of Spirit*, two anthologies based on Buber's philosophy. His essays have appeared in books such as *Ethics after the Holocaust; After-Words: Post-Holocaust Struggles with Forgiveness, Reconciliation, Justice*, and *Fire in the Ashes: God, Evil, and the Holocaust.*

Patrick Hayden is Lecturer in Political Theory at Victoria University of Wellington, New Zealand. His research interests include international ethics and human rights, theories of war and peace, democratic theory, and the application of social and political theory to the study of international relations and global politics. Hayden's books include *Cosmopolitan Global Politics; America's War on Terror; John Rawls: Towards a Just World Order*; and *The Philosophy of Human Rights.* His scholarly articles have appeared in *Human Rights Review, Theoria*, and *International Studies.*

David H. Jones is Professor of Philosophy Emeritus at the College of William and Mary. He has taught and published primarily in the areas of ethics, social and political philosophy, and the philosophy of law. He continues to teach a course on genocide and is the author of *Moral Responsibility in the*

Holocaust. His current research interest is in the prevention of genocide and crimes against humanity.

Berel Lang is Professor of Humanities at Trinity College (Connecticut). He has also held appointments as Professor of Philosophy at the University of Colorado and the State University of New York at Albany; Visiting Professor at Wesleyan University and the Hebrew University, Jerusalem. Lang is the author or editor of more than twenty books, including: *Act and Idea in the Nazi Genocide; The Future of the Holocaust; Heidegger's Silence;* and *Post-Holocaust: Interpretation, Misinterpretation, and the Claims of History*. His research and writing have been supported by fellowships from the National Endowment for the Humanities, the American Council of Learned Societies, the Remarque Institute, and the United States Holocaust Memorial Museum.

Sander H. Lee is Professor of Philosophy at Keene State College, where he has chaired the Department of Communication, Journalism, and Philosophy. In addition to serving on the editorial boards of *The Journal of Value Inquiry* and *Film and Philosophy*, Lee has served as president of the Society for the Philosophic Study of Genocide and the Holocaust. Lee is the author of *Eighteen Woody Allen Films Analyzed: Anguish, God, and Existentialism* and *Woody Allen's Angst: Philosophical Commentaries on His Serious Films* as well as numerous scholarly essays on issues in aesthetics, ethics, social philosophy, and the Holocaust.

Michael Mack holds the Sesqui Fellowship, 2004–07, at the University of Sydney, Australia. Along with his many scholarly articles, he is the author of two books: *Anthropology as Memory: Elias Canetti's and Franz Baermann Steiner's Responses to the Shoah* and the award-winning *German Idealism and the Jew: The Inner Anti-Semitism of Philosophy and German Jewish Responses*, which uncovers the deep roots of antisemitism in the German philosophical tradition.

Michael L. Morgan is the Chancellor's Professor of Philosophy and Jewish Studies at Indiana University, Bloomington. His research interests include the history of philosophy, especially ancient philosophy and modern philosophy, the philosophy of religion, Jewish philosophy, and the Holocaust. The recipient of several teaching awards, he is also the author of numerous books, including *Platonic Piety; Dilemmas in Modern Jewish Thought; Interim Judaism;* and *Beyond Auschwitz*. In addition, he has edited *Classics of Moral and Political Theory; The Jewish Thought of Emil Fackenheim: A Reader; A Holocaust Anthology; The Collected Works of Spinoza;* and he has translated and edited, with Paul Franks, *Franz Rosenzweig: Philosophical and Theological Writings*. Morgan is currently working on a book about Emmanuel Levinas.

David Patterson holds the Bornblum Chair of Excellence in Judaic Studies at the University of Memphis, where he directs the university's Bornblum Judaic Studies Program. The author of scores of journal articles and book chapters, he has also published more than fifteen books, including: *The Shriek of Silence: A Phenomenology of the Holocaust Novel; Sun Turned to Darkness: Memory and Recovery in the Holocaust Memoir; Along the Edge of Annihilation: The Collapse and Recovery of Life in the Holocaust Diary*, which received the 1999 Koret Jewish Book Award for Jewish Thought and Philosophy; and *Hebrew Language and Jewish Thought*. Patterson is also the translator and editor of the English edition of *The Complete Black Book of Russian Jewry* and co-editor of the *Encyclopedia of Holocaust Literature*.

D. Z. Phillips is the Danforth Professor of Philosophy of Religion at Claremont Graduate University and Professor of Philosophy Emeritus and Rush Rhees Professor Emeritus, University of Wales, Swansea. Much of his research concentrates on issues pertaining to evil. He is the author or editor of more than forty books, including *The Concept of Prayer; Faith and Philosophical Enquiry; Death and Immortality; Religion Without Explanation; Faith after Foundationalism; Interventions in Ethics; Wittgenstein and Religion; Introducing Philosophy: The Challenge of Skepticism; Philosophy's Cool Place; Religion and Friendly Fire;* and *The Problem of Evil and the Problem of God*.

John K. Roth, the editor of *Genocide and Human Rights: A Philosophical Guide*, is the Edward J. Sexton Professor of Philosophy and the Director of the Center for the Study of the Holocaust, Genocide, and Human Rights at Claremont McKenna College, where he has taught since 1966. In addition to service on the United States Holocaust Memorial Council and on the editorial board for *Holocaust and Genocide Studies*, he has published hundreds of articles and reviews and more than forty books, including, most recently, *Will Genocide Ever End?; After-Words: Post-Holocaust Struggles with Forgiveness, Reconciliation, and Justice; Genocide in Rwanda: Complicity of the Churches?;* and a revised edition of *Approaches to Auschwitz: The Holocaust and Its Legacy*. Roth has been Visiting Professor of Holocaust Studies at the University of Haifa, Israel, and his Holocaust-related research appointments have included a 2001 Koerner Visiting Fellowship at the Oxford Centre for Hebrew and Jewish Studies in England as well as a 2004–05 appointment as the Ina Levine Invitational Scholar at the Center for Advanced Holocaust Studies, United States Holocaust Memorial Museum, Washington, DC. In 1988, Roth was named U.S. National Professor of the Year by the Council for Advancement and Support of Education and the Carnegie Foundation for the Advancement of Teaching.

Paul C. Santilli is Professor of Philosophy at Siena College. An award-winning teacher, he is particularly interested in law and jurisprudence, the moral imagination, ancient philosophy, film studies, and business ethics. His numerous papers and articles, including "On the Strange Relation between Heroic Socrates and Wise Achilles," concentrate on these fields. Presently he is writing a book about the late Polish film maker, Krysytof Kieślowski.

Thomas W. Simon is Professor of Philosophy at Illinois State University. Trained in law as well as in philosophy, he focuses his research and teaching on political philosophy, ethics, philosophy of law, genocide, and human rights. He has served as a consultant on human rights issues for the United Nations and the American Bar Association. The author of *Democracy and Social Injustice: Law, Politics, and Philosophy*, Simon is also the editor of *Law's Philosophies: An Anthology of Contemporary Comparative Jurisprudence*. In addition, he is the founder and co-editor of *Injustice Studies*, an electronic refereed journal.

Frederick E. Sontag is the Robert C. Denison Professor of Philosophy at Pomona College, where he has taught since 1952. He has held visiting appointments at the College of Sant' Anselmo in Rome, the Center for the Study of Japanese Religions in Kyoto, and as a Fulbright scholar in India and East Asia. His research interests have focused on issues about evil. Sontag is the author or editor of some thirty books, including: *The God of Evil: An Argument from the Existence of the Devil; What Can God Do?; Emotion: Its Role in Understanding and Decision; 2001: A Spiritual Odyssey*; and *The Mysterious Presence*.

Colin Tatz, a specialist in race politics, founded and directed the Centre for Australian Indigenous Studies at Monash University in Melbourne from 1964 to 1970. He then founded the Political Science Department at the University of New England, where he taught from 1971 to 1982. He took the chair of Politics at Macquarie University, Sydney, in 1982, where, in 1993, he established and directed the Center for Comparative Genocide Studies. The Center has since relocated to the Shalom Institute, University of New South Wales, as the Australian Institute for Holocaust and Genocide Studies. Tatz is the author or editor of eighteen books, including: *Race Politics in Australia: Aborigines, Politics, and Law; Genocide Perspectives II: Essays on the Holocaust and Genocide*; and *With Intent to Destroy: Reflecting on Genocide*.

Laurence M. Thomas is Professor of Philosophy and Political Science at the Maxwell School in Syracuse University, where his scholarly interests focus on ethics, political theory, and social philosophy. He is the author of many articles, and his books include *Living Morally: A Psychology of Moral Character; Sexual Orientation and Human Rights*; and *Vessels of Evil: American Slavery and the Holocaust*. Currently he is at work on a book about family and children, and he is editing a volume on social philosophy.

James R. Watson is Professor of Philosophy at Loyola University, New Orleans. He is President of the Society for the Philosophic Study of Genocide and the Holocaust (SPSGH). He has published numerous essays and books on philosophy and the Holocaust, including *Between Auschwitz and Tradition: Postmodern Reflections on the Task of Thinking* and a co-edited volume entitled *Contemporary Portrayals of Auschwitz and Genocide*. His current book project is

Metaphysics and the Degradation of Labor: Philosophy's Repression and Its Uninvited Return in Psychoanalysis.

Paul Woodruff is the Darrell K. Royal Professor in Ethics and American Society and a Distinguished Teaching Professor in the Department of Philosophy at the University of Texas, Austin. The author of influential articles on Socrates and Plato, he has also published critical editions of Plato's *Hippias Major, Ion*, and (with Alexander Nehamas) *Symposium* and *Phaedrus*. He has also written on topics in aesthetics and ethics. His recent publications include: *First Democracy: The Challenge of an Ancient Idea; Reverence: Renewing a Forgotten Virtue; Thucydides on Justice, Power, and Human Nature*; and contributions to *Essays on the Philosophy of Socrates; The Cambridge Companion to Early Greek Philosophy*; and *Facing Evil*. Woodruff has been Visiting Professor at the University of Pittsburgh and has twice directed seminars on ancient philosophy for the National Endowment for the Humanities.

Edith Wyschogrod is the J. Newton Rayzor Professor of Philosophy Emerita at Rice University. Her books include *An Ethics of Remembering: History; Heterology and the Nameless Others; Saints and Postmodernism: Revisioning Moral Philosophy; Spirit in Ashes: Hegel, Heidegger, and Man-Made Mass Death;* and a second edition of *Emmanuel Levinas: The Problem of Ethical Metaphysics*. Her current work is centered on philosophical responses to biological and psychological theories of altruism.

Prologue: Philosophy and Genocide

John K. Roth

On 2 October 1938, less than a year before Nazi Germany's invasion of Poland began the Second World War, the British philosopher R. G. Collingwood put the finishing touches on his autobiography. Its observations underscored his belief that "the chief business of twentieth-century philosophy is to reckon with twentieth-century history."[1] Collingwood's primary intention was to urge philosophers to pay more attention to the discipline of history—its methods, consciousness of context, and attention to detail—so that philosophy might be less abstract, more aware of its own historical heritage, and directed more fully to inquiry about problems raised by historical thinking (e.g., how is historical knowledge possible?). At least by implication, this call for an up-to-date philosophy of history meant that philosophy's responsibilities included paying close attention to twentieth-century events as well.

Unfortunately, twentieth-century philosophy did relatively little to meet Collingwood's expectations. Whether philosophy will do better in the twenty-first century remains to be seen. Illustrative evidence for those latter judgments can be found by noting that the late December 1985 meeting of the American Philosophical Association's eastern division featured a symposium on the Holocaust. An article in the prestigious *Journal of Philosophy* provided a prelude for that event. Authored by Emil Fackenheim—with a brief commentary by Berel Lang—the essay was entitled "The Holocaust and Philosophy." As if echoing Collingwood in a minor key, it began with a lament: "Philosophers," wrote Fackenheim, "have all but ignored the Holocaust."[2] Twenty years on, Fackenheim's indictment is less devastating than it was in 1985. Philosophical attention to the Holocaust has grown and continues to do so.[3] To that degree, philosophers have not ignored genocide entirely, for the Holocaust is a paradigmatic instance of that crime, but when one thinks of philosophy and genocide before and after the Holocaust, a version of Fackenheim's judgment remains valid. To a large extent, philosophers have ignored and still overlook genocide. This book responds to that fact by indicating how philosophers can correct that unfortunate situation and why it is important for them to do so.

While the Holocaust raged in the 1940s, Raphael Lemkin, a Jewish lawyer who fled from Poland, coined the term *genocide*. Initially defining it to mean "the destruction of a nation or of an ethnic group," he observed that the term denoted "an old practice in its modern development," for the plight of the

Jews under Hitler was not a simple repetition of past historical patterns.[4] From the slaughter of Armenians in 1915 and the Holocaust to the Rwandan genocide in 1994 and, arguably, what has happened in the Darfur region of Sudan as this book went to press in 2005, genocide's modern development has taken an immense toll on human life and civilization in the twentieth century and now in the twenty-first as well. It is no exaggeration to say that we live and philosophy exists in an age of genocide.

Writing in the December 2002 issue of the *International Social Science Journal*, the Holocaust historian Omer Bartov argued persuasively that the modern development of genocidal catastrophes can neither be understood nor prevented in the future unless one grasps that "scholars have played a prominent role in preparing the mindset, providing the rationale, and supplying the know-how and personnel for the implementation of state-directed mass violence."[5] Philosophers and philosophy are not exempt from Bartov's indictment. The passage from Genesis that serves as this book's epigraph—"What have you done? Listen; your brother's blood is crying out to me from the ground!"—accuses and indicts, provokes and challenges them as well. For even though the history of philosophy shows that philosophers have done much to advance human rights and to defend human equality, the same history shows that genocide has been aided and abetted by philosophies that have advanced racism and antisemitism and by philosophers who have encouraged—inadvertently if not explicitly—political regimes and cultural agendas that turned genocidal. When the topics are philosophy, genocide, and human rights, the ones highlighted in this volume, the problem is not simply that philosophy has ignored genocide and that philosophers need to pay more attention to that crime. The problem is also that philosophy and philosophers must bear more responsibility for genocide than they have usually admitted. In our post-Holocaust world, nations, businesses, churches, and professions such as medicine and law have been called to account for their complicity or for bystanding while Nazi Germany committed genocide against the European Jews.[6] To some extent philosophers have been held accountable too, but when the history of genocide is taken into account, philosophy and philosophers have not been sufficiently self-critical about their bystanding and complicity. The contributors to this book hope that their work will do its part to reverse that deficiency.

Generally speaking, philosophy and philosophers have high estimates of themselves. Philosophy depicts itself as occupying high moral ground. Philosophers tend to see themselves—I include myself in these judgments—as extending a tradition that serves free inquiry, truth, goodness, beauty, and justice. But philosophy and philosophers have darker sides, and they have been less than forthcoming about them, especially with regard to genocide. As the history of the Holocaust shows, and other genocides follow similar patterns in this regard, the expertise and cooperation, or at least the passivity, of virtually every professional group within a state and a society—teachers, professors, scholars, and philosophers among them—are needed for genocide to take place. Philosophy and genocide exist in the same world. Unfortunately, their relationship has not always been one of opposition. Philosophy's association with genocide does not leave philosophy unscathed and untarnished. For the sake of humanity's well-being and philosophy's integrity, philosophers should come to grips with that reality.

Although philosophy often highlights characteristics shared by all persons, its history contains theories that have negatively emphasized differences—religious, cultural, national, and racial.[7] Such theories have encouraged senses of hierarchy, superiority, and "us versus them" thinking in which genocidal policies may assert themselves, especially in times of economic and political stress. If philosophy is divided between views upholding that all people are equal members of humanity and others stressing differences between groups as fundamental, how can philosophy contribute to stopping or mitigating genocide?

Philosophy is critical inquiry about reality, knowledge, and ethics. It explores what is, what can be known, and what ought to be. Germany has produced some of the world's greatest philosophers, including Immanuel Kant, G. W. F. Hegel, Friedrich Nietzsche, and Martin Heidegger. Regrettably, neither in Germany nor elsewhere have philosophers done all that they could to protest genocide and other crimes against humanity. On the contrary, as Heidegger's case reveals, philosophy can expedite genocide.[8]

Hitler rose to power on 30 January 1933. Three months later Heidegger joined the Nazi Party. On 27 May 1933, he was inaugurated as rector of Freiburg University. Although Nazi book burnings and the dismissal of many so-called non-Aryan academics had taken place a few weeks earlier, Heidegger's inaugural address advocated stepping-into-line with the times, which was at least an implicit embrace of Nazi antisemitism. He also stressed that the Führer's leadership was crucial for Germany's future. In February 1934, Heidegger resigned his rectorship, but he never became an obstacle to the Third Reich's genocidal policies.

Living for more than thirty years after Hitler's defeat in 1945, Heidegger neither explicitly repudiated National Socialism nor said much about the Holocaust. When he did speak about that genocide, his remarks were, at best, problematic. Debate continues about his philosophy as well as about the man himself. In *Being and Time* and other major works, Heidegger analyzed human existence, its significance within Being itself, and the need for people to take responsibility within their particular times and places. Arguably, his philosophy includes a fundamental flaw: The abstract, even obscure, quality of its reflection on Being and "authentic" action precludes a clear ethic that speaks explicitly against racism, antisemitism, genocide, and crimes against humanity.

Typically, philosophers have not given genocide priority as a field of study. However, as this book helps to show, there are some twenty-first century signs that a welcome change may be taking place. A small but growing number of philosophers are focusing on evil.[9] More than that, they recognize that the paradigmatic cases of evil are not only produced by human beings but also are to be found in the Holocaust and other genocides. This emphasis also drives home the importance of human rights, but with a difference that Bartov captures when he argues that it cannot be credible to philosophize "by applying, as if nothing had happened, the same old humanistic and rational concepts that were so profoundly undermined" by genocidal catastrophes.[10] Genocide puts profound challenges before philosophers. Much depends on how contemporary philosophy meets them. This book shows that even the few philosophers who are grappling with genocide are still in the relatively early stages of that work. While providing a glimpse of the work about philosophy and genocide that is under way early in the twenty-first century, this book also makes clear that much remains for philosophers to do in this field.

Genocide and Human Rights: A Philosophical Guide tries to show what philosophers can do when they begin to meet the challenges that genocide produces for philosophy. The chapters in Part I of this book consider how genocide does or should affect philosophy. More specifically, these essays illustrate how a confrontation with genocide affects philosophy's traditional understandings of evil and suffering. Part II contains reflections about philosophy's involvement in genocide. They consider the degree to which philosophy can be found innocent or guilty of complicity in genocide. In Part III the philosophers take up genocide's challenge to philosophy, assessing, in particular, how philosophy needs to focus and change if it is to confront genocide effectively. Finally, Part IV considers how genocide makes it particularly important for philosophy to develop credible views about universal human rights, to criticize forms of thought and action that undermine such rights, and to defend institutions that support international justice.

The contemporary philosophers who have contributed chapters to this book represent diverse traditions.[11] They employ different philosophical approaches as well. Some have worked on the Holocaust and other genocides for some time; others have come to these concerns more recently. While the writers may disagree, as philosophers are often likely to do, and some have written at greater length than others, as philosophers are also likely to do, they share the commitment that philosophy cannot be what it ought to be unless it confronts genocide directly, honestly, and boldly. As the book's editor, as one who nudged and pressed the book's contributors, I express thanks to each and all for accepting the challenges of working with me and of writing about philosophy, genocide, and human rights.

Many other good people also labored long and hard to bring this book into existence. At Palgrave Macmillan, it was Jennifer Nelson who initially encouraged me to develop this book. Her successor, Luciana O'Flaherty, focused the project further, and then Daniel Bunyard managed the final editorial and production process, which was also facilitated efficiently by Vidhya Jayaprakash. I am indebted to each of them for professional expertise and friendly support. At Claremont McKenna College, my research assistant, Garrett Hodge, helped on correspondence, documentation, preparation of the manuscript, and countless other details pertaining to the book. Both he and the book's superb copyeditor, Sarojini Solomon, also deserve my thanks.

Major parts of my writing and editing for the book were done at the United States Holocaust Memorial Museum in Washington, DC, where I was privileged to spend the 2004–05 academic year as the Ina Levine Scholar in Residence at the Center for Advanced Holocaust Studies. I am immensely grateful to Paul Shapiro, the Center's dedicated director, and to his superb staff. They make the Center a wonderful place to work. My thanks also go to Sara J. Bloomfield, the director of the United States Holocaust Memorial Museum, and to the Center's scholars, visiting and permanent, who did so much to create a stimulating, challenging, and congenial exchange of ideas and research. I am particularly grateful to Lisa Yavnai and Lisa Zaid, who coordinated the Visiting Fellows Program in 2004–05, and to Ellen Blalock, who helped to organize lectures and seminars where the book's ideas were discussed. Jerry Fowler, who works persistently and creatively on genocide prevention as he guides the Museum's influential Committee on Conscience, also gave encouragement and guidance when they were much needed.

This book is dedicated to Carol Rittner, William S. Levine, and to the memory of his late wife, Ina Levine. An accomplished scholar of the Holocaust and genocide, Carol has been my close friend and colleague for almost twenty years. We have worked together on numerous books, including two on genocide. As much as any other person, she has urged me to think about philosophy in relation to genocide. Such work has been difficult and unsettling but very much worthwhile. Bill Levine's thoughtful generosity endowed the Ina Levine Scholar in Residence Fellowship, which it was my honor to hold at the Center for Advanced Holocaust Studies in 2004–05. As the epigraph attached to my dedication indicates, when I think of these special people, I am reminded that they are part of the light and their light is good. My debts to the three of them are far more than I can ever repay, but if this book can help philosophy and philosophers to make a contribution to the prevention of genocide, then I hope that result will pay tribute to the memory of Ina Levine and grant both Bill Levine and Carol Rittner at least some of the encouragement that work on these pages has given me.

Notes

1. R. G. Collingwood, *An Autobiography* (Oxford: Oxford University Press, 1939), p. 79. The opening paragraphs of this prologue draw on my book *Holocaust Politics* (Louisville, KY: Westminster John Knox Press, 2001), pp. 27–32.
2. Emil Fackenheim, "The Holocaust and Philosophy," *The Journal of Philosophy* 82 (October 1985), p. 505.
3. In addition to Fackenheim, Lang, and most of the contributors to this volume, a representative list of philosophers whose work has been centrally concerned with the Holocaust would include the following: Theodor W. Adorno, Giorgio Agamben, Jean Améry, Robert Antelme, Hannah Arendt, Alain Badiou, Richard Bernstein, Maurice Blanchot, Martin Buber, Albert Camus, Jacques Derrida, Jonathan Glover, Philip Hallie, Karl Jaspers, Hans Jonas, Steven Katz, Sarah Kofman, Emmanuel Levinas, Jean-François Lyotard, Avishai Margalit, André Mineau, Susan Neiman, Gillian Rose, and Alan Rosenbaum. Depending on how broadly the term *philosopher* is understood, the list above could be augmented by very important thinkers such as Charlotte Delbo, Primo Levi, Richard Rubenstein, and Elie Wiesel.
4. Raphael Lemkin, *Axis Rule in Occupied Europe: Laws of Occupation, Analysis of Government, Proposals for Redress* (Washington, DC: Carnegie Endowment for International Peace, 1944), p. 79.
5. Omer Bartov, "Extreme Violence and the Scholarly Community," *International Social Science Journal* 54 (December 2002): 509.
6. For more on this topic, see Richard L. Rubenstein and John K. Roth, *Approaches to Auschwitz: The Holocaust and Its Legacy*, rev. edn (Louisville, KY: Westminster John Knox Press, 2003).
7. Several of the following paragraphs, including my discussion of Heidegger, are adapted from my contributions to Dinah L. Shelton, ed., *The Encyclopedia of Genocide and Crimes against Humanity* (Detroit, MI: Macmillan Reference, 2004).
8. In books and articles, numerous philosophers have taken Heidegger to task. One of the best accounts is provided by Hans Sluga, *Heidegger's Crisis: Philosophy and Politics in Nazi Germany* (Cambridge: Harvard University Press, 1993), which places Heidegger in the context of German philosophy during the Third Reich and argues that Heidegger was the most prominent example of a large number of German philosophers who were willing and eager to cooperate with the Nazi regime.
9. See, for example, Richard J. Bernstein, *Radical Evil: A Philosophical Interrogation* (Cambridge: Polity Press, 2002) and Susan Neiman, *Evil in Modern Thought: An Alternative History of Philosophy* (Princeton, NJ: Princeton University Press, 2002).
10. Bartov, "Extreme Violence and the Scholarly Community," p. 511.
11. Most, but not all, of the contributors are scholars who do their research and teaching as members of university or college departments of philosophy. Such an identification, of course, is not a necessary condition for being counted as a philosopher, and the category is used in a broader sense than that in this book. For more detail about the contributors, see the biographical information at the beginning of the volume.

Part I

The Problem of Evil: How Does Genocide Affect Philosophy?

John K. Roth

In his classic Holocaust memoir called *Night*, Elie Wiesel succinctly describes the deportation of Jews from Sighet, his hometown in Nazi-occupied Hungary, during the spring of 1944. That genocidal railroad journey reduced his world to "a cattle car hermetically sealed."[1] Wiesel recalls "the heat, the thirst, the pestilential stench, the suffocating lack of air" but emphasizes that they were "as nothing compared with [the] screams which tore us to shreds."[2]

The screams were those of a middle-aged woman whom Wiesel identifies only as Madame Schächter, although he adds that he knew her well. She was imprisoned in the cattle car with her ten-year-old son, but her husband and two older boys had been deported earlier. "The separation," says Wiesel, "had completely broken her. ... Madame Schächter had gone out of her mind."[3] Her disorientation was revealed not only by moans and increasingly hysterical screams but also by the visions that provoked them.

Madame Schächter could not see outside, but on the third night of the seemingly endless journey she saw flames in the darkness. " 'Jews, listen to me' she kept exclaiming, 'I can see a fire! There are huge flames! It is a furnace.' "[4] At first the screams led some of the men to look through the small windows that allowed a little air into their cattle-car prison, but they saw no flames. "There was nothing there," reports Wiesel, "only the darkness."[5]

Some took pity and tried to calm Madame Schächter. Others were less kind. Wanting her quiet, they bound, gagged, and even struck Madame Schächter—"blows," Wiesel acknowledges, "that might have killed her." Meanwhile, he observes, "her little boy clung to her; he did not cry out; he did not say a word. He was not even weeping now."[6] Dawn's arrival stilled the bewildered woman. She remained quiet throughout the next day, but the fourth night again brought her screaming visions of fire. On the following day, the train stopped at a station. None of Madame Schächter's flames were to be seen, but signs indicated that the train had reached Auschwitz. "No one," says Wiesel, "had ever heard that name."[7]

For an afternoon and on into the evening, the train did not move, but with nightfall Madame Schächter's mad cries were again renewed. At last the train began to move, and as it took the rail spur that had been recently constructed to facilitate the arrival of transports at Birkenau, the killing center at Auschwitz, Madame Schächter once more became quiet, but other voices echoed hers with terrible screams of their own. They accurately reported what could be clearly seen. " 'Jews, look! Look through the window! Flames! Look!' "[8] Lighting up the darkness as they reached skyward from Birkenau's crematorium furnaces, these flames turned Jewish lives into smoke and ash.

Wiesel's memory of Madame Schächter did not leave him. Decades after writing *Night*, Wiesel recalled her in his 1995 memoir, *All Rivers Run to the Sea*. "Certain images of the days and nights spent on that train invade my dreams even now," he wrote, "anticipation of danger, fear of the dark, the screams of poor Mrs. Schecter [*sic*], who, in her delirium, saw flames in the distance; the efforts to make her stop; the terror in her little boy's eyes."[9] Such recollections make Wiesel wonder: "And what of human ideals, or of the beauty of innocence or the weight of justice? And what of God in all that? ... Why all these deaths? What was the point of this death factory? How to account for the demented mind that devised this black hole of history called Birkenau?"[10] Wiesel says that he and other Holocaust survivors wanted and tried to understand, but, he adds, "perhaps there was nothing to understand."[11]

The Holocaust was genocide or nothing could be. Every genocide, moreover, involves countless scenes of horror and suffering, each one particular and distinctive but all of them related by immense injustice and a vast wasting of human life. In the midst of such devastation, in a confrontation with genocide, what can and cannot, should and should not be said about human ideals, about what Wiesel calls "the beauty of innocence or the weight of justice," about God, and about humanity's condition and future? Is there anything more than darkness to report? What understanding, if any, can be found? In a word, when the problem of evil is grounded in history and made very specific by reference to the threats and realities of genocide, what does philosophy have to say?

Focused on the question "How does genocide affect philosophy?" the chapters in Part I wrestle with two problems. First, for the most part and sadly, genocide does not affect philosophy. Mostly, philosophy goes on as if genocide never happens. Philosophers have not confronted genocide persistently and in detail, even when they have concentrated on evil. Second, if and when philosophers do consider genocide seriously and sensitively, the impact of its devastation is unsettling. It cannot be simple, let alone self-evident, to determine what philosophy's response to genocide ought to be. When it confronts genocide, philosophy is driven back to "ground zero," not in Descartes's sense of identifying certainties that are beyond all doubt but in the sense of responding to atrocity that produces anguished questions and profound uncertainties about how, if at all, answers can be found that are hopeful, credible, and convincing.

Reflection on these issues and others related to them begins with Berel Lang's observation that genocide "arguably appears now as the most serious offense in humanity's lengthy—and, we recognize, still growing—list of moral or legal violations." Genocide involves double murder, not only that of individuals but also that of a group. Insofar as groups are imperiled, the very conditions of human life itself are besieged, for no one is a human being in general. Each of us has particularities that are related to group identities. Furthermore, Lang contends, the wrong that is done in genocide is done knowingly, not out of ignorance or primarily because the perpetrators are pursuing what they take to be good aims. From these dimensions of evil, however, it may be possible to salvage some good, especially if philosophers can accurately detail and convincingly defend the idea that there are group rights as well as rights that belong to individuals.

Much of Lang's long and distinguished career as a philosopher has been devoted to the study of the Holocaust and genocide. As Sander Lee points out, however, Lang's example tends to prove the rule that "the Holocaust and other genocides have had relatively little impact on the work of philosophers, including ethicists." While lamenting that fact, Lee directs his attention to philosophers who have considered the Holocaust and genocide, and he does so to respond to skeptical claims that some of them have made about the post-genocide credibility of traditional views of human rights and God. Lee, too, has doubts that are intensified by the Holocaust and other genocides, but he seeks in sensitive ways to recover affirmations about rights and religion that are needed to resist the threats of genocide.

For decades, Frederick Sontag has been thinking about radical evil and, in particular, its implications for understanding God and religion. He argues that genocide's impact on philosophy should be to impel philosophers to try "to understand evil more adequately and to cope with it more effectively." History shows that human beings are capable of eliminating some of the conditions that produce suffering and injustice, but genocide makes us wonder what will happen next in a world where suffering and injustice still know no end. Sontag senses that the questions that genocide raises for philosophy may be better known in the early twenty-first century than they have been before, but he wisely acknowledges that philosophers "are only at the beginning in taking up their responsibility to consider how genocide should affect philosophy."

Stephen T. Davis indicates that one of genocide's impacts on philosophy should be that genocide is not surprising. His claim denies neither that genocide is shocking nor that it is morally outrageous, but it does mean that philosophy must study human existence in ways that focus on humanity's propensity to commit genocide or to stand by while it takes place. As Davis reflects on these matters, he finds that the moral outrage that genocide rightly provokes may imply the existence of a God who also finds genocide outrageous. Davis presents this finding tentatively but hopefully. Indeed, he thinks that unless such a God exists, "our grounds for hope in the light of genocide are limited."

Under the influence of Ludwig Wittgenstein and other philosophers of language, twentieth-century philosophy took what has been called a "linguistic turn," which continues to be highly visible in much contemporary philosophy, especially in its Anglo-American expressions. Without language, neither philosophy nor genocide could exist; language is fundamental for them both. The philosopher of language D. Z. Phillips focuses on the ways in which genocide and the Holocaust in particular affect language, especially our senses of its limitations and our awareness of what it is appropriate or inappropriate to say in ordinary discourse. Phillips emphasizes a cautionary note that should keep philosophy vigilant about itself: "As philosophers," he says, "we need to be mindful of the fact that in writing about evil, we may add to it."

Part I concludes with Thomas W. Simon's suggestion that genocide could affect philosophy by making the latter a more "relevant intellectual force in an increasingly global world." If philosophers turn their questioning minds more intently to injustice and to genocide in particular, they may contribute to keeping genocide at bay. Drawing on his expertise as a philosopher of law and jurisprudence, Simon urges philosophy to pay attention especially to issues about international systems of justice and global ethics. "The campaign against injustice," he concludes, needs to involve "philosophers and philosophies that focus eyes on obvious scourges and engage minds and bodies in the intricacies of prevention, accountability, and punishment."

After Auschwitz, after genocide, Elie Wiesel has wondered: "And what of human ideals, or of the beauty of innocence or the weight of justice? And what of God in all that? ... Why all these deaths? What was the point of this death factory? How to account for the demented minds that devised this black hole of history called Birkenau?"[12] As the chapters in Part I suggest, genocide should affect philosophy by giving priority to questions such as those.

Notes

1. Elie Wiesel, *Night*, trans. Stella Rodway (New York: Bantam Books, 1982), p. 22. My discussion of *Night* draws on my contributions to David Patterson and John K. Roth, eds, *Fire in the Ashes: God, Evil, and the Holocaust* (Seattle, WA: University of Washington Press, 2005).
2. Wiesel, *Night*, p. 24.
3. Ibid., p. 22.
4. Ibid., p. 23.
5. Ibid., p. 22.
6. Ibid., p. 24.
7. Ibid., p. 24.
8. Ibid., p. 25.
9. Elie Wiesel, *All Rivers Run to the Sea: Memoirs* (New York: Alfred A. Knopf, 1995), p. 76. The change in the spelling of Madame Schächter's name is Wiesel's.
10. Ibid., p. 79.
11. Ibid.
12. Ibid.

1

The Evil in Genocide

Berel Lang

A different title that I decided *not* to use for this chapter would have been more explicit—but also offensive: *"What's so bad about genocide, anyway?"*[1] That wording sounds flippant, and the topic of genocide warrants something more than that. The flippancy, however, has a serious side to it. Although what is bad or wrong in genocide is often regarded as self-evident, it is in fact far from that; the assumption that it *is* obvious has led to both overuse and misuse of the term and to distortions in understanding its meaning. The question of the evil in genocide—what *is* so bad about it—is, at any rate, my subject here, with my premise the claim that genocide is indeed "so bad": evil, if any human act is or can be. Nobody is likely to find this assessment surprising or contentious. On any ranking of crimes or atrocities, it would be difficult to name an act or event regarded as more heinous. Genocide arguably appears now as the most serious offense in humanity's lengthy—and, we recognize, still growing—list of moral or legal violations. The evil in genocide ought to make an impact on philosophy. The following reflections show some of the ways in which philosophical work can respond to that proposition.

My view about genocide's public standing is supported by two pieces of evidence in particular. The first is that the charge of genocide has become a metaphor for atrocities in general, some of them clearly not genocide even when we make allowance for vagueness in that phenomenon's formal definition. For example, poverty, disease, and slavery have at times been labeled genocide or genocidal, and although these have sometimes been *associated* with genocide, it is doubtful that there is any *intrinsic* connection between the two. Human history includes many terrible acts and events—but not all of them, indeed relatively few, are or were genocidal. Nonetheless, *genocide* has become a virtual synonym for atrocity, the equivalent of a curse other than which nothing is more damning. And this figurative expansion has been possible, I suggest, only because the term's *literal* meaning made it so; figurative expression, after all, is anchored in the world as it is.

The second piece of evidence for the extreme character of genocide stems from the history of the word itself: the fact that a new term had to be coined (as recently as 1944) to name the crime it denoted—implying also that a new concept had to be *thought*, one that reflected new circumstances or old circumstances newly pushed to an extreme or, perhaps, an expanding moral consciousness or imagination. To be sure, this relatively brief history does not mean that genocide had not *occurred* previously (events often take place without being named), and there is continuing disagreement on genocide's historical status—with claims on one side, for example, that the Holocaust, the Nazi genocide against the Jews, was the first of its kind or (more strongly) unique; on the other side (here, with majority opinion), that earlier occurrences of genocide, from biblical and classical times onward, had all its requisite features, however distinctive the *scale* of the Holocaust as genocide turned out to be.

There is no disagreement, however, about the novelty of the *term* genocide or (by implication) of the concept at its basis. These were shaped largely by the efforts of a single person, the Polish–Jewish jurist and then émigré to the US—Raphael Lemkin—who, after a number of other starts at the concept in the 1930s, in his 1944 book, *Axis Rule in Occupied Europe*, applied the term as we now know and use it.[2] During this period, Lemkin was working his way toward a definition of his new term as a needed development, since, in his view, no other term or phrase available in the legal or moral vocabulary adequately expressed its meaning: not *murder*, not *mass murder*, not even the catchall but also vague phrase of *crime against humanity*. Genocide, the phenomenon of *group murder* (joining the Greek and Latin roots: *genos* and *cide*), was, in his view, distinct from all of these, distinct as an act and distinct also in its moral weight, its evil—the latter, both for the wrong *specific* to its occurrences and also (as I shall attempt to show) for widening the scope of the nature of evil as such.

First, then, I turn to the evil specifically in genocide. To represent this evil adequately requires retracing certain steps in the concept's history, with a focus on the *gap* that it was meant to fill. Legal and moral thinking—like nature in its classical formula—at once abhors a vacuum and seems to do nothing in vain. When a new concept appears, then, it is reasonable to assume that it does so because something had been found missing in the extant array of legal and moral categories. Just such a lack stands behind the formulation of the concept of genocide as a distinctive crime that Lemkin set out to identify, beginning with his initial effort at an international congress in Madrid in 1933, and moving then to a fuller articulation in the 1944 book just mentioned, which he wrote in full view of the Nazi atrocities, including the murder of 49 members of his own family. The concept of genocide that emerged from this process was subsequently put to use in the construction of the Nuremberg trials (the International Military Tribunal) of 1945–46 and the many war trials that followed in Germany and the countries it had occupied or attacked (although genocide as a formal prosecutorial charge figured only rarely in the immediate postwar trials).[3] This phase of the new concept's history culminated in actions taken by the newborn United Nations, first in a General Assembly resolution in 1946 and then in the 1948 Convention on the Prevention and Punishment of the Crime of Genocide. A further development in this continuing history was the formation of the permanent International Criminal Court established for prosecuting the crime of genocide, which has been active since July 2002. Other tribunals initiated earlier under the auspices of the United Nations (for the former Yugoslavia and for Rwanda) have also conducted hearings on charges of genocide in those locations—the best known of which is the case of Slobodan Milosevic.

The extraordinary figure of Raphael Lemkin affected *all* these stages of thinking and legislation about genocide. The crime he labored to bring to the world's attention seems now so obvious that we might well conclude that there were reasons (not necessarily good ones) why it had not been identified earlier—with one such reason especially relevant to understanding the concept itself. International law in its modern history has viewed the nation-state as its basic structural unit; international crimes—which nations had always regarded warily because of the possibility that any legislation they agreed to might later be turned against them—were on the standard model crimes committed by one nation against another or others. The implications of this taboo were straightforward: within the boundaries of a given nation, no other country had a recognizable interest in the first country's treatment of its citizens or minorities. As far as the individual inhabitants of *another* country were concerned, the obligations even of nations at war were primarily to other nations, with little thought to spare for the other's citizens and none at all for individuals or groups that were stateless. To be sure, international conventions had been adopted for protecting prisoners of war and "civilian populations" in conquered and occupied territories. Omitted from that protection, however— as revealed more graphically in the Second World War than ever before—was protection for groups who either had never been citizens of a host country, or had been citizens of that or another country but were then persecuted because of some group-feature either after having been disenfranchised or after having an alleged (negative) group-feature judged sufficient to override whatever rights they had. These groups, Lemkin saw, were quite without internal protection—since a reigning government could believe itself entitled to do as it wished to its own populace (as the Turks made clear in persecuting the Armenian minority in Turkey in 1915–17, and as also the Nazis did to German Jews, beginning in 1933—both of these under a fig leaf cover of internal legality). On the other hand, such groups were also unprotected externally from an *occupying* power, since the legal apparatus imposed by an occupying power might override whatever protections the occupied country itself had set up—the more readily, of course, if no such legislation had existed.

The concept of genocide verged on a distinctive, if not novel domain of law—breaching the traditional boundaries of national and international law by rejecting the "hands-off" doctrine that gave nations free rein with respect to members of their own populace and by disputing the premise of international law that granted full standing only to nations. The UN's Convention on Genocide thus moved toward a conception of "*meta*-national" law that would protect groups *aside* from (and sometimes, of course, against) the political authority that had formal jurisdiction over them. Admittedly, a lengthy theological and philosophical tradition of natural law and natural rights antedated this development[4]—as had earlier been demonstrated, for example, in such prominent political texts of the Enlightenment as the American Declaration of Independence (1776), and the French Declaration of the Rights of Man and Citizen (1789). These documents, however, did not disrupt the readily applied dualism between national and international law, leaving groups that were other or less than nations to fend for themselves. Those political texts did indeed speak of "natural" or "unalienable"—that is, *inherent*—rights as more fundamental than any granted by national affiliation or citizenship, asserting that every person, quite apart from the question of national citizenship, possessed such rights which *could* then have been extended to associations or groups of citizens within the body politic. In practice, however, such rights, important as they were as a rationale for the American or French revolutions, gave way in practice to a less generous model which associated them with the national citizenship of individuals—in effect abandoning groups of citizens as groups to the space between individual and nation, a space that remained quite empty.

It was these unprotected groups, outside the law as groups even in supposedly enlightened societies, that Lemkin saw as requiring protection against the threat of genocide—the murder or destruction of a group *qua* group. The act of genocide thus rests equally on the two parts of the term itself: on *genos* (people in the sense of groups), and on *cide* (murder). The first of these parts raises more complex conceptual issues than the second (what, after all, *is* a group?), but much might be said about the latter as well. Lemkin and the UN Convention found, for example, that the destruction of a group did not require the physical killing of its members. A group *could* be destroyed by killing, of course, and this remains the term's most definitive application—the reason why the Nazi genocide against the Jews remains a paradigm, if one can use that term, of genocide. (There could be no clearer expression of genocidal intent than Heinrich Himmler's words to the SS in 1943: "that people" [the Jews] must be made "to disappear from the earth.") But there are also other ways of destroying groups of people, and if these are less certain or their results less easily determined, their consequences may be equally destructive. Thus, the UN Convention includes four means of genocide in addition to physical killing: the forcible transfer of children, imposing measures to prevent births within the group, inflicting conditions of life on the group calculated to bring about its destruction,[5] and causing "serious bodily or mental harm" to the members of the group. These means differ in the range of their immediate cruelty, but any one of them, it is evident, could lead to the destruction of the group over a period of time— and it is clearly *this*, the demise of the group, the death of potential future members, against which the formulation of the crime speaks.

In addition to the differences among these means, there is also some unclarity in the terms that identify them (as there is most obviously in the Convention's stipulation that genocide may be directed against a group "in whole or in part"). The need for greater precision in the Convention's wording has been widely acknowledged, and undoubtedly the Convention will be progressively modified, if only through the weight of precedents as these emerge from actual genocide trials. Its essential principle, however, is clear and unambiguous: genocide entails the intended destruction of a group—and it differs in this not only from the destruction of individuals, but also from destruction or murder on a large scale where that act is directed at individuals as individuals and not as members of a group. (Genocide is thus not a function of numbers; mass murder that is not genocide may account for larger numbers of victims than particular instances of genocide.) What is distinctive about the murder in genocide is not killing, then, but its object: namely, the group. For it is the intent of genocide, as Himmler's statement makes clear, to destroy the group, with the group-identity itself, apart from its individual bearers, "made to disappear." Of course, the surest and quickest way to destroy a group is by the physical destruction of its members— but the latter is the means to the end represented by the former, with a recognizable distinction between the two.

Here, then, is the first aspect of the evil in genocide: As in the Holocaust, genocide's most explicit example, this evil involves a twofold murder, killing at two levels: the murder of individuals, but that murder as the means to a second murder—that of the group to which the individuals belong. This twofold murder is the basis, again, for distinguishing it from individual murder, on the one hand, and from mass murder, on the other. The murder committed is of two kinds of beings: individuals—yes; but also, and distinctively, the group of which the individuals are members. Certain objections to this formulation may appear quickly. Are not groups only the assembly of a number (and an indefinite one at that) of individuals? How can groups be substantively distinguished from the individuals who make them up? Something more will be said about this issue later, but the short response to it is that we make the distinction referred to *all the time*. For groups—at least, some of them—are not simply individuals added to each other; at times they have an identity larger than and separable from the individuals who make them up. They appear, in effect, as corporate or collective persons that are capable of actions and achievements, sometimes in ways that individuals by themselves or even randomly assembled together are not. To be sure, groups do not have the *physical* "vital signs" of individual human beings, but they do constitute lives and histories apart from the lives and histories of their individual members. As genocide makes clear, they can also suffer death. (The analogy to the threatened deaths of biological species is only approximate—but the various movements to protect animal species are so confident in the justification for their cause that it typically goes unstated.[6])

A pressing question recurs here as to *which* groups can be subject to genocide, since the definition of what counts as a group is so elastic: they may, for example, have as few as three or four members or as many as millions (Henry David Thoreau, we recall, could think of himself as a majority of one). Membership in a group, furthermore, can be fixed by an indefinitely large number of indicators—from eye color or occupation to the first letter of last names, and so on. Genocide as defined in the UN Convention, however, referred to groups with special significance in social and cultural life. Such definition, of course, does not mean that the murder of *any* group would not be criminal or evil—only that it might nonetheless be distinguishable from genocide. And although there has been disagreement about which groups *should* be covered by the Genocide Convention, there has been relatively little about the groups that the Convention *does* name: that is, "national, ethnical, racial or religious groups."

Why should these groups in particular be singled out for protection? The UN Convention itself offers no justification or explanation, but the reasoning behind its choices seems clear enough: These groups contribute more essentially to social structure and life (collective or individual) than others within the indefinitely large number of groups that might be named—from the College Class of 2005 to the residents on Main Street to Sherlock Holmes's "red-headed" league. (The most contentious exclusion debated in the United Nations was that of "political" groups; that category was finally excluded—on what were patently political grounds.) And indeed, whatever other candidates might be added to the UN's list, it seems indisputable that the groups presently on that list have indeed been primarily instrumental in shaping cultural and individual identity in contemporary societies: West or East, the First World or the Third World. A test of this claim would be the thought-experiment of imagining what societies or individuals would be like without such groups. It seems clear that the outcome would be social and individual life radically different from anything familiar to us—indeed, a life difficult even to imagine. The difference made evident in this way would not be due to the absence of this or that feature or individual, but to the absence of a *group*-identity as that shapes individuals in a way that no other influence on them—including biology itself—can do.

The first aspect of the evil in genocide, then, comes to this: that the types of groups against which genocide is directed—those *"eligible"* for genocide— are types in the absence of which the lives of individual (and collective) humanity would be inconceivable or, at the very least, radically diminished.

And this, it seems, is a principal justification for thinking of genocide (as such) as the murder referred to by the term: not only that genocide may involve individual murder as a means to its corporate end, but that the goal is murder aimed at the destruction of the group-identity without which individuals would not have been, and could not have been, the individuals they were. In effect, genocide in this sense represents the group as a "person"—arguably, as Aristotle proposes for the polis in the *Politics*, an entity *prior* to the individual person: life-*giving*—and understood in this way, reflecting the difference between death and life as well for the individual. This claim might seem exaggerated if we think of ethnic or religious or national groups and identity as made up of many small and discreet parts, a large number of which might be altered or excluded with no *essential* loss. But it is important to keep in mind that the destruction intended in genocide is total, not piece-meal. (Individuals may also "lose" parts of themselves without ceasing to be the same individuals.) Murder here, in the first evil of genocide, involves the destruction of the means of existence or personhood.

A second and different facet of the evil in genocide is only obliquely related to the first: The intent of genocide is to destroy members of a group not because of anything they have *done*, but solely because of their identification *as* members of the group. In other words, genocide kills individuals not after finding them responsible for doing or failing to do some specific thing, but just because of their identity—with the determination of that identity to a large extent externally imposed. What I mean by this is that identification of the group and its members is typically determined for the purposes of genocide by the agent of genocide, not by its victims—since here as elsewhere, the social power-structure also controls the categories or labels of identity. What results is typically a process of imposed identification which is also, to that extent, arbitrary. For example, the 1935 Nuremberg Laws, which defined Jewish identity within Nazi Germany, held that anyone with three Jewish grandparents was fully Jewish. This specification, however, represented a substantial reduction in the ruling issued two years earlier according to which *one* Jewish grandparent sufficed. But there is ample evidence that the basis for this change, which by the stroke of a pen sharply reduced the total number of German Jews, was pragmatically driven and largely arbitrary. The earlier, more inclusive definition would have made law enforcement much more difficult, however odd it may seem that the Nazis would under any circumstances object to having "too many" Jews to persecute. Or again, to show how the process of group-identification can come even closer to absurdity, we recall the alleged (disputed, but alleged) Khmer Rouge policy of identifying for genocide those of their Cambodian countrymen who wore eye-glasses—a mark that was taken to identify the dangerous group of "intellectuals." What happens in these cases is that within the vague initial boundaries of a group marked for genocide, further specifica-tion may be made—but these decisions identify group members neither by their own assent nor for reasons related to the group-identity itself. Nevertheless, a death sentence emerges.

This grounding of genocide on involuntary identity or character—the denial of individual autonomy—appears also in relation to the question of how individual membership in the four groups named by the UN Convention is determined. For although membership in those groups is voluntary in principle (race, to be sure, the least so, but also there, insofar as the definition of race is a social construct), to a great extent the reality of those identities is involuntary, certainly initially (ethnicity, for example, is transmitted first and strongly through language and the home)—but then with continuing external pressure too. Religion and nationality, to be sure, are more clearly voluntary features of individual identity than the other categories, but in those cases as well the pressures against "opting out" are often intense and at times overwhelming: many people manage to do it, but many more do not—and even for those who do, it is often a difficult process. For those subjected to genocide, the group-identification that is the necessary first step in the process (and a universal mark of it), is largely, if not entirely, imposed. Even at their most free, these elements of identity are distinguishable from other, fuller decisions or choices made by members of the group—which means that genocide acts against its victims, once again, on grounds for which they have at best only limited responsibility.

To be sure, the perpetrators' justification for genocide often cites the responsibility of the targeted group, claiming that its decisions or actions have caused harm or represent a danger to others. But even the semblance of evidence for these claims is usually lacking, and a stronger objection still is that on this justification, the targeted group is held responsible for dispositions or conduct for which they are not in fact responsible—in the sense that they were unable *not* to engage in the acts or conduct they are charged with. This is one reason, it seems clear, why the language of genocide so frequently turns to medical or biological metaphors: the Jews, in Hitler's language, were "germ carriers," "a virus," and "a racial tuberculosis." This representation of the Jews' conduct as symptomatic of a dangerous disease would then justify genocide as surely as the menace of any other deadly pestilence would warrant the steps to eradicate it. One does not *"blame"* a virus or bacillus for the harm it causes; the moral issue simply does not arise.

Admittedly, societies do act against even involuntary conduct when that appears as a menace. But such measures are based on individual *conduct*, not on a presumption of group-identity—which is at once larger than anything the individual does but also smaller in the sense that there is no necessary connection, where genocide emerges, between the group and the action initiated against it. Genocide, in these terms, adds to the destruction of the group-identity because the genocidal murder rejects the humanity of its victims by denying their autonomy or freedom of decision. They are killed *not* for choices they have made or acts they have committed, but either for alleged dispositions beyond their control or for others which they might have acted upon even though they have not actually been shown to do so. The action against them, then—the genocide—is first (whatever else ensues) a denial of them as persons, as responsible moral agents—a denial otherwise intimated in genocide's twofold murder, but distinctive enough in this second aspect to stand by itself. In the first facet of the evil in genocide, the denial of the victims' humanity appears as a prior condition or preventative, declaring that there shall be no such group or individual members of it *in the future*. The second aspect of evil in genocide denies or reduces humanity in the group *at present*, as and when it exists. Whatever else can be said against the Nazi denial that the Jews were human at all, the internal logic leading to its consequences was rigorous: given their essentialist—biological—conception of Jewish group-identity, genocide was not simply the *"Final* Solution" but also the *only* solution.

If one asks how these two facets of the evil in genocide fit into or reshape any more general conception or understanding of evil, it seems to me that in one way they conform to a standard view—and in another way, they challenge it. Both facets conform to what seems a minimal standard view of evil as value destroyed with no commensurate recovery—the destruction affecting not only the potential that exists in any human being, but also the *means* (through group-identity) by which, and only by which, that potential can be realized. But genocide also goes further, it seems to me, by undermining a common view of evil, which holds that evil has an intrinsic relation to ignorance, to an absence of deliberation or intention. According to this view, when people do evil or wrong, it is not because they have chosen these goals fully cognizant of the evil or wrong in them, but because they mistakenly believe that what they are doing is good—or at least, that it is better than the alternative. Thus, this position argues—standing on the shoulders of Plato and the Platonic tradition, of the seventeenth-century rationalism of Spinoza and Leibniz, and of at least a part of the Judeo-Christian heritage—if people who do evil only knew better, if they *really* understood what they were doing, they would not do it; they would choose differently.

There is much to be said—and much that has been said—about this view of evil. Some of what is at issue here was dramatically focused on genocide in Hannah Arendt's analysis of Adolf Eichmann's character and role in the "Final Solution," an account that is remembered especially for her views about "the banality of evil," which claimed that Eichmann managed to do great evil although neither his intention nor he himself was at all great.[7] He was neither an Iago, Arendt suggested, nor a Richard III. He did not think enough about what he was doing to qualify as authentically or radically evil—indeed, he hardly thought at all. In her words, he was "thoughtless," a "clown"—unfortunately finding himself (he spoke of his own "bad luck") in a position that placed fateful decisions in his hands. That thoughtlessness, Eichmann's reliance on clichés not only in speaking but also in *thinking*, was his, and his evil's, banality—with the clear implication, according to Arendt, that if he *had* been capable of thought, he would not have done what he did. Iago and Richard III, after all, in the forms that we know them best, are products of Shakespeare's imagination: there and there only, we infer from Arendt's account, is where radical evil, evil deliberately chosen, is to be found—in fictional worlds, not in the course of ordinary human agency and responsibility. She had come to realize, Arendt concluded not long afterward in a letter to Gershom Scholem (just before he cut off all communication with her) that "*all* evil is banal."

Insofar as this alleged impossibility of voluntary or willed evil is open to verification at all, however, the phenomenon of genocide seems to me to provide certain counterevidence, or at the very least to raise doubts about it. As the UN Convention indicates, genocide is always intentional. Although in this respect, genocide may seem no different from other premeditated acts, an implication of what I have been saying here *also* suggests that genocidal intention is not only directed at the destruction of the group, but also aims at that destruction *knowing* the act's wrongfulness. In other words, those who commit genocide both recognize the wrong and do what they do at least in part for that reason—in effect making that knowledge itself an element of the intention. This is obviously a large claim to make good on, both about genocide in general and its specific instances. I have elsewhere attempted to show how an awareness of their wrongdoing figures in the Nazis' "Final Solution"—arguing that the moral "quality" of that process appears in the conscious "style" of Nazi expression and actions where, in addition to their specific wrongdoing, the will to transgress itself is also evident.

Here I can rehearse that argument only in an abbreviated form, relating it at the same time to the still more difficult challenge of showing that genocide as such involves conscious wrongdoing. On that point, I would claim that the rationale for killing on the basis of an imposed group-identity always betrays itself—can never be undertaken in good faith—because of the evident disproportion between the object and the act: it is the group traits that are condemned, but it is individuals who are killed, and the disparity between those two, no matter how much effort is made to align them, cannot be eliminated in fact or theory. This contention seems to me to be supported by certain apparently accidental, albeit typical features of genocide—which are, in my view, not accidental at all: the invariable practice of secrecy and denial on the part of those carrying it out; the elaborate—and one has to say, imaginative—efforts at dehumanization that typically accompany it (not simply direct physical or brute torture but measures directed against the person as a member of the *genos*); the subsequent psychopathologies that appear in its agents. All these features of genocide require explanation—and *one* such explanation points to the perpetrator's awareness that wrong or evil is being done. Some of the features mentioned, to be sure, may appear in atrocity as such—but the requirement in genocide of imposing and then annihilating group-identity increases both the opportunity and the need for the consciousness of transgression. I realize that the broad thesis of intentional and knowing wrongdoing (inside or outside genocide) requires more evidence and argument than I provide here, but even its possibility seems important to me as a basis for questioning the view that wrongdoing can never be fully voluntary—a basis to which genocide may contribute as distinctively as genocide itself is a distinctive historical occurrence.

At the beginning of this chapter, I suggested a probably offensive alternate title to the one mentioned—and I would balance that now, in concluding, by another probable offense, proposing that beside what I have described as the evil in genocide, we would do well also to look for the good in it. The immediate response to any such proposal will undoubtedly be, "No! No good at all has come or could come out of genocide, no redeeming features, no, none!" But a more deliberate response, which begins with the same condemnation, might turn its attention to one historical aspect of the conceptualization of genocide that promises—I can think of no other way of describing them—positive or even good consequences. In this age of social self-consciousness, the relationship between immoral practice and moral prohibition hardly needs re-telling. As even the gentle skepticism of Montaigne reminds us, the history of religious prohibitions or cultural taboos shows that banned practices have in fact occurred—and with sufficient frequency to be regarded as a danger. There *would be* no prohibitions against murder, robbery, adultery, incest—unless they had first been part of the moral (or immoral) landscape, and unless they had occurred. Furthermore, for all these prohibitions and their attendant punishments, something more seems to be going on than only the delineation of individual offenses. What occurs is also a stirring—and further construction—of the moral imagination, a development that in some way anticipates specific violations and prohibitions but comes into full view only as the pair—act and prohibition together—appear. Together, they then shape further the extent of the moral domain which, it should by now be clear, has a history and is even, in its own qualified way, a progressive history. This is not to say that wrongs as they are singled out and identified *become* good or right in this process, or even that, if we had the choice, it would be right or good (whatever that might mean in the context) to choose a world with evil and moral imagination in it over the world without them—but only that in *this*, that is, our world, wrong and evil can be, and sometimes are, met by right and good.

Something like this sequence has appeared, I would argue, in relation to genocide as it has been conceptualized, identified, and then expressed in legal, moral, and common discourse. For a concurrent event has been the emergence, also in legal, moral, and common discourse, of "group rights": first and foremost, the right of groups to exist, to *be* groups that are self-determining, a concept that can be extended to other rights implied by or built on that first one. The contemporaneous recognition of genocide as a crime and of group rights as a condition of moral and political justice—both emerging in the aftermath of the Second World War—is not, *could not* be accidental: they are too closely related conceptually and chronologically, too much history had passed with neither of them identified, for their simultaneous emergence to be coincidental. Even if one sees the historical progression as moving first from the crime of genocide to the recognition of the new group's right-to-exist—first, violation, then virtue or justice—there is nothing startling in this; much moral history, perhaps all of it, follows a similar pattern.

Admittedly, all talk about "group rights" faces substantial objections—but so does, after all, talk about *individual* rights (which, we remember, Jeremy Bentham unkindly characterized as "nonsense upon stilts"). Furthermore, there has for long been a widely held presumption that group rights, if they are acknowledged at all, are only individual rights bundled together: since I as an individual have the right to free speech, so, too, any group of which I am a member (together with other individuals) has the same right, but only because of the individual rights of its individual members. Nevertheless, an alternative view of group rights raises the possibility that, in certain cases, they may precede rather than follow individual rights, or that the two may be co-temporal or co-logical. Such concepts suggest a "deep structure" for society that is quite different from the individualist conception of human nature and social structure that is deeply embedded in contemporary Western political ideology. In certain respects, the practice of group rights has advanced more quickly than its theory, since many aspects of contemporary political life—from issues of affirmative action to church–state relations to issues of property rights and taxation—seem dependent not only on the possibility but also on the actuality of group rights. Those possibilities, however, are a topic for another time. I mention them only to illustrate that, even in relation to the extreme act of genocide, moral history and analysis do not escape the reach of dialectic.

The appearance of group rights as underwriting the identification and criminalizing of genocide is not at all meant to provide a concluding "uplift" to the terrible story of genocide that remains, I should argue, the dominant motif of twentieth-century history as a whole. Nevertheless, these developments have taken place close together, if not quite simultaneously. Thus, they need to be viewed together, or at least close to one another. Group rights, yes—because, first, group wrongs. And at the very beginning of that beginning: genocide.

Notes

1. A version of this chapter appeared in Berel Lang, *Post-Holocaust: Interpretations, Misinterpretations, and the Claims of History* (Bloomington, IN: Indiana University Press, 2005).

2. Raphael Lemkin, *Axis Rule in Occupied Europe* (Washington, DC: Carnegie Endowment for International Peace, 1944).
3. The charge of genocide was not formally part of the charges brought at Nuremberg. Arguably the first appearances of the charge in formal juridical argument occurred in Poland, in discussions and judgments rendered by the Supreme National Tribunal. Consider, for example, the trials of Amon Leopold Goeth (1946) and Rudolf Hoess (1947), which are summarized in *Law Reports of Trials of War Criminals*, Volume VII (London: Published for the United Nations War Crimes Commission, 1948). I am indebted to Raul Hilberg for this reference. On the history of genocide, see also Samantha Power, *"A Problem from Hell": America and the Age of Genocide* (New York: Basic Books, 2002). On the evolution of the United Nations Convention on the Prevention and Punishment of the Crime of Genocide, see especially William A. Schabas, *Genocide in International Law: The Crime of Crimes* (Cambridge: Cambridge University Press, 2000).
4. See, for examples, Richard Tuck, *Natural Rights Theory* (Cambridge: Cambridge University Press, 1976).
5. In its verdict of 2 September 1998, the United Nations Tribunal for Rwanda identified under this heading the systematic rape of Tutsi women by the Hutu as a genocidal act, although the wording of the verdict suggested the possibility that systematic rape might also be considered an independent modality of genocide.
6. Certain implications concerning this parallel seem unavoidable. During the more than twenty-year struggle in the United States to win Senate confirmation for the UN Genocide Convention, the Endangered Species Act (1977) passed without dissent and on its first presentation.
7. See Hannah Arendt, *Eichmann in Jerusalem: A Report on the Banality of Evil* (New York: Viking, 1963), especially the Epilogue.

2
Rights, Morality, and Faith in the Light of the Holocaust

Sander Lee

Should philosophers discuss the Holocaust?

When I mentioned to a colleague from the social sciences that I would be developing a course in philosophy and the Holocaust, he responded by suggesting that it should be easy to design such a course given the enormous impact that the Holocaust must have had on the field of philosophy, especially ethics. Indeed, he proposed that the course focus on ethics after the Holocaust, emphasizing the major changes in ethical theories that have resulted from an awareness of the horrors of the Holocaust. I am sorry to confess that my first response to my colleague's suggestion was to laugh. As a scholar outside of the field who has a great respect for philosophy, my colleague simply assumed that an event as devastating as the Holocaust must have had a profound effect on moral philosophy. Wouldn't all ethicists, he assumed, feel the need to respond to the murder of millions and the calculated attempt to extinguish European Jewry in its entirety?

Unfortunately, as those of us within the field of philosophy know all too well, the Holocaust and other genocides have had relatively little impact on the work of philosophers, including ethicists. For the most part, philosophy and ethics look much the same after the Holocaust as they did before. The same basic divisions that existed prior to the Holocaust (between Anglo-American and Continental philosophy, for example, or between teleology and deontology in ethics) continue to develop along the same lines as before. Few prominent figures in the field have issued public calls to re-examine the foundations of ethical thinking as a result of the Holocaust and genocidal situations that came after Auschwitz. Indeed, one could even argue that most philosophers have gone out of their way not to mention the Holocaust and genocide in their scholarly work, even on occasions when such references would appear to be appropriate.

In my view, the main reasons for this somewhat shocking oversight are twofold. First, we philosophers tend to be extremely argumentative. One of the few claims that can be made with absolute certainty about the field of

18

philosophy is that any assertion made by any philosopher on any topic whatsoever at some point in time will be vehemently attacked at another point in time by some other philosopher. While we philosophers recognize that these attacks are rarely mean-spirited, and that the launching of such attacks is in fact the highest form of flattery one philosopher can offer another, to those outside the field, scholarly attacks of this sort can appear to be vicious and unfeeling. When the topic at hand is the verifiability criterion of meaning or the ever popular accusation of solipsism, then the apparent viciousness of these debates seems only puzzling to those outside the field; however, if the issue at hand is related to the Holocaust, then such philosophical debates are capable of eliciting public outrage.

I saw this reaction firsthand a number of years ago when I participated in the process of establishing the first American society made up of philosophers for the study of issues relating to the Holocaust: The Society for the Philosophic Study of Genocide and the Holocaust. While most sessions held in conjunction with the American Philosophical Association attract at the most one or two dozen philosophers, the meeting set to establish this new society elicited a large audience, a fact that is not inconsistent with the description I have offered above. The audience included many non-philosophers, some of whom were survivors or the offspring of survivors, and most of whom had very strong feelings about the establishment of the society and every aspect of its operation, including its name. The expression of opinion at that session ran the gamut from those who claimed that only survivors are qualified to speak about the Holocaust to those who objected to the establishment of any society that confined its interest to the experiences of Jews in the Second World War without taking into account the plight of some other group or groups (Sinti and Roma, for example, or homosexuals, African Americans, Native Americans, Armenians, and so on). Without going into the details of this interesting discussion, I will simply observe that issues related to the Holocaust can attract a much broader audience of non-philosophers, many of whom are quick to feel offense if the topics under discussion are not approached in a manner that they deem to be appropriately respectful to their particular concerns. An unwillingness to offend such individuals and groups has, in my opinion, contributed to the silence of many contemporary philosophers on these issues.

A second and more significant reason for this silence is theoretical. While the events of the Holocaust shocked the world when they were revealed in their full horror at the end of the Second World War, many philosophers believe that those events, horrible as they were, added no new information to the scholarly study of ethics and social philosophy. After all, they would argue, most philosophers have always acknowledged that human beings are capable of committing acts of great evil and that political societies governed by such individuals are equally capable of investing their acts with the appearance of legitimate governmental authority.

Beginning with Plato and Aristotle, and continuing through Hobbes, Locke, Kant, the Utilitarians, Hegel, Marx, and beyond, the history of Western philosophy is filled with theories examining these problems from a variety of differing philosophical perspectives. Many philosophers working on these issues believe that while the Holocaust presents us with an appalling example of the consequences of the misuse of political power, perhaps even the most appalling example in history, the issues raised by the Holocaust may be sufficiently dealt with in the context of the standard approaches already used within philosophy and that there is nothing in particular to be gained by focusing on the Holocaust in the context of these ongoing philosophical debates.

There are, of course, exceptions to this silence within the field of philosophy. In this chapter I focus on the arguments made by a number of those thinkers. While I disagree with some of their claims, I wish, first, to praise them for their willingness to promote serious consideration of the ramifications of the Holocaust and other genocides for the work of contemporary philosophy. They realize that even if there may be some merit to the claim that the Holocaust raises no entirely new philosophical issues, the shocking enormity of the horror of those events recasts traditional philosophical problems in ways that demand a fundamental re-evaluation of our most cherished beliefs. Thus, I agree with Irving Greenberg when he argues that "failure to confront it [the Holocaust] makes repetition all the more likely. So evil is the Holocaust, and so powerful a challenge to all other norms, that it forces a response, willy-nilly: not to respond is to collaborate in its repetition."[1]

What is the status of rights after the Holocaust?

In "Returning Home: Reflections on Post-Holocaust Ethics," his essay in *Ethics after the Holocaust*, John Roth examines the impact of what he calls "Rubenstein's Dilemma," the claim made by Richard L. Rubenstein that the fact of the Holocaust demonstrates once and for all that so-called "human rights" are merely the result of agreed upon societal conventions and that their justification, and very existence, depends entirely on the power that is expended to uphold them. In this sense, according to Rubenstein, "until ethical theorists and theologians are prepared to face without sentimentality the kind of action it is possible freely to perpetuate under conditions of utter respectability in an advanced, contemporary society, none of their assertions about the existence of moral norms will have much credibility."[2] As Roth points out, Rubenstein concludes that when it comes to even the most fundamental human rights, there is often "little or no penalty for their violation. And, norms that can be freely violated are as good as none at all."[3]

Roth responds to Rubenstein in the following way:

> The answer to Rubenstein's dilemma, if there is one, will not be found in some clinching intellectual argument or irrefutable philosophical

analysis, for the best responses to this challenge are not that easy or simple. Instead they involve sustained reflection on the memories people should share, the emotions we should express, the beliefs we should hold, the decisions we should make about how to live after Auschwitz, and the questions we ask about all of those aspects of our experience, individually and collectively.[4]

Roth goes on to compare the heroic actions of the French rescuers of Jews in Le Chambon to those of the character of the doctor in Albert Camus's novel, *The Plague*. Echoing Phillip Hallie, Roth points out that those in Le Chambon who risked their lives on a daily basis to save innocent people did so in a spontaneous and largely unreflective way. Roth quotes Magda Trocmé as saying, "None of us thought we were heroes. We were just people trying to do our best."[5] In the end, Roth agrees with the doctor of Camus's novel that, "there are more things to admire in men than to despise."[6] While the fight against "terror and its relentless onslaughts [is] never ending," Roth implies that if most of us have the courage to act in accordance with the inherent goodness innately within each of us, we could help to ensure that evil does not once again gain the upper hand in society as it did during the Holocaust.[7]

In his essay, "Teleology as the (frustrated) Pursuit of Happiness: Meister Eckhart on 'living without a why,' " John M. Connolly points out that the Medieval theologian Meister Eckhart held a similar view.[8] He quotes Eckhart as follows: "[The just man] wants and seeks nothing, for he knows no why. He acts without a why just in the same way as God does; and just as life lives for its own sake and seeks no why for the sake of which it lives, so too the just man knows no why for the sake of which he would do something."[9]

With due respect to the position I have attributed to Roth and the outlook that Connolly underscores from Eckhart, over reliance on such a belief in humanity's innate goodness can lead to disastrous consequences if that belief is not backed by effective government sanctions. This point is dramatically illustrated in Primo Levi's famous description of an encounter with a guard in Auschwitz, an account that suggests the polar opposite of Eckhart's position in words that are "eerily similar."[10] Levi's statement is as follows:

Driven by thirst, I eyed a fine icicle outside the window, within hand's reach. I opened the window and broke off the icicle but at once a large, heavy guard prowling outside brutally snatched it away from me. "*Warum?*" I asked him in my poor German. "*Hier ist kein warum*" (there is no why here [in Auschwitz]), he replied, pushing me inside with a shove.[11]

Unfortunately, the inner sense that calls some people to act morally without concern for a "why" does not appear to operate in everyone. Indeed, it would seem that some people experience an inner sense that leads them to evil rather than good—Adolf Hitler comes to mind—while many others appear to possess no inner moral sense whatsoever.[12]

I shall discuss further the ramifications of such ethical intuitionism, but first I want to add a few comments concerning Roth's presentation of "Rubenstein's Dilemma." Roth quotes Rubenstein as saying that *"rights do not belong to men by nature.* To the extent that men have rights, they have them only as members of the polis, the political community. ... Outside the polis there are no inborn restraints on the human exercise of destructive power."[13] No one can dispute Rubenstein's claim that the Holocaust makes clear that individuals, governments, and indeed entire societies are capable of acting systematically in ways that deny the most fundamental human rights. If, in fact, the claim that certain natural rights are "inalienable" implies that it is objectively impossible to deny such rights, then Rubenstein would have succeeded in disproving their existence.

Advocates of rights-based theories, however, do not claim that the inalienability of certain natural rights makes it objectively impossible to deny them. When Thomas Jefferson, following in the footsteps of Hobbes, Locke, and perhaps Hume, made his claims about the nature of rights in the Declaration of Independence, he was not claiming that rights could not be violated. In fact, the justification for issuing the Declaration lay precisely in the claim that the British *had* violated these rights and that these violations legitimized the decision of the American colonies to proclaim their political independence.

In other words, the fact that the Nazis and their collaborators regularly violated human rights does not demonstrate the nonexistence of those rights. What that history does show, yet again, is that the mere existence of rights does not ensure their protection in the absence of governmental mechanisms that have the authority and power to enforce them. This analysis, it turns out, is not an argument against Rubenstein's position, for his conclusion is remarkably similar. In arguing that, "to the extent that men have rights, they have them only as members of the polis, the political community," Rubenstein does not oppose a rights-based theory, he merely echoes the positions of the originators of such theories, especially those who interpret the status of rights without resorting to a natural law position. When Rubenstein contends, moreover, that "norms that can be freely violated are as good as none at all," his position does not necessarily imply an extreme moral relativism or nihilism as Roth seems to suggest.

Instead Rubenstein's claim could be accepted in the context of those, such as me, who argue that the responsible nations of the world (including the United States) should publicly accept the legitimacy of institutions such as the International Criminal Court. Such mechanisms will not only empower the international community to investigate and respond appropriately to genocide but will also serve to ensure, by means of their powers of deterrence, that crimes similar to those committed during the Holocaust are less likely to recur.

I have argued elsewhere that the commonly accepted natural law justification for war crimes tribunals is inaccurate and misleading and that the positive law account of war crimes tribunals is a more honest description of such trials as it recognizes that some past trials, such as Nuremberg, made use of retroactive law, a legal practice usually forbidden in many legal systems (including the Constitution of the United States). Despite this use of retroactive law, I argue that past war crimes trials can be justified on the basis of a variety of differing moral theories. At the same time, recognition and honest acceptance of the use of retroactive law in such cases enables us to identify important issues that await resolution.[14] Rather than revisiting those inquiries, however, I want to return to a point that is fundamental for this chapter and arguably for this entire book: I believe that Roth is correct in suggesting that the horror of the Holocaust throws into doubt the wisdom of accepting absolutist theories of morality.

Should we value autonomy or obedience in the light of the Holocaust?

What exactly is it that disturbs Richard Rubenstein so much about the realization that rights depend on man-made sanctions for their effectiveness? If one is lucky enough to live in a country that actively defends the rights of its citizens, or if the International Criminal Court is eventually able to act as a global governmental authority defending the rights of all people, then what difference does it make whether that defense relies on physical or metaphysical force? Does it really matter that rights are respected because of autonomous choices to act in accordance with human-made positive laws and not solely in obedience to the laws of nature or God?

David Patterson believes that it makes an enormous difference. In his essay "Nazis, Philosophers, and the Scandal of Heidegger," Patterson maintains that "the Nazi project to exterminate the Jews came about not in spite of but, in part, because of the sophisticated German civilization as it had been shaped by German philosophy."[15] Specifically, Patterson claims, "there is, then, a line of progression from the will to make the maxim of one's action into law, to the will to power, to resolve. The thread running through this progression is the accent on the autonomy of the self as the basis for freedom, a notion that was part of the thinking of all Nazi philosophers—and a notion antithetical to Jewish teaching. For Jewish teaching places its accent not on freedom but on justice, not on ontology but on metaphysics, not on being but on being ethical, which means living in a manner in keeping with God's Torah, and not setting oneself as the author of good and evil."[16] Later, Patterson concludes that "the cornerstone of the argument lies in the opposition ... between Kantian autonomy and religious heteronomy, between power and truth, between expedience and ethics—in short, between Nazi and Jew."[17] Thus, for Patterson, it is not enough that people autonomously choose to respect the rights of others for reasons of their own making. For him, justice can result only from obedience to God's law. The decision to reject absolutism in favor of free will is the first step on the road to Nazi disdain for the rights of others.

Yet, one could point out that there is a movement within Judaism itself which advocates the very sort of autonomous thinking that Patterson, unfortunately, associates with Nazism. The Reform movement in Judaism has its roots in the philosophy of Moses Mendelssohn, a philosophy that influenced Kant in its advocacy of reason and Jewish assimilation as opposed to traditional beliefs and obedience to religious rituals that seemed no longer relevant in the modern world. Indeed, most of the German Jews who were the victims of Nazism considered themselves to be followers of the German Reform movement. Today many Jews throughout Europe and North America accept the tenets of Reform Judaism.

Patterson is aware of this criticism and incorporates a response to it in his essay. For Patterson, Reform Jews (such as myself) are not really Jews at all: "But inasmuch as it rejects the Covenant with Abraham, the prophecies of the Messiah, the resurrection of the dead, the chosenness of the Jews, and other teachings essential to Judaism," Patterson contends, "German Reform Judaism becomes more German than Jewish."[18] Patterson concludes his attack on autonomy by stating that "only by opposing an ethics grounded in metaphysics—only by using absolutist justice to limit autonomous freedom—can we even begin to speak of a post-Holocaust ethics."[19]

I could not disagree with Patterson more. Indeed, one of the most striking moral implications of the Holocaust lies in the fact that it vividly demonstrates that human beings can violently disagree about issues of morality. Debates and disagreements over such issues characterize much international communication. In the contemporary world, there currently exist great disagreements over such issues, not just between governments, but also between the world's many religious and cultural movements. For example, it is very hard for many of us to conceive of religious or moral principles that could motivate people to engage in suicide bombings against innocent civilians, yet, as we have been reminded too often in the past few years, such attacks not only take place but they are also motivated by religious or moral principles of one kind or another.

We know that some people consider such acts justified. They even see themselves as making heroic sacrifices that have been sanctioned by God. In fact, some even believe that they would be violating God's law if they did not engage in these kinds of activities. Thus, perhaps the most difficult problem facing absolutists such as Patterson is not just deciding what objective moral laws to advocate, but also persuading others to adopt them or forcibly imposing them on people who disagree. If allegedly objective moral laws are not agreed upon democratically, how can we be sure we are correct in asserting their validity? There is the danger that an acceptance of absolutism could result in some individual, or some small groups of individuals, or even an oppressive majority of individuals seeking to serve as the ultimate judges of this morality.

Indeed, I would argue, this is exactly what the Nazis attempted to do. The evil of the Nazis' ideology derived not from any respect for individual autonomy, as Patterson claims, but from a fervent belief in the very sort of unthinking obedience that he advocates. The Nazis killed people for asserting their rights to individual autonomy and rewarded those who blindly obeyed their immoral imperatives. The essence of democracy lies in a realization that different individuals may construct their moral values (within limits) in accordance with differing perspectives.

Partially because of the Holocaust, many people, unlike Patterson, have come to reject traditional beliefs in a universal set of objective moral principles. For example, in his response to Roth's essay on Rubenstein, Leonard Grob states that "following in the tradition of Jean-Paul Sartre, and his fellow existential philosophers, I contend that we humans are more verb than noun, that we do not *have* a nature, but we are a nature in question for ourselves. We are always in process, always making and remaking ourselves, morally speaking."[20] Peter Haas concurs with this rejection of absolutism when he says that "we can no longer call on the assumptions invoked in the past that there exists some supernatural 'Good' or some essence of humanity that provides us at least in principle with some objective way of measuring right and wrong. These types of assumptions are simply not part of the intellectual possibilities open to us in the modern world."[21]

We cannot escape the horror of the Holocaust by claiming that only heirs of a certain cultural environment (German philosophy, for example) have the capacity for such acts. Such an attitude displays aspects of the same kind of blind prejudice that produced the Holocaust. Events in the Balkans, Rwanda, the former Soviet Union, Cambodia, and elsewhere have shown us repeatedly that non-Germans are also capable of mass atrocities and genocide. Thus, the absolutist claim that all people share a common set of objective moral principles, which are innate in all of us, has been empirically disproved.

What about God?

Drawing these reflections to a close, I want to comment briefly about some related issues addressed by both Roth and Rubenstein. In *Holocaust: Religious and Philosophical Implications*, the editors include some of Rubenstein's best-known analysis concerning how the Holocaust compels people and Jews in particular to re-evaluate their thinking about and relationship with God. Famously, as a result of his interview with Dean Heinrich Grüber, Rubenstein concludes, correctly in my view, that the Jewish community must "recognize that we are, when given normal opportunities, neither more nor less than other men, sharing the pain, joy, and the fated destiny which Earth alone has meted out to all her children. ... As long as we continue to hold to the doctrine of the election of Israel, we will leave ourselves open to the ideology expressed by Dean Grüber, that because the Jews are God's Chosen People, God wanted Hitler to punish them."[22]

I agree with Rubenstein that those who continue to choose to have religious faith are hard-pressed, in the light of the Holocaust, to believe in a God of history, one who intervenes directly to rescue the people of the Covenant from oppression as He supposedly did during the time of the biblical Exodus. ("I have often stated," says Rubenstein, "that the idea that a God worthy of human adoration could have inflicted Auschwitz ... is obscene."[23]) Yet, I cannot agree entirely with Rubenstein's arguments when he goes on to make the following claims:

> But, notice the terrible price one must pay if one rejects the God of the Covenant. If the God of the Covenant exists, at Auschwitz my people stood under the most fearsome curse that God has ever inflicted. If the God of history does not exist, then the Cosmos is ultimately absurd in origin and meaningless in purpose. ... Like Kierkegaard, I have had to choose between a world without the biblical God and the leap into faith. I have had a slightly different "Either-Or" than Kierkegaard. I have to decide whether to affirm the existence of a God who inflicts Auschwitz on his guilty people or to insist that nothing the Jews did made them more deserving of Auschwitz than any other people, that Auschwitz was in no sense a punishment, and that a God who would or could inflict such punishment does not exist. In other words, I have elected to accept what Camus has rightly called the courage of the absurd, the courage to live in a meaningless, purposeless Cosmos rather than believe in a God who inflicts Auschwitz on his people.[24]

I respect Rubenstein's initial claim to accept a form of existential secularism (although I personally prefer a Sartrean account to one based on Camus). I even respect his claim (later in the same work), that his true "confession of faith" would reveal him to be a "pagan."[25] What I do not accept is his assertion that a choice to have faith in God necessarily requires one to believe in an intervening God who either inflicted Auschwitz upon us or who deliberately stood by and allowed the Holocaust to proceed when He had the power all along to intervene at any point and stop it from happening. I would contend that there are other approaches to God that fundamentally alter the character of this dilemma.

In my view, and that of others such as Elie Wiesel, it is possible to approach the problem of theodicy in other ways. I am constantly engaged in an ongoing internal dialectical debate between existential secularism and some form of religious faith. At those times when I do believe, the God I address is not the God of history, in fact it is not an intervening God at all. Echoing Martin Buber, the God I address at these times is an intimate, a confidante, one who might assist me in the search for solace, consolation, or meaning, but God is not a being capable of intervening directly to prevent individual evil acts much less enormous systematic evils such as the Holocaust.

While in a way my view resembles that of the Deists, bringing us back full circle to our earlier discussion of Thomas Jefferson, I do not view God as a being of pure rationality. The God described by theorists such as Buber or Joseph Soloveitchik is a being more like us, composed of both rational and emotional elements. Sometimes I even agree with those who suggest that this notion of God is no more than a renaming of the best parts of oneself, just another way of referring to one's personal attempt to re-create oneself as one wishes oneself to be. In any case, I think Elie Wiesel's response to Rubenstein is philosophically more interesting than Rubenstein's supposed paganism, especially when Wiesel suggests that

> to be a Jew is to have all the reasons in the world to destroy and *not to destroy!* To be a Jew is to have all the reasons in the world to hate the Germans and *not to hate them!* To be a Jew is to have all the reasons in the world to mistrust the church and *not to hate it!* To be a Jew is to have all the reasons in the world not to have faith in language, in singing, in prayers, and in God, but *to go on telling the tale, to go on carrying on the dialogue,* and to have my own silent prayers and quarrels with God![26]

In the postscript to this exchange we are told that after listening to Wiesel, Rubenstein indicated that he wished to speak. Rather than continuing the debate, he simply told Wiesel, "I as a rabbi want to give you my blessing."[27] Thus, in opposition to Patterson's notion of rights backed by an objective knowledge of God's will, I would propose the possibility of a less arrogant faith based more on hope than certainty, respect for individual autonomy, and the attempt to find common ground for agreement on notions of rights acceptable to all of us despite our many differences. These tasks challenge philosophers to wrestle with the destruction of the Holocaust and the devastation of genocide as they respond with the best reflection and insight they can provide.

Notes

1. See Irving Greenberg, "Cloud of Smoke, Pillar of Fire," in John K. Roth and Michael Berenbaum, eds, *Holocaust: Religious and Philosophical Implications* (St. Paul, MN: Paragon House, 1989), p. 313.
2. Richard L. Rubenstein, *The Cunning of History* (New York: Harper Torchbooks, 1987), p. 67. Quoted in John K. Roth, ed., *Ethics after the Holocaust* (St. Paul, MN: Paragon House, 1999), p. 291.
3. Rubenstein, *The Cunning of History*, p. 88. Quoted in Roth, ed., *Ethics after the Holocaust*, p. 291.
4. Roth, ed., *Ethics after the Holocaust*, pp. 291–2.

5. Ibid., p. 292.
6. Ibid.
7. Ibid.
8. "Teleology as the (frustrated) Pursuit of Happiness: Meister Eckhart on 'living without a why,' " by John M. Connolly (Smith College), p. 5. This essay was presented at the annual conference of the Northern New England Philosophy Association (NNEPA) held on the campus of Keene State College in Keene, New Hampshire, 20 September 2003.
9. Meister Eckhart, Sermon 41,*Qui sequitur justitiam* (They who pursue justice), German Works, vol. II, (Stuttgart: Verlag W. Kohlhammer, 1936).
10. In the discussion following Connolly's NNEPA presentation, Jeffrey Buechner (Rutgers University) was the first to point out this problem.
11. Primo Levi, *Survival in Auschwitz: The Nazi Assault on Humanity*, trans. Stuart Woolf (New York: Touchstone Books, 1996), p. 29.
12. According to John Connelly, "while Eckhart may believe in 'man's innate goodness' (we are after all God's creations), he would surely acknowledge that this innate goodness is something we are generally not in touch with, and we quite routinely act selfishly and unjustly. So I don't think Eckhart disagrees with you, and he would be horrified that the guard in effect, even if unintentionally, quotes him to Levi."
13. Roth, ed., *Ethics after the Holocaust*, p. 288.
14. See my essays, "Never Again: The Protection of International Human Rights," in Yeager Hudson and W. Creighton Peden, eds, *The Social Power of Ideas* (Lewiston, NY: Edwin Mellen Press, 1996) and "The Law and Morality in War Crimes Trials," in Diane Sank, ed., *To Be A Victim: Encounters with Crime and Injustice* (New York: Plenum Press, 1991).
15. Roth, ed., *Ethics after the Holocaust*, p. 167.
16. Ibid., p. 159.
17. Ibid., p. 204.
18. Ibid., p. 207.
19. Ibid., p. 209.
20. Ibid., p. 298.
21. Ibid., p. 302.
22. See the selections from Richard L. Rubenstein's *After Auschwitz*, in Roth and Berenbaum, eds, *Holocaust: Religious and Philosophical Implications*, p. 287.
23. See Roth and Berenbaum, eds, *Holocaust*, p. 355.
24. Ibid., p. 355.
25. Ibid., p. 360.
26. Ibid., p. 369.
27. Ibid.

3

How Should Genocide Affect Philosophy?

Frederick Sontag

In the twentieth century, it could be said that evil caught up with philosophy, has called philosophy to account, but to what extent has philosophy recognized and responded to that impact? If the twentieth century has aptly been called an age of genocide, to what extent has genocide affected philosophy and its views about evil, goodness, human existence, and God in particular? Has genocide changed how we must think about humanity and God? Have genocide and its possible relationship to God affected how we should think about evil? Viewed with humanity's genocidal impulses in mind, must evil now become a key concept for self-understanding, including philosophy's understanding of itself? Philosophy is as good as the questions it asks. These questions are among the ones that philosophy most needs to ponder if it is to make its best contributions in the twenty-first century.

As far as American life is concerned, full of optimism and hopes for progress as it tends to be, I think it has never deeply occurred to us Americans, at least not deeply enough, to use evil as the key concept, and as a central historical fact, when we want to assess where we stand in our search for self-understanding. The concept of evil, in fact, is difficult, even elusive, to define simply, for evil comes in so many forms. If genocide is not evil, however, it is difficult to imagine anything that could be. The issue is whether awareness and analysis of genocide can help us to understand evil more adequately and to cope with it more effectively. With that point in mind, it is important to note that the most devastating attempts at massive human massacres came, in fact, just after human ingenuity had placed the modern, scientific, human intellect "on high." Scientific discovery had immensely empowered human beings, but typically it was not expected that, as optimism grew, evil would do likewise and complicate self-understanding.

As one major example, consider how concepts of God may be required to change in the twenty-first century. At least in American life, "God" often plays a central part in our high self-evaluation, but if evil looms larger than ever, reappraisals about God's relation to history and American life in particular will also be required. On the other hand, optimism about human power and its potential have also resulted in pushing God to the sidelines of national life. New awareness of evil "after Auschwitz," however, is unlikely to lead people back to a simple, loving God. If God is to be found in genocidal times, our understanding of God's nature will need to change to incorporate a more radical sense of evil than traditional views have suggested.

Biblical narratives suggest that evil, leading to brother murdering brother, took place in the Garden of Eden. At least in that sense, the world was not created perfect, even if (or perhaps even because) it contained human freedom. Along with human freedom, God allowed evil to enter at the world's inception. Now it seems that, in accounting for human nature, we too must include evil—and so attribute to God the knowing ability to conceive and to create a world plagued by evil as well as good. Surely God can still be seen as creating a good world for humans to start with. Yet, even the original humans were just as clearly inclined to do evil as to try to improve human nature. At the world's beginning the seeds of genocide were sown.

Thus, if we try to pray to an all-good God, we are not speaking about or to the one who created this mixed world of ours. Take evolution as an example. Anyone interested in religion and in our human creative forces must now give God at least some credit for the suffering incorporated in evolution, such as animals that came to life and were mercilessly eliminated. We understand evolution scientifically now, but we must admit that it includes vast suffering. God, it seems, could have created a more perfect world had God wanted it. Our knowledge of science tells us that. True, we have many good and helpful instructors of religion trying to perfect us, but now we must also give our divine Creator at least some credit for all the malfunctions and evils that seem to grow equally well in the divinely created order.

In the twenty-first century, if we give God credit for the beauties and perfections that have developed from an evolutionary creation, we may have to give God credit for at least a share of all the evils too. The grandeur of our evolving natural order is that it contains beauties and almost unlimited creative possibilities, except that we must accept—when and if we thank God for nature's marvelous potentials as they lead us in our ability to create—that evil and destruction occurred at nature's massive inception too and increased as human understanding developed. The creative intelligence that was set within us, plus our free ability to control nature's massive power potential, allowed major possibilities for improvement. Yet we must also open ourselves to all of nature's dangers—including human freedom itself—in our human search to control natural power.

The world's various religions have often been a counterbalancing force that can help to control humanity's tendency to seek the power that so easily gets us into evil ways. Arguably, it would be better for human nature (and for the divine nature too) if God's creation had limited us to a single religion that would be universally persuasive and peace-seeking. Instead, our inherited religions are multiple, often unpersuasive and at odds, and problematic with respect to peace-making even when their impulses go in that direction.

Religions not only serve humankind but also play parts in destroying it, including parts that are intertwined with genocide.

Cain's killing of his brother Abel signifies that human life had barely begun before murder took place. Nor has it ceased. On the contrary, humanity's murderous destruction has escalated over time even while men and women have tried to build perfect world orders. But particularly since the rise of modern science, humanity has tended to call more attention to its successes than to its failures. We had good reason to believe that, in growing scientific eras, we could create new societies which would be at least relatively free of evil's destruction.

So evil was not the most noted thing since Genesis, given what humans had learned to create. Small-scale genocides had existed and continued, but the human optimism that was driven by science was not thoroughly called into question until Nazi Germany, which rose out of one of history's most scientific and culturally advanced societies, unleashed the Holocaust, a genocide whose massive scope still boggles human minds. "After Auschwitz" it no longer makes sense to say that science and culture can ensure that humanity will move beyond the evils of genocide. Thus, the twenty-first century faces a new situation with more massive evil than modern cultures can escape easily. Philosophers and theologians who fail to put that fact at the center of their agendas can scarcely be said to do their work responsibly.

Not only must we ask if genocides will continue, even supported by modern scientific cultures, but also: Do we face increasingly sophisticated evils that we do not have the will and the power to eliminate? Philosophers, who have often been captivated by humanity's creative potential, have to confront more directly than ever the likelihood that evil, including genocide, can never be eliminated. That realization highlights other issues that urgently need attention, including philosophical attention: How can we draw on humanity and the power in modern societies to restrict or at least to lessen the evil of genocide? How can we use education and communication to alert humanity better about the potential destruction we continually face and to see if the nearly universal agreement we need, at least to control if not to eliminate the evils of mass destruction, can be more easily found?

We know how to heal and even to eliminate many physical illnesses that for centuries could not be treated. Perhaps we thought that the increased education needed to control medical evils could be extended to human nature in general. But we know that such developments did not take place in Germany, and the Nazis rose to power by convincing many highly educated people to support the mass destruction of the European Jews. Why? Perhaps we can really learn that power was and is the necessary goal of countries and politicians, and that power tends to corrupt absolutely. Education, including philosophy, has crucial parts to play in this task. The history and threat of genocide can and should motivate philosophers to fulfill and to help others to feel the importance of the Socratic injunction, "Know thyself."

As previously noted, some have thought religions could be counted on to draw people away from the quest for power and to bring peace. Sometimes we have seen this happen: those accomplishments should be celebrated. But we have already faced enough warfare and human destruction in the twenty-first century to know that we cannot expect all religions to abandon power goals. As much good as some religious groups accomplish, our new situation with evil deepens the realization that we cannot count on religion to accomplish good at all times. The quest for power, moreover, seems almost as pervasive inside religions as in secular groups. So must we abandon all hope that religious growth can offer control of evil itself?

Millions, of course, have emigrated thousands of miles to try to find homes in societies less affected by power and therefore less evil. The United States would never be what it has become if her immigrants had not thought they could largely leave evil behind. Nowadays, however, speed of travel and communication leave no place on earth invulnerable to evil. It can be imported and exported everywhere, as terrorism and the world's war against it reveal. We may have early warnings about genocide, but it does not follow that it will be checked. Advances in such social scientific understanding rarely result in political agreement.

Increased social and economic inequality escalates genocide's threat, and such inequality continues to increase, not decrease or stop altogether, as the twenty-first century unfolds. Where evil is concerned, we must not give up the hope and expectation many held to lessen the causes of genocide. True, knowing what we know about movements in society, we can work harder in our new century for increased understanding. The trouble is that those seeking power, evil's greatest cause, seem blinded about how close their power seeking is to pervasive evil under different names and aims. Revolutions, those events starting new nations and social orders, also hide evil more easily in their announced and accepted goals.

It is difficult to grasp that those killed in genocide are usually not slaughtered for anything they have done but mostly for how they are identified. Genocides intend to destroy a national, ethnic, racial, or religious group; their victims are not killed for what they have done but because of the group they belong to. Religiously and philosophically grounded education that seeks to underwrite the preciousness of individual life and individual rights is particularly challenged by genocide, which undercuts those values and efforts, not by theory or ideology alone but by devastating violence. Genocides depend on an "essentialism" that rejects individuality. The group is all alike in its alleged threat. So they must all be killed. Historically, philosophy has long been preoccupied with essences and with what is essential. Where those concepts are concerned, genocide adds troubling and perplexing dimensions for philosophy to consider and criticize.

Unless the future can be made different from the past, intellectuals and academics, including philosophers, cannot be counted on to reject authoritarian rule and other destructive uses of power, since we know that they often play a key role in the ideological rationalization for genocide. Its aim is "to make killing the necessary and the right thing," and academics are far from 100 percent innocent where that goal has been in play. There is no automatic guarantee that intelligence or education will oppose evil. Many perpetrators of genocide have been highly educated. A study of history can show us artistic and intellectual advancements. But history also shows how individuals and societies become murderous, and the arts and sciences have made lethal contributions to those circumstances. To check evil in the twenty-first century we cannot assume that human beings are naturally ethical, let alone making moral progress. In an age of genocide, philosophy should be affected by and responsive to that reality.

Twenty-first century evil has its roots in Cain's murder of Abel. In that regard, contemporary circumstances are not completely different from those that came to life in the beginning. Nevertheless, in the twenty-first century we must give up all modern, scientific hope of creating a world in which evil, perhaps even massive evil, does not exist. What one would hope is that, with modern technologies, we would develop more sophisticated ways of dealing with it. In our personal and cultural worlds, we can hope for advances in dealing with evil, even the massive evil of genocide, but we cannot count on the sheer passage of time or on optimistic assumptions about cultural progress to eliminate evil. On the contrary, penetrating analysis of humankind's propensity to do evil, and to do it in ever more ingenious ways, is crucial lest goodness be outclassed and overcome by human destructiveness.

If violence, including genocide, is to be checked, permanent international institutions have to be developed and empowered to act, but such unified action is no easier to develop and support than is unified action in the government of the United States or the corridors of the United Nations. Yet that is just where it seems a good portion of our search to control evil and mass destruction lies. Given advances in communication, we should be better able to expose the deception and disinformation used to confuse the public and to maintain secrecy. Yet we should be rendered unsure when we realize how intractable the modern nation state remains when involved in horrible crimes of war and genocide. This alone should make us unsure of counting on any cultural advance where controlling evil is concerned.

If we support the various religious groups to which we are attracted, we need to remember the often violent roles that religious fundamentalism and militancy have continued to play in the twenty-first century. We may support our new abilities to contain evil, even if we cannot eliminate it. But an ultimate question remains: Do we really have any new understanding of evil if we cannot really hope to escape genocide? Are we really any better off, as human beings, if we do not understand and cannot control evil?

As the twenty-first century starts, philosophers must ask, "After Auschwitz, what now?" Have we investigated evil enough to feel that we have some advice to offer which might lead us to increased understanding, and thus also increase our effectiveness in doing our part to expose and oppose the evil still threatening us in the twenty-first century and beyond? Particularly, in America's future, how can we best deal with these matters? Must we accept a divine and natural order that is less than perfect? What would such acceptance mean and what should it not mean? This chapter has offered some preliminary responses to those questions. More beginnings need to be made, for philosophers—and too few of them at that—are only at the beginning in taking up their responsibility to consider how genocide should affect philosophy.

4

Genocide, Despair, and Religious Hope: An Essay on Human Nature

Stephen T. Davis

Occasionally we have experiences that make us proud to be members of the human race. When we watch a play by Shakespeare, or listen to a Mozart symphony, or look at a Rembrandt painting, or admire an Ansel Adams photograph, or benefit from a medical discovery—in those moments we feel thrilled and uplifted. We sense that this sort of thing is the work of *homo sapiens* at its best.

But our feelings are not quite the same when we think of the Holocaust of 1939–45, in which some six million Jews and millions of others were murdered by the Nazis. As with all acts of genocide, when we think about the Holocaust, we feel profoundly ashamed to be members of the human race. We ask: How could it have happened? How could the hatred of the perpetrators, as well as the indifference of the bystanders, have reached such a shocking level? We sense that this sort of thing is the work of *homo sapiens* at its worst. For that reason, and others that I will explore in this chapter, genocide should affect philosophy and, in particular, its responsibility to grapple with the problem of evil.

A thought experiment

In the contrast I have described at the outset, we see, *par excellence*, the dual nature of human beings. We can create and discover things that are breathtaking in their beauty, goodness, and utility. We can do things that are outrageously evil and that will stain the pages of history for millennia. We are capable of the loftiest heights and the most hellish depths. This seems an inexplicable mystery. Virtually all religions, and many philosophies, try to explain this tendency toward evil in the hearts of human beings.

Let's perform a *Gedankenexperiment*. A term from physics, a "thought experiment" is simply a situation where we do not have the money or the technology to actually perform the test, so what we do is try to imagine, as best we can, what the likely result would be if we *were* able to perform it. The ancient Greek Archimedes was conducting a thought experiment when he said, "Give me a long enough lever and a place to stand and I will move the earth."

My thought experiment is not from the realm of geometry or physics but morality. It concerns a crime that has been called *omnicide*. Suppose human beings possessed the technology to destroy the entire universe. Is there any doubt that there are people who, if they could lay their hands on that technology, would use it? There is no such doubt in my mind. I believe that such people do exist. Just as there are people who would kill another human being in a given situation if the technology (a handgun, let's say) were readily available, so there are people (doubtless a much smaller number) who would destroy the universe, including themselves, if they could.

Genocide appears to be a crime that is situated somewhere between the crime of murder and the crime of omnicide. Genocide is the crime of intentionally destroying or attempting to destroy an entire group of people, usually a racial, ethnic, national, or religious group.[1] Just as there are people who would commit murder if they could, and just as there are people who would commit omnicide if they could, so there are people who would commit genocide if they could.

The moral of this depressing story is this: *genocide should not surprise us.* (I am not saying that it should not horrify us.) Occasionally there will be people who (a) hate another group enough to kill all its members, and (b) are able to seize control of the technology and social organization necessary to achieve that end. Most fortunately, not all human beings are guilty or even potentially guilty of genocide. Most of us are not. But it is troubling that genocides are typically carried out by ordinary people who have adopted an ideology of hatred for the persecuted group or else see themselves as simply obeying the orders of their superiors.

As far as we know, mass slaughter and perhaps even genocide have been part of history ever since human beings first organized themselves into social groups. But something changed in the twentieth century. It was during that period that human hatred began to be allied to governmental bureaucracies, propaganda machines, transportation services, and technologies for mass killing. Nevertheless, I doubt that the fairly late appearance of that sort of systematic genocide on the human scene is because people before (roughly) 1900 were morally superior to those after that date. Surely it is because genocide in the fullest sense was not technically possible then.

But, alas, the mechanisms and technologies of genocide are now available. So we can almost say this: human beings and human progress are such that *genocide or at least attempted genocide is now something that is to be expected* (as well as, of course, resisted with all the power at our command).

Another way of making the point, one that relates more to human communities rather than individuals, is this: If human group A has complete control over human group B, it is very possible that the members of A will oppress the members of B and perhaps even engage in genocide against the members of B. (Note that the victims of genocide are almost always politically and militarily powerless.) It will be the first if the B people are economically useful to the A people, the second if the A people hate the B people sufficiently.

A perplexing question

Why are human beings capable of moral evil and indeed of gross moral outrages like genocide? To try to answer that perplexing question, I am going to appeal to two of the foundational myths of Western culture, the story of Cain and Abel and the story of the Tower of Babel. Both stories are found in the biblical book of Genesis. They are terse, and each raises important questions that the text does not attempt to answer. But as Albert Camus said, "Myths are made for the imagination to breathe life into them."[2] I will supply my own interpretation of the stories, doing something like what Jewish tradition calls *midrash*. Taken together, I believe the two texts illuminate the phenomenon of genocide.

In Genesis 4, the Bible tells us that Adam and Eve, the first human beings, had two sons whom they named Cain and Abel. Abel, the younger, was a keeper of sheep, and Cain, the firstborn, was a farmer. The text proceeds as follows:

> In the course of time Cain brought to the Lord an offering of the fruit of the ground, and Abel for his part brought of the firstlings of his flock, their fat portions. And the Lord had regard for Abel and his offering, but for Cain and his offering he had no regard. So Cain was very angry, and his countenance fell. The Lord said to Cain, "Why are you angry, and why has your countenance fallen? If you do well, will you not be accepted? And if you do not do well, sin is lurking at the door; its desire is for you, but you must master it." Cain said to his brother Abel, "Let us go out to the field." And when they were in the field, Cain rose up against his brother Abel, and killed him. Then the Lord said to Cain, "Where is your brother Abel?" He said, "I do not know; am I my brother's keeper?" And the Lord said, "What have you done? Listen; your brother's blood is crying out to me from the ground! And now you are cursed from the ground, which has opened its mouth to receive your brother's blood from your hand. When you till the ground, it will no longer yield to you its strength; you will be a fugitive and a wanderer in the earth." (Genesis 4:1–16, New Revised Standard Version [NSRV])

When Cain complained that his punishment was too great for him to bear and that anyone who met him might kill him, God placed a mark on him so that no one would kill him. As the story concludes, Cain leaves the presence of the Lord and settles in the land of Nod, east of Eden.

This story describes the first murder. It is a crime of fratricide. The text presupposes, but does not attempt to explain, the tendency toward pride, arrogance, envy, and oppression of the weak (what the rabbis called *yetzer ha-ra*) that seems to reside in the human heart. Murder is different from, and far more serious than, most other crimes and offenses. There are two related reasons for this: first, since no human being has the power to bring the dead back to life, a crime of murder can never be made good again in the sense of reversing its effect; second, since no human being has the power to create life, it follows that life and death belong to God alone. Murder, then, is a crime both against the victim and his family and friends, and also (and most importantly) against God.

We do not know why God preferred Abel's sacrifice to Cain's. Perhaps there was no reason other than God's sovereign choice. After all, we read in Exodus 33:19 that God said to Moses: "I will be gracious to whom I will be gracious and will show mercy upon whom I will show mercy." But the story contains hints of prior religious or even moral culpability on the part of Cain: Cain, it says, brought only "an offering of the fruit of the ground" while Abel brought "the firstlings [or 'the choicest'] of his flock." Perhaps Abel took the ritual more seriously than his brother did. Maybe Cain's sacrifice was a mere outward act while Abel's was sincere and heartfelt. Moreover, when Cain's countenance fell because God dishonored his sacrifice, God asked him, "If you do well, will you not be accepted?" as if he had failed to do well. What he had failed to do, it turns out, was to prevent sin from lurking at his door.

The story is clear that Cain, even in his fury at Abel, had freedom of choice. Sin was lurking at his door—so God advised him—but "you must master it." Here we see the Lord appealing to Cain's better motives: God gave him a chance to amend his ways. The myth is apparently saying that we human beings are able to resist our murderous impulses; it is up to us to decide whether we will do good or evil. But sin in the Bible seems to have a kind of positive power, a way of gaining control over human beings. This inclination explains the human tendency to kill, or at least to want to kill, our enemies. Cain did not master his murderous impulse.

We do not know how Cain did the deed. Since the killing involved spilling his brother's blood, we naturally think of a stone or club. Whatever the tool, a technology of death was available to him. He lured Abel out into the field where he thought the act would not be observed, and struck him down.

In the end, we learn from the Cain and Abel story that murder, and all crimes greater than murder (such as genocide), are morally wrong. They are evil for three reasons. First, murder is wrong because no human being has the right, out of self-centered motives like anger or jealousy, to take the life of another. Second, murder is wrong because even nature itself, in receiving Abel's blood, cried out in protest to God over what Cain had done. Human life is sacred. Third, murder is wrong because once that crime is introduced into human history, it is liable, like an infectious disease, to spread. Even Cain recognized as much. In protesting his punishment, he said to God: "I shall be hidden from your face; I shall be a fugitive and a wanderer on the earth, and anyone who meets me may kill me."

The implications of Cain's act are still with us today. In the year 2001, there were 13,653 persons arrested for murder (in its various degrees) in the United States.[3] In that same year, there were 15,980 victims of murder (in its various degrees) in the United States.[4] In the year 2000, 8600 people were convicted of murder in the United States.[5] Since 1976 (when the Supreme Court reinstated the death penalty), 885 people have been executed by the various states (71 in 2002; 65 in 2003), the vast majority for murder.[6] As of 1 July 2003, there were 3517 prisoners under sentence of death in the United States.[7] Murder has been with us ever since Cain, and shows no sign of going away.

Murder also seems to corrupt the murderer even further. After his deed, Cain's heart was hardened to such an extent that he lied to God. When God asked him the whereabouts of his brother, Cain replied, "I do not know." This was also the point where Cain posed his famous sarcastic question, "Am I my brother's keeper?" I think Cain was trying—as most criminals do—to find somebody else to blame. I think he was saying to God, "It's not my job to protect Abel from all the dangers that might prove fatal to him in this world that you created: that's your job." So murder and lying about it were now parts of human experience, and would remain so. Cain was condemned to the life of a wanderer or nomad in the land of Nod ("restlessness").

In Genesis 11, we read about a great tower:

> Now the whole earth had one language and the same words. And as they migrated from the east, they came upon a plain in the land of Shinar and settled there. And they said to one another, "Come, let us make bricks, and burn them thoroughly." And they had brick for stone, and bitumen for mortar. Then they said, "Come, let us build ourselves a city, and a tower with its top in the heavens, and let us make a name for ourselves; otherwise we shall be scattered abroad upon the face of the whole earth." The Lord came down to see the city and the tower, which mortals had built. And the Lord said, "Look, they are one people, and they have all one language; and this is only the beginning of what they will do; nothing that they propose to do will now be impossible for them. Come, let us go down, and confuse their language there, so that they will not understand one another's speech." So the Lord scattered them abroad from there over the face of all the earth, and they left off building the city. (Genesis 11:1-9, NRSV)

The story concludes that the city was called Babel, because that is where the Lord confused the language of all the earth.

This deep and puzzling myth also presupposes the human tendency toward self-aggrandizement and rebellion against God, although it interprets that tendency in a more corporate or social way than the Cain and Abel story does. Here technology is an explicit part of the story, and technology becomes an aid to the evil tendency in human beings. The human race had developed to the point of living in cities, using bricks to build with, and erecting great towers. Genesis wants us to understand that the attempt to build the great tower at Babel was an act of pride on the part of the people who lived there. They wanted to "make a name" for themselves and even to reach "the heavens." That is, they wanted no longer to have to serve God. They wanted to equal God or even *be* God. They reached too high.

God saw that human beings were now capable of great evil. God grasped immediately that "this is only the beginning of what they will do." Those are prophetic words indeed. In our own age, a time not only of genocide but of nuclear weapons, worldwide terrorism, genetic engineering, and global degradation of the environment, we see the truth of God's words, "Nothing that they propose to do will now be impossible for them." Human beings now have powers that people once sensibly thought that only God possessed. It is depressing to contemplate how those powers have been used thus far, and sobering, if not terrifying, to wonder how they will be used.

At Babel, God intervened. God confused the language of the people, and thus their ability to continue building. Unable to understand each other, they could no longer organize themselves to complete the project, or even stay together in one place. The crisis—at least at that moment—was averted. But now it seems to us that the God of the Bible, after the great flood in Genesis 6–9 and the confusion of the languages in Genesis 11, no longer intervenes to prevent gross evils. Evil runs rampant. What the Bible calls sin has become a landslide. After the murder of Abel and the episode at Babel, genocide is not only possible but actual.

Relativism is wrong

Before turning to the problem of genocide and hope, I must discuss further a point about genocide that I just claimed we can learn from our two biblical texts. It is the claim that murder, in all its forms (one of which is genocide), is wrong. In one sense, this claim seems perfectly obvious. But I need to point out that moral relativism has a long history in the discipline of philosophy, and has made a strong comeback in recent decades.

What exactly is moral relativism? Let's define it as the philosophical position which says that nothing is morally right (or wrong) per se. There are no trans-personal normative truths in morality. If I say, "Murder is morally wrong," I am only reporting my own opinion that murder is morally wrong. And of course murder *is* morally wrong if I believe it is morally wrong, but that means only that it is morally wrong "for me." Other people might think that murder is morally right, and of course that view is correct too— for them. The theory is called moral relativism because it crucially claims that the truth or falsity of normative moral claims is relative to the person or group making them.[8]

It seems to me that genocide is the *reductio ad absurdum* of moral relativism. Indeed, I believe we all *know* that murder in all its forms is morally wrong. When we read Genesis 4, we recognize as much in our revulsion at Cain's behavior. We *are* our brothers' keepers. Abel's blood *does* cry out from the ground. Here is the strongest thing that a moral relativist can say against genocide: *I hold that genocide is morally wrong.* Or perhaps: *I hold, and my community holds, that genocide is morally wrong.* But the problem is that such a position allows the perpetrator of genocide (a Nazi, perhaps) to reply: *Sorry, but my community holds that genocide is morally right.*

It is painful even to ponder such an exchange. We want to cry out: "It isn't a matter of what people *think* is right or wrong: *Genocide is just plain morally wrong.*" That is, it is morally wrong per se, morally wrong no matter what any person or community may think. I would make so bold as to claim that anyone who holds that genocide is morally wrong only for those who believe it is morally wrong is either badly confused, malicious, or insane.

Genocide and God

Does God exist? Theists say yes; atheists say no; and agnostics neither agree nor disagree. But let me now try to argue, on the basis of what I have said thus far, that God exists. My proof, which we might call "the Genocide Argument for the Existence of God," can only be convincing to those who agree with me that moral relativism is false and that genocide is morally wrong. The argument I give is related to the traditional "moral argument" for the existence of God, but is also different at crucial points.[9]

Suppose it is true that genocide is morally wrong. Now those things that we consider to be morally wrong constitute departures from the way (so we believe) that things ought to be. And those things that *are* in fact wrong *are* in fact departures from the way that things ought to be. That is at least part of what we mean by "morally wrong." It follows, then, that genocide is a departure from the way that things ought to be. And if that much is true, then it follows that there *is* "a way that things ought to be." In other words, certain things are morally right and certain things are morally wrong quite apart from what anybody believes. And if that much is true, it then follows that there exists what we might call a "design plan" for human life and experience. A full design plan would simply be a list of all those things that constitute the ways that things ought to be (presumably it would include items like compassion, truth-telling, promise-keeping, and so on) and a list of all those things that should not be (presumably it would include items such as cruelty, lying, murder, and of course genocide).

Now if there is a design plan for things, then there must be an author of the design plan, a designer, a sentient agent of some sort. I can make no sense of the notion of an authorless design plan or a design plan that emerged merely from nature or the cosmos. The cosmos is the way that things *are*; it has nothing whatever to do with the way that things *ought to be*. If then there is a designer, we can call it "God." Of course the Genocide Argument does not prove that the designer possesses all the properties that the God of theism is traditionally said to have—oneness, omnipotence, omniscience, benevolence, etc. Certainly the moral designer that we have just proved to exist *could* have all those properties; the point is just that the Genocide Argument by itself does not prove that it *must*. Still, if the Genocide Argument is sound, then God, the moral designer of the universe, exists.

Here then is the way the argument can be summarized:

1. Genocide is a departure from the way that things ought to be.
2. If genocide is a departure from the way that things ought to be, then there is a way that things ought to be.
3. If there is a way that things ought to be, then there is a design plan for things.
4. If there is a design plan for things, then there is a designer.
5. This designer we call "God."

How should we assess the Genocide Argument? Is it convincing? Where does it lead, so far as genocide and hope are concerned?

Grounds for hope

Nothing in human experience is more disgusting and profoundly depressing than genocide. To turn to the question that I have postponed until now, let me ask: Is there any sense in which genocide can be a springboard for hope? Or even: Is there any room for hope in a world in which genocide occurs?

My central answer is this: *Unless God exists, our grounds for hope in the light of genocide are limited indeed.* I recognize that this bold claim will meet with disapproval in many circles. But it seems that if no creator or higher power such as the God of theism exists, the only hope we can sensibly have in the light of genocide is tenuous. It is the hope that some day we can so design our educational, social, political, and diplomatic systems in such a way that no more genocide occurs.

I have no doubt whatsoever that this goal is one which all right-thinking human beings, believers in God or not, must pursue. My wife and I instructed our own children that they were to hate no one, and that they were never to be a party to, or in any sense to support, any acts of genocide. Much, much more is required than that, of course, but it is at least a place to start. We can think of places in the world where children are apparently not taught along those lines.

But if God does not exist, a genocide-free world is the best for which we can hope. Those who believe in inevitable human progress will find it a possible hope. Those, like me, who do not share that belief will reply that we can certainly *hope* for such a world, but that it will be something like a hope that continental drift will cease. Certainly, if God does not exist, there is no hope whatsoever for any experience of reparation or even joy by the victims of genocide. They are gone forever. That sort of hope only makes sense if God exists. If one holds that God does not exist, and if one's assessment of human nature is such that the possibility of genocide can never be excluded ... well, that reasoning seems to me to lead to despair.

Note that there are hints of grace even in our two dark biblical stories. God does not kill Cain, even though Cain had killed his brother, and when Cain protests that his punishment is too severe, God acts to protect him. He places a mark on Cain, perhaps a tattoo on his forehead (the rabbis thought it was one letter of the divine name), in order to protect him. The fact that he continues to live gives him the time and opportunity to repent of his crime. I think God was saying to Cain: "There is still time, Cain; it is not too late; you can still master the evil that you have allowed to lurk at your door." God is merciful. And the denizens of Babel, despite their arrogance and desire to worship themselves instead of God, are not killed. Nor are they so afflicted that each one speaks a different language. They can continue to live in communities based on language groups, and they too are given time and opportunity to amend their ways and learn again to worship only God. God is merciful.

Is it possible for evil to be redeemed? Is it possible that all the acts of genocide ever committed can be redeemed? That of course will depend in part on how we define words such as *evil* and *redeem*.

Let us simply define *evil* as *undeserved human suffering*. I actually believe that the category of *evil* is broader than that (it is sometimes evil when animals suffer, for example, and it is possible to do an evil deed that does not cause any suffering), but here I ignore those sorts of complications. The notion of undeserved human suffering will suffice to cover all that I want to say about genocide. Undeserved suffering might be caused by another human being or other human beings, or by natural, non-human causes such as earthquakes, hurricanes, diseases, famines, etc. We can call the first "moral evil" and the second "natural evil." Both sorts of evils can equally cause pain and death, but moral evil is more troubling because human beings are culpable in bringing it about. Genocide is clearly an instance of moral evil; it is about as bad as moral evil gets. Natural evils can wipe our entire populations of people, but such events do not constitute genocide.

If "redeeming genocide" means restoring conditions so that an act of genocide such as the Holocaust never occurred, then obviously genocide cannot be redeemed. This outcome follows from the metaphysical principle that the past is fixed and unchangeable. It is too late for anyone, even God, to do anything about the fact that the event occurred. Nor can the Holocaust be redeemed, in my opinion, in the sense that we will one day understand that it was really *good*. Some evils can surely be redeemed in that sense. Probably all human beings have experienced undeserved suffering where they later came to understand that it was for the best that it occurred.

But this hardly applies to the Holocaust. Good did come out of it, one supposes. It is sometimes said that the State of Israel would never have existed had the Holocaust not occurred. That may be true. And I regard the existence of Israel as a good thing (this does not mean that I always support that nation's policies). Perhaps the Holocaust also strengthened the resolve of Jews, and of many non-Jews, that there shall be no more genocide against Jews. If so, that too is in my opinion a good thing. But do those goods produced or caused by the Holocaust outweigh the evil of the Holocaust? Of course not. The very suggestion seems absurd, almost obscene.

Well then, is there any sense in which genocide *can* be redeemed? The answer is, yes, but only if God exists. If no God exists, genocide cannot be redeemed at all. But if a perfectly good and all-powerful Supreme Being exists (as Jews and Christians claim), a sort of redemption is possible. Suppose that such a Being provides punishment for the perpetrators of genocide and a limitlessly good afterlife for murder and genocide victims (as well as for others, of course) in which their horrific earthly experiences fade further and further away in memory and eventually pale into insignificance in the light of the goodness then revealed and experienced. If that occurs, it will I think amount to something like redemption of genocide.[10]

Religious skeptics will dismiss talk like this as sheer silliness. And certainly they are allowed to declare with bravado their credo—that this life is all that there is, that death is the final and complete end for human beings, and that we had best just get used to the idea that we live in a radically unjust world. There simply is no redemption of genocide—so they will insist—or compensation for its victims.

But there is no denying that most human beings have a deep longing for justice, and a hope that our world will turn out just. I believe that the reality of genocide in our world for most people increases, rather than decreases, that longing. For those of us who wish to avoid despair, that hope is appealing. For those of us who believe in God, it is not just a hope but a conviction.

Notes

1. That the term *genocide* is exceedingly difficult to define precisely—for both conceptual and political reasons—is made clear in the essays in part I of Carol Rittner, John K. Roth, and James M. Smith, eds, *Will Genocide Ever End?* (St. Paul, MN: Paragon House, 2002). But since I believe the concept is clear at its core (as opposed to the margins), I will leave the definition I just provided at its present broad level.
2. Albert Camus, *The Myth of Sisyphus and Other Essays*, trans. Justin O'Brien (New York: Vintage Books, 1955), p. 89.

3. Federal Bureau of Investigation, U.S. Department of Justice, Crime in the United States 2001, Uniform Crime Reports, Table 29, p. 233; http://fbi.gov/ucr/cius01/01crime4.pdf.

4. Federal Bureau of Investigation, U.S. Department of Justice, Crime in the United States 2001, Uniform Crime Reports; http://www.fbi.gov/ucr/cius01/01crime2.pdf.

5. Bureau of Justice Statistics, U.S. Department of Justice, Felony Sentences in State Courts, 2000, Table 1, p. 2; http://www.ojp.usdoj.gov/bjs/pub/pdf/fssc00.pdf.

6. Death Penalty Information Center; http://www.deathpenaltyinfo.org/article.php?scid=8&did=145.

7. NAACP Legal Defense and Educational Fund, Inc., as reported by the Death Penalty Information Center; http://deathpenaltyinfo.org/article.php?scid=9&did=145.

8. The motivation for being a relativist seems often to be the desire to promote the moral value of tolerance. After all (so the reasoning apparently goes), if one moral view is right per se and all others false, those who hold the true view (or think they do) will be tempted to persecute those who don't. If moral relativism is true, no one has the moral right to impose his or her views on anybody else. But this ignores the possibility that moral theories that are true per se might have built into them a recommendation or even command to be tolerant of those who differ.

9. In the form in which I use it, the argument that follows is due to Douglas Geivett of Talbot Theological Seminary, and I use it with his permission. The only major difference is that while I focus on genocide, Geivett argues that anything that is genuinely evil is evidence for theism in the sense that it is a departure from the way things ought to be. See the brief discussion of the classical "Moral Argument," in my *God, Reason, and Theistic Proofs* (Edinburgh: Edinburgh University Press, 1997), pp. 146–50.

10. Of course the traditional problem of evil can still be raised—why did a good and all-powerful God allow genocide to happen in the first place?—and will have to be answered. Doing so is not the project of this chapter. See, however, my contributions to Stephen T. Davis, ed., *Encountering Evil*, 2nd edn (Louisville, KY: Westminster John Knox Press, 2001).

5
The Holocaust and Language

D. Z. Phillips

Two friends of long-standing fulfill their ambition to see the Grand Canyon together. As they stand before it, one says, "Magnificent!" The other responds, "Yes, magnificent!" The first says, "Awesome!" and the other replies, "Yes, awesome, and very pretty, too." The first looks at his compatriot with perplexed amazement. In this moment, their friendship is forever changed.

What did the first friend find out about the second? Note that they agreed in their first two reactions to the Grand Canyon, but diverged in the third. When the second friend is prepared to connect "magnificent" and "awesome" with "and very pretty, too," the first friend wonders what his companion meant by "magnificent" and "awesome" in the first place. For the second friend, nothing is revealed or threatened by the connection he is prepared to make, but the first realizes they have never shared a common sense of magnificence and awe. This revelation altered their friendship irreparably.

Making connections

What light can that simple story throw on the question how does, or should, genocide affect philosophy? This chapter reflects on that topic not in a general way but by focusing on a particular genocide—the Holocaust—and on why I want to link it with considerations of language. The concerns and points that I underscore pertain to relationships between genocide and philosophy, but the issues are put in especially bold relief by directing attention to the Holocaust and to issues about language that surround philosophical and theological reflection about that catastrophe.

At the outset, note that the concerns of Holocaust survivors regarding the limitations of the spoken word help to explain why many were reticent to share their experiences. Elie Wiesel says that there was a fear "that ... in the very process of telling the tale, they would betray it. ... So we didn't speak about it because we were afraid of committing a sin."[1] We hope, with a considerable degree of confidence, that most people will agree that to connect the Grand Canyon with mere "prettiness" is comically inappropriate. The Canyon deserves better than that. Analogously, there are reactions to the Holocaust that are agreed upon as inappropriate. Some, who are mercifully few in number, are prepared to connect descriptions of the Holocaust with words such as "exaggeration," "lies," "conspiracy," and "propaganda." Our reaction to their readiness to reach such conclusions is not to wonder whether there have been slips in Holocaust scholarship or whether hasty conclusions have been drawn from the facts. Rather, as Ludwig Wittgenstein would say, the connections we are being asked to make are "too big for a blunder." Our reaction is one of horror. The language used is a sin against the Holocaust, infinitely greater than that which occurred against the Canyon. Similarly, the minimal disagreement over objectionable syntax in regard to the Grand Canyon pales in comparison to the multitude of varied reactions to the Holocaust. Some make connections concerning the Holocaust to which others react with bewilderment, incomprehension, rage, and disgust.

It is not uncommon to hear it said that the story of the Holocaust can never be fully told. Partly, this is because it is unclear what "completeness" would mean when one thinks of the connections between the Holocaust and the lives of those it touched. That idea is somewhat different from Wiesel's concern that our language may betray the Holocaust. The point is not that we first have a conception of the Holocaust and then make appropriate or inappropriate connections. Rather, our conception of the Holocaust shows itself in the connections we make when we speak of it. Those connections divide as often as they unite. Is that where matters must be left, with a raggedness that cannot be tidied?

Can philosophy be of help in this situation? After all, was there not a revolution in the subject in the twentieth century, when it was said to have taken "a linguistic turn"? If philosophy is truly the "guardian of language," should it not be able to sort out appropriate from inappropriate language in regard to the Holocaust?

Unfortunately, such an optimistic view of philosophy is unfounded. The very philosophy that called itself "linguistic" has been accused of "a distrust of language."[2] Moral philosophy, for example, retreated into a narrow, restricted language of its own, preferring its "thin" concepts to the "thick" ones applicable to people's lives. Philosophy of religion, for the most part, discusses the Holocaust in consequentialist terms. Though it calls itself "analytic," the prospects for analysis are not good. Confronted by the Holocaust, philosophers of religion often connect it to some greater good, for the sake of which God has allowed it to happen. Surrounded by such reactions, it seems to me as though the majority, confronted by the Canyon, were to say: "and very pretty, too." Let me say that I am well aware of the bewildered looks that turn in my direction when I say this. All this goes to show that one cannot appeal to philosophy as though it were a formal method to decide whose language sins against the Holocaust.

Are we simply confronted with a philosophical Tower of Babel? Can we just say, "To each his own," and rest content with the variety of personal perspectives? Despite what I have said, such a conclusion would be premature. In relation to the Holocaust and other genocides, philosophy must walk a tightrope. On the one hand, it must not neglect its core commitment to distinguishing between sense and nonsense, clarity and confusion, integrity and corruption. It follows that philosophy cannot allow just any kind of language about the Holocaust, no matter what. On the other hand, philosophy cannot pretend that it possesses the criteria that determine an appropriate language to describe the Holocaust. It must do conceptual justice to the various reactions people have. Unfortunately, this begets dangers of its own. Philosophy can slide easily into a relativism that says that all reactions to the Holocaust are equally valid. In walking the tightrope, philosophy has to present the different reactions, not simply with their imperatives, but also with their criticisms of other kinds of reactions. As Peter Winch has pointed out, this places an enormous moral burden on the philosopher who has strong views about the Holocaust, which may stand in the way of appreciating the language in which very different views are expressed.[3]

The perspicuous representations philosophy is called on to provide will be relevant to related philosophical issues. How are differences about the Holocaust to be understood? Are they theoretical differences? What is it to accept one of these as true? Can any view be one which has the backing of philosophy? These questions are part of philosophy's contemplative task. It is easy to see how one is walking a tightrope in pursuing it.[4]

The Holocaust and "free" language

Why, despite the danger of sinning against the Holocaust, have Jews discussed it from about every aspect imaginable? Wiesel replies: "We believe in transmission, we believe in sharing. I think the single factor in Jewish existence is the need to communicate."[5] But this task of communication has been said to involve a fundamental difficulty of language. Our language is a "free" language. How can it convey the experiences of the supremely "unfree" conditions of the Holocaust? The Auschwitz survivor Primo Levi argued that this fundamental problem exists even in relation to the most elemental experiences of the Holocaust. He writes,

> Just as hunger is not that feeling of missing a meal, so our way of being cold has need for a new word. We say "hunger," we say "tiredness," "fear," "pain," we say "winter" and they are different things. They are free words created and used by free men who lived in comfort and suffering in their homes. If the Lagers [camps] had lasted longer a new, harsh language would have been born; and only this language could express what it means to toil the whole day in the wind, with the temperature below

freezing, and wearing only a shirt, underpants, cloth jacket and trousers, and in one's body but weakness, hunger and knowledge of the end drawing near.[6]

The harsh language needed to capture what happened in the Holocaust did not develop. How then is a bridge to be built between our "free" language and what Levi is talking about? Is that the right way to express the problem? Read in one way, the required "building" becomes impossible. In their writings, Wiesel and Levi want to tell us something they hope we will not forget. However, if there is a radical linguistic discontinuity between our "free" language and experiences of the Holocaust, the appeal not to forget would be futile, since there would be nothing we could remember. But those writing about the Holocaust are not reporting a failure to show us anything—they write to show us something, and they write in our language.

This does not mean that Levi and Wiesel were saying nothing in emphasizing a discontinuity between our "free" language and the Holocaust. However, we need to probe further to bring out what is important in what they say. There are two reasons for their emphasis on the discontinuity, but I want to argue that neither of these should lead us to think that our problem is one of bridging a gap between our "free" language and a language that we do not have but which, unlike ours, would be adequate to express the experiences of the Holocaust.

First, Levi and Wiesel want to emphasize the discontinuity that exists between being a victim of the Holocaust and being someone who simply reflects on it. The importance of this discontinuity may be disputed. For example, it may be argued that if we appreciate the spectrum of behavior that occurred during the Holocaust, why cannot it be said that we understand what occurred? This argument need not be accompanied by foolish predictions about how we would have behaved under those circumstances. Neither need it be accompanied by a rush to judge those who were broken by the camps. Furthermore, it may be questioned how one reflecting on the Holocaust from a distance may understand certain aspects of it better than some of its victims.

All the above considerations may be granted, but an essential distinction remains between survivors of the Holocaust and those who simply research it. The former have to come to terms in their lives with what they have endured. There is a "coming to understand" or a "failure to understand" that is inseparable from the need to analyze what one has gone through. Victims are marked in a way others are not. That is a discontinuity worth remembering.

The second reason for emphasizing the difference between victims and researchers of the Holocaust involves why it is worth remembering—not only the fact of suffering, but also what those trials entailed. In the midst of the Shoah, an exerted attempt was made by the perpetrators to negate the very conditions of a "free" language. That is one explanation for why some victims described their experiences as a loss of trust in the world. Part of such trust is our elemental belief that others will come to help us in our hour of need. Jean Améry writes,

> The expectation of help is as much a constitutional psychic element as is the struggle for existence. Just a moment, the mother says to her child who is moaning from pain, a hot-water bottle, a cup of tea is coming right away, we won't let you suffer so! I'll prescribe you a medicine, the doctor assures, it will help you. Even on the battlefield, the Red Cross ambulances find their way to the wounded man. In almost all situations in life where there is bodily injury there is also the expectation of help; the former is compensated by the latter.[7]

One of the first shocks for those sent to concentration camps was the denial of this belief. Recalling the torture that was inflicted upon him, Améry continues:

> At the first blow, however, this trust in the world breaks down. The other person, *opposite* whom I exist physically in the world and *with* whom I can exist only as long as he does not touch my skin surface as border, forces his corporeality on me with the first blow. He is on me and thereby destroys me. It is like a rape, a sexual act without the consent of one of the two partners.[8]

There is no reciprocity present, not even the kind involved in "an eye for an eye." The tortured one is nothing; the torturer is everything. As Améry puts the point:

> If from the experience of torture any knowledge at all remains that goes beyond the plain nightmarish, it is that of a great amazement and a foreignness in the world that cannot be compensated by any sort of subsequent human communication. Amazed, the tortured prisoner experienced that in this world there can be the other as absolute sovereign, and sovereignty revealed itself as the power to inflict suffering and to destroy ... Whoever has succumbed to torture can no longer feel at home in the world.[9]

The desire to destroy the Jews cannot be equated with the desire to annihilate them. If it could, the humiliations to which they were subjected would be illogical. Yet, this degradation is an essential part of what is meant by a loss of trust in the world. Terrence Des Pres explained,

> Why this was necessary is not at first apparent, since none of the goals of the camp system—to spread torture, to provide slaves, to exterminate

populations—require the kind of thoroughness with which conditions of defilement were enforced. But here too, for all its madness, there was method and reason. ... The mere act of killing is not enough; for if a man dies without surrender, if something within him remains unbroken to the end, then the power which destroyed him has not, after all, crushed everything. Something has escaped its reach, and it is precisely this something—let us call it "dignity"—that must die if those in power are to reach the orgasmic peak of their potential domination.[10]

Wiesel makes the same point,

What the Germans wanted to do was not only to exterminate the Jewish people physically; first of all, they wanted to exterminate them *spiritually*. ... The Germans wanted to deprave, to debase the Jew, to have him give up all values and dehumanize him. That was the first thing. Even the language in the camp—what kind of language was it? The most obscene language you could imagine, meant to create a climate, to impose an inhuman concept of man and of the universe upon the Jewish people.[11]

We have seen two interrelated forms of discontinuity in discussing the Holocaust. First, there is the divide between those who were its victims and those who were not. Second, the victims experienced systematic attempts to create a chasm between a sense of their own humanity and the conditions created to destroy it.

Full weight must be given to these discontinuities. The way to do so, however, is not by postulating the existence of two languages: one "free" and the other which would have given adequate expression to the experiences of the Holocaust. This is because our language already possesses a concept adequate to express a sense of horrendous evil: the concept of the unthinkable.

In many circumstances, if one discovers that what one once thought impossible actually came to be, one has to say that it is not unthinkable. At one time, it would have been unimaginable to take seriously someone's claim to have been on the moon. Today, as we know, this statement is no longer unthinkable. In morality and religion, matters are different. When people do things to each other that we once regarded as impossible, we do not conclude that those things are not unthinkable after all. We call them "unthinkable" to express the enormity of what has been done, making a moral or religious judgment.

It is important not to confuse the two senses of "unthinkability." Some people believed that an occurrence such as the Holocaust was unthinkable; it could not happen. Believing in the mythology of the inevitability of human progress, many who lived prior to the Shoah did not believe it was possible for people to perpetrate an atrocity of such magnitude. However, when the Holocaust occurred and was recognized for what it truly was, such people had to admit that it was not unthinkable after all. But in the moral or religious sense of "unthinkability," people had to address the fact that the unthinkable had actually happened.[12] Neither notion of unthinkability calls for a new language; they are both present in our own. This, as we shall see, does not mean that everyone accords them the same place in their lives.

Our problem, then, is not one of relating our "free" language to the experiences of the Holocaust, which it finds difficult to express. Our question is how the presence of "the unthinkable" in the Holocaust is related to the ordinary contexts of human life. This question, of course, is much more than theoretical—life went on after the Holocaust. But how did it go on, and how does it continue to go on for those who were victims of, and those who reflect on, the fact that "the unthinkable" occurred? We should not be surprised to find that the question does not elicit simply one answer.

Connecting the Holocaust and human life

Survivors' conceptions of the Holocaust are illustrated through the connections they are, or are not, prepared to make with respect to it. How it fits into the context of their ongoing lives makes itself known through the language they use. Consider three extreme examples of the types of connections I have in mind.

Minimal connections

Clearly, many people behaved in the camps in ways they would never have imagined themselves acting in their previous lives. Some did things of which they normally would have been deeply ashamed or horrified. When asked why they behaved in this way, many often cite "the need to survive." Perhaps they followed advice akin to that given to the young Wiesel by the head of his prisoner block at Buchenwald, the camp to which Wiesel and his dying father were sent when the Germans evacuated Auschwitz in late January 1945:

> Listen to me, boy. Don't forget that you're in a concentration camp. Here, every man has to fight for himself and not think of anyone else. Even of his father. Here, there are no fathers, no brothers, no friends. Everyone lives and dies for himself alone. I'll give you a sound piece of advice—don't give your ration of bread and soup to your old father. There's nothing you can do for him. And you're killing yourself. Instead, you ought to be having his ration.[13]

Given that such things happened, what of life after the Holocaust? How is the memory of behavior of that kind taken up into ongoing life? Could the connection be minimal? One has to say that it could, and sometimes has been, if the following words are read as an expression of such a minimal connection.

> The Holocaust was an aberration, a prolonged but unreal nightmare which is over and I keep it that way—over. It had nothing to do with anything, except history and politics. Certainly in no way was it connected with my religious behavior and beliefs. The Holocaust was a detour in the pathway of the progress of civilization and the Holocaust was a detour in my personal life. I am back on safer ground now and I'll never even glance down that horrible road again if I can help it ... [14]

One remarkable feature of the language in this testimony is the retention of a belief in progress. For many people, the Holocaust shattered that belief, but, obviously, not for all. Regarding it as a detour in the path of progress, the speaker is able to bracket off the Holocaust, which keeps it from being an obstacle to faith in progress. In this case, Albert Camus's lesson has not been learned:

> As he listened to the cries of joy rising from the town, Rieux remembered that such joy is always imperiled ... the plague bacillus never dies or disappears for good; that it can lie dormant for years and years ... and that perhaps the day would come when, for the bane and enlightening of men, it roused its rats again and sent them forth to die in a happy city. [15]

A second feature of this minimal connection with the Holocaust is that it is seen not only as a detour in the path of progress but also as a detour in the speaker's personal life. One's conduct in the Holocaust is bracketed off from the rest of one's life. But if someone wants to describe life after liberation as being morally or religiously "safer ground," how is such circumvention to be understood? Of course, someone may say of his conduct in the Holocaust, "That was not really me." Nevertheless, one dimension of the situation remains the case: *he did whatever he did.* No questions need be begged about how the actions should be described, or about what third person judgments should be made of them, if any. It cannot be denied that people block out aspects of their past. The problem is in the language being used in reflecting on the Holocaust. It seems as though life is "put on hold." But it makes no sense to speak of the demands of morality or religion as demands one can "put on hold," or as a detour in one's personal life. In that context, such a view would be a case of moral or religious evasion.

All-consuming connections

The second example of the connections between the Holocaust and the life which followed it could not be more different from the first. So, far from the

Holocaust's being seen as a detour in personal life, it engulfs that life. Three examples can illustrate how this has happened in different ways.

Paralyzing effects   Experiences in the Holocaust may engulf one's life in that it consumes the possibility of building up one's life after it in any positive way. For example, in Wiesel's short novel called *The Accident*, a woman wants her lover, a survivor of the Holocaust, to look forward to a life together. He cannot do so. Instead, he is haunted by what he witnessed in the camps. She tells him that he must choose between life and death. He replies, saying that he chooses death because it is more real. When I speak of the "paralyzing" effect of the Holocaust, I am not using the term pejoratively. No doubt a preoccupation with the Holocaust can take perverted forms, but those are not the cases I have in mind. We are talking of people whose encounter with it marks them in such a way as to make anything else unreal by comparison. I do not see that philosophy as such has any right to pass judgment on such a reaction.

Ultimate moral judgment   So far from viewing the Holocaust as a detour in their personal experience, there are those who could never forgive themselves for their conduct during it. To draw on a fictional example, which has its real counterparts in the history of the Holocaust and genocide, Sophie, in William Styron's novel *Sophie's Choice*, is degraded by an SS officer who gives her the choice of handing over one of her children to prevent both from being killed. In handing one over, she did what she felt she had to do, but she never forgives herself for doing so. Sometime after liberation, she commits suicide. We, as observers, feel pity and compassion for her, but part of that pity and compassion involves appreciation of why she cannot forgive herself. For her, an ultimate judgment on what she has done cannot be avoided.[16] Again, the philosopher cannot reverse or modify that judgment in the name of his subject.

Desire for unity with the dead   Under this subheading, I am thinking not of those who commit suicide because of what they have done, but about those who do so simply because they feel guilty about being alive and want to be one with their dead comrades. This response is not a form of escapism. It is not like the confused suicide of an officer who wanted to avoid facing his huge gambling debts. In a suicide note, he said he preferred death to dishonor. But, as R. F. Holland says, "What he ends up with is both the death and the dishonor."[17] In the case we are considering, what is desired is unity with the dead.

Some philosophers of religion speak of resources, offered by faith, that help one to go beyond the urge to suicide. If the existence of such resources has been denied, the philosophical reminder of their reality has its point. What such philosophers cannot do, however, is to give a philosophical demonstration of the superiority of such resources over a desire to be with the dead.

Someone may argue that the sought-for unity with the dead cannot be achieved in any suicide *after* the Holocaust, because the dead died *in* the Holocaust. Another may argue differently, saying that the experiences of the survivor in the Holocaust, and his or her subsequent reactions, are sufficient for suicide to be seen as an expression of unity with the dead. Again, philosophy itself cannot arbitrate between these judgments. When it attempts to do so, personal judgments are masquerading as general philosophical theories.

A voluntaristic claim for continuity and a denial of discontinuity

The previous examples emphasize discontinuities between experiences in the Holocaust and ordinary, day-to-day lives. An extreme voluntarism denies this discontinuity, claiming that moral freedom in decision-making is in no way impaired by the conditions of the Holocaust. Thus, Viktor Frankl tries as follows to explain why some people acted well, while others acted badly: "Man has both potentialities within himself: which one is actualized depends on decisions but not on conditions."[18] How does Frankl's voluntarism stand against examples such as the following?

> Two days after Christmas, a Jewish child was born on our block. How happy I was when I saw the tiny baby. It was a boy, and the mother had been told that he would be taken care of. Three hours later, I saw a small package wrapped in cheese cloth lying on a wooden bench. Suddenly it moved. A Jewish girl employed as a clerk came over, carrying a pan of cold water. She whispered to me "Hush! Quiet! Go away!" but I remained for I could not understand what she had in mind. ... She took the little infant and submerged its little body in the cold water. My heart beat wildly in agitation. I wanted to shout "Murderess!" but I had to keep quiet and could not tell anyone. ... The woman held its head in the water. After about eight minutes the breathing stopped. The woman picked it up, wrapped it up again, and put it with the other corpses. Then she said to me, "We had to save the mother otherwise she would have gone to the gas chamber." The girl had learned well from the SS and became a murderess herself.[19]

According to Frankl, "Psychological observations of the prisoners have shown that only men who allowed their inner hold on their moral and spiritual values to subside eventually fall victim to the camp's degenerating influences."[20] It is an understatement to say that critical reactions to Frankl's view are understandable, but critical reactions to his voluntarism can create problems of their own. Consider Lawrence Langer's response to Frankl's words:

> How do we present this sanctimonious view to the woman who was forced to drown an infant to save the mother, or the other woman who

could only stand by in silence? ... The need to equate moral activity with continued existence and moral passivity with death reflects a desperate desire to retain some ethical coherence in a chaotic universe ... and may betray nothing more than a misuse of what Primo Levi called "free words": using language to create value where none exists.[21]

To enforce his point, Langer asks a number of questions:

How is one to pass judgment on such an episode, or relate it to the inner freedom celebrated by other commentators on the death camp experience? Does moral choice have any meaning here? The drama involves the help-less infant, whose fate is entirely in someone else's hands ... the absent mother, who may or may not have approved of the action; the "agent" who coolly sacrifices one life to preserve another, as a deed of naked necessity, without appeal, not of moral choice; and the author, sole wit-ness to a crime that is simultaneously an act of charity and perhaps of lit-eral secular salvation to the mother. Conventional vocabulary limps through a situation that allows no heroic response, no acceptable gesture of protest, no mode of action to permit *any* of the participants, including the absent mother, to retain a core of human dignity.[22]

The problem with both Frankl's and Langer's language is that it trades in unearned generalities. Nevertheless, it is important to try to understand why they speak as they do. Each wants to preserve something that we ignore at our peril. Frankl's voluntarism wants to avoid a determinism that makes the conditions in the camps wholly determinate. On the determinist's view, given the conditions, certain consequences follow. According to Langer's reaction, the conditions specified make moral choice, protest, inner free-dom, human dignity, impossible, because we are trying to invoke value where none exists. This reaction simply does not do justice to the *variety* of responses one finds to the *same* conditions in the Holocaust. Frankl wants to leave room for the autonomy of the individual, for the role of character in the responses people make. Even in the narrative as presented by Langer, fur-ther questions need to be asked. What are we to make of his description of the clerk as *coolly* sacrificing one life to preserve another? When Sophie had to make her "choiceless choice," wouldn't any such description of her action be grotesque? What of the relation of the deed to the mother who, we are told, may or may not have approved of it, a fact that allows that she would *not* be devoid of any moral or religious reactions? And is justice done to the witness in saying that *she* saw an act of charity? What she actually says is that the clerk had learned well from the SS and had become a murderess her-self. My point in raising these questions is neither to suggest that the answers to them are obvious or easy nor to claim that there always are answers. But the very possibility of asking the questions is enough to show that one should not simply accept Langer's general conclusion, that here is a chaotic condition in which no ethical coherence could exist. Frankl wants to allow a space for such coherence. The problem lies in the extent of the space he thinks is allowable.

Frankl, too, propounds a general thesis. His extreme voluntarism claims that strong characters were not degraded by the Holocaust, whereas weak characters suffered degradation. Furthermore, whether one is strong or weak depends on a power of decision that no condition, however horrendous, can affect. This claim can degenerate into an empty tautology: only strong characters are not degraded; therefore, anyone who was degraded was not a strong character. This result will not do for Frankl, since he claims to be offering an *explanation* of moral and spiritual survival. As such, however, it flies in the face of the facts. It gives no recognition of the power of conditions horrendous enough to break the strongest person. It also ignores the fact that many would not want to judge those broken in such circumstances. They would not say, "They could have pulled themselves together had they wanted to!" Frankl's voluntarism, moreover, falsifies the way in which those who emerged from the Holocaust speak of themselves, or others, in this respect. For the most part, one does not find them invoking a strength that they say the victims lacked. Rather, we find them speaking of luck and good fortune or testifying to God's help and the help of those around them. Often, they offer no explanation for their survival, let alone the kind that Frankl seeks.

In all three examples of connections made between the Holocaust and the life which followed it, we have simply revealed a minute part of what is shown in the language in which people express themselves. In its contemplative task, philosophy, in its *own* language, has to be faithful to the variety to be waited on.

Connecting God with the Holocaust

The nature of people's belief in, or denial of, God will also show itself in the kind of language they use. Versions of Frankl's voluntarism, for example, loom large in the way most contemporary analytic philosophers of religion discuss horrendous evils, including the Holocaust. They ask why God allows such evils to occur, and proceed to give a consequentialist answer. God does so, we are told, because in facing such evils, people are given an opportunity to develop their characters in ways God thinks desirable. It would be fatal to such an argument to admit that afflictions may crush a person, since, in that event, there is no opportunity for character development. To what most people would regard as the obvious fact that some people *are* crushed by affliction, Richard Swinburne replies,

> Which one? Presumably one who has collapsed morally under the suffering—God "has gone too far for him." But that follows if we know

that he couldn't help collapsing, that he hasn't given in to forces which he could have resisted—and that's just what we don't know until philosophers and scientists together have solved the free will problem.[23]

The distinction between what is and what is not too much for people to bear does not, generally speaking, wait on the findings of philosophers and scientists. It enters into our common understanding of human conduct. There may not be agreement in all judgments, but, within broad parameters, some excuses offered are regarded as ludicrous, while some circumstances are accepted as constituting varying degrees of mitigation for people's conduct. Some horrendous circumstances would be thought of as overpowering for *most* people, while others would be regarded as too much for *anyone*. These are not makeshift judgments awaiting a theory. They are constitutive of our understanding of each other. We cannot assert, in an a priori fashion, that *any* evil, no matter how horrendous, affords an opportunity for good character development. If someone said that, one would wonder what world he was living in. Rush Rhees rightly asks, "What was the value of the degradation that belonged to the sufferings in the concentration camps? When, for instance, a man is going to pieces morally and knows it. If I could put my questions more strongly, I should do so. For I think that religious apologists have generally been irresponsible and frivolous in writing about this matter."[24]

Rhees goes as far as to say that such apologists have deceived both themselves and others. Voluntarism blames those who were morally crushed in the Holocaust and praises the self-sufficiency of those who were not. It thinks this is the language of human dignity and autonomy, whereas it is the language of the worst of all the religious sins—the sin of pride. Rhees comments, " 'They could have refused?' Could they? 'We who have not fallen'— the fall that there is in *that*. Circumstances by which people are crushed."[25]

The language employed by the apologists negates the very concepts they think they are propounding. If I say, for example, that the sufferings of others are *justified* because they give me an opportunity to be morally responsible and to develop a conscience with respect to wrongdoing, the language shows a grotesque emphasis on oneself instead of a concern for the sufferings of others, which should be the hallmark of conscience. Further, if the sufferings are God's means of developing character in others, the instrumental use of the sufferer shown in such language reveals a God who makes human beings the object of experiments.

The language of a covenantal relation with God may show itself to be a language concerning *contracts*.[26] If the people do x, God promises to do y. The people did x, but, instead of y, along came the Holocaust! Can any sense be retained in such a language? Remarkably, some Jews reacted to the Holocaust within the terms of the contract as envisaged above.

The Holocaust had come, instead of *y*, because not enough Jews had done so!

> The message to the Jew was that he should keep the Torah and all the commandments, and if and when he fails to do so, the savages will be unleashed against him ... The Holocaust had a message. The Holocaust was saying that Jews who keep the mitzvot are doing the right thing and Jews who do not are doing the wrong thing, a terribly wrong thing, but that we will all suffer and be punished alike, the innocent and the guilty together, until we all become religious and observant Jews. We Jews are all responsible one for the other.[27]

In this language, there is an external relation between sin and its consequences. If you sin badly enough, the savages are released against one. On such a view, to ask God to spare you from his wrath would be to ask, "Don't do that to me." The deeper religious view is to see it as meaning, "Don't let me become that." To see this is to appreciate the *internal* relation between sin and its consequences. If one sins, God does not distance himself from one as an external consequence of the sin. The sin *is* the distance. On this understanding, it would make no sense to speak of God's punishing the innocent. Punishment, conceived in the external way I have criticized, was enough in itself to lead, in some, to a loss of belief in God when that punishment proved to be the Holocaust!

"I refuse to believe God is a horrible sadist."[28] In the language of that testimony there is a severance of responsibility from desert, the kind of severance that puzzled Job so much. On the other hand, to try to *keep* the connection intact, can lead to the view that one survived the Holocaust because one kept one's contract with God. Hence, the following startling testimony:

> I'd pray to God and He would hear me. And I made vows that if I would survive this selection I'd eat only kosher after I was free. And when the next came I'd say if I will survive this selection I will keep the Sabbath 100 percent. ... During the long death march, when so many others fell aside, I kept promising so many vows to God, and I had resolved to be a very pious Jew. And I am that today, as you can see.[29]

We are not told what this "pious Jew" thought of the prayers of those others on the death march who "fell aside." Would we prefer his language, or that of a survivor who spoke as follows? "In the camps people prayed for a miracle to deliver them from death. I know I'd never expect one and could not pray for one because now I know for certain what I'd vaguely felt before, that there is no God at all."[30] The severance of one's fate in the Holocaust from any strict correlation with desert seems to be an admission that no such correlation could be sustained. A faith that depends on such a correlation obviously should go up with the smoke from the camps, as it did for Elie Wiesel in *Night*.

An important Jewish tradition, which I have not mentioned explicitly thus far, is one that continued more than ever after the Holocaust—I refer to the tradition of questioning or even quarrelling with God. I am not sure that I understand this tradition, and so my remarks are tentative. Sometimes, it seems, God is being told that he must improve. I confess to finding that notion problematic. It seems far removed from the notion of an eternal, Creator—God. But, at other times, the questioning can be seen as a form of *seeking* God. After all, isn't the growth and development in the idea of God in the Hebrew Bible the result of such seeking? If so, the questions, even when they appear as rebukes, may be saying, not, "You can't *do* that," but, rather, "You can't *be* that."[31]

I have left until last a sense of what God is, which does not figure prominently in contemporary philosophical discussions of the Holocaust and other horrendous evils. This sense of God is not arrived at, however, by means of cumulative moral judgments of him, based on an appraisal of God's good and bad qualities. Rather, one is offered a given conception of God, a light or an element, in terms of which one is invited to think of human life. This does not mean that the light offered is not answerable to life; it is. But its answerability is via the illumination it offers. Not everyone will see what the illumination amounts to. Not everyone who sees what it amounts to will be able to accept it, or even approve of it. Philosophy's task is to try to do conceptual justice by it.

One central religious attitude to life is to see it under the aspect of a gift. This perspective is essential to the distinction between the Creator and creatures. The gift of life is undeserved and, in that sense, is seen as a gift of love. Gratitude for existence is the form taken by acceptance of such a belief, a gratitude that includes gratitude for and therefore love of one's neighbors. But what does one say when the actual neighbors are the perpetrators of the Holocaust or some other genocide? Incredibly, we find some believers saying and showing that even the horrors inflicted on them do not render the things of God pointless. In fact, one's sense of the horror can only be explicated by reference to the things of God being defiled. There is no instrumentalism involved in this faith. It has no truck with the view that the horrendous evils are suffered *in order that* the things of God are loved. The things of God inform the sufferings in that their point and value is not lost despite the pain.

Nothing in what has been said of this faith in the things of God guarantees that human life and behavior will not be crushed or broken by circumstances. How could one think otherwise faced by the realities of the Holocaust? In that case, it may be asked, can it mean anything to say that God was still with those victims—a very present help in trouble? Doesn't that language collapse? It certainly cannot mean that the victims are consciously sustained in death by their faith, since I am referring here to those whose spirit has been broken despite their faith. As far as I can see, to say that God is with them is to say that *their story cannot be taken from them*. The things of God are shown *in* their story, and, in that sense, it intercedes for us in showing us what love of God can be. What we see is witness *in extremis*; a witness that becomes a sacrifice for us.

Isaiah knew that many would find this conception of faith unbelievable, since its language is at odds with a faith in compensations and worldly triumph. He asks, "Who hath believed our report? and to whom is the arm of the Lord revealed?" After all, what is revealed in the sufferer "hath no form or comeliness; and when we shall see him, there is no beauty that we should desire him." Is not the sufferer "a man of sorrows and acquainted with grief"? For many, this scene of suffering is simply too much to contemplate, and to see in it any religious revelation of faith in God, or the face of God, seems perverse. If we feel like this, we say that "we hid as it were our faces from him; he was despised, and we esteemed him not." Surely, when we look at what happened in the Holocaust, it may be said that what we need is an honest realism: "He was oppressed, and he was afflicted, yet he opened not his mouth: he is brought as a lamb to the slaughter, and as a sheep before her shearers is dumb, so he opened not his mouth." Yet, though as realistic as one can imagine, Isaiah speaks of one who has "poured out his soul unto death," and says that as such he is "wounded for our transgressions," "bruised for our iniquities," and that "with his stripes we are healed."

I am arguing that this language, found in the tradition of the Suffering Servant, has purchase, if we see in it an emphasis on what is shown in the story of people of faith who, nevertheless, are broken in the Holocaust. In them, it is possible to see what love of God is, and what can happen to it. It is in this sense that the death of many "made intercession for the transgressions"; the showing of what love of God is, *is* that intercession.

I have deliberately interwoven my analysis with the language of the Suffering Servant presented by Isaiah. I am not competent to judge how prominent this language has been in Jewish discussions of the Holocaust. My impression is that it has not been all that prominent.[32] Some thinkers have pointed out parallels between the story of the Suffering Servant, and the Passion in Christianity, where we also have one "broken for our sakes."[33] Others have suggested that there is an important difference between the *voluntary* acceptance of the Cross by Jesus, and the *involuntary* fate of those herded to their deaths in the Holocaust.[34] Two points need to be made in this connection. First, as Wiesel has pointed out, it is wrong to think that there are no instances of martyrdom in the Holocaust. Many went voluntarily to the camps to share the fate of their fellow Jews when they could have been free.[35] Second, it is a mistake to equate the Crucifixion with martyrdom. The martyrs die a death informed by one who went before them. It is true that Jesus goes to the Cross willingly, but the cry that rings out from it, "My God, my God, why has thou forsaken me?" is not a product of the will. Here is the cry of one whom Christians regard as having been broken for our sakes. Both the Holocaust and the Crucifixion, in what they show, are said to make intercession on our behalf.

There is one more important point to be made in this context. In my preceding remarks, I have emphasized the way in which the story of the Suffering Servant and the Passion can be seen as making intercession for the living. This should not lead to the conclusion, however, that if the stories of the victims of the Holocaust were forgotten, they become futile. The story is what it is, whether anyone actually gets to know of it or not. After all, how many stories of compassion and love of God in the Holocaust have been lost to us? Their significance is no less because of that fate, any more than a decent act is less decent because no one knows of it. The religious expression of this point is to say that even when no one listens, God listens. Again, it is a philosophical mistake to seek for a justification of this religious faith. Philosophy's task is to note its existence, and the relation of its language to that of other reactions to the Holocaust we have considered.

Connections and conclusions

In the connections people are or are not prepared to make, we see what the Holocaust means to them. No general philosophical theory emerges that embraces them all. That there is no such theory is one important lesson to be learned when one considers how genocide does, and should, affect philosophy. That itself, someone may say, is a general conclusion, if not a theory. I have been told that I have a "no–theory theory." I am content to let that clever claim be itself, as long as it recognizes how far my conclusions are from anything that could pass for a general theory in philosophy. We have asked how philosophizing may sin against the Holocaust. We have seen examples of its doing so. As I have said elsewhere, as philosophers we need to be mindful of the fact that in writing about evil, we may add to it.[36] That thought brings us back to this chapter's beginning. To those who think concern about the language in which we speak is unimportant, Wiesel's words are worth repeating: So we didn't speak about it because we were afraid of committing a sin.[37]

Notes

1. Elie Wiesel, "Talking and Writing and Keeping Silent," in John K. Roth and Michael Berenbaum, eds, *Holocaust: Religious and Philosophical Implications* (St. Paul, MN: Paragon House, 1989), p. 367.
2. See Cora Diamond, "Losing Your Concepts," *Ethics* (January 1988). For a parallel accusation in contrasting the tidiness of moral theories with the complexities of life shown in literature, see "Allegiance and Change in Morality: A Study in Contrasts," in my *Interventions in Ethics* (Albany, NY: State University of New York Press, 1992).

3. Peter Winch, "Doing Justice or Giving the Devil His Due," in D. Z. Phillips, ed., *Can Religion Be Explained Away?* (Basingstoke: Macmillan, 1996).
4. For my elucidation of a contemplative conception of philosophy see, *Philosophy's Cool Place* (Ithaca, NY: Cornell University Press, 1999).
5. Wiesel, "Talking and Writing, and Keeping Silent," p. 368.
6. Primo Levi, *Survival in Auschwitz: The Nazi Assault on Humanity*, trans. Stuart Woolf (New York: Collier Books, 1969), pp. 112–3.
7. Jean Améry, *At the Mind's Limits: Contemplations by a Survivor on Auschwitz and Its Realities*, trans. Sidney Rosenfeld and Stella P. Rosenfeld (New York: Schocken Books, 1986), pp. 28–9.
8. Ibid., p. 28.
9. Ibid., pp. 39–40.
10. Terence Des Pres, *The Survivor* (New York: Oxford University Press, 1976), pp. 59–60.
11. Wiesel, "Talking and Writing and Keeping Silent," p. 366.
12. For a discussion of "unthinkability," see my "Minds, Persons and the Unthinkable," in Anthony O'Hear, ed., *Minds and Persons* (Cambridge: Cambridge University Press, 2003).
13. Elie Wiesel, *Night*, trans. Stella Rodway (New York: Bantam Books, 1982), p. 105.
14. Quoted in Reeve Robert Brenner, *The Faith and Doubt of Holocaust Survivors* (New York: Free Press, 1980), p. 48. I want to make it clear that I am not imputing any *actual* behavior to the person who is quoted in this way in Brenner's survey of testimonies. I am simply reflecting on what such language *would* amount to were it a reaction to the kind of behavior I describe.
15. Albert Camus, *The Plague*, trans. Stuart Gilbert (London: Penguin, 1965).
16. For a parallel discussion of Oedipus's judgment on himself for unknowingly killing his father, and marrying his mother, see Peter Winch, "Moral Integrity," *Ethics and Action* (London: Routledge and Kegan Paul, 1972).
17. R. F. Holland, "Suicide," *Against Empiricism* (Oxford: Blackwell,1980), p. 147.
18. Viktor Frankl, *Man's Search for Meaning* (New York: Pocket Books, 1963), p. 213.
19. Judith Sternberg Newman, *In the Hell of Auschwitz* (New York: Exposition Press, 1963), pp. 42–3.
20. Frankl, *Man's Search for Meaning*, p. 110.
21. Lawrence L. Langer, "The Dilemma of Choice in the Deathcamps," in Roth and Berenbaum, eds, *Holocaust*, p. 231.
22. Ibid., p. 225.
23. Richard Swinburne, "Postscript" (to a symposium on The Problem of Evil with D. Z. Phillips) in Stuart Brown, ed., *Reason and Religion* (Ithaca, NY: Cornell University Press, 1977), p. 132.
24. Rush Rhees, "Suffering," in *On Religion and Philosophy*, edited by D. Z. Phillips, assisted by Mario von der Ruhr (Cambridge: Cambridge University Press, 1997), p. 304.
25. Rush Rhees, "Difficulties of Belief," in *On Religion and Philosophy*, p. 149.
26. For a fuller discussion of covenants as contracts see, D. Z. Phillips, *The Problem of Evil and the Problem of God* (London: S. C. M. Press, forthcoming).
27. Quoted by Brenner, *The Faith and Doubt of Holocaust Survivors*, p. 58.
28. Ibid., p. 111.
29. Ibid., p. 71.
30. Ibid., p. 108.
31. See my *The Problem of Evil and the Problem of God* (forthcoming), part 2, chapter 7.

32. For my discussion in the context of Wiesel's *Night*, see "Beyond the Call of Duty," *From Fantasy to Faith* (Basingstoke: Macmillan, 1991).
33. See, for example, Irving Greenberg, "Cloud of Smoke, Pillar of Fire" in Eva Fleischner, ed., *Auschwitz: Beginning of a New Era? Reflections on the Holocaust* (New York: KTAV, 1977).
34. See, for example, Richard L. Rubenstein and John K. Roth, *Approaches to Auschwitz: The Holocaust and Its Legacy*, rev. edn (Louisville, KY: Westminster John Knox Press, 2003), pp. 336–7.
35. Elie Wiesel, "Talking and Writing and Keeping Silent," pp. 356–7.
36. The closing remark of my *The Problem of Evil and the Problem of God*.
37. Wiesel, "Talking and Writing and Keeping Silent," p. 367.

6

Genocide, Evil, and Injustice: Competing Hells

Thomas W. Simon

> We have been flooded with historical reports but philosophical reflection has been slow in coming ...
>
> Susan Neiman, "What's the Problem of Evil?"[1]

Does philosophy have anything to say about the horrors of the world? Does philosophy matter? On a scale that compares the good and the bad, philosophy goes from one side to the other depending on which philosophers we choose to weigh. More broadly, an overall assessment of philosophy's contribution to civilization eludes philosophers and historians. It proves difficult to demonstrate the effects that philosophy and philosophers have had on history. Did Aristotle, for example, change the course of history when he tutored Alexander the Great? Even in cases where philosophers have achieved considerable fame and notoriety, historians disagree about philosophy's accomplishments overall.

In a few cases, the status of philosophers has been raised to mythological proportions. Often one hears assertions that John Locke, the seventeenth-century British philosopher, constructed the theoretical principles for the American Revolution. On a parallel track, the "citizen of Geneva" Jean Jacques Rousseau has been credited for providing the conceptual weapons for the French Revolution. Despite the generally positive contributions to history made by theorists such as Locke and Rousseau, philosophers do not like to dwell on the seedier side of these Great Thinkers who populate their canon. The relationships between Locke's thought and slavery or between Rousseau's "tyranny of virtue" and the French Revolution's "reign of terror," although not completely suppressed, rarely receive full attention among professional philosophers. Contemporary philosophers not only ignore or reject politically embarrassing pieces of the writings of the Great Thinkers but also rehabilitate them, as happened in the cases of Friedrich Nietzsche and Martin Heidegger.

An investigation into some current "Lesser Thinkers" in philosophy might expose blemishes worse than the flaws found among its Great Thinkers.

Some philosophers have played a rarely acknowledged role in promoting world conflicts and global injustices. The recent nationalist wars in the Balkans provided soil for philosophical wrongdoing. Serbian academics, including professional philosophers, helped Slobodan Milosevic construct a vicious, extreme form of nationalism. The works of Mihailo Markovic, a leading member of a socialist humanist group (*Praxis*) in the former Yugoslavia, carried considerable prestige until he began to promote a Greater Serbia ideology. Markovic advocated the suppression of the Albanians in Kosovo through an infamous memorandum for the Serbian Academy of Arts and Sciences.[2] Markovic proclaimed that only an ethnically pure Serbian state could be democratic. As one commentator noted,

> Markovic became not a passive spectator, but a significant player on behalf of Milosevic's rise to power. Markovic helped navigate his fellow Serbs into the jaws of racist nationalism. He became a key ideologue for Milosevic. The role that Markovic played on behalf of the Belgrade regime, now accused of genocide and crimes against humanity, must not be understated.[3]

Sadly, rather than having situations where philosophers help us to understand injustices, we may have far more cases where professional philosophers stand accused of aiding and abetting atrocities. These circumstances suggest that philosophers need to think about their own discipline in relation to the problem of evil and, in particular, about the relationships between philosophy and genocide.

Such reflection might show that philosophers face a fate worse than condemnation. Philosophers and their work may prove entirely irrelevant to the affairs of men and women. Despite the blemishes of applied philosophy, the thought that philosophy has played only a minor role in the theoretical and practical affairs of politics appears worse than acknowledging tainted Great Thinkers and condemnable Lesser Thinkers. While the jury remains sequestered, philosophers seem more likely to stand charged with political irrelevance than with immoral activism. Unfortunately, philosophers have had little reason to cite their fellow philosophers for their valor in the global battles against injustices.

How can philosophy become more of a relevant intellectual force in an increasingly global world? Oddly enough, genocide may provide the answer. Philosophers should embrace the study of genocide and other injustices. The challenge ahead lies in sorting out the many forms that injustice can take. How does genocide differ morally from other grave injustices? Are all instances of genocide morally equivalent? The proliferation of genocides and other grave injustices throughout the twentieth century provides a wealth of cases for philosophers to examine. Cases of genocide provide a key and sure place for philosophers to find materials needed to establish universal moral principles. International jurists have come to regard the prohibition against genocide as universal. The crime of genocide has become the lynchpin in the ongoing construction of an international justice system. Philosophers should follow suit by exploring how to use prohibitions against genocide as the foundation stones for building global ethics.

Genocide studies

Given that philosophers have devoted relatively little time to the study of injustices, it should come as no surprise that new fields of study such as genocide studies have relegated philosophy to a minor role. For a relatively new academic discipline, the field of genocide studies has matured rather quickly. Numerous institutes devoted to the study of genocide now operate around the world.[4] Other centers focus on Holocaust studies and other specific genocides. The new field of study now has its own professional organization, an encyclopedia, and scholarly journals.[5] Recently, as a sign that it has truly arrived, scholars from this previously fledging discipline produced a volume devoted to the history of its founders. *Pioneers of Genocide Studies*, however, has a notable gap in its coverage of academic disciplines.[6] The list of pioneers includes historians, political scientists, sociologists, jurists, and psychologists. Except for one theologian (the volume's coeditor, Steven Jacobs), the work excludes representatives from the humanities. Elie Wiesel and Berel Lang—both humanities professors—number among the missing pioneers.

While academics, irrespective of their fields of study, typically complain when they find their discipline underrepresented, this case of unequal disciplinary representation raises deeper questions. Should social scientists dominate genocide studies? What contributions, if any, can philosophy and other branches of the humanities make to genocide studies? Philosophy offers a vantage point from which to reveal and question hidden value assumptions made in studies of genocide. Value assumptions often mold choices of research programs. Values shape the questions researchers ask. Value commitments also affect how seriously researchers take challenges to their work. Holocaust scholars, for example, use value judgments to decide how seriously to take claims made by those who deny the Holocaust. Scholars make decisions about whether to reply to the claims of deniers on political grounds more than on scientific grounds. Subtler examples come from the different degrees of seriousness mainstream genocide scholars have given to issues raised by non-mainstream researchers. Consider the following: Genocide scholars have given considerable attention to studies that compare the Holocaust to other genocides. However, the literature makes only passing reference to another type of comparison. Discussions about the Rwandan genocide often highlight the problem of moral equivalence. The "problem" or strategy treats various instances of mass killings of two groups by each other as morally equivalent. According to the moral equivalency thesis, the prior (and subsequent) incidents of Tutsis killing Hutus in Rwanda and Burundi deserve the same degree of moral condemnation as the 1994 Hutu slaughter of Tutsis. Scholars have addressed attempts to elevate or degrade the horror of the Holocaust relative to other mass killings, but they have not paid a great deal of attention to other comparisons such as the appeal to moral equivalency that downplays the horror of the Rwandan genocide. Genocide scholars, in effect, tend to take threats to the privileged position of the Holocaust on the scale of horrors more seriously than they take attempts to diminish the horror of the Rwandan genocide. What accounts for different degrees of attentiveness scholars give to such issues? A sound philosophical analysis of different value (and not scientific) judgments made by social scientists and others might help to clarify, explain, and criticize the attention that scholars give to such issues.

Although scholars typically present themselves (particularly to those outside academic circles) as politically neutral, it should come as no surprise that those people who study horrific conflicts across the globe encounter many objections. Anyone even remotely connected with the study of genocide has some academic (and perhaps some nonacademic) "war stories" about external political reactions to their work. Almost inevitably, any study that compares various instances of genocide will meet some highly charged criticisms. Comparative analyses of genocide cases often contain value judgments about different events. Even if an investigator assiduously tries to avoid making value assessments, there are likely to be critics who will find that the study gives too much weightage to one case of genocide and too little to another. Despite the risk of entering treacherous waters, genocide scholars might find some solace in an overall decrease in some types of these accusations. The recent establishment of the new field of genocide studies attests the progress made over the issue of whether scholars should compare the Holocaust to other horrific events. Some Holocaust scholars found early attempts to compare the Holocaust to other horrors barbaric. For them, the Holocaust stood apart from all others as a unique and incomparable event. As Holocaust studies have become more mainstream and as the Holocaust has attained considerable international attention, the sting felt from denials of its uniqueness has dissipated. This state of affairs has not signaled an end to the "uniqueness debate."[7] Rather, it has meant that sympathy for the uniqueness claim no longer serves as a litmus test for the legitimacy of comparative studies that do not explicitly subscribe to the uniqueness thesis.

While the uniqueness controversy may no longer act as an impediment to some comparative projects that include the Holocaust, comparative studies of different cases of genocide face a more general problem. Comparisons seem bound to make value judgments—however benign, tacit, and innocent— that often raise the ire of friend and foe. Members of one victim group often feel that any comparison will devalue the horror of their experiences. They seem to think that making their trauma a part of a study of two or more other cases of genocide dilutes their victimization. Again, an established, recognized discipline of genocide studies might provide some comfort to future scholars engaged in comparative studies. The name of this field of study, genocide studies, indicates a commitment to projects that compare instances of genocide. Yet, despite the progress made in the acceptance of studies that compare genocides, the discipline has not matured to a point where it readily welcomes projects that compare instances of genocide with some other misdeeds or wrongdoings. Projects that compare genocide to other types of injustices, including violations of human rights, present important challenges to the dominant view that bristles at comparisons of genocide to anything else.

Holocaust scholars should become genocide scholars because the relatively bright flames they have lit for the Holocaust can help to light other torches of remembrance, and these other genocides desperately need illumination. Unlit torches provide further excuses to overlook other grave injustices, which cause victims to spiral into deeper despair. Scholars, including philosophers, should attend to grave injustices because they occur and because their recurrences threaten humanity. For balance, let us turn the gadfly loose on philosophy itself, particularly in a case where philosophers have tried to regain territory taken over by social scientists and theologians.

Philosophies of evil

The concept of evil often enters into discussions of genocide. I propose a drastic solution to challenge projects that rely on the concept of evil. Philosophers should discard the notion of evil since it seldom advances and often hinders an understanding of genocide. Typically, evil comes packaged as a theological problem, so much so that theology and religion seem to have a monopoly on the concept. Some philosophers have launched a campaign to "recover the concept of evil for contemporary thought."[8] I shall treat those contemporary theorists who have focused on the concept of evil as part of an intellectual movement that I shall dub "reconstructionism."[9] However, reconstructionists are not the primary targets. The real villain is the commonplace appeal to the idea of evil when discussing genocide. The so-called reconstructionists begin their project with Kant, one of the first philosophers to secularize the concept of evil. Kant saw evil as a human failing, a deviation from the acceptance of universal moral maxims. Evil arose when self-love snatched control over moral sensibilities. The Holocaust, however, radically altered the background conditions that Kant and other Enlightenment thinkers had assumed. Kant's sense of evil as a type of immoral maxim failed to capture the depths of depravity that went under the heading of evil in the twentieth century. As Hannah Arendt put the point, "the men of the eighteenth century did not understand that there exists goodness beyond virtue and evil beyond vice."[10] Arguably, more than any other twentieth-century philosopher, Arendt boldly confronted the daunting task of reconceptualizing Kant's sense of evil to make it applicable to the magnitude of contemporary horrors, including genocide. At first, she saw evil as a demonic, systematic dehumanization. Perhaps at the urging of Karl Jaspers, she altered her emphasis and referred to what she called "the banality of evil." Reconstructionists carry on this Kant-to-Arendt lineage.

Ideally, philosophical analysis should clarify the meanings of terms such as *evil* and produce helpful distinctions. Until relatively recently, theorists placed all types of harms—from natural catastrophes (such as the 1775 Lisbon earthquake)[11] to moral failings—under the category of *evil*. Instead of one sense of evil to cover all horrors, philosophers then developed a typology of evils. Arendt added a further distinction by suggesting that these historical senses of evil differed from an altogether new and modern sense of *radical evil*. For Arendt, "radical evil" meant the systematic dehumanization of human beings first carried out under the Nazi regime.

A philosophical analysis of evil should not only produce clear distinctions among types of evil but must also preserve a strong sense of moral outrage about evil.[12] This additional moral requirement places the secular theorists in a dilemma: It lands them in the same religious domain that they set out to escape, for moral outrage, historically, finds its expression in religious language. Arendt fell back into this religious domain when she tried to clarify the meaning of "radical evil." For Arendt, it implied "something beyond the pale of human sinfulness."[13] To make sense of radical evil, she found herself resorting to religious language by comparing it to sin. Secular theorists of evil, in general, have great difficulty in discarding entirely the historically entrenched religious framework that supports the concept of evil.

Philosophers of evil, at a minimum, should distance themselves from religion and especially from Christianity. First, given its primary theological roots, the concept of evil lends itself to totalizing and determinative judgments. Condemnation of something as evil precludes making nuanced distinctions about it. Judgments becomes absolute; condemnations, inescapable. Augustine's transformation of the Greco-Roman just war traditions offers an illuminating example of how religion totalizes the secular. As Paul Christopher suggests: "Beginning with Augustine, war ... became more than just a legal remedy for injustice; it became a moral imperative."[14] After Augustine, the concepts of good and evil began to taint and supplant the concepts of the lawful and the unlawful. As a result, "[Augustine's] just war was thus total and unlimited in its licit use of violence, for it not only avenged the violation of existing legal rights but also avenged the moral order injured by the sins of the guilty party regardless of injuries done to the just party acting as a defender of that order."[15] Religious senses of evil, in general, lend themselves to sweeping condemnations. As long as secular attempts to understand evil remain tied to religious ones, secular versions cannot escape the wholesale approach associated with religious concepts and create a more refined sense of evil.

Second, when philosophers use the concept of evil, they often follow, unwittingly and unfortunately, a path first carved out by theology. Although the enormity of the Holocaust made a few theologians question God's existence, most of them dealt with Auschwitz within the framework of the age-old problem of evil. Theologians faced the task of reconciling the evil of Auschwitz with divine creation and providence. While theologians could fit Auschwitz into their religious paradigms, philosophers tried to describe and explain it without having the comfort of a traditional framework that theologians had. Philosophers did not have a powerful secular vocabulary to describe and analyze Auschwitz. Concepts such as "vice," "wickedness," and "cruelty" seemed wholly inadequate. The concept of evil gave philosophers a way to deal with Auschwitz, for the term *evil* seemed to capture the extreme moral outrage needed to describe Auschwitz.

The acceptance of the label of "evil" for Auschwitz marked an endpoint for philosophers. This ready incorporation of the concept of evil into philosophy stops conceptual analysis and stifles political action at just the places where they should begin.[16] The concept of *evil* substituted for analysis by fostering the pretense that to label a phenomenon is to explain it. The concept of evil, under the guise of making the incomprehensible comprehensible, stops the analysis at just the point where it should begin. Even a refurbished concept of evil still leaves us with important unanswered questions about the nature of the horror and its relationship to other horrors, the nature and responsibility of the perpetrator, and the designation of the victims.

A third reason that philosophers should avoid using the religious idea of evil is that it would enable them to escape the tangles of theological conundrums and to formulate their own goals. The religious paradigm contextualizes evil in the form of a puzzle embedded, quite naturally, in religion. Within Christian doctrine, evil presents a phenomenon that needs to be explained away. How can a world created by a benevolent God contain so much evil? The philosophical reconstructionists also think of evil in the context of a puzzle. How can some humans be so deplorably cruel to other humans?[17] Reconstructionists set out to establish a (nonreligious) moral and political philosophical foundation for judging evil acts and evildoers. Reconstructionists extrapolate from individual psychology to social psychology and from individual ethics to political philosophy. Only after they have delved into social psychology and political philosophy do they entertain any legal questions. Maria Pia Lara expresses the task, order, and hope of this project: "If we can construct moral and political concepts that best comprehend the meaning of evil deeds, and the agency and responsibility of cruelty, then legal institutions must proceed to translate these meanings into the realm of positive law ..."[18]

Often philosophers uncritically accept a conceptual hierarchy within their discipline. In value theory, political philosophers build on a prior foundation of ethics. Only after these philosophers have laid a foundation of moral theory and then constructed a first floor of political philosophy do they issue permits to build a second floor of legal philosophy. I want to use a somewhat reversed "natural" disciplinary order of importance by placing legal philosophy at the center of a philosophical approach to the study of genocide and other injustices.

If a critical component of any approach to evil is to establish grounds for judging evil acts and evildoers, then legal philosophy should play the central role in the analysis. A much more nuanced analysis should result when we situate the problem within the context of legal institutions. Legal codification has produced refined distinctions, such as that between genocide and crimes against humanity. In effect, a different puzzle requires a different paradigm than the ones provided by theologians and Reconstructionists. If the challenge is not to explain evil theologically or philosophically but to ascribe legal responsibility, then we need an entirely different paradigm. To position themselves to make contributions to international justice and global ethics, philosophers not only should distance themselves from religious senses of evil but also they should abandon the idea of evil entirely and focus on injustices.

Injustice studies

Injustices[19]

An injustice paradigm cures the previously noted defects of both genocide studies and philosophies of evil. The new discipline of genocide studies has found a relatively comfortable niche in the social sciences. Injustice studies would have a more interdisciplinary reach that gives greater prominence to philosophy, particularly value theory. The implicit and often hidden value judgments that underlie genocide studies would come to the forefront as explicit, debatable claims in injustice studies. In addition, with injustice studies closely connected (as we shall see) to legal issues, political stands become central to injustice studies rather than unwelcome intrusions that they are in genocide studies. Injustice studies, also, would diverge from current attempts to construct a theory of evil. Although studies of injustices may lack the sweeping grandeur of theories of evil, an injustice framework would produce more precise terms and richer, more variegated concepts. In making these contrasts, I do not mean to imply that injustice studies would abandon or completely replace the empirical orientation of genocide studies or the grand visions of philosophies of evil. On the contrary, injustice studies could provide a more meaningful theoretical framework to conduct empirical studies as well as a more practical base for constructing bold visions. Further, I am not dismissing the valuable work done by genocide studies or philosophies of evil.

Philosophers should fully embrace genocide. This odd proposal, obviously, does not mean that philosophers should relish and applaud genocide. Instead, philosophers should give genocide its due and give detailed analyses of it. I faulted philosophies of evil for not producing the needed clarity. Philosophies of injustice do not fall victim to the same criticism. Genocide, in a sense, saves the day for injustice studies. First, philosophers of injustice can point to the paradigmatic injustice, namely, genocide. Of course, they cannot simply leave matters there. They would need to demonstrate that genocide is the most odious wrong. To many, attempts to compare horrible wrongs seems to be a misguided enterprise at best. However, if the comparative project is undertaken within a framework of international criminal law, then it makes perfect sense. Simply in terms of assessing the seriousness of various crimes, international jurists must distinguish and rank, for example, the crime of genocide and crimes against peace.

A second way that philosophies of injustice differ from philosophies of evil is that it would be incumbent upon the former to produce an in-depth analysis of genocide. Rather than proclaiming Auschwitz incomprehensible, the philosopher of injustice would make genocide and other injustices as comprehensible as possible. They would spell out, in excruciating detail, the exact nature of genocide. Again, this becomes a feasible project if done within the context of international law by, for example, specifying the elements of the crime of genocide.

As the late political theorist Judith Shklar observed, "Philosophers rarely talk about cruelty. They have left it to the dramatists and historians who have not neglected it."[20] Injustice is far too prevalent and too important for the philosopher in each of us to ignore. Once we accept the centrality of the concept of injustice, then we can try to ground a philosophy of injustice to avoid a charge of irrelevance. The law, as I have hinted, provides the anchors.

Law

The law gives practical mooring to studies of injustices. By examining injustices within the context of law, social scientists would have to pay closer attention to definitions. International law has a relatively exact definition of the term *genocide*. Social scientists do not need to accept that definition. However, social scientists should begin with something relatively precise such as the legal definition of *genocide*. Disagreements over the legal definition of genocide, then, would take place within the context of long and continuing legal debates over the meaning of genocide. These analyses could then take advantage of previous debates over, for example, whether mass killings of members of political groups should count as genocide when the legal definition specifies only "religious, racial, ethnic, and national groups."

The law per se does not provide a panacea. Certainly, we must recognize the law's role in maintaining the Nazi regime. However, it is another matter with international law. While it is easy to chide international law for not doing enough to address global problems, it has made considerable strides especially since the Second World War. Amazingly, the international community has reached a consensus over a number of human rights treaties. The International Covenant on the Rights of the Child became the fastest implemented human rights treaty in history, signed by all nations except two, the United States and Somalia. The Ad Hoc War Crimes Tribunals for the Former Yugoslavia and Rwanda have produced a rich jurisprudence that has widespread implications for a global ethics. The newly established International Criminal Court (ICC) has begun the daunting philosophical and legal task of constructing an international criminal code.

International law, then, provides a sensible way to ground philosophical analyses of genocide and other horrors. Let us illustrate this by outlining an injustice studies approach to criminal intent, one of the key elements required to convict someone of the crime of genocide. International jurists unwittingly transfer concepts that prosecutors use in national criminal law systems to international criminal law. In national legal systems, a conviction for premeditated murder requires proof of intent. Similarly, a successful prosecution of the international crime of genocide requires proof of intent. In this way, jurists transposed the notion of intent from national to international law. Nevertheless, the concepts that prosecutors use in national criminal law often prove inadequate when extended to international criminal law.

To see this, let us return to Hannah Arendt, who provided a rich and insightful analysis of the legal aspects of Adolf Eichmann's trial. While her work is seen as primarily contributing to philosophies of evil, *Eichmann in Jerusalem* had more to do with theories of law than it did with theories of evil. Her infamous phrase "the banality of evil" actually signified Arendt's frustration with standard legal categories. Ironically, normal legal concepts fail to capture both the normality (banality, ordinariness) of perpetrators like Eichmann and the ab-normality of their crimes. The ordinary concept of criminal intent, by its very nature, makes Eichmann out to be something that Arendt had trouble portraying. If we examine Eichmann's deeds by using the notion of criminal intent, we would be led to conclude that murder on the scale of genocide had to stem from a demonic mind. Yet, a banal, non-demonic individual like Eichmann does not fit this picture.

We can begin to reconcile Eichmann's banality and the Holocaust's distinctiveness by questioning the individualistic assumptions that guide criminal law. Individuals are the primary responsible agents in both national and international criminal law systems. For international systems, the focus on individual responsibility leaves open a wide, festering gap. Although everyone acknowledges that Eichmann did not act alone, the law has not fully focused on the organizations that made Eichmann's and other perpetrator's deeds possible.

Unfortunately, Nuremberg stands alone among all war crimes tribunals for its indictments of organizations. After Nuremberg, war crimes tribunals have focused exclusively on individual criminal guilt. The tribunals dealing with genocide in the former Yugoslavia and in Rwanda have no jurisdiction over organizations. Similarly, the statutes governing the formation of the International Criminal Court do not include procedures for declaring organizations criminal. Yet, organizations typically play key roles in perpetrating the crimes over which international tribunals have jurisdiction. International criminal systems typically deal with the most widespread and severe crimes. Genocide, for example, surely qualifies as an exemplar of organized violence. It is difficult to imagine how killings on the scale of genocide were carried out without organizations. Questions about organizational responsibility are essential in cases where international law is applied to genocide and crimes against humanity. Yet, the history of war crimes tribunals reveals approaches to responsibility dominated by concepts of individual criminal responsibility.

What effects would the Nuremberg judgments have had if the Tribunal had held Nazi organizations fully (but not exclusively) responsible for war crimes? An important difference between Germany after the Second World War and Rwanda after the 1994 genocide strengthens the case for holding organizations criminally responsible for crimes like genocide. After the Second World War, Nazis criminal organizations were completely disbanded. After the Rwandan genocide, organizations that should have qualified as criminal continue to wreak havoc in the region. Today, these organizations such as the Interhawame still play a major role in destabilizing Central Africa through their operation in the Democratic Republic of the Congo. The genocide militia, the Interhawame, reestablished itself in UN-sponsored refugee camps and continues to commit atrocities throughout the region. The failure to confront the responsibility of organizations for war crimes has had and will continue to have disastrous consequences.

It would have been ingenuous, at best, to ascribe demonic intent to Eichmann. Yet, we should not fall into the opposite trap of seeing Eichmann merely as a cog in a huge bureaucratic machine. Eichmann played a critical role in a despicable organization. It is at the intersection of individual and organizational responsibility that we begin to understand what Arendt tried to capture with the idea of the banality of evil. An injustice paradigm embedded in law provides a fruitful theoretical way to enrich empirical studies of genocide. It further anchors philosophical thinking about atrocities in the practical realm of legal responsibility.

This brief account of organizational responsibility provides at least a glimpse of what I have in mind by advocating a new paradigm of injustice studies. A nation's criminal code reflects the morality of that nation. Likewise, an international criminal code reflects global morality. With the recent establishment of the ICC, the construction of an international criminal code is under way. This aspect of law provides an excellent (but certainly not exclusive) focus for philosophers who are concerned about how genocide should affect philosophy.

Conclusion

Philosophers have moral and political obligations as scholars, as philosophers, and as global citizens. On their deathbeds, few philosophers will regret not producing one more article or book, but philosophers should have deep pangs if their work, implicitly or explicitly, gives aid and comfort to injustice. Philosophers should be able to look back at some instances where their philosophy and philosophizing contributed, if only in small ways, to the fight against injustice. "The truth," as the philosopher Emil Fackenheim once proclaimed, "is that to grasp the Holocaust whole-of-horror is not to comprehend or transcend it, but rather *to say no to it*, or *resist it*."[21] Yet, to do something about injustices by preventing and punishing them requires a great deal of comprehension. A battle against an injustice does not mean a campaign for the eradication of some unknown thing that possesses certain people or particular nations and groups. Nor does the stand against injustice need to elevate itself to some cosmological platform. The campaign against injustice has a rather banal quality. It involves philosophers and philosophy that focus eyes on obvious scourges and engage minds and bodies in the intricacies of prevention, accountability, and punishment.

Notes

1. See Susan Neiman's article in Maria Pia Lara, ed., *Rethinking Evil* (Berkeley, CA: University of California Press, 2001), p. 41.
2. Keith Doubt, "Intellectual Betrayal and Agony of Bosnia and Herzegovina," *Centre For Historical Studies* (22 May 2001). See also http://www.ifbosna.org.ba/engleski/documenti/historija/57/index.html and http://www.ifbosna.org.ba/engleski/pocetna/index.html
3. Maga Branka, *The Destruction of Yugoslavia: Tracking the Break-up 1980–92* (London: Verso, 1993).
4. Among other places, they can be found in Jerusalem, Israel; Sydney, Australia; Montreal, Canada; Copenhagen, Denmark; and New York City in the United States.
5. These include the Association of Genocide Scholars, *Encyclopedia of Genocide*, and *Journal of Genocide Research*.
6. Samuel Totten and Steven Jacobs, eds, *Pioneers of Genocide Studies* (New Brunswick, NJ: Transaction Publishers, 2002).
7. Alan S. Rosenbaum, ed., *Is the Holocaust Unique?: Perspectives on Comparative Genocide*, 2nd edn (Boulder, CO: Westview Press, 2001).
8. Maria Pia Lara, "Introduction," in Lara, ed., *Rethinking Evil*, p. 1.
9. A few of the more recent works that focus on the concept of evil are the following: Ronald D. Milo, *Immorality* (Princeton, NJ: Princeton University Press, 1984);

Paul Woodruff and Harry A. Wilmer, eds, *Facing Evil: Light at the Core of Darkness* (LaSalle, IL: Open Court, 1988); Nel Noddings, *Women and Evil* (Berkeley, CA: University of California Press, 1989); John Kekes, *Facing Evil* (Princeton, NJ: Princeton University Press, 1990); Mary Midgley, *Wickedness: A Philosophical Essay* (London, New York: Routledge, 1992); Jonathan Glover, *Humanity: A History of the Twentieth Century* (New Haven, CT: Yale University Press, 2000); Lara, ed., *Rethinking Evil*; Amelie Rorty, ed., *The Many Faces of Evil: Historical Perspectives* (New York: Routledge, 2001); Claudia Card, *The Atrocity Paradigm: A Theory of Evil* (New York: Oxford University Press, 2002); Susan Neiman, *Evil in Modern Thought: An Alternative History of Philosophy* (Princeton, NJ: Princeton University Press, 2002).

10. Hannah Arendt, *Eichmann in Jerusalem* (New York: Viking Press, 1964).

11. The Lisbon earthquake of 1 November 1775 killed about 15,000 people. As the center of the Inquisition, the event stirred considerable controversy among Catholics, Protestants, and philosophers (including Voltaire, Rousseau, and Kant). "It was the last time that the ways of God to man were the subject of general public debate and discussed by the finest minds of the day." Judith Shklar, *The Faces of Injustice* (New Haven, CT: Yale University Press, 1990), p. 51.

12. Raimond Gaita finds that "the moral dimensions are sometimes only adequately represented by a distinctive concept of evil." Raimond Gaita, *A Common Humanity* (New York: Routledge, 1998), p. 52.

13. Hannah Arendt, *The Origins of Totalitarianism* (New York: Harcourt, 1951), p. 459.

14. Paul Christopher, *The Ethics of War and Peace: An Introduction to Legal and Moral Issues*, 3rd edn (Upper Saddle River, NJ: Prentice-Hall, 2003), p. 38.

15. Frederick Russell, *The Just War in the Middle Ages* (London: Cambridge University Press, 1975), p. 19, as quoted in Christopher, *The Ethics of War and Peace*, p. 38.

16. See Inga Clendinnen, *Reading the Holocaust* (Cambridge: Cambridge University Press, 1999).

17. "The challenge is to create a meaningful concept of evil that allows us to comprehend why we are capable of exercising cruelty upon our fellow human beings" (Lara, "Introduction," p. 2).

18. Ibid., p. 14.

19. In this section, I draw on chapter 1 of my *Democracy and Social Injustice* (Lanham, MD: Rowman & Littlefield, 1995).

20. Judith Shklar, *Ordinary Vices* (Cambridge: Harvard University Press, 1984), p. 7.

21. Emil Fackenheim, *To Mend the World: Foundations of Post-Holocaust Jewish Thought* (New York: Schocken Books, 1989), p. 239.

Part II

Innocent or Guilty? Philosophy's Involvement in Genocide

John K. Roth

In the summer of 1880, the French sculptor Auguste Rodin (1840–1917) was commissioned to create a monumental door for an art museum in Paris. Inspired by Dante's *Divine Comedy*, Rodin called his project *The Gates of Hell*. Although the door remained unfinished, its centerpiece, *The Thinker*, became one of the world's best known artworks.

Sarah Lisl Waller, a talented Scripps College alumna who studied the Holocaust with me in the autumn of 1999, has produced a thought-provoking interpretation of Rodin's masterpiece. It appears on this book's cover. In a simple but striking black-and-white style, Waller depicts a thinker—a philosopher—who is ambiguously situated with regard to lines of barbed-wire that front the figure. The barbed-wire suggests the boundaries of a prison, a concentration camp, a deportation center, or some other enclosure whose ominous presence might be a warning about genocidal threats or a sign of genocidal intentions.

While I worked on this book about philosophy, genocide, and human rights, I often thought of Waller's image. I did so, in particular, with respect to the volume's second part, which contains chapters that explore questions about philosophy's involvement in genocide. As is true of philosophy's relationship to genocide, ambiguity surrounds the position and perspective of Waller's thinker. Is he or she behind barbed-wire barricades that have formed hellish places such as concentration camps and killing centers? If so, in what sense? Has he or she paid a price for resisting crimes against humanity? Is this thinker, this philosopher, unjustly imprisoned? Is he or she even waiting to be killed for taking a bold and courageous stand against genocide? Or is the thinker outside the barbed-wire's constraints but neither innocent nor free because he or she may be "behind" the barbed-wire in ways that implicate him or her wrongdoing.

Waller's thinker invites multiple interpretations of place and posture, but each implies that genocide and human rights abuses ought to provoke philosophical thinking of the most penetrating and ethical kind. They should do so because humankind's capacity—including philosophy—to make plans, pursue goals, and enact decisions not only creates injustice and inflicts suffering but also can reduce them both. Much depends on how well people think, for thinking well and acting well go hand in hand. For those reasons, much also depends on how philosophers do their work.

As the six chapters in Part II bear witness, philosophy has not done all that it could to prevent or check genocide. On the contrary, philosophical reflection—implicitly and inadvertently if not explicitly and consciously—has often aided and abetted genocide. That tarnished record is one for which philosophy and philosophers should take responsibility and make amends.

Discussion of these issues begins with Colin Tatz's analysis of a variety of philosophical trends and thinkers and on their part in what he calls "the doctorhood of genocide." Tatz is particularly interested in how eighteenth- and nineteenth-century philosophies of science, broadly construed, had genocidal implications that found their way into public policy in the twentieth century, particularly but not only in Nazi Germany. Most of the thinkers he discusses are not primary figures in the canon of Western philosophy, but during their careers and through their writings they exerted significant and, at times, lethal influences nonetheless.

David Patterson follows with a chapter that finds philosophical warrants for genocide running deeply in the mainstream of Western philosophy, especially in movements linked to the Enlightenment. Patterson finds that, at least since Descartes and Kant, Western philosophy has largely been hostile to God and Judaism while it has glorified the human self. In Patterson's view, the consequences have been dehumanizing. As the case of Martin Heidegger's Nazism suggests, philosophy and genocide can all too easily become bedfellows unless philosophy thinks deeply and self-critically about where it ought and ought not to go.

While Tatz explores philosophies of science and Patterson traces key moves in the history of philosophy, Michael Mack's chapter indicates how Western philosophies of history have played parts in genocide. One of their consequences has been a tendency to legitimate war, mass violence, and the destruction of so-called inferior races as part of civilization's progress and even of Reason's fulfillment, as Hegel's outlook suggested. In an age of genocide that it helped to create, philosophy can reform and rehabilitate itself only through self-examination that explicitly confronts genocide and philosophy's involvement in it.

Emmanuel C. Eze pushes the inquiry further by appraising what he calls the epistemological conditions of genocide, the features and structures of thought itself that must be active for genocide to be possible. His analysis focuses on three types of ideas: instrumental, justificatory, and historical. Eze shows how the human capacity to think and especially to categorize can have genocidal implications. Philosophy must emphasize the fallibility and vulnerability of human thought, including philosophy itself, to check its destructive tendencies.

Taking his inspiration from Emmanuel Levinas's philosophy, Leonard Grob suggests that recognition of the fallibility and vulnerability of human thought supports ethical impulses that can save philosophy from the temptation to develop totalizing claims and theories. Grob believes that a Levinasian framework, or some version of it, can help philosophers to understand that philosophy is "more verb than noun." It should free itself—and us—from presumption and dogmatism, which are usually key factors in the epistemic conditions that foster and unleash genocide.

Part II concludes with Robert Bernasconi's argument that philosophy, often unwittingly but destructively nonetheless, contributed to the formation of what he calls "a culture of genocide." Concentrating especially on Kant and Hegel, his account can be read as a description, a summary, and a warning about what can go wrong when philosophy and philosophers, including the greatest among them, lend legitimacy, however inadvertently, to "the idea that some lives are of more value than others, even to the point of tolerating genocide."

Rodin's thinker embodied resistance at the gates of hell. From inside or outside the barbed-wire, the chapters in Part II suggest, philosophy may do so as well by warning that thinking, including its own, can waste lives and by urging that the action inspired by good thinking can save them.

7

The Doctorhood of Genocide

Colin Tatz

Genocide is neither spontaneous nor episodic. Emerging from biological sciences and from philosophies that encourage and reflect those perspectives, ideas accrete and culminate in racial policies and practices that often become genocidal. These biological and philosophical antecedents began in earnest in the late eighteenth century. By the time of the Nazi rise to power, established thought-patterns about racial hierarchies had come to the fore— as "science"—in Europe and particularly in Britain and the United States. Biological race theory, which is the primary basis of modern genocide, came from *within* the scientific, medical, and academic communities—not from *without* as a political imposition by totalitarian governments. In the twentieth century, the members of the "doctorhood" that formulated, legitimized, and justified biological solutions to social and political problems not only thought, expounded, and wrote about their findings but also acted out their beliefs.

The steps of accretion

As events in the twentieth century attest, genocide is neither unique nor abnormal. Where genocide has occurred—and will occur again—there is a historical explanation of the (inevitable?) steps leading to the event. Genocide occurs as if by an organic growth, by an accretion or aggregation of human experience and precedent—mechanically, medically, physically, politically, psychologically, and, of course, ideologically. The Holocaust scholar Raul Hilberg has said that when he looked at bureaucracy in the destruction process against the European Jews he saw "a series of minute steps taken in logical order and relying above all as much as possible on experience."[1] Little was new until the Nazis went beyond that which had been established by precedent—and "inventiveness" came only with their decision to build industrial death camps.

The Nazi Judeocide could not have happened without a number of accretions: *völkisch* antisemitism and the demonization of Jews over the

82

centuries; the fatal mix of that "longest hatred" with "scientific" racism in the nineteenth century; a perpetrator nation intent on developing an ethnic rather than a civic nationalism; some earlier experience within the nation regarding genocide, as in Germany's earlier twentieth-century activity in south-west Africa (now Namibia) and Turkey[2]; and finally, an ideological imperative that received philosophical justification and political legitimacy. Metaphorically speaking, the building blocks or engine parts were assembled over time, and the genocidal motor was switched on at an opportune moment. That the engine needed a radical driver to turn the key is clear, but the assembly had to be ready and fueled for Adolf Hitler to do what he did.

The Nazi Judeocide followed sequential steps: the formulation of the idea that Jews should disappear, *so oder so* (one way or another), was followed by its exposition, justification, legitimization, adoption, and implementation. Often there is also post hoc rationalization and then a final step, negation— the genocide never happened. Much the same pattern can be found in the Armenian genocide that preceded the Holocaust. In these various steps, only one of the processes, implementation, is primarily a physical action. The others are largely intellectual and philosophical.

We need to find the sources for these ancient hatreds, these ideological imperatives that propel genocide. That search leads to philosophy and to philosophers—that is, to those who specialize in the synthesis of knowledge and who seek final, overarching truth, especially about the nature or essence of human life, which they claim to find through logical, scientific reasoning. I am interested in those investigators and scholars who seek to discover the innermost essence of reality, who by reason of their skill and knowledge teach and expound authoritatively on the fields of knowledge. More specifically, I want to identify some of those who could be called, broadly speaking, philosophers of science: thinkers who used their scientific training and findings as a foundation for philosophical views or thinkers who claimed that their philosophical views especially reflected scientifically grounded claims about the nature and value of human life. Using the terms *philosophy* and *philosopher* broadly, as I am indicating, this chapter focuses on a variety of philosophical trends and thinkers and on their part in what I call the *doctorhood of genocide*. As will be seen, I use that term for multiple reasons, and one of them is that so many of these philosophers of science, as I call them, held advanced degrees in the arts and sciences of their day. They took pride in the status and recognition they enjoyed as people entitled to be called "Doctor." When considering the movements under examination here, we may think that their proponents perverted the good and the virtuous, but we also need to understand that they took themselves to be pursuing truth and reality. Unfortunately, their work, its implications and effects, led to Anatolia, Auschwitz, and other genocides that have followed those disasters.

The heart of darkness

The UN's definition of genocide lists the targeted victims as ethnic, racial, national, or religious groups. It also specifies that a key factor in genocide is the *intent to destroy* such groups *because* they are those groups.[3] Despite its flaws,[4] the UN's Genocide Convention is the major forensic tool we have for dealing with genocide. It is also a framework for analysis of many things, including the apportionment of legal responsibility in trials. But the UN document does not help to explain what the novelist Joseph Conrad called "the heart of darkness," the human tendency to arrive at the simple-sounding answer to "problem" peoples—to "exterminate all the brutes."[5]

Christian Pross came close to the essence of modern genocide when he described nineteenth-century race theory as an ideological tool that justified "exterminating the brutes" by having recourse to biological "solutions" to social or political problems.[6] He did not go far enough, however, in exploring and identifying those who were the ideologues, the articulators, and the justifiers of the Holocaust. Were they the philosophers of science or the politicians? Were only the nineteenth- and twentieth-century race theorists the malignant ones? Today we deride these men as racists, but in their time they were in the revered vanguard of "scientific" research and academic writing, adorned with all manner of degrees and professorial recognition at universities such as Cambridge, Oxford, the Sorbonne, Göttingen, Jena, Harvard, Stanford, and Columbia.

There are numerous well-documented and critical social histories of medical and scientific involvement in race theory and practice.[7] There is, however, a problematic and disturbing perspective to add from that otherwise fine historian Eric Hobsbawm. As if the Nazis alone had invented race theory, he asserted that Nazi Germany's racial policies "horrified serious geneticists." Only under Nazism and Soviet Communism, he wrote, were scientists forced into "ideological straightjackets," with racial–biological science driven by political agendas.[8] This questionable statement raises two issues. First, has "good" scholarship been perverted, twisted, and manipulated at specific political moments only by (German, Soviet, Turkish, or Serbian) political decision-makers, or has philosophical-scientific involvement in destructive race matters been continuous and widespread since the eighteenth century? Second, has the doctorhood been central or peripheral to the work of the *genocidaires*?

David Hume *et alia*

In one form or another, ideas of racial superiority are arguably as old as human history. Plato, Aristotle, Herodotus, Thucydides, Augustine, Aquinas, Machiavelli, Montesquieu, Locke, Rousseau, Kant, and Hegel all developed theories that traded on racial and national differences. Prior to the eighteenth century, the always morally dubious history of racial thinking lacked a scientific legitimacy that could establish with finality the "natural" hierarchy of the races and correlate "race" with history, culture, language, psychology, nationalism, and imperialism. Problematic though it was, this legitimacy began with the development of modern science and philosophy, including the work of the Scottish philosopher David Hume, one of the founding fathers of the social sciences, who wrote as follows in 1770: "I am apt to suspect the negroes ... to be naturally inferior to the whites. There scarcely ever was a civilized nation of any other complexion than white ... No ingenious manufactures amongst them, no arts, no sciences ... In Jamaica, indeed, they talk of one negro as a man of parts and learning; but it is likely he is admired for slender accomplishments, like a parrot, who speaks a few words plainly."[9]

Hume's comment, which contained views that were by no means his alone, tells us something about the prevailing culture of the time.[10] For as long as naturalists, physicians, anatomists, physical anthropologists, and philosophers divided human anatomies into Lapp, Tartar, Ethiopian, European, Caucasian, Negroid, and Mongoloid, the term *race* was reasonable.[11] Categorizing the variety of human forms, creating taxonomies of physically different people or races, was not necessarily fatal, but doing so was a step on the path to a "new reality" in which "science" would link temperamental, intellectual, cultural, and social characteristics to specific physical types. In eighteenth- and nineteenth-century Europe and America, a major literature flourished, one which made immutable the equation of physical traits with socially important characteristics. Spurious, untested, and unverifiable generalizations became racial lore—and later, law. Africans were black: therefore phlegmatic, indulgent, lazy, devious, promiscuous, and unable to govern themselves. *Europaeus Albus*, however, was found to have the special traits of liveliness and creativity, which made him superior to all others.

The "Hume tradition" had been bolstered by the earlier "Locke tradition," which held that only civilized people understood and valued property and knew what to do with land. Hunter-gatherers, as in the United States and Australia, failed to understand the politics of property—hence their inevitable demise. Meanwhile, Voltaire—the Frenchman who devoted his life to tolerance, justice, and humanity—predated several eminent scientists in arguing that racial differences were the result of separate origins, that not all men were the descendants of Adam and Eve.[12] Following in Voltaire's footsteps, the essentially American "polygenecists" concentrated on the singular defectiveness of the black American—then (and since) considered another species, biologically and mentally. These versions of "science" held that blacks were not simply different or diverse but truly "other," that is, other than fully human.

The craniologists

Polygenecists and monogenecists—who defended multiple and single basic sources of human life, respectively—used at least two methods of race classification. The former concentrated on characteristics such as skin color, stature, hair, and optic, nasal, and facial forms. The latter often studied the skull in what, for more than half a century, was to become the smug and certain "science" of craniometry or craniology. One of this movement's leaders was Philadelphia's Samuel Morton. Intelligence came from the brain, and if he could not measure intelligence or the brain precisely, Morton and his followers could at least measure the casing of that intelligence. His "scientific" contribution was to rank humans according to the mean internal capacity of the skull, of which he collected more than a thousand. By 1839, Morton proclaimed the superiority of the white race by appealing to the brain capacity of the "typical" Caucasian skull, which he found to be, on average, nine cubic inches greater than that of the Ethiopian—a "fact" that could still be found in some Western school texts at the end of the twentieth century.[13]

Paul Broca, the French surgeon, "cerebrologist," and prince of the French Academy of Sciences, perpetuated Morton's nonsense from 1860 to 1880, after which virtually all European and then American scientists engaged in systematic rankings of the sub species. Typically, they agreed that differences between humans—such as race, sex, or class—were *inborn* and that society is but an accurate reflection of biology. Increasingly, biological determinism became established: one's worth as an individual or race member could be assigned by measuring intelligence as a single quantity, entity, unity—first by craniology and later by its equally problematic successor, intelligence testing.

As Stephen Jay Gould has argued, biological determinism is a theory of limits: the external imposition of a number that ascribes intelligence or ability, falsely identifying such characteristics as lying forever within one and with no hope of change.[14] As late (or as recently) as the 1960s and 1970s, William Shockley, the 1956 Nobel physics laureate, and Arthur Jensen, the Berkeley educational psychologist, agitated against treating black Americans as equal to other groups in health, education, and welfare programs. While they agreed that black Americans should be granted benefits, they argued that those benefits should be of a kind suitable to their biologically determined and inferior station in life. Obviously, the eugenics cult of 1920s and 1930s America remained alive more than half a century later.

The English imperialists

As the twentieth century dawned, the philosophy of biological determinism was deeply entrenched in Britain and, slightly later, in the United States. Scientist-philosophers such as the anatomist Robert Knox insisted that "race is everything: literature, science, art, in a word, civilizations depend on it." He also contended that "no race exceeds [the Anglo-Saxons] in an abstract sense of justice, and a love of fair play."[15] The Cambridge University historian John Seeley saw something "intrinsically glorious in an Empire 'upon which the sun never sets' " and in whose natural growth there was "a mere normal extension of the English race into other lands."[16] Even the historian Lord Bryce, a quintessential democrat, believed that in the thought and imagination of every civilized people "there is an unquestionable racial strain," and that the British were the most civilized of people.[17] In 1868, Sir Charles Dilke described Anglo-Saxons as destined to conquer the world. That "race" was the "only extirpating race," one that would eventually displace the backward colored peoples. The English in India, for example, were the "dearer race," the officers controlling the foot soldiers of the "cheaper race." In Australia, too, the English were triumphant, "the cheaper races excluded from the soil"—and, he might have added, from life itself.[18]

Thomas Carlyle's *Occasional Discourse on the Nigger Question*, first published in 1849, proposed a "Law of the World" in which "the more foolish" had to obey their superiors—or else the price to be paid would be "futility and disappointment."[19] From these perspectives it was but an easy step toward Benjamin Disraeli's racist imperialism and to Rudyard Kipling's eminence as the high priest of an Anglo-Saxon cultism. "Truly," Kipling told his country-men, "ye come of The Blood." Vague, yes, and certainly hematologically silly, but Kipling popularized and helped to legitimate the political philosophy that native races could never attain the high standards of the Anglo-Saxons.

For Charles Darwin there was no end to the desperate struggle in which the strong, the fit, and the talented come to rule while the meek and the weak—as Thucydides once said—suffer what they must: to become the tools of those with greater vitality. Those unfortunates, it seems, were not only doomed to die but also the progress of the universe virtually demanded their elimination. Sir Francis Galton and arch-eugenicist Karl Pearson followed, but with heredity rather than the environment as the key to their understanding.

The American eugenicists

By the start of the nineteenth century, thinkers such as the French educator Alfred Binet came to see the glaring nonsense of craniology. In 1904 he developed appropriate techniques for children needing remedial education. Devising tests to measure the age levels at which certain tasks should be achieved, he also emphasized that intelligence was too complex to capture by a single number or intelligence quotient (IQ). He was rightly afraid that his tests would be perverted, used to label worth indelibly rather than serving as a guide to identify and assist children with specific problems.

His devices were indeed perverted. Three American scholars—Henry Herbert Goddard, Lewis Terman, and Robert Yerkes—ignored his cardinal principle that the tests were never to be used on normal children. Anxious to establish the primacy of white, American Protestants, Goddard began his IQ testing in public schools in 1910. By 1913 he was testing immigrants at Ellis Island. The trio's work produced the "Stanford-Binet" test of intelligence, which was used on 1.75 million American soldiers in the First World War. In the minds of Goddard, Terman, and Yerkes, the results confirmed and vindicated their discriminatory views about heredity, race, and eugenics.

Eugenics is a term pertinent to animal husbandry. It involves the study and science of pedigree and breeding. In the late nineteenth century and early twentieth century, a eugenics movement—centered in Great Britain and the United States but extended to other nations as well—gained considerable influence. An early form of genetic engineering, the eugenics movement wanted to control human breeding to maximize superior characteristics and to diminish negative ones. Goddard's 1912 monograph, *The Kallikak Family*, was an influential example of eugenics philosophy. It purported to prove the devastating social consequences of marriage and breeding practices that passed so-called feeblemindedness from one generation to another.[20] By 1940, most of American psychology questioned this research, but the maladies inherent in the approach lingered on. The various tests for intelligence and other characteristics were used to maintain and justify gaps between the rich and the poor, to restrict immigration, and to defend Jim Crow segregation laws. Laws were passed to prohibit marriages of and between sub-IQ people and to sterilize or institutionalize "morons," the term Goddard coined for some mentally impaired people. These developments helped to provide the seedbed in which the advocates and practitioners of Nazi Germany's so-called "euthanasia program" did their work. Both American and pre-Weimarian intellectual traditions gave succour and support for these apprentice *genocidaires*.

Henry Osborn, the "dean" of American racialists, the Harvard psychologist William McDougall, who promoted eugenics and disparaged immigration, the Princeton professor Carl Brigham, and Robert Yerkes were all instrumental in the passage of the US Immigration Act of 1924 whereby annual immigration quotas for each European country were effectively reduced from 3 percent of people from each nation recorded in the 1890 census to 2 percent. While some of these men recanted in the mid-1930s, the damage was done. Eugenics propaganda, as Gould argues, barred Jews even when American immigration quotas went unfilled: "We know what happened to many who wished to leave but had nowhere to go. The paths to destruction are often indirect, but ideas can be agents as sure as guns and bombs."[21]

The German racial hygienists

The reality that philosophical ideas can be agents of death is nowhere better illustrated than in the case of the German pre-Nazi nationalist quest for a "warrior" identity. Rooted in ethnic homogeneity, twentieth-century nationalism needed "scientific racism" for validation of what were seen as two possibilities: either the assimilation of those not "ethnically pure" or their exclusion or extrusion—by one means or another. So-called racial hygiene played a central part in these initiatives.

Key roots for the racial hygiene movement can be found in philology and its search for a common ancestral language. In 1788, Sir William Jones believed that the similarities between the Greek, Sanskrit, Persian, Celtic, and German languages could only be explained by a common origin. He called these languages "Indo-European," a term that soon changed to "Indo-Germanic." Meanwhile, the Anglo-German philologist, Friedrich Max Müller, invented the term "Aryan" to replace "Indo-Germanic" because the people who invaded India and spoke Sanskrit called themselves Arya. Following from the assumption that language and race were interconnected, these philological theories led to the view that there must have been a pure Aryan race, although neither Müller nor any other scholars offered proof of its existence. In 1888, he recanted the whole theory, but the ethnic nationalists and "scientific" racists would not relinquish the Aryan myth.

The doctrine of Aryanism received a major boost from the French diplomat, Joseph Arthur, Comte de Gobineau, whose four-volume *Essai sur l'inégalité des races humaines* became the racial bible in 1855. His thesis was that all human races were anatomically, physically, and psychologically unequal. Civilizations degenerated and died when the primordial race-unit was broken up and swamped by the influx of foreign elements. Racial differences were permanent. Of the three races—white, yellow, and black—white was superior. Purity of blood was essential to maintain that power, and purity had to be protected from the dangerous germ plasmas, the bacilli, who were the Jews. Gobineau's racial theories and Aryanism were mutually supportive.

Twenty-four years later, in 1879, the Prussian historian-philosopher-prophet, Heinrich von Treitschke, penned the one-liner that was to become such a propelling force in nineteenth- and twentieth-century German antisemitism: "The Jews are our misfortune." Even Friedrich Nietzsche, who despised the vulgarity of antisemitism, prophesied that European Jewry had reached its Rubicon and that the twentieth century would decide its future: "either they will become masters of Europe or they will lose it."[22]

Along with the musician Richard Wagner, a professor named Ludwig Schemann introduced Gobineau to the German public: "All good Germans," he said, "regard Gobineau as one of the most extraordinary men of the nineteenth century, one of the greatest God-inspired heroes, saviors and liberators sent by Him across the ages." "Gobineau societies" proliferated in Germany, and in due time his reprinted works made him a philosopher much revered in Nazi ideology. Wagner's son-in-law, Houston Stewart Chamberlain, who had helped to popularize Gobineau's thinking, also pushed racial philosophy by blending the Aryan myth with his call for the superiority of a Nordic–Teutonic race. In the late nineteenth and early twentieth centuries, his influential writings argued as follows: "To this day these two powers—Jews and Teutonic races—stand, wherever the recent spread of the Chaos had not blurred their features, now as friendly, now as hostile, but always as alien forces face to face ..." The "alien elements" in Teutonism had not yet been exorcised "and still, like baneful germs, circulate in our blood ..." The "sacredness of pure race" was the underlying tenet of his work.[23]

These ideas greatly influenced Ludwig Woltmann and Alfred Ploetz, founders of *Rassenkunde* and *Rassenhygiene* in the early 1900s, the hereditarian specialists Eugen Fischer, Erwin Baur, and Fritz Lenz, the academic ideologues Hans F. K. Günther, Otmar von Verschuer, Walter Gross, Wolfgang Abel, and Alfred Rosenberg. The latter was to become the philosophical *Führer* of Nazi intellectualism. *The Myth of the Twentieth Century* was his scientific-philosophical justification for the Nazi blood myth. "The Mythus is the Mythus of the blood," he wrote, "which under the sign of the Swastika, released the World Revolution. It is the Awakening of the Soul of the Race, which, after a period of long slumber, victoriously put an end to racial chaos." The real Christ, he contended, was an Amorite Nordic, aggressive and courageous, a man of true Nordic character, a revolutionist who opposed the Roman and Jewish systems and who, with sword in hand, brought not peace but war.[24] This German "science" and the philosophy intertwined with it was portrayed as having racial and "earth-rooted" values as opposed to "Jewish science," which was invidiously portrayed as abstract, neutral, internationalist, or cosmopolitan.[25]

The doctorhood in *Aktion*

Norman Naimark contends that one feature of twentieth-century racial nationalism was that it was driven from the top downwards, from the political leadership above, rather than from fanatical, seething mobs below.[26] I largely agree but also contend that racial nationalism was also driven by the nationalistic scientist-philosophers of the time. They were not so much "conscripted" by political leaders as they were the "fuelers" of political ideology. Several of these ideas-men engaged in *Aktionen* as "fieldworkers."

Eugen Fischer and Alfred Ploetz, for example, were instrumental in establishing the *Gesellschaft für Rassenhygiene* in 1905. Following Fischer's work on the "problems" of miscegenation, the German colonial authorities in South-West Africa had forbidden mixed marriages. These steps were consistent with Fischer's philosophy which urged protection for inferior races only so long as they were useful. When they no longer had such utility, it was best to let "free competition" and nature see to their destruction. In this climate in 1904, General Lothar von Trotha and his forces committed the twentieth century's first genocide by murdering 65,000 of the 80,000 indigenous Herero and Damara peoples after they rebelled against Germany's colonial rule in South-West Africa. "No prisoners will be taken," said von Trotha. Herero women and children were a disease-threat to German troops;

feeding those natives was impossible. It was more appropriate for them to perish. Here, indeed, was fulfilment of the philosopher Eduard von Hartmann's theme—that "the true philanthropist, if he has comprehended the natural law of evolution, cannot avoid desiring an acceleration of the last convulsion [of the savages], and labor for that end."[27]

In Turkey, the turbine of a virulent Turkish nationalism was Mehmed Ziya, also known as Ziya Gökalp, a writer, poet, and senior intellectual of the nationalist movement. In 1912 he took the chair of sociology at Istanbul where he developed his nationalism and his revolutionary ideals. In essence, he preached as radical and as ethnic a nationalism as anything yet emanating from Germany: a Pan-Turkism, a Pan-Turanism producing a Turkish solidarity and a pride in Turkishness based on a trinity of race–religion–language, which echoed what the philosopher Johann Fichte, a leading proponent of German nationalism, had advocated a century earlier.

A cadre of physicians, many of them holding senior university and political party posts, were directly involved in the ensuing Armenian genocide—as ideologues and as killers. Behaeddin Sakir and Mehmed Nazimas, as the Courts Martial Extraordinary of 1919–20 later documented, were pivotal in the formation, deployment, and direction of the Special Organization units, the lethal instrument of that particular genocidal "solution."[28] German officers, very much involved as advisers and leaders in Turkey at the time of the Armenian genocide, testified to the "exterminations" carried out "with animal brutality" by Sakir and his men.

Nicknamed, the "execution governor," Mehmed Resid was renowned for nailing horseshoes to victims' hearts with hot nails, smashing skulls, and crucifying people on makeshift crosses. His rationale for Armenian murder was stark: "Even though I am a physician, I cannot ignore my nationhood. I came into this world as a Turk. My national identification takes precedence over everything else ... Armenian traitors had found a niche for themselves in the bosom of the fatherland; they were dangerous microbes. Isn't it the duty of a doctor to destroy the microbes? ... My Turkishness prevailed over my medical calling." This particular Turkish doctorhood—Sakir, Nazim, Resid, and others—let loose bands of specially released brigands to kill people in death marches, injected live typhus serum in medical experiments, slaughtered people on butcher's hooks, experimented with elementary "steam-bath" gas chambers and mass poisonings, and blinded beautiful young girls under anaesthetic in infinitely delicate surgical operations.

From the excesses of South-West Africa and Turkey it was not a long leap for the jurist Karl Binding and the psychiatrist Alfred Hoche to publish *Die Freigabe der Vernichtung lebensunwerten Lebens* (The release and destruction of lives not worth living) in 1920. In Nazi Germany, the next "logical" steps were the sterilization program that began in the summer of 1933 and the euthanasia program that followed in 1939. These steps were precursors and precedents for the Nazi death camps.

Meanwhile, some further detail about the previously mentioned Eugen Fischer is instructive. In his July 1933 inaugural address as rector of the University of Berlin, Fischer, who had presided over the dismissal of Jewish colleagues, declared that only a biological framework was possible to "safe-guard the hereditary endowment and our race." In 1939 he rejected "Jewry with every means in my power, and without reserve, in order to preserve the hereditary endowment of my people." In December 1941, at the time of the earliest uses of industrialized death machines for Jews—the mobile gas vans at the Chelmno death camp—Fischer was lecturing to the French intelli-gentsia in Paris about the indivisibility of Bolshevism and Judaism and the "scientific necessity of the final solution." He concluded that "the morals and actions of the Bolshevist Jews bear witness to such a monstrous mentality that we can only speak of inferiority and of beings of another species."[29] As Fischer spoke, the "Final Solution" was well under way.

It soon became possible for the doctorhood and the professoriate—includ-ing German men such as Karl Brandt, Rudolf Brandt, Karl Gebhardt, Waldemar Hoven, Wolfram Sievers, Fritz Fischer, Gerhard Rose and, of course, Josef Mengele and Fritz Klein—to engage in experiments on the living, such as the effects of low pressure and supercooling, forced seawater drinking, injection of typhus and epidemic hepatitis viruses, bone transplantations, phosgene and mustard gas inhalations, twin engineering, surgery without anaesthesia, *und so weiter*.[30] In sentiments akin to Mehmed Resid's, the Nazi doctor Fritz Klein placed himself in the pantheon of those doctor-philosophers who saw "killing as a therapeutic imperative." As a doctor, and out of "respect for human life," Klein said, he wanted to preserve life—but just as he would "remove a gangrenous appendix from a diseased body," so he removed Jews "as a gangrenous appendix in the body of mankind."[31]

The unbroken *continuity* of this biological–philosophical–biomedical vision and framework was not coerced by political powers that required doctors of philosophy, science, and medicine to do their bidding. On the contrary, these philosophers of science freely developed their outlooks and urged that they be politically implemented. They did not have or need *Gauleiters* or commisars to guide or coerce them. They needed precedent—of which they had a great deal.

Never again?

In the 1990s rape centers were established in Bosnia, places where forced impregnation of Serbian "seed" would biologically displace Bosnian "Muslimness" once and for all. The doctorhood, under the direction of the notorious Radovan Karadzic, a medical psychologist and poet, gave us a new invention, but one still very much within the cultural configuration of a "biological solution" for those who are a "problem" people: the cholera, bacilli, baneful germs, "brutes," "gangrenous appendixes," mongrels, and microbes in the German or Turkish or Serbian bodies politic. Thanks to the long history that the doctorhood of racism, atrocity, and mass death and its philosophers of science have compiled, a history that may expand still further, philosophy cannot credibly claim to be innocent of complicity—or worse—in genocide.

Notes

1. Raul Hilberg, author of the seminal three-volume *The Destruction of the European Jews*, 3 vols. rev. edn (New Haven, CT: Yale University Press, 2003), in an interview with Claude Lanzmann in the latter's documentary film, *Shoah*, 1985. See Claude Lanzmann, *Shoah: An Oral History of the Holocaust* (New York: Pantheon, 1985), p. 70.
2. See Vahakn N. Dadrian, *German Responsibility in the Armenian Genocide: A Review of the Historical Evidence of German Complicity* (Watertown, MA: Blue Crane Books, 1996).
3. *The Convention on the Prevention and Punishment of the Crime of Genocide*, United Nations, 1948.
4. Article II equates the five (unequal) acts of genocide. For example, killing is placed on a par with the forcible removal of children from one group to another. Article III makes the actions of conspiracy and incitement to genocide, the attempt to commit the crime, and complicity in it, equal in seriousness with the physical commission of the crime.
5. Sven Lindqvist, "*Exterminate All the Brutes*," trans. Joan Tate (London: Granta Publications, 1997), pp. ix–x.
6. Götz Aly, Peter Chroust, and Christian Pross, *Cleansing the Fatherland: Nazi Medicine and Racial Hygiene*, trans. Belinda Cooper (Baltimore, MD: Johns Hopkins University Press, 1994), p. 1.
7. Especially pertinent in this regard are the works by Götz Aly, Michael Burleigh, Robert J. Lifton, George Mosse, Benno Müller-Hill, and Robert Proctor that are cited in this book's bibliography.
8. Eric Hobsbawm, *The Age of Extremes* (London: Michael Joseph, 1994), pp. 532–3.
9. As Hume is quoted in Peter Rose, *The Subject is Race* (Oxford: Oxford University Press, 1968), p. 18.
10. Robert Palter, "Hume and Prejudice," *Hume Studies* 21 (April 1995): 3–23.
11. Among others, Carl von Linnaeus (1707–78), the Swedish botanist, George Louis Leclerc (1708–88), the French naturalist, and Johann Blumenbach (1758–1840), the German physician.
12. Rose, *The Subject is Race*, pp. 33–9. The major "polygenecists" were Samuel Morton (1799–1851), a Philadelphia physician and professor of anatomy, Josiah Nott (1804–73), the Alabama physician and a founding father of American anthropology, and Louis Agassiz (1807–73), the Swiss-American naturalist.
13. The term *Caucasian* derives from a "perfect" (white) skull found in the Caucasus Mountains.
14. Stephen Jay Gould, *The Mismeasure of Man* (New York: W. W. Norton, 1981), p. 28. See also Leon Kamin's *The Science and Politics of I.Q.* (Harmondsworth: Penguin, 1977).
15. As Knox is quoted in Louis Snyder, *The Idea of Racialism: Its Meaning and History* (Princeton, NJ: Von Nostrand, 1962), p. 137.
16. As Seeley is quoted in ibid., pp. 140–1.

17. As Bryce is quoted in ibid., p. 32.
18. As Dilke is quoted in ibid., pp. 138–9.
19. As Carlyle is quoted in ibid., p. 57.
20. Leila Zenderland, *Measuring Minds: Henry Herbert Goddard and the Origins of American Intelligence Testing* (Cambridge: Cambridge University Press, 2001).
21. Gould, *The Mismeasure of Man*, pp. 232–3.
22. J. L. Talmon, "European History as the Seedbed of the Holocaust," in Jacob Sonntag, ed., *Jewish Perspectives—25 Years of Modern Jewish Writing* (London: Secker & Warburg, 1980), p. 11.
23. As Chamberlain is quoted in Snyder, *The Idea of Racialism*, pp. 48–50.
24. As Rosenberg is quoted in ibid., p. 84.
25. Robert Proctor, *Racial Hygiene: Medicine under the Nazis* (Cambridge: Harvard University Press, 1988), p. 291.
26. Norman Naimark, *Fires of Hatred: Ethnic Cleansing in Twentieth Century Europe* (Cambridge: Harvard University Press, 2001).
27. Eduard von Hartmann, *Philosophy of the Unconscious*, 2 vols. (London: n.p., 1884), 2, p. 12.
28. For more detail, see Vahakn N. Dadrian, "The Role of Turkish Physicians in the World War I Genocide of Ottoman Armenians," *Holocaust and Genocide Studies*, 1, 2 (1986): pp. 169–92.
29. Benno Müller-Hill, *Murderous Science: Elimination by Scientific Selection of Jews, Gypsies and Others in Germany, 1933–45*, trans. George Fraser (Oxford: Oxford University Press, 1988), p. 46.
30. A. Mitscherlich and F. Mielke, *The Death Doctors*, trans. James Cleugh (London: Elek Books, 1962).
31. Robert J. Lifton, *The Nazi Doctors: Medical Killing and the Psychology of Genocide* (London: Macmillan, 1986), pp. 15–16.

8

The Philosophical Warrant for Genocide

David Patterson

The first novel to emerge from the Auschwitz experience was *Sunrise over Hell* by Ka-tzetnik 135633. In this harrowing account, Harry Preleshnik, an inmate of Auschwitz modeled after the author, discovers the corpse of his friend Marcel Safran. "Prone before his eyes," writes Ka-tzetnik, "he saw the value of all humanity's teachings, ethics and beliefs, from the dawn of mankind to this day ... . He bent, stretched out his hand and caressed the head of the Twentieth Century."[1] The value of humanity's teachings and of the human image itself meet this fate at the hands not of ignorant brutes but of highly educated people who acted in a meticulous, calculated, and systematic manner. It is well known, for example, that three of the four commanders of the *Einsatzgruppen* killing units had doctoral degrees, as did eight of the thirteen men whom Reinhard Heydrich summoned to the Wannsee Conference on 20 January 1942. The purpose of this meeting of great German minds? To discuss the logistics of murdering the Jews of Europe.

Although these men were not philosophers, they were educated in Europe's finest universities and were therefore versed in a philosophical tradition that had undertaken the project of philosophical deicide. And there we have the philosophical warrant for genocide. From the ascent of German Idealism to the assault on logocentrism, it buds with modernism and blossoms with postmodernism. The process is characterized by a philosophical erasure of God from the framework of thought and the increasing centrality of the thinking ego. As the ego dominates and becomes identified with thought, the thinker slips away from the combination of human-to-human and human-to-divine relationships that alone can determine the sanctity of a human life. Because genocide entails the murder of human beings, it requires this philosophical draining of holiness from the human image; it requires the subsequent collapse of human relations as a defining element of humanity. Because the warrant entails the question of what is permitted, it requires the philosophical erasure of the divine prohibition against murder. Whereas it once was thought that truth held sway regardless of power, philosophy's innovations were inclined, however inadvertently, to make power the ultimate reality. Whereas human freedom was once defined in terms of an adherence to a divine commandment, much of philosophy's history determined that freedom lies in human autonomy.

Franz Rosenzweig comments on this philosophical folly by saying, "It is nothing but a prejudice of the last three centuries that in all knowledge the 'I' must necessarily accompany it, ... [for] the standard philosophical claim that the I is omnipresent in all knowledge distorts the content of this knowledge."[2] To be sure, that claim does more than distort knowledge—it eliminates the absolute nature of the prohibition against murder. For more than three hundred years, a certain mode of philosophical understanding has assumed a position no longer inherently inconsistent with genocide. If history has proven anything in this regard, it has shown that philosophy is not only powerless to prevent genocide, but—at least in its speculative, ontological, and postmodern forms—it has provided the warrant for genocide. But how has this come about?

The foundations of the warrant

Ever since the Enlightenment, philosophy has harbored hostility toward revealed religion in general and to Judaism in particular. While its funda-mental forms are contrary to this philosophical movement, Christianity does not pose the same problem that Judaism does, because Christianity preaches individual salvation through a personal belief in the Christ. Judaism, on the other hand, seeks a communal salvation through an adher-ence to the commandments of Torah—commandments that arise from out-side the thinking ego. Emil Fackenheim correctly pointed out that in Christian thinking as it develops in philosophers such as Hegel, "divinity comes to dwell, as it were, in the same inner space as the human self."[3] Once this collapse of God into the self takes place, the self is "as God," self-legislating and self-determining. Soon, says Fackenheim, "the denial of the living God was an essential aspect of man's scientific and moral self-emancipation. If man was to be fully free in his world, God had to be expelled from it. ... The living God had to become a mere 'Deity,' a 'Cosmic Principle'—remote, indifferent, and mute."[4] From the perspective of modern and postmodern philosophy, any embrace of the living God of Moses and His command-ments is taken to be not only superstitious but also dangerous to this "self-emancipation."

Because Judaism maintains that the self cannot emancipate itself, Jonathan Sacks rightly makes the following points:

> it is no accident that almost all the great continental philosophers of the eighteenth and nineteenth centuries—Voltaire, Kant, Hegel, Schopenhauer and Nietzsche—delivered sharp attacks on Judaism as an anachronism. Voltaire described it as a "detestable superstition." Kant

called for its euthanasia. Hegel took Judaism as his model of a slave morality. Nietzsche fulminated against it as the "falsification" of all natural values. In the twentieth century, Sartre could see no content to Jewish existence other than the defiance of anti-Semitism. Martin Heidegger, the greatest German philosopher of his time, became an active Nazi. Modern Western philosophy, promising a new era of tolerance, manifestly failed to extend that tolerance to Judaism and the Jews. Against this background, the transition from Enlightenment to Holocaust is less paradoxical than it might otherwise seem.[5]

Berel Lang adds to Sacks's analysis: "There are few figures of the Enlightenment in fact who in their common defense of toleration do not qualify that principle where the Jews are concerned. This fact alone would be significant for assessing the Enlightenment in relation to its ideals; it becomes still more significant in the light of evidence that this attitude toward the Jews was not accidental or simply the recrudescence of earlier prejudices, but was engendered by the doctrines of the Enlightenment itself."[6] And those doctrines proved to be just what the warrant for genocide required.

Emphasizing the self's autonomy, authenticity, and resolve, the philosophy that arose in the Enlightenment and paved the way for genocide follows a clear line of development from Immanuel Kant onward. If the Cartesian *cogito* situates being within the thinking ego, the Kantian critique deduces everything from the thinking ego and thus, as Rosenzweig astutely pointed out, "reduces the world to the perceiving self."[7] Far from glorifying the human being, however, the reduction of the world to the perceiving self is radically dehumanizing. "Corresponding to the Copernican turn of Copernicus which made man a speck of dust in the whole," says Rosenzweig, "is the Copernican turn of Kant, which, by way of compensation, placed him upon the throne of the world, much more precisely than Kant thought. To that monstrous degradation of man, costing him his humanity, this correction without measure was, likewise, at the cost of his humanity."[8] Refashioning himself after his own image, the human being loses his humanity, the sanctity of which can be determined only from beyond the human being. This loss of holiness with the human is dehumanizing and leads to the murder of the *other* human being. And so genocide happens.

In the aftermath of Enlightenment philosophy, then, all values, moral and otherwise, are soon viewed as a product of either natural accident or human will, so that nothing outside the self is left with any inherent or absolute value. Kant himself sets the stage not only in his *Grounding for the Metaphysics of Morals*, where the ongoing theme is that autonomy is the key to freedom,[9] but also in his *Anthropology from a Pragmatic Point of View*, where he ascribes certain inherent characteristics to various peoples of the world according to the accidents of nature.[10] One soon recognizes in this thinking the rudimentary ingredients of what is now termed "postmodernism": namely, the idea that the "nature" of a human being is determined by race, gender, culture, and other "systems of signs," and that neither the world nor humanity has any absolute, inherent meaning. Inasmuch as modern and postmodern thought eliminates all that is absolute and divine—everything that has meaning *outside* of any context—such thinking provides the warrant for genocide. For if all meaning is contextual, then all meaning is contingent. And where one's resolve is powerful enough,[11] contingencies can be willed away.

With regard to the differences between Kant and Hegel, Edith Wyschogrod makes an important point: "Moral decisions," according to Hegel, "are not to be made by subjecting the agent's subjective maxim to the criterion of universalizability as Kant claims, but rather by determining whether the agent's will is in harmony with the will of the community."[12] And genocide requires precisely this aligning of the agent's will with the will of the community. Indeed, precisely in the community—in the *Volk*—one finds the "life of the Spirit," which, says Hegel, "is not the life that shrinks from death and keeps itself untouched by devastation, but rather the life that endures it and maintains itself in it."[13] In contrast to Kant's view of time as a function of the subject, Hegel views time in terms of death and destruction as part of a process of becoming. Subsequently, when Martin Heidegger went on to identify being with time, the only thing that concerns the human being is his own death, which he must confront both for the sake of his own authenticity and for the sake of the *Volk*.[14] For the one whose project is authenticity—and Western philosophy's dominant history from Kant to Heidegger has left us with no other project—nothing else matters. With the emergence of Heidegger, then, we have the emergence of postmodern thought, since the holy has been thought out of the picture. And with Heidegger's entry into the Nazi Party, philosophy and genocide become bedfellows.

The Heideggerian warrant for genocide

Thinking God out of the picture, philosophy thinks the human being out of the picture; the Nazis are the paradigm—and Heidegger makes them a *philosophical* paradigm—for genocide, because genocide entails not only the murder of human beings but also the philosophical obliteration of the holiness of the human being as one created in the image and likeness of the Holy One. Therefore, while we may look back and call, say, the case of the Native Americans a genocide, it cannot be understood as such in philosophical terms, since, in principle, one could "kill the Indian but save the man," as the slogan went, through education. For even the Indian was created in the image and likeness of God. Here there may have been political and economic warrants for genocide, but there was no philosophical warrant. Here philosophy had not yet extinguished the divine spark of the Holy One that makes every life sacred.

Undertaking precisely the project of erasing the image of the Holy One from the human, the SS implemented what the philosophers had conceived.

At the June 1939 meeting of the National Socialist Association of University Lecturers, Dr Walter Schultze declared before the assembly, "What the great thinkers of German Idealism dreamed of, and what was ultimately the kernel of their longing for liberty, finally comes alive, assumes reality. ... Never has the German idea of freedom been conceived with greater life and greater vigor than in our day."[15] Schultze was a physician; he was no ignoramus, and he thought philosophically: he saw as clearly as most of Nazi Germany's philosophers the link between the German philosophical tradition and the genocidal agenda of National Socialism. In fact, by 1940, when the Nazis' intentions toward the Jews were clear, nearly half the philosophers of Germany were members of the Nazi Party. True, the Nazi philosophers were quite varied in their philosophical positions, but they all represented the defining philosophical ingredient in the warrant for genocide: the embrace of a philosophical tradition that is fundamentally hostile toward divine prohibitions and that takes individual autonomy to be the measure of human freedom and authenticity.

Emmanuel Levinas accurately describes this thinking that begins in Kant and culminates in Heidegger: "Heideggerian philosophy precisely marks the apogee of a thought in which the finite does not refer to the infinite (prolonging certain tendencies of Kantian philosophy: the separation between the understanding and reason, diverse themes of transcendental dialectics), in which every deficiency is but weakness and every fault committed against oneself."[16] Therefore, says Levinas, "a philosophy of power, ontology is, as first philosophy which does not call into question the same, a philosophy of injustice. ... Heideggerian ontology, which subordinates the relationship with the Other to the relation with Being in general, remains under obedience to the anonymous, and leads inevitably to another power, to imperialist domination, to tyranny."[17] And Heideggerian ontology is the bedrock of postmodernism. Continuing to ground freedom in autonomy and authenticity in resolve, postmodernism continues this philosophical strain that situates freedom beyond the Law and is therefore lawless. To be sure, lawlessness is a necessary, if not a sufficient, condition for genocide. Where does it find its philosophical expression? Initially it is in the exaltation of the Nietzschean "will to power." "The expression 'will to power,' " says Heidegger in his study on Nietzsche, "designates the basic character of beings; any being which is, insofar as it is, is will to power. The expression stipulates the character that beings have as beings."[18] And history has shown that it stipulates the character beings have as mass murderers.

For genocide to be justified, the prohibition against murder has to be relativized, which is precisely what happens when the prohibition is situated within "a semiotic web of interlinking pieces," as it happens in postmodernism.[19] The value of human life and therefore any ethical value attached to our treatment of human beings are lost from the moment philosophers begin to spin the web of semiotics. Heidegger makes the deadly move from a modern to a postmodern warrant for genocide when he asserts, "If one takes the expression 'concern' ... in the sense of an ethical and ideological evaluation of 'human life' rather than as the designation of the structural unity of the inherently finite transcendence of *Dasein*, then everything falls into confusion and no comprehension of the problematic which guides the analytic of *Dasein* is possible."[20] To be sure, one of the central features of the Heideggerian thinking that characterizes the philosophical warrant for genocide is the elimination of the other human being from its concern. "*Das Dasein existiert umwillen seiner*," Heidegger declares: "*Dasein* exists for the sake of itself."[21] Which means: neither the Armenians nor the Jews nor the Tutsis have anything to do with me. Nor, in the solitude of my being, do I have anything to do with them. Thus modern and postmodern philosophy provides the warrant for murder by giving the excuse for the bystander.

Here the other human being is excluded—and ultimately annihilated—from consideration. Neither the inner resolve that determines our authenticity nor the system of signs that shapes our reality has anything to do with an absolute relation; for they have nothing to do with any absolute ethical obligation that precedes all resolve and every system. Diametrically opposed to the genocidal being-for-oneself is the being-for-the-other represented by Jewish teaching and tradition. Whereas Heideggerian ontology sees the death that concerns me, for example, as *my* death,[22] the Jewish view of ethical obligation to and for the other person takes the death that concerns me to be the death of the other human being—the widow, the orphan, and the stranger, who are of no concern to Heidegger. Indeed, once the world is reduced to the perceiving self, once thinking for oneself is a matter of seeking the highest touchstone of truth in oneself, once knowledge becomes the appropriation of the other by the same, then the only contradiction is a contradiction of self-interest, where self-interest is understood in terms of power and resolve. There we have Heideggerian evil underlying genocide.

Of course, what is referred to here as "Heideggerian evil" cannot be seen as evil from the standpoint of postmodernism, since such a category implies a divinely determined good, which, like the very notion of evil, has no place or significance in postmodern thought. Here lies one of Heidegger's chief contributions to postmodernism: it is the final erasure of vertical, "logocentric" categories that would enable us to speak of anything holy or evil. With the removal of the dimension of height, we are left only with the horizontally defined power struggles of culture and ideology that are invoked to justify genocide, which bring us back to the fundamental philosophical hostility toward revealed religion in general and Judaism in particular. Inasmuch as Judaism insists upon the dimension of height and holiness, postmodern thought *has to be* anti-Judaic, if not antisemitic. For opposed to postmodernism's erasure of absolutes is the Jewish insistence on absolutes—from dietary laws to moral sanctions—that are neither culturally determined nor ideologically dictated but are given from on high. This height—and not the accidents of culture—is what opens up truth and meaning in life. In Judaism the capacity to make such distinctions—between high and low, God and humanity, good and evil, sacred and profane—is the basis of the holiness from which the human sanctity derives.

With the postmodern leveling of these distinctions, being itself is leveled into a flatland of neutrality. This collapse of all into the same is characteristic of the postmodern thinking, for which even genocide is "all the same." Heidegger himself illustrates this leveling by equating technologically driven agriculture with the technologically driven murder of the Jews.[23] Commenting on Heidegger's view in this regard, Jürgen Habermas wrote, "Under the leveling glance of the philosopher of Being, the extermination of the Jews, too, appears as a happening, where everything can be replaced as one likes with anything else."[24] The world in which everything can be replaced as one likes with anything else is precisely the postmodern world, and genocide is part of the landscape of that world. Since everything is all the same, anyone can take the place of another, and everyone is expendable. Thus, with the postmodern loss of the dimension of height, we also lose the absolute nature of the prohibition against murder. Genocide, then, is a logical outcome of a line of philosophical thinking traceable from Kant's Idealism to the postmodernism spawned by Heidegger.

Concluding reflections

During a conversation I had in 1991 with Yehiel De-Nur, the author known as Ka-tzetnik 135633, I asked him what role philosophy might play in the response to the Holocaust. "*Philosophy*," he grimaced in response. "It's a *shabby* word." While I was initially taken aback by his remark, I think I have come to understand why he made it. The reason lies in a tearing of meaning from the word, just as the divine image has been torn from the human being. For *philosophy* means "love of wisdom." But what do we love when we love wisdom? Do we not love first of all the *other* human being as one in whom something holy abides? And in that love do we not love something higher—something holier—than ourselves, something that sanctifies and therefore *commands* that relation? Without the human relation expressive of a higher relation, *philosophy* is indeed a shabby word. The issue that confronts us, then, is whether we can return meaning to the word, which entails returning God to our thinking and our thinking to God.

Once God is eliminated from our thinking, then power is the only reality and weakness is the only sin, so that the perpetrators are not in error; no, the victims are in error for being weak. From this perspective, in order to be in the right, we need not become more righteous; we only have to become more dangerous. Once God is eliminated from our thinking, then each of us—every culture, society, and ethnic group—is as god, but of no *intrinsic* value and therefore of equal value. Yes, as god—not as the God of Abraham, who is loving and longsuffering, but as the false god of our egocentric aspirations, the god who can do what he or she wants and who gets what he or she wants. Once the God of Abraham is thus eliminated from our thinking, what remains are "belief systems" in the place of divine injunctions, so that, no longer the measure of a culture, religion is equated with culture. Yet when philosophers appeal to systems of belief or equate religion with culture, they lose all but expedient grounds for objecting to genocide. Here genocide is not evil—it is merely contrary to my interests. If philosophy is to find a way to object to genocide—if philosophy is truly to be the love of wisdom—then it must answer a fundamental question: *In the name of what* does it raise that objection? In the name of reason or human decency, lofty concepts or semiotic systems? Has history not shown that these are very flimsy structures indeed?

The anti-religious and anti-Judaic stance that characterizes much of philosophy has led many thinkers to shift the blame for genocide from philosophy to religion, particularly to the so-called religions of Abraham. Here they discover what they take to be the "proto-genocidal intent" in Judaism and view it as "the most familiar of all localized religions."[25] The implication is clear: Whereas Christians blame the Jews for the murder of God, philosophers blame the Jews for the murder of humanity. Christians cite Scripture, which they take to be truth, to prove that the Jews killed God in the person of Jesus. Similarly, intellectuals cite the Scripture, which they regard as myth, to prove that the Jews are behind genocide. Leonard Glick, for example, points out that "as the Hebrews, under Joshua's leadership, undertake the conquest of Canaan, they massacre everyone who stands in their way."[26] Leo Kuper makes a similar observation.[27] What makes genocide not only horrible but also *evil*, however, is precisely the God who prohibits murder (Exodus 20:13) and commands love for the stranger (Deuteronomy 10:19)— *absolutely*, from beyond all cultural contexts, all ontological contingencies, localized and otherwise. Once we reject the divine prohibition against murder, we have no grounds for objecting to the divine commandment to wage war.

Further, in the interest of intellectual honesty one should at least note the reason for the divine commandment to wage war. It is because among certain tribes "even their sons and their daughters do they burn in the fire to their gods" (Deuteronomy 12:31). Thus they renounce the holiness of human life that is proclaimed in the Torah and that makes genocide evil. Once we get rid of God, then passing our children through fire in the interest of power can easily be justified; it is not wrong—it is simply a cultural peculiarity. Which is to say: once the category of holiness is out of the picture, all that remains is human autonomy and an "authenticity" that is rooted in resolve. And, contrary to the covenantal commandment, human resolve knows no limiting principle.

Here we do have a key to a possible connection between religion and genocide. Wherever a religion divides humanity into believers and infidels, into the saved and the damned—wherever a religion insists that only those of a certain faith have a place with God—then there is indeed a potential for mass murder, if not for genocide. Contrary to such creeds, Judaism does not demand that a person become a Jew in order to have a place with the Holy One. From the standpoint of Judaism, one is righteous not in the light of having embraced a certain doctrine but because of engaging in certain actions, beginning with saving lives, as exemplified by the Righteous among the Nations during the Holocaust. Nevertheless, there is a crucial difference between revealed religion and ontological thinking in their contributions to genocide. The difference between the Crusaders' slaughter of Jews and Muslims, for example, and the megamurder perpetrated by Hitler, Stalin, and Mao does not lie in the technology at their disposal. It lies, rather, in the limiting principle at work in the religious teaching. At any point during the Christian blood bath one could still be a Christian and suggest that the killers were going too far, precisely by invoking Christian teaching. If, as Kuper rightly points out, "the teachings of the Church provided no specific warrant for genocide,"[28] it is because such a warrant would be contrary to other stated teachings, as for instance, the commandment to love one's enemies (Matthew 5:44). With the advent of modern and postmodern philosophy, the limiting principle is lost.

If a philosophical imperative prohibiting genocide can be determined, then it must somehow be grounded in an absolute, divine prohibition against murder, such as we have from the God of Abraham. For without that absolute prohibition, the human being has no absolute value. Without that commandment from the Holy One, the human being has no holiness. To be created in the image and likeness of God is to be commanded by God, so that, as the Ten Commandments are laid out on the tablets, the affirmation "I am God" parallels the injunction "Thou shalt not murder." Genocide is evil because genocide amounts to the most radical assault against the God of Abraham. It is no accident that, more often than not, genocidal regimes are also antisemitic regimes. They are antisemitic because, in order to pursue the genocidal program, they have to eliminate the divine prohibition against murder that comes to the world through the Jews. All too often philosophy has played into genocide's hands.

Notes

1. Ka-tzetnik 135633, *Sunrise over Hell*, trans. Nina De-Nur (London: W. H. Allen, 1977), p. 111.
2. Franz Rosenzweig, *Franz Rosenzweig's "New Thinking,"* trans. and ed. Alan Udoff and Barbara E. Galli (Syracuse, NY: Syracuse University Press, 1999), p. 80.
3. Emil L. Fackenheim, *Encounters between Judaism and Modern Philosophy* (New York: Basic Books, 1993), pp. 190–1.
4. Emil L. Fackenheim, "Jewish Existence and the Living God: The Religious Duty of Survival," in Arthur A. Cohen, ed., *Arguments and Doctrines: A Reader of Jewish Thinking in the Aftermath of the Holocaust* (New York: Harper & Row, 1970), p. 260.

5. Jonathan Sacks, *Crisis and Covenant: Jewish Thought after the Holocaust* (Manchester: Manchester University Press, 1992), pp. 268–9.
6. Berel Lang, *Act and Idea in the Nazi Genocide* (Syracuse, NY: Syracuse University Press, 2003), p. 185.
7. See Nahum Glatzer's introduction to Franz Rosenzweig, *Understanding the Sick and the Healthy*, trans. Nahum Glatzer (Cambridge: Harvard University Press, 1999), p. 24.
8. Rosenzweig, *Franz Rosenzweig's "The New Thinking,"* p. 96.
9. See Immanuel Kant, *Grounding for the Metaphysics of Morals*, trans. James W. Ellington, 3rd edn (Indianapolis, IN: Hackett, 1993).
10. See Immanuel Kant, *Anthropology from a Pragmatic Point of View*, trans. Victor Lyle Dowdell, ed., Hans H. Rudnick (Carbondale, IL: Southern Illinois University Press, 1978).
11. "*Dasein is its own self*," Heidegger maintains, "in the original isolation of silent resolve." See Martin Heidegger, *Sein und Zeit* (Tübingen: Max Niemeyer, 1963), p. 322.
12. Edith, Wyschogrod, *Spirit in Ashes: Hegel, Heidegger, and Man-Made Death* (New Haven, CT: Yale University Press, 1985), p. 78.
13. G. W. F. Hegel, *Phenomenology of Spirit*, trans. A. V. Miller (Oxford: Oxford University Press, 1979), pp. 18–19.
14. See, for example, Heidegger's Rectorial Address of 27 May 1933 in Martin Heidegger, "The Self-Assertion of the German University," in Guenther Neske and Emil Kettering, eds, *Martin Heidegger and National Socialism* (New York: Paragon, 1990), p. 10.
15. Quoted in George L. Mosse, *Nazi Culture* (New York: Grosset & Dunlop, 1966), p. 316.
16. Emmanuel Levinas, *Collected Philosophical Papers*, trans. Alphonso Lingis (Dordrecht: Martinus Nijhoff, 1987), p. 52.
17. Emmanuel Levinas, *Totality and Infinity*, trans. Alphonso Lingis (Pittsburgh, PA: Duquesne University Press, 1969), pp. 46–7.
18. Martin Heidegger, "Will to Power as Art," in *Nietzsche*, Vol. 1, trans. David Krell (San Francisco, CA: Harper & Row, 1979), p. 18.
19. See Zachary Braiterman, *(God) after Auschwitz* (Princeton, NJ: Princeton University Press, 1998), p. 166.
20. Martin Heidegger, *Kant and the Problem of Metaphysics*, trans. J. S. Churchill (Bloomington, IN: Indiana University Press, 1962), p. 245.
21. Martin Heidegger, *Vom Wesen des Grundes*, 5th edn (Frankfurt am Main: Klostermann, 1965), p. 38.
22. Heidegger, *Sein und Zeit*, p. 118.
23. See John D. Caputo, "Heidegger's Scandal: Thinking and the Essence of the Victim," in Tom Rockmore and Joseph Margolis, eds, *The Heidegger Case: On Philosophy and Politics* (Philadelphia, PA: Temple University Press, 1992), p. 265.
24. Quoted in the introduction to Neske and Kettering, eds, *Martin Heidegger and National Socialism*, p. xxxi.
25. See, for example, Leonard B. Glick, "Religion and Genocide," in Israel W. Charney, ed., *The Widening Circle of Genocide*, Vol. 3 (New Brunswick, NJ: Transaction Publishers, 1994), p. 47.
26. Ibid., p. 46.
27. Leo Kuper, "Theological Warrants for Genocide: Judaism, Islam, and Christianity," *Terrorism and Political Violence*, 2 (1990): 356.
28. Ibid., p. 371.

9
The Rational Constitution of Evil: Reflections on Franz Baermann Steiner's Critique of Philosophy

Michael Mack

> What is *really* irrational and what truly cannot be explained is not evil, but contrarily, the good.
>
> Imre Kertész, *Kaddish for a Child Not Born*

This chapter contributes to an analysis of philosophy's involvement in genocide by exploring the work of Franz Baermann Steiner (1909–52), a Prague poet and Oxford anthropologist whose critique of philosophy was developed against the background of the Holocaust. The epigraph from Imre Kertész's novel goes to the heart of Steiner's philosophical investigation of philosophy, which emphasizes that, far from being irrational, evil is impregnated by and with reason.

Evil and the history of reason

According to Kertész, Auschwitz reflects Hegel's philosophy of history. Interpreting Hegel's famous equation of the real and the rational, the narrator of Kertész's *Kaddish for a Child Not Born* puts the Nazi genocide squarely within the context of the historical realization of Hegel's World Spirit:

> the only facts that cannot be explained are those that don't or didn't exist. However, I most likely continued my train of thought, Auschwitz did exist, or, rather, *does* exist, and can, therefore, be explained; what could not be explained is that no Auschwitz ever existed, that is to say, one can't find an explanation for the possibility that Auschwitz didn't exist, hadn't occurred, that the state of facts labeled Auschwitz hadn't been the materialization of a *Weltgeist* ...[1]

Kertész's narrator suggests that Hegel's rational explanation of the factual coincides with a philosophy of history that represents nothing if not the history of evil. The refinement of reason goes hand in hand with the development of the mindset that made Auschwitz possible. Kertész's narrator continues:

> Consequently, Auschwitz must have been hanging in the air for a long, long time, centuries, perhaps like a dark fruit slowly ripening in the sparkling rays of innumerable ignominious deeds, waiting to finally drop on one's head. After all, what is, is; and its very existence is necessitated by the fact that it is. The history of the world is the image and deed of cognition (to quote Hegel), because to see the world as a series of arbitrary chance occurrences would be a rather unworthy view of the world (to quote myself).[2]

Reason's implication in genocidal violence requires that the mind reflects upon its own cunning, to use Hegel's term for ways in which reason can make history a slaughter-bench. Ironically, the history of genocide demands a return to a Hegelian perspective on the question as to how to explain historical facts: precisely because history reveals reason's progress, it also delineates the progression of evil and violence in particular. The interrelationship between reason and violence calls for thinking that reflects critically upon certain philosophical systems that show themselves to be indifferent or hostile to the well-being of humanity's embodied life.

Violence and the philosophy of history

Throughout history, philosophy has served as an accomplice to violations of human rights. From Aristotle's philosophical defense of slavery onwards, philosophy has repeatedly offered rational justifications for harmful social and political practices. An even more disturbing set of issues emerges from investigations into the possible presence of violent implications and inclinations at the heart of much philosophical thought. My 2003 study, *German Idealism and the Jews: The Inner Anti-Semitism of Philosophy and German Jewish Responses*, analyzes the subterranean tremors and aftershocks of certain ideational paradigms that not only incorporate prejudices widespread in the general public of a given time, but also shape and sharpen these prejudices into a seemingly rational, systematic, self-consistent whole.

To embark on such an analysis, the critic has to historicize philosophy, an approach that has often been interpreted as a violation of philosophy as such. Philosophy *qua* philosophy seems to reside in a realm removed from the contingencies of historical events. It is important to understand, however, that this enforced separation from the unpredictability of various historical realities sets the stage for the violent imposition of predictable, therefore "rational," schemata onto the infinite diversity of both individual actors and anthropological communities.

Philosophy often seems unwilling, if not unable, to bear the thought of that which could potentially unhinge the pure, stable, and unchangeable order established by reason. The diverse changes brought about by history seem to shake philosophical cohesion at its foundations. As Berel Lang has pointed out, "the image of philosophical thought as atemporal and undramatic, as itself non-representational, has been very much taken for granted in the historiography of philosophy since the nineteenth century; it has in certain respects been part of the profession of philosophy since its origins."[3] Lang focuses on both time and drama as elements that run counter to philosophy's self-understanding.

Meanwhile, up to the eighteenth century *historia* was concerned with the representation and explanation of particular events as they unfold with the passing of time, endlessly generating the emergence of new, varied social and cultural formations. However, at the end of the eighteenth century and throughout the nineteenth century, philosophers turned to history not to historicize their thinking but rather to differentiate thought from the contingencies of historical time. As this philosophical project unfolded, philosophy attempted to free history of unpredictability through a process of assimilation. The philosophical destruction of the historical and its contingencies coincided with the birth of a philosophy of history; the *cognitio philosophica* made history commensurable with philosophy.[4]

By contrast, in focusing on both time and drama, a philosophy such as Lang's implicitly discusses the historical within the broader context of the literary. Both trace the actions of particular agents and are thus immersed in the realm of the unpredictable, the diverse, and the potentially new.[5] Philosophical systems, by contrast, reside in a realm beyond time and drama, claiming to be universal and rational. Even while he emphasized the limits of human reason, Immanuel Kant accentuated these philosophical trends by underscoring what he took to be the universal and permanent nature of rational judgment and ethical duty and by revealing his lack of positive concern for the diversity of human life. In *German Idealism and the Jew*, I trace how this radicalization of philosophy as the atemporal and the undramatic prepared the way for the exclusion of groups of people from the universality of the human. At the end of the day, philosophy's detachment from the historical coincides with the history of genocide. But how can this be? Analyzing Franz Baermann Steiner's anthropological response to the Holocaust will highlight some of the insights that follow from that question.

The philosophical progression of history and the universal division of humanity

Steiner explored the culture of Western philosophy, its responsibility for human rights abuses, and the ways in which philosophical concepts inform and encourage genocidal practices. His penetrating outlook can be discerned in his instructive poem "Elefantenfang" (Elephant capture) and his aphoristic essay, "On the Process of Civilization," which was written in 1944 when Steiner was a refugee from Nazi-occupied Europe. At the time, he was completing his comparative study of slavery,[6] which, as part of an anthropological response to the Holocaust, criticizes what Edward Said would later call "Orientalism." In this study he calls into question the ethical validity of certain theoretical foundations that underpin various nineteenth-century philosophies of history. Instead of depicting the progression of the good, he delineates the progress of evil. For example, Steiner's reflections on slavery included the following observations:

> If we accept the continuity of slavery from Mediterranean antiquity down to the colonial slavery of modern times, if we recognize that slavery played an important role in Mediterranean economies through the ages, and was tied to the money economy in all parts to which Mediterranean capitalism (Roman, medieval or modern) spread, we have to regard modern colonial slavery as the culmination of this tendency and as the consummation of a European inheritance; and that it developed in the wake of the cultural Renaissance of Europe, is hardly surprising.[7]

The terms *culmination* and *consummation* clearly refer to a philosophical theory about the essence of history according to which the self-sufficiency of reason enables its self-generation and growth throughout the ages. That process, it follows, finds its apotheosis in the establishment of modern rational society. Steiner's descriptive analysis, however, is also a telling critique of such outlooks, for it shows how such philosophies of history provide a kind of legitimation for evil. If a theory legitimates evil, Steiner suggests, it is rendered suspect and deserves rejection.

How does Steiner's ironic critique of slavery as the true hero of modern philosophical progress respond to genocidal violence? He characterized his work on slavery as a sacrifice for surviving the Holocaust as a refugee in England.[8] Before embarking on this topic, however, he worked on what might be called the sociology of elephants. Instead of a theoretical or scholarly treatise, the outcome of this research was one his most powerful poems, "Elefantenfang." This poem highlights Steiner's literary critique of philosophical paradigms that support, justify, and even enable, at least theoretically, the perpetration of genocidal violence. By likening the human realm to the animal realm (i.e., the world of elephants) in a writing style that draws on the parable, "Elephantenfang" undermines the common contrast between humanity as the epitome of rationality and the animal as the embodiment of the irrational. Through this poem, Steiner communicates his understanding of racism as well as slavery.

"Elefantenfang" depicts the quasi-genocidal murder of wild elephants by tame ones. The murderous elephants, Steiner emphasizes, do not kill out of utilitarian considerations, a point that bears a striking resemblance to Hannah Arendt's analysis of totalitarianism, wherein she contrasts the "idealism" of totalitarian regimes with the utilitarianism of traditional societal structures.[9] Instead, the tame elephants murder out of purely "rational" and idealistic motivations, which emerge from a belief that they are fundamentally different than their wild counterparts. Bodily needs (hunger, thirst, or sex) play no role in the instigation of these quasi-genocidal killings. On the contrary, the tame ones are well-fed (*wohlgenährt*), but their hatred is inflamed by theoretically driven constructions and perceptions of difference. Steiner's poem captures some of these points as follows:

> *Erbarmungslos der wohlgenährten hass*
> *Dem waldgeruch galt, dem fernherkommen:*
> *Strafte mit lust.*

> [And pitiless the hatred of those well-fed
> Turned on the forest smell, provenance from afar,
> Punished with relish.][10]

Significantly, the smell of the wild elephants' bodies arouses the tame elephants' hatred. Likewise, socially constructed perceptions of odor functioned as a major justification for hatred and violence in mainstream antisemitic writings.[11] Indeed, versions of the contrast between tame and wild were among the standards to which antisemites referred when they differentiated the non-Jew from the Jew. At the heart of this contrast lies the opposition between the civilized and the uncivilized, which, in turn, opens the philosophical divide between the rational mind and the body. Steiner sees that a result of such philosophical theory is that the tame ones attack the wild ones "with relish."

This outcome is as ironic as it is devastating, for Steiner's poem also emphasizes that the groups are related, as the last stanza makes clear:

> *So schlachten sie die eigne, kleine wildheit*
> *Im bruderleibe mal um mal …*

> [So in their brothers' bodies again and again
> They butcher the lesser wildness that's their own …][12]

The tame elephants reject their wild brothers, denying their rights as family members. Thus Steiner illustrates his understanding of the way in which philosophical theory leads to the exclusion of certain groups from the human family, which renders them socially, if not physically, dead. This exclusion results from the philosophical attempt to overcome the "lower," nonrational aspect of the human condition, including those elements that may be part of ourselves as well as characteristics of those who are deemed "other." The extermination of the "other" presumably coincides with the elimination of our own irrational shortcomings. In this way, genocidal violence seems to work hand in hand with the rational perfection of humanity. Steiner's poem unmasks the deception of such violence, whose roots include philosophical theory. While attempting to liberate themselves from their own wildness, the tame elephants succeeded only in murdering their brothers and discrediting their own senses of rationality, although the latter awareness may have escaped them until it was much too late.

In his aphoristic essay "On the Process of Civilization," Steiner analyzes further the disturbing relationships between the rational organization of genocide and human attempts at liberation from the lowly sphere of bodily wildness. He introduces the reader to his way of argumentation by shedding light on how presumably objective, and thus detached, scholarship almost willfully misreads the social consequences of an increase in the power potential a given society acquires with the advance of scientific knowledge. He makes clear that his writing concerns the whole of humanity:

> In the lives of those peoples whom we are thinking of there is only one variety of power: power over other groups of people—that is to say military, political, economic power, power which guarantees the exploitation of other groups or permits their annihilation. In the head of a scholar it may well be that a new technological advance (including the sociological adaptations which this enforces) means an increase in the power of "Man." In the life of the planet and at the present moment, it simply means an increase in power over other people.[13]

Owing to divisions that open up around and between different segments of humanity, an increase in human power does not support the living conditions of every human being. Philosophers may talk and write about a seemingly all-encompassing human community, but then everything depends on one's understanding of what constitutes the human. Is humanity distinguished by its differences from the animal world? The latter would then denote the wildness and bodily "smelliness" of Steiner's captured elephants. As a poet and cultural critic, Steiner approaches the philosophical problem of the mind–body divide from the perspective of a social anthropologist. As illustrated in the quotation above, he emphasizes that the debate about how to define the human has consequences far beyond the realm of a specialized scholarly analysis: The debate and its consequences, as Steiner sees them, have profound implications for human rights.

Steiner's response to the Nazi genocide against the European Jews sharpened his insight that the exploitation and annihilation of specific groups are among the offspring of certain kinds of philosophical rationality. Like Hannah Arendt, he questions the ethical validity of philosophy's detachment from the bodily sphere of social life. This critical perspective differentiates the post–Second World War era from that which followed the First World

War. As Anson Rabinbach has acutely observed, "World War I gave rise to reflections on death and transfiguration, World War II to reflections on evil, or on how the logic of modernity since the Enlightenment, with its legacy of progress, secularism, and rationalism, could not be exculpated from events that seemed to violate its ideals."[14] Rabinbach's account, however, is not entirely fair to the Enlightenment, for at least some critical reflections on the violence within a detached type of philosophical reason were already part and parcel of the emerging Enlightenment in the latter part of the eighteenth century.

This more reflective stance found its voice in some of the emerging discourse in anthropology, which clearly paid attention to the social consequences of a philosophical way of reasoning that harbored hostility toward human diversity. Disagreements about human diversity that can be found in the philosophies of Kant and Johann Gottfried Herder are at the heart of Steiner's literary and anthropological–historical critique of philosophy's dehumanizing elements. Following Rousseau, Kant differentiated between natural and rational societies. The distinguishing feature of the latter is the sacrifice of individual preferences for the greater good of the community. As Wolfgang Pross has recently shown, this dualistic image of the human goes hand in hand with Kant's reception of Christoph Meiner's polygenetic division of humanity into two races: "The dichotomy between *the state of nature* and *the state of culture*," Pross cogently observes, "resolves into the dichotomy between two types of humans, which are in their physical disposition completely different."[15] The rational type embarks upon the process of civilization and thus establishes culture, while, by contrast, the opposed type remains passively, and thus immutably, imprisoned in the realm of nature. Arguing against this view, Herder maintained that every human type— "savage" or "civilized"—has been born with reason: "Ein'und dieselbe Gattung ist das Menschengeschlecht auf der Erde" (The human race is one and the same species throughout the earth).[16]

In his review of the second part of Herder's *Ideen*, Kant harshly criticized this conflation and its concomitant abolition of the universal division of humanity into natural and rational. One result was that Kant, in effect, denied human rights to the inhabitants of Tahiti, asking of Herder:

Meint der Herr Verfasser wohl: dass, wenn die glücklichen Einwohner von Otaheite, niemals von gesitteten Nationen besucht, in ihrer ruhigen Indolenz auch Tausende von Jahrhunderten durch zu leben bestimmt wären, am eine befriedigende Antwort auf die Frage geben könnte, warum sie denn gar existieren, und ob es nicht eben so gut gewesen ware, dass diese Insel mit glücklichen Schafen und Rindern, als mit im blossen Genusse glücklichen Menschen besetzt gewesen wäre.

[Does the author mean that if it were the case that the happy inhabitants of Otaheite, having never been visited by civilized nations, would be destined to live in their quiet indolence for another thousand of centuries, one could then give a satisfactory answer to the question why they exist and whether it would not be as well that these islands were occupied with happy sheep and cattle rather than with humans who are happy with sheer consumption/pleasure (*Genuss*)?][17]

On this view, *Genuss*, that is to say the sheer pleasure of consumption, makes the human mutate to the bodily level of the animal. As a consequence, Kant argues that Tahiti might as well be "cleansed," its inhabitants replaced by sheep and cattle. The latter would be as happy as the former but more useful for the subsistence of human society.

Sympathetic to Herder's justification of empirical pleasure, which Kant clearly demoted as animalistic, Steiner points out that so-called primitive ways of life do not blindly obey bodily impulses. Rather those ways of life constitute pleasurable modes of adapting to specific environments. Steiner refers to his outlook as "unsystematic empiricism," which he contrasts with philosophy that stresses "system and theory." Nevertheless, his approach differs from Herder's in that Steiner does not focus his analysis so much on providing a rationale for primitive societies' adapting to the demands of natural necessities. Instead, Steiner's concern clearly centers on power and danger. The difference in perspective reflects his situation as a Jewish refugee from Nazi-occupied Europe. Thus he compares "the so-called adaptation to nature with its control."

What distinguished the primitive from the civilized has to do with divergent attitudes toward power/danger. Indeed, Steiner first developed what has become known as the sociology of danger, which defines power as that element by which one can threaten to endanger the life of another.[18] Far from romanticizing "the natural way of life," Steiner locates power/danger within nature. Whereas primitive societies avoid contact with nature's power/danger—with natural demons, for example—by establishing a variety of taboo mechanisms, the progress of civilization immensely expands the boundaries of the dangerous and the powerful: "Yes, indeed, human society has expanded," says Steiner. "It has expanded the demonic sphere."[19] This expansion both reflects and enables the empowerment of certain segments of humanity while, more significantly, equating other communities with the demonic. These demoted groups thus replace the uncanny demons, which primitive society had detected strictly in the taboo zones located outside of the human community. Steiner specifically analyzes Europe's Christian society during the Middle Ages because that process of civilization strikingly coincided with the replacement of natural demons by members of particular non-European/Christian groups, primarily Jews:

It would be helpful to treat Christian-European society in the Middle Ages as a society, which constantly felt itself threatened by the non-Christian peoples surrounding it. In so doing they equated the heathendom with the demonic sphere to such an extent that the heroic deeds performed by the crusades were considered a legitimate, unbroken continuation of those mythical deeds which had to be performed in heathen or semi-heathen days against dragons and demons.[20]

With the progress of civilization, the "primitive" contrast between human beings and nature's demons dissolves. Instead, a divide opens between a philosophic—rational—humanity and those demoted, quasi-primitive groups that represent merely natural life. The latter are the new demons of the rational age. Significantly, they are by and large those who do not hold positions of power. For Hannah Arendt, as for Steiner, the persecution of the powerless by the powerful arises from a rationalist definition of the human: "What makes men obey or tolerate real power and, on the other hand, hate people who have wealth without power, is the rational instinct that power has a certain function and is of some general use."[21]

Kant's demotion of the Tahitians has serious ramifications for philosophy's implication in genocidal violence. Philosophy's exclusionary tendencies helped to pave the way for the Nazis to depict the Jews as a lethal threat that had to be eliminated. Other genocides, before or after the Holocaust, have reflected similar tendencies. Steiner characterized the "trapping" of "human masses in close-knit nets," past which " 'healthy' life floods by," as an utterly new form of "torment."[22] With the progress of civilization, the violence against those who are perceived as less than fully human or inferior to other superior groups had grown to such an extent that Steiner was compelled to embark on an analysis of the history of reason. To a large extent, it turns out that this history turns out to be a history of the progression of evil. Steiner finds philosophy guilty of complicity in genocide. His analysis leaves philosophy and philosophers to ask: How can philosophy be reformed and rehabilitated? Steiner suggests that the response to that question begins with philosophy's self-examination.

Notes

1. Imre Kertész, *Kaddish for a Child Not Born*, trans. Christopher C. Wilson and Katharina M. Wilson (Evanston, IL: Northwestern University Press, 1997), p. 28.
2. Ibid., p. 28.
3. Berel Lang, *The Anatomy of Philosophical Style: Literary Philosophy and the Philosophy of Literature* (Oxford: Blackwell, 1990), p. 22.
4. See, for example, John H. Zammito, *Kant, Herder and the Birth of Anthropology* (Chicago, IL: University of Chicago Press, 2002), p. 313.
5. In this context Edith Wyschogrod has defined life as the unpredictable: "The everyday structures of our lives are promissory notes: their coming due constitutes the horizon of our 'blissfully earthly' expectations." Edith Wyschogrod, *Spirit in Ashes: Hegel, Heidegger, and Man-Made Mass Death* (New Haven, CT: Yale University Press, 1985), p. 11.

6. For a detailed examination of the importance of Franz Baermann Steiner's work as poet and cultural critic see, Michael Mack, *Anthropology as Memory: Elias Canetti's and Franz Baermann Steiner's Responses to the Shoah* (Tübingen: Niemeyer, 2001).
7. Franz Baermann Steiner, "Slavery," in Jeremy Adler and Richard Fardon, eds, *Franz Baermann Steiner: Selected Writings*, Vol. II, *Orientpolitik, Value, and Civilization* (New York: Berghahn Books, 1999), pp. 155–9, and especially p. 158.
8. For a detailed discussion of this point, see Mack, *Anthropology as Memory*, pp. 106–18.
9. Like Steiner, Arendt focuses her analysis not on violence as such but on the conceptualization that prefigures genocidal murder.

> The trouble with totalitarian regimes, is not that they play power politics in an especially ruthless way, but that behind their politics is hidden an entirely new and unprecedented concept of power, just as behind their *Realpolitik* lies an entirely new and unprecedented concept of reality. Supreme disregard for immediate consequences rather than ruthlessness; rootlessness and neglect of national interests rather than nationalism; contempt for utilitarian motives rather than unconsidered pursuit of self-interest; "idealism," i.e., their unwavering faith in an ideological fictitious world, rather than lust for power—these have all introduced into international politics a new and more disturbing factor than mere aggressiveness would have been able to do.

> Hannah Arendt, *The Origins of Totalitarianism* (New York: Harcourt, Brace and Company, 1951), pp. 396–7.

10. Franz Baermann Steiner, "Elephant Capture," trans. Michael Hamburger, in *Modern Poetry in Translation* 2 (special issue on Franz Baermann Steiner with translations and an introduction by Michael Hamburger) (Autumn 1992), p. 31.
11. For a detailed discussion of smell, in particular, and the body, in general, as the target of attack in various antisemitic constructions, see Sander L. Gilman, *The Jew's Body* (New York: Routledge), 1991.
12. Steiner, "Elephant Capture," p. 31.
13. Franz Baermann Steiner, "On the Process of Civilization," trans. by Jeremy Adler and Michael Mack, in Adler and Fardon, eds, *Franz Baermann Steiner*, pp. 123–8, and especially p. 123.
14. Anson Rabinbach, *In the Shadow of Catastrophe: German Intellectuals between Apocalypse and Enlightenment* (Berkeley, CA: University of California Press, 2000), p. 9.
15. Wolfgang Pross, "Anmerkungen zu Seite 389," in Wolfgang Pross, ed., *Johann Gottfried Herder: Band III/2.Ideen zur Philosophie der Geschichte der Menschheit. Kommentar* (Darmstadt: Wissenschaftliche Buchgesellschaft, 2002), p. 594.
16. Pross, ed., *Johann Gottfried Herder*, p. 229.
17. Immanuel Kant, "Rezension zu Johann Gottfried Herders Ideen," in Wilhelm Weischedel, ed., *Schriften zur Anthropologie, Geschichtsphilosophie, Politik und Pädagogik* (Frankfurt a. M.: Suhrkamp, 1964), pp. 781–806, and especially p. 805.
18. See Mary Douglas, ed., *Rules and Meanings: The Anthropology of Everyday Knowledge* (Harmondsworth: Penguin, 1977), p. 113, and Talal Asad, *Genealogies of Religion: Discipline and Reason of Power in Christianity and Islam* (Baltimore, MD: Johns Hopkins University Press, 1993), p. 146.
19. Steiner, "On the Process of Civilization," p. 127.
20. Ibid., p. 126.
21. Arendt, *The Origins of Totalitarianism*, p. 5.
22. Steiner, "On the Process of Civilization," p. 127.

10

Epistemic Conditions for Genocide

Emmanuel C. Eze

This chapter assumes that there is a widely shared definition of genocide.[1] What I explore are the deepest origins of that devastating crime. The claims I make about the relationships between philosophy and genocide—including the way in which I construe the idea of the *philosophical*—are likely to be more controversial than the usual definition of genocide, but I hope they will be persuasive nonetheless.

At the outset, I suggest that most, if not all, of my readers will accept Norman Cohn's well-researched argument that perpetrators of genocide— "however narrow, materialistic or downright criminal their own motives may be"—could not accomplish their genocidal programs "without an ideology behind them."[2] Cohn's argument rests on the premise that, unlike an individual's committing a crime without the assistance of others, the organized, dedicated, and political nature of genocidal acts requires collective justification. Genocide thus necessitates that its perpetrators explain the reasoning behind their programmatic intent to destroy, completely or in part, a targeted population.

Furthermore, I suggest that most, if not all, of my readers will also agree that the public justifications for genocide advanced by its architects need not correctly describe the external causes or truthfully explain the alleged provocations that the perpetrators identify as requiring them to act. Perpetrators, moreover, are known to deny flatly that genocide has taken place, let alone that they intended it. By most scholarly accounts, however, a genocidal ideology is unlikely to advance its aims unless it enables the perpetrators and their sympathizers to *believe* that the ideology's justifications for genocidal acts, or their reasons for genocide denial, are true. From the perpetrator's point of view, reasons produced to explain or deny genocide thus function as "ideological warrants" that legitimate genocidal behavior. Many scholars believe that without such warrants, perpetrators would have no choice but to see themselves for what they really are: dedicated thieves and murderers.[3]

Philosophy, ideology, and genocide

Arguably, the psychological and political functions of ideological warrants for genocide are well understood. Nevertheless, insight about the genocidal mindset may be deepened if we distinguish between *ideology* and *philosophy*. The differences between the two can be identified in various ways, but a common approach draws on the idea that whereas philosophy is purely rational and scientific—it involves, for example, objective and open-ended inquiry—ideology is not because it already "knows" what is true and strives only to legitimate or defend its fixed beliefs. Thus, to raise questions about philosophy's role in promoting genocide (by means of complicit actions or explicit justifications) or about philosophy's opposition to genocide (via the production of moral and ethical counterarguments) is a matter more complex than the simple question of whether or not genocide requires ideological pretexts.

Owing to philosophy's self-presentation as scientific and beholden to reason and rational inquiry alone, it is not easy to explain how philosophy's traditional functions could be related—as subtexts or pretexts—for genocidal initiatives. Indeed, if philosophy is scientific and beholden to reason and rational inquiry alone, it becomes nearly impossible to imagine that anyone could raise questions about "philosophy and genocide" or about "philosophy and human rights"—the key topics of this book—except in ways that would be praiseworthy or that would also apply, for instance, to other sciences, such as physics, chemistry, biology, sociology, or anthropology. The situation, however, is much more complicated. Although philosophy and philosophers have not faced the facts as seriously and honestly as they need to do, the very status of philosophy as a science and, more importantly, philosophy's tendency to claim a purity of existence in reason above ordinary or "applied" sciences, properly creates suspicions about philosophy's relations to ideology and to genocide as well.

It is the allegedly scientific nature of philosophy that makes especially important any questions about philosophy's relations to genocide and also to defenses of human rights. Such questions arise because the very idea of "science" is subject to abuse and also because the hope runs strong that domains of science exist that are free from corruption. Thus, to argue that philosophy is a science in the sense of being based on free inquiry and open pursuit of truth, whereas ideology is "truth" tailored to particular motives regardless of the objective rightness or wrongness of those motives and their consequences, is to recognize the need to distinguish philosophy from ideology. Our capacity to criticize ideology, it seems to me, depends on the recognition that there are, or at least can be, spaces where reason is exercised freely, critically, and self-critically. I reserve the terms *philosophy* and *philosophical* for those systematically reflective activities of thought that are carried out from such critical spaces of reason.

An easy, comfortable, and comforting analysis would argue that, yes, we sometimes misuse philosophy, or do not remain faithful to its discipline, a point that could be made about any use of scientific method or body of established knowledge. This position would find nothing problematic about philosophy itself. A much more difficult, uncomfortable, and discomforting analysis would argue—as Max Horkheimer and Theodor Adorno did in their *Dialectic of Enlightenment*—that there *is* something problematic about philosophy itself, at least in its modern, scientific development.[4] The chief problem stems from seeds that were planted in ancient Greek rationalism but which flowered only in modern science and philosophy. The procedures emphasized in those outlooks stressed forms of rationality that sought comprehension and control of nature, human subjectivity, and even of reason itself. Adorno and Horkheimer were not alone in attacking these tendencies in modernity. Friedrich Nietzsche's criticism of philosophy's "will to truth" anticipated some of what they had to say. Martin Heidegger's identifications with Nazism continue to cast long shadows over him and philosophy as well, but he did understand that much previous philosophy had helped to create, however inadvertently, a mass humanity no longer capable of ontological depth or consciousness of the self as a "shelter," "house," or "shepherd" of Being. Michel Foucault's pioneering archeological and genealogical expositions of the historical structures of reason also showed how modern philosophy is much less objective and purely scientific than it has imagined itself to be. Modern philosophy, he argued, is deeply embedded in networks of historical and bio-political power.[5]

Defenders of modern—often specifically Enlightenment—models of rationality often point out that such criticisms of philosophy and reason are "totalistic." These defenders may concede that a one-sided conception of scientific reason—as instrumental and technological—may have led to philosophical positivism and scientism, to colonization of the life-world by problematic systems of technology, or to a commercial rationality intent on economic exploitation of human persons as mere economic resources or as abstract objects of nature. But they propose a different critique of modernity and its forms of reason—a critique that is differentiated rather than totalistic. Thus, we find Jürgen Habermas celebrating modernity for both its destructive and constructive aspects.[6] Modernity may have destroyed traditional mythical, religious, and tribal world views and the forms of life dependent on them, but modernity also provides alternatives to the institutions of myth, religion, and tribe in the forms of constitutional democratic political institutions; civil societies, both local and global; and greater self-expression for individuals in the spheres of morality and art that are newly independent of religious and political control.

It would be unwise to side completely with either side in this debate, because the division of opinion appears to inscribe itself entirely within the history of postmodern Western thought.[7] Our choices and decisions need to be framed beyond these intra-European debates about reason and the sciences. Other perspectives, such as those derived from postcolonial criticism, also yield important insights. These further insights are crucial not only for understanding the material contents of the formal issues at stake in the intra-European debates (e.g. the ways in which both the rise of capitalism and the growth of civil societies in Europe depended on imperialism and colonialism); they are also necessary for a fuller understanding of the possible relationships of modern sciences and the humanities to genocidal practices. Thus, in addition to the intellectual difference a postcolonial perspective might make, the practical account that comes from postcolonial outlooks might also shed light on the very idea of genocide. Not all colonial crimes, for instance, rose to the level of genocide. A postcolonial analysis can help us to avoid oversimplified analyses of the relationships among philosophy, ideology, genocide, and human rights.

If we are to find the right grounds for raising questions about the relationships of philosophy, ideology, genocide, and human rights, we need to identify the specifically philosophical issues. For example, if we accept that philosophy stands as a science in relation to truth and that ideology stands as pseudo-science in relation to untruth, the purpose of our questions about philosophy and genocide becomes clearer. We would ask: presupposing, but going beyond, the psychological studies of the genocidal mind, what are the objective ideas, as well as the historico-epistemological structures within which those ideas arise, that may constitute "genocidal knowledge"? That question would focus our search on what I shall call the *epistemology of genocide*.

As I use the concept, the epistemology of genocide does not refer primarily to an existing body of knowledge but to a program of research. One of its governing questions is as follows: Are there systems of thought that could be said to constitute either necessary or sufficient conditions for genocidal acts? No sooner is that question raised, however, than two others also loom large. First, how should one understand the relationships between thought and action? Second, how can one best clarify key concepts—such as those of psychological or historical "causality"—that are implicit in the idea of necessity or sufficiency of condition? Whereas the first problem is cognitive-psychological, the second is historico-epistemological. If the first studies structures of subjectivity, the second inquires about the historical structures under which subjective and inter-subjective conceptions of truths about self and action are possible. While the first focuses on internal conditions of cognition (or "miscognition") of truth in relation to an act, the second studies the history and social or political patterns of uses (and abuses) of ideas of truth.

In much of the analysis of genocide, the first perspective predominates. The psychological dispositions to genocide (for instance, the role of fear: "If we do not do this, it will be done to us";[8] or pride: to preserve "purity of the race" or "purity of the nation," which necessarily requires stereotypical construction of genocide's target-population as "outsiders"[9]) are well known and documented. Studies of the cognitive requirements for genocidal thought are also abundant; for example, the target-population must be perceived as less than human—members of the group are "dogs" or "vermin."[10] Finally, the moral and ethical issues involved in these psychological and cognitive considerations of conditions of genocide have also received attention.[11] What has been lacking, however, is a credible account—that is, a sound theory—of the historically constructed character of the epistemological conditions of genocide, particularly insofar as some necessary ideas may be said to grow out of these conditions. What we would contribute through rigorously exploiting the initial distinction suggested between ideology and philosophy is thus a historically grounded epistemic critique of genocide.[12]

Ideas have power

Are there epistemic conditions that are predisposed to unleash genocidal crimes? If ideas have power, the answer to that question should be *yes*. If power (e.g. access to material resources or "authority" to execute a genocidal program) is a necessary requirement for genocidal acts, then, to the extent that ideas may share in or advance this conception of power, they could be instruments of genocidal acts.

Immediately, however, another question follows: what exactly is an idea? We easily, though indirectly, grasp the answer to this question by noting the main epistemic forms or qualities that anything identifiable as an idea will possess. Furthermore, since the goal is a direct demonstration that ideas have power, it will be helpful if, in the course of establishing the main epistemic forms or qualities that an idea will possess, we show the modes of power that ideas can reasonably be said to display. If these tasks can be accomplished, we can see more clearly how an idea may or may not be causally linked, directly or indirectly, with actual genocidal acts. To advance this inquiry further, consider three kinds of ideas.

Instrumental ideas

I call an idea instrumental when the knowledge we claim about an object in relation to the idea is causal-naturally derived. We study and come to know causal relations in nature and treasure ideas and concepts associated with them because we have needs and uses for such knowledge, which allows us to manipulate natural relations in such a way that either nature bends to our will or we adjust our expectations to conform to causal laws. Emerging from this kind of knowledge, the ideas we develop and employ in the form of concepts or theories are instrumental precisely because they are treasured largely for service in realization of our purposes. When, for example, we conserve ideas in the concepts of "space," "gravity," "length," or "weight," we believe that these concepts are not only derived experimentally as generalities but also as laws (i.e. they are valid anywhere and at any time natural objects act as expected). On account of such generality and universality, we claim that the ideas embody or reflect laws of the natural world.

Historically, the power of the natural sciences largely depends upon this understanding of general ideas as forms of natural law. Scientific ideas that represent, for example, the causal relations among material elements of nature could easily be constituted into a body of knowledge on the basis of which humans can successfully intervene—instrumentally, for our profit— in the material conditions of the world. The phrase "science and technology" communicates *par excellence* our view of science as an exploitable body of ideas for production of intended and predictable results.

Justificatory ideas

Ideas are justificatory when their form includes the fact that they are derived from social, rather than, natural law. In the distinction between the natural and the social, we should understand the source of authority that underwrites the "law" in question. In natural law, we appeal to nature; in social law, we appeal to acts of human judgment. The natural is not distinct from the social; rather, the difference between the natural and the social resides in the nature of the "reason" that governs the different appeals to law. The natural sciences regard nature as largely dictating what constitutes "rationality" or "causality," but in the human sciences social and cultural interests (a legislative resolution, for example, or a court order) are part of the constituting rationality. In the world of technological effectiveness, for example, natural "law" predetermines the ideas, at least the valid ones. In the case of justificatory ideas, their authority derives from moral or legal structures that form the context in which they work. While the natural sciences appeal to the natural world for their grounding, justificatory ideas typically refer to the human world where social "law" must be seen to be compatible with the free agency of the intellect and will.

Whether moral or social law is ultimately grounded in natural law and, if so, how this grounding should be (naturally) explained or (socially) interpreted are crucial questions that are beyond the scope of this chapter.[13] Awareness of their import and the consequences of possible answers to them, however, need to be kept in mind to appreciate our main arguments about the possible relations between (1) philosophy as science and (2a) genocide as morally unacceptable and legally criminal behavior or (2b) human rights as morally worthy and legally defensible. For the task before us, however, it is important to distinguish between the idea of "law" as grounded in nature and the idea of "law" as socially grounded. Whereas we regard the former as related primarily (though not exclusively) to instrumental interests, the latter functions largely for purposes of justification— to support our claims, for example, that we are "in the right" morally or politically.

We also noted that if the grounds of natural law primarily require causal explanation, the grounds of social law usually call for hermeneutical interpretation. In explanation, we focus on presenting or re-presenting those relations that we claim to have discovered in nature; in interpretation, we appeal to values, customary laws, traditions, and other social realities in attempts to produce or solidify reasons that will support the norms that authorize or prohibit action. If the goal of explanation is to produce a reflective representation of non-human, objective relations in nature, the goal of interpretation is to formulate ideas that justify the actions of human agents. While the instrumental character of natural ideas requires their rationality to be measured in terms of material (technological) effectiveness, the rationality or reasonableness of an interpretation depends on inter-subjective evaluation: Does the justification persuade? Are rational and free individuals who share the value-orientation disposed to agree about the persuasive—and coercive—power of the law?[14]

While the effectiveness of instrumental ideas depends on their congruence with the natural order, the effectiveness of justificatory ideas depends on their congruence with social reality. Instead of thinking of justification in opposition to inflexible laws of nature, however, it should be seen, rather, as "practical." Justificatory ideas are deployed to explain events that human beings, largely through their choices, cause to happen. The assumption on which the power of these ideas rests is that human actions are neither determined nor predictable in ways that would be applicable to natural objects. Human actions are expressions of the will. In short, moral freedom is absolutely necessary if we are to think of ways in which philosophical ideas—products of human thought and will—may epistemically dispose a person or group toward or against genocidal acts.

Historical ideas

I call ideas historical when their sources and forms of expression cannot be singularly traced to one of the forms already discussed. Instead, historical ideas emerge from a variety of sources, and analysis of those combinatory relations is what yields the epistemic insights that such ideas offer. Historical ideas derive from already-constituted ideas—that is, from relations among already existing simple ideas or bodies of ideas. Historical ideas may also be called "historical insights," which occur when we reconstitute known theories, or even scientific traditions, in a fashion that produces new understanding about what we knew in the past and what we could not have known from the previous state of knowledge alone. But, it may be asked, can new insight really be obtained merely by examining individual pieces or sets of information, each of which—one might think—had been exhaustively studied and understood before? The answer is *yes*, for this new insight emerges from, even constitutes, *learning*—the use of formal intelligence to "connect the dots." Often, the proverbial "dots" do not, in and of themselves, contain complete information. Further study reveals patterns of interaction among them. Comparative perspectives produce insights that would otherwise elude one who saw only the constituent parts separately.[15]

It is important to note another aspect of historical ideas and the insights they provide. Old ideas appear in new light not only in combination with each other but also when gaps between the past and the present are recognized. Over time we may come to see that (what we knew about) x is related to (what we now know as) y. We notice now, for example, that Arabic numerals relate to Roman numerals in such and such a way. Or, from my current standpoint, I can see how the results might have varied when I acted toward Peter as I did five years ago, or when I acted toward Paul as I did last year. Such insight is historical because it could not occur except in the light of a history of previous, largely independent actions. To arrive at these historical insights, we weave together objects, characters, and ideas to produce historical knowledge in the form of (a) narrative.[16]

What does this analysis suggest as far as the epistemology of genocide is concerned? First, no single type or pair of idea types alone is sufficient to motivate genocidal initiatives. That outcome arises because historical ideas are necessary for genocide to occur. Exclude them, and there can be no rationale that eventuates in the distinction between a targeted population and those who are potential perpetrators. Distinctions between *us* and *them* are necessary for genocide to happen. They are rooted in historical considerations. On the other hand, historical ideas cannot be understood for what they are unless instrumental and justificatory ideas are taken into account, for the latter are constitutive of historical ideas, although neither singly nor together are they identical with historical ideas. Thus, the three types of ideas are needed and necessary for genocide to be possible. One hastens to add, however, that even in combination these ideas are not sufficient to produce genocide. They have to be packaged ideologically in terms of *us* and *them* to ramp up their potential for genocide. In addition, the determination of the human will has to be in the mix, along with social and political structures that can implement that determination. When all of those pieces are in place, genocide may well be on its way.

Epistemic conditions of genocide: A triumph of *Dóxa* over *Logos*?

Echoing some of Hannah Arendt's and Aimé Césaire's arguments in *The Origins of Totalitarianism* and *Discourse on Colonialism*, respectively, the Ugandan political scientist Mahmood Mamdani has argued that "the idea that 'imperialism had served civilization by clearing inferior races off the earth' found widespread expression in nineteenth-century European thought, from natural sciences and philosophy to anthropology and politics."[17] Along with political theorists, philosophers have not been inattentive, at least not completely, to this essentially modern problem. From the radical critiques of the Enlightenment by Adorno and Horkheimer to Foucault's "archeology," Jacques Derrida's deconstructive thought, and postcolonial theory, the notion of "epistemic violence" has gained intellectual currency in recent social, literary, and philosophical criticism. As Martin Jay pointed out in his study of the totalitarian character of Soviet ideology and the National Socialists' racism, "while it may be questionable to saddle Marx with responsibility for the Gulag archipelago or to blame Nietzsche for Auschwitz, it is nevertheless true that their writings could be misread as justifications for these horrors in a way that ... John Stuart Mill or Alexis de Tocqueville could not."[18] Discussing Nietzsche, Derrida more delicately remarked that although Nietzsche's "utterances are not the same as the Nazi ideologists' and not only because the latter grossly caricature the former to the point of apishness," one still should ask "how and why what is so naively called a falsification was possible."[19]

Hume, empiricist naturalism, transatlantic African slavery, and anti-black racism; Marxism and the Gulag; Nietzsche, Nazism, and Auschwitz; civilization and genocide: these "ands," these conjunctions, require philosophers to give an account of philosophy and to hold philosophy accountable. Basically, I believe, there are two stark choices: Either *logos* (rationality) is disposed to terror or *dóxa* (belief and opinion) is disposed to triumph over *logos*.

In their varied ways, Joseph Conrad, Jean-Paul Sartre, Franz Fanon, Chinua Achebe, and Albert Memmi have shown that it is not only when a "foreign" people are targeted to be forcefully divested of their autonomy and sovereignty that the members of the group so identified must be theorized as less than human. What we are not sure about—and need to investigate further—is how such epistemological violence is a necessary condition for genocide. After all, one could argue—as the individual who commits a horrible crime in a heat of passion is likely to do—that he or she was suffering from momentary insanity. Could we not describe genocides as mere acts of communal passion, conceived and executed in a fit of collective insanity, and thus absolve reason, including any form of philosophical rationality, from responsibility for genocidal crimes? Certainly, if we cannot equate insanity with reason, why should one saddle reason in general—even dialectically, as Horkheimer and Adorno did—or philosophy in particular, with an act of provable insanity?

Convenient though such an analysis might be for philosophy, it has to be resisted, for genocides are not haphazard, idiosyncratic expressions of passion. Typically they have historical antecedents and develop along similar lines: conception and incubation, planning and organization, and execution, usually in the form of mass murder. Whereas an individual's intellectual or moral faculty may fall apart under the stress of overpowering passion, it is difficult to imagine an analogous convulsion and collapse of a culture and its social order. After all, the very ideas of culture and its moral values or of society's law and order mark that point of no return in which a human community, as a culture or civilization, irrevocably transcends the "natural" state of existence. That point is both marked and embodied in functioning institutions of morality (e.g. family, schools, and religion) and of law and order (the state). Historical evidence suggests that genocides have occurred not simply because of the collapse of institutions of morality, such as family, educational, and religious structures, or because of the failure of systems of law and order. Rather, genocides emerge where institutions of morality and law use their immense powers to co-opt and develop complex activities and ritual exercises—constructing concentration camps; transporting victims; experimenting on human beings; establishing national communications networks and broadcasting genocidal propaganda from them; importing and stockpiling machetes; and so on. These same institutions lend an air of authority to acts of genocide, allowing perpetrators to believe they are engaged in "normal" and "legal" activities, thus permitting them to clear their consciences and excuse their actions by believing they were merely following orders and doing their jobs.

Genocide should not be excused as collective irrationality or madness resulting from the breakdown of culture and law and order. There are neither scientifically established, causal relations nor historical correlations to warrant such excuses. Still, what of philosophy itself, which once claimed to be "queen of the sciences" and still likes to think of itself as the guardian of reason? What does it have to do with the offense of genocide? What might it contribute to the defense of human rights?

Earlier I distinguished between philosophy and ideology. Now we should also distinguish between scientific philosophy and "folk" philosophy. Philosophy is not merely "belief"—however principled or strongly held belief may be. The term *philosophy* should be reserved to refer to ideas that are justified—ideas that interconnect to form a defensible system or systems of beliefs. The primary vehicle of such belief-justification is argumentation—hence the significance of words. In philosophy, language is the expression of the persuasive power of reason. On account of the uses or abuses of language, and at least since the time of Socrates' encounters with the Sophists in Athens and the confrontation of the purist Mbari artist with the Janus-faced devotee of Agwushi among the ancient Igbos, we know that philosophy and rhetoric have had a very ambiguous and yet inseparable relationship. Rhetoric is indispensable for philosophy, even as it is assumed that, unlike the Sophist or Agwushike, the philosopher or Mbarike—the "lover of wisdom," the "artist of reason," the "seeker of knowledge"—intends to persuade his or her audience on the basis of reason alone, through the power of his or her ideas.

Given the unavoidable and often problematic relationship between philosophy and rhetoric, as illustrated by Socrates and the Sophist, Mbarike and Agwushike, I would suggest that a potentially fruitful avenue for this inquiry into philosophy's abuses of reason—especially those used for genocidal ends—would concentrate on the intersection of reason and the uses of language. The emphasis on language is crucial, for arguably neither reason nor philosophy can exist independently of language. Nevertheless, language may corrupt reason, or, we could say, reason and philosophy may corrupt themselves. One might think that such lines of thought require a metaphysics of language or even a theodicy of the natural (causal) or social (hermeneutical) reason and will, but such excursions are unnecessary.[20] It is sufficient to study the historical uses and abuses of reason in language.[21]

The power of ideas and crimes of genocide

Although genocidal acts have been widespread in the twentieth and twenty-first centuries, it is remarkable that relatively few persons have been indicted and tried explicitly for committing the crime of genocide. At the time of this writing, an international tribunal in The Hague has been prosecuting Slobodan Milosevic and others for genocide in the wake of the ethnic cleansing in the former Yugoslavia. Only in the late 1990s was the first genocide case prosecuted before an international court, which convened in Arusha, Tanzania, to deal with the 1994 Rwandan genocide. What is even more remarkable—and the point bears directly on the issues raised in this chapter— is the fact that so many of the trials and convictions that took place after the Rwandan genocide did not hold the criminals directly responsible for acts of genocide.

Three men, for example, were found guilty because they "had used a radio station and a newspaper published twice a month to mobilize Rwanda's Hutu majority against the Tutsi, who were massacred at churches, schools, hospitals and roadblocks." These people may not have killed anyone directly; instead, they were criminally responsible for inflaming hatred in a large population—"poison[ing] their minds," as the court said—against another, supposedly racial group. Without this use of ideas and language, it is scarcely conceivable that the Rwandan genocide would have taken place.[22]

Thus, it is noteworthy that the first victims of the genocidal mind-poisoning were the group intended to profit from it: the Hutus. Radio stations and newspapers were also used to disseminate deceptive and false information that led Tutsis, sometimes by name, to Hutu death traps. Again, those who spoke or wrote such words may not have murdered anyone directly, but the court in Arusha saw this use of language as a key part of the genocide. What we can conclude, therefore, is that the court held these men responsible for a massive distortion of language: that is, the use of words with intent to incite the mass killing of a racial group.[23]

If words, language, argumentation, and even logic can be genocidal weapons, how does philosophy wield or resist them? Could we characterize a philosopher's deployment of language as either "neutral," "offensive," or "defensive"? If so, how would this characterization work, in relation to whom or what? Furthermore, if the media in all its forms could be employed for genocidal ends, how do books, scientific journals, philosophical treatises, and the like, thought-up and produced by scientists, philosophers, and their publishers, imagine and portray both the people the books are meant to educate and the world of others (natural things and human societies or cultures) about which students and readers are being educated?

If a book or a philosophical work is not recognizably ideological upon an initial reading, it can be too easy to conclude that it must be "scientific," "true," and therefore "objective." It seems that when a scientific work meets all these criteria, we are more than ready to say "let the truth fall where it may" or "the truth will set us free." In technology, a related disposition often leads people to conclude "If we can, we should and must." But the question is whether truth tells us what truth is for, whether truth shows how not to deploy knowledge abusively against others and against ourselves. What would be the truth-status of a discipline that promises to teach us the universally moral uses of truth? Such questions are integral to the inquiry that characterizes what I am calling the epistemology of genocide. It is an inquiry far from finished. Indeed, it has barely begun and is much needed.

Philosophy has often been portrayed—frequently by philosophers—as a rational, disinterested, and neutral method for obtaining truth. These narratives advocate that the philosopher must put the epistemological will to truth first and foremost. Such advocacy, we should concede, has its place; it has reasonable justifications in its favor. Not to think of philosophy in this way is to take steps that blur the distinction between philosophy and ideology all over again.

On the other hand, disenchanted with the idea that philosophy should or even can be "pure" in these ways, philosophers have also argued that science and philosophy are inexorably, even ontologically, connected to human interests and cannot escape deep moral questions about the status of truth and the ways in which human understanding of it may do immense harm. This way of thinking about philosophy complicates matters because it raises questions about both truth and philosophy and, in doing so, tends to deny that any of the answers to those questions are self-evident. When philosophy accepts its own fallibility and vulnerability, it surrenders long-held assumptions about its authority as the guardian of reason and rationality. Yet the choices that remain are not restricted to saying only that "truth" is a term masking human interests and that philosophy is really ideology and nothing more, or that truth is a mental reflection of universally pure ideas—ideas that are, or should be, independent of human needs and interests. Philosophy as critical inquiry—particularly in terms of the epistemology of genocide that I have outlined here—remains available to explore and test the theories and practices that lead to genocide and also to the defense of human rights.

Notes

1. The 1948 United Nations Convention on the Prevention and Punishment of the Crime of Genocide defines *genocide* as: "any of the following acts committed with intent to destroy, in whole or in part, a national, ethnical, racial, or religious group, as such: (a) killing members of the group; (b) causing serious bodily or mental harm to members of the group; (c) deliberately inflicting on the group conditions of life calculated to bring about its physical destruction in whole or in part; (d) imposing measures intended to prevent births within the group; and (e) forcibly transferring children of the group to another group." For variations on this widely accepted definition, see, for example, Colin Tatz, *With Intent to Destroy: Reflecting on Genocide* (London: Verso, 2003).
2. Norman Cohn, *Warrant for Genocide: The Myth of the Jewish World-Conspiracy and the Protocols of the Elders of Zion* (New York: Harper and Row, 1967), p. 263.
3. Ibid., p. 264.
4. See Max Horkheimer and Theodor W. Adorno, *Dialectic of Enlightenment*, trans. John Cumming (New York: Continuum, 1999).
5. Michel Foucault, *Discipline and Punish: The Birth of the Prison*, trans. Alan Sheridan (New York: Vintage, 1995) and *The Order of Things: An Archaeology of the Human Sciences* (New York: Vintage, 1994).
6. Jürgen Habermas, *A Theory of Communicative Action*, 2 vols. trans. Thomas McCarthy (Boston, MA: Beacon Press, 1984–87).
7. Heidegger's theoretical and practical complicities with Nazism, or Foucault's or Habermas's pregnant silences on questions about racism or colonialism, highlight the ambiguity of framing questions about genocide and human rights as if they were problems entirely interior to the cultures of the Western worlds or exclusively topics for dialogue only within "mainstream" Western traditions of thought. Because the problems of genocide and human rights are universal, presenting themselves diversely in various cultures and in different modes, we can grasp the necessary causes or sufficient conditions of the phenomena only if we consider the historical and cultural components from broad perspectives.
8. See: Mahmood Mamdani, *Good Muslim, Bad Muslim: America, the Cold War, and the Roots of Terror* (New York: Pantheon, 2004), pp. 3–16.
9. See, for example, Florence Mazian, *Why Genocide? The Armenian and Jewish Experiences in Perspective* (Ames: Iowa State University Press, 1990), and Peter du Preez, *Genocide: The Psychology of Mass Murder* (New York: Boyars/Bowerdean, 1994).
10. See, for example, Alexander Laban Hinton, ed., *Annihilating Difference: The Anthropology of Genocide* (Berkeley, CA: University of California Press, 2002). For other studies of "rational" pretexts for genocide, see Karla Poewe, *The Namibian Herero: A History of Their Psychological Disintegration and Survival* (Lewiston, NY: Edwin Mellen, 1985) and Samuel Totten, William S. Parsons, and Israel W. Charney, eds, *Genocide in the Twentieth Century: Critical Essays and Eyewitness Accounts* (New York: Garland, 1995). In the case of the racially targeted Africans, David Hume, Immanuel Kant, and G. F. W. Hegel were explicit in theorizing the slave as a "dog" or "beast of burden."
11. See, for example, Eve Garrard and Geoffrey Scare, eds, *Moral Philosophy and the Holocaust* (Burlington, VT: Ashgate, 2003); John K. Roth, ed., *Ethics after the Holocaust: Perspectives, Critiques, and Responses* (St. Paul, MN: Paragon House, 1999), Ervin Staub, *The Roots of Evil* (Cambridge: Cambridge University Press,

1989), and Laurence M. Thomas, *Vessels of Evil: American Slavery and the Holocaust* (Philadelphia, PA: Temple University Press, 1993).

12. By *epistemic* or *epistemological* I shall mean the mental and historical *forms* in which we know things, including the *meta-forms* in which the production of justifications *that* we know a thing can be found.

13. Kant, of course, famously attempted to formulate and answer some of these questions. For insightful exploration of the problem in our time and with "postmodern" sensitivities, see, for example, John McDowell, *Mind and World* (Cambridge: Harvard University Press, 1996) as well as *Mind, Value, and Reality* (Cambridge: Harvard University Press, 1996). For alternative conceptions or direct critiques of McDowell, see, for example, Donald Davidson, "On the Very Idea of a Conceptual Scheme" [1974], in Davidson, *Truth and Interpretation* (New York: Oxford University Press, 2001), pp. 183–98, R. E. Nisbett, ed., *Rules of Reasoning* (London: L. Erlbaum, 1993), and Arnold Silverberg, "Psychological Laws," in *Erkenntnis* 58 (2003): 275–302.

14. As already indicated, our broader arguments about power and genocide do not require us to explore at this time the question of whether the law of the social is ultimately, somehow, grounded in the law of nature. For example, it would be interesting to explore whether there are naturally prescribed limits, and if so what those limits are, with regard to the capacity of the human mind to be persuaded. Is the effectiveness of persuasion determined by non-human, natural conditions— conditions of the brain and of the rest of the nervous system about which science could tell us? Is it possible that even the rotation of the earth or the movements of the moon or the stars influence the human capacity to make judgments? But we do not need to have answers to these larger questions in order to know that genocide is wrong or that the moral and legal defense of human rights is good.

15. If one objects to us that such "new" knowledge is not a *form* of knowledge, because it is obtained only from a whole new level of abstraction (the comparative sphere), we should answer: How do we know exactly where to draw the line between primary and secondary forms of abstraction? How do we know that the insight from one may be more "real" than the other? Is it possible that the higher the level of abstraction, the more reliable the theoretical, and perhaps also practical, intellectual grasp we have of the matters under study? Or, is it possible that we do, in the "comparative" historical insight, create an entirely new need to which the new knowledge then is a response? If this is the case, how do we assess the value of the needs, except from the perspective of the purposes of the inquirer? What if these purposes are diverse and differentiated and thus met by various levels of knowledge? In short, we need to recognize this comparative level of thinking as a legitimate domain that, even if it is not as empirically or locally rooted as the first two, nevertheless allows us to explore other needs we might have for knowledge, and how these other needs for knowledge are met. The criteria for scrutiny of the truth or untruth, the validity or invalidity, of such meta-forms of knowledge should be as rigorously testable as any other claims to truth or proper knowledge.

16. Bringing it all together, the relationships between and across our three forms of ideas are fairly obvious. For example, one could argue that all knowledge is temporal (time-bound) and therefore, in lesser or greater degrees, shares the historical character of the third form of ideas. The typical time-bound expression "If p, then q" could be used as a general index for rationality—an index that should cut across

scientific procedures or propositions without regard to the natural or social contexts of inquiry. This reconstructive mode of reasoning seems best suited for understanding, for example, relationships between quite distant and, on the surface, unconnected events. In historical research—say, about the relationships of similarities and differences that might exist between ancient Egyptian and ancient Igbo–Ukwu religions, or between ancient Greek and colonial American architectural practices—there can only be the historical perspective on the evidence.

17. Mamdani, *Good Muslim, Bad Muslim,* p. 6.
18. Martin Jay, *Fin-de-Siècle Socialism and Other Essays* (New York: Routledge, 1988), p. 33.
19. Jacques Derrida, "Otobiographies: The Teaching of Nietzsche and the Politics of the Proper Name," in Christie V. McDonald, ed., *The Ear of the Other: Otobiography, Transference, Translation,* trans. Peggy Kamuf and Avital Ronell (New York: Schocken, 1985), pp. 30, 24. For an insightful discussion of Nietzsche and Nazism, see Jacob Golomb and Robert S. Wistrich, *Nietzsche, Godfather of Fascism? On the Uses and Abuses of a Philosophy* (Princeton, NJ: Princeton University Press, 2002).
20. Or so I have argued in "Philosophy, Science, and the Anthropological Principle of Reason," in Emmanuel Eze, *Word and World: Reason, Language and History* (forthcoming).
21. Before a United States congressional committee, and in justification of his request for a budget to militarize space, Secretary of Defense Donald Rumsfeld told the committee that "humans have used against themselves land, air, and water," and he did not believe that "space would be an exception." We should add that among the earliest weapons humans have used against themselves are *words.* The expressive and assertive power of language, and the rhetorical manipulations of that power, are vast.
22. The court's findings, which include the quotations in this paragraph, are available at: http://www.ictr.org/ENGLISH/cases/Barayagwiza/judgement/Summary%20of%20judgment-Media.pdf.
23. Specifically, the court was told that in less than a hundred days in 1994, "about 7 out of 10 of Rwanda's Tutsis were wiped out with a brutal efficiency." See the website noted earlier for more detail.

11
Genocide and the Totalizing Philosopher: A Levinasian Analysis

Leonard Grob

In the face of the Socratic charge to examine the nature of all that is, the failure of philosophers to pay little more than passing attention to genocide should give us pause. Although a number of contemporary thinkers have begun to attend to that evil, and although a few, such as Hannah Arendt and Theodor Adorno, had done so much earlier than most, philosophers have usually gone about their business as if the genocidal events that bloodied the twentieth century, and still loom large in the twenty-first, simply had not occurred.[1] How are we to account for this glaring omission in philosophy's history?

Inspired by the work of the contemporary French Jewish philosopher, Emmanuel Levinas (1906–95), this chapter speaks to the silence of philosophers in an age of genocide. Surprise at the silence of philosophers in the face of genocide pales, however, in comparison with yet another realization: Contemporary philosophers have not merely avoided a subject matter that they should have addressed; in addition, the tradition of philosophizing in the West may well have served *to foster a mode of thinking that gives subtle encouragement to genocide.* What arguments might be proffered to substantiate this claim?

With Levinas, I contend that the proper response to this query is rooted in the realization that "Western philosophy has most often been an ontology."[2] If we look to the grand systems of Western philosophy from Aristotle to Hegel and beyond, we see that within this tradition *to know* is *to "comprehend"*—literally, to "take together"—all that exists within the bounds of a conceptual structure, a structure that reflects the ideal of the adequacy of the knower to that which is known. Utilizing the mediating force of the concept, the grand ontological scheme poses as its ideal the reduction of the otherness of the other to the realm of what Levinas calls "the same": the realm subject to the all-embracing vision of a sovereign ego. In its endeavor to unify the multiplicity of beings within the reach of this subject, philosophy-as-ontology attempts to include within the realm of reflection the egoist grasp of things that characterizes our pre-reflective appropriation of the world. That which appears to be independent of me is to be subsumed under such mediating categories as, for example, substance or cause and effect. Even twentieth-century phenomenological thought—an allegedly "radical reflection"—merely continues what Levinas terms the "imperialist" thrust deeply embedded within traditional Western philosophy. The endeavor, as Edmund Husserl would have it, to "return to the things themselves" preserves the traditional equation of philosophy with the comprehension of being. Indeed, for the phenomenologist, to disclose the world is to actualize its sense: Being is equated with being-meant. Throughout the course of the history of Western philosophy, from Plato's immortal soul and Aristotle's *Nous* to the Sartrean "for-itself," the solitary subject, according to Levinas, is understood to be sufficient unto itself.

In this ontological tradition, to realize oneself is to approach all beings as instances of concepts that derive their meaning from me and thus, ultimately, to achieve that autonomy of being in which the "I" is limited by nothing other than itself. Although I will inevitably fail to realize the goal of a full appropriation of my world—Western philosophers have most certainly been aware of the gap that exists between the ideal and the real—all that exists remains *in principle* subject to my appropriative powers: "In the last analysis," Levinas claims, "*everything* is at my disposal, even the stars if I but reckon them. ...."[3] If I fall short—as indeed I must—of realizing the totalizing aim of the philosophical enterprise, the aim itself remains impervious to radical critique. Although the ego may be humbled by the magnitude of the task before it, its humility is a humility that is not humble enough. The enterprise of calling into question one's ability to know is engendered solely by the realization on the part of the subject that he or she has failed to achieve the goal of self-sufficiency, a goal that itself remains unexamined.

This critique is not to say that the totalizing tradition of thought in the West has been bereft of what Levinas terms "prefigurings" or adumbrations of that which transcends, in principle as well as in fact, the appropriative grasp of the ego. Allusions to what is unknown—and, indeed, unknowable— are most certainly to be found within that tradition. The Platonic notion of "the good beyond being" and the Cartesian idea of "thinking infinity" herald the vision of an otherness that can never be incorporated into the sphere of my meaning-giving acts, the sphere of "the same." These are but two instances of what Levinas terms "traces" of that "heteronomous" or fundamentally "alien" experience to which the ego is otherwise "allergic." Foreshadowings of an otherness-beyond-being, such as those offered by many religious philosophers, are duly noted by Levinas. Although harbingers of the other-who-remains-truly-other are found in many instances of religious writings through the ages, Levinas argues that both religious and philosophical thought remains *essentially* impervious to any *other* that is radically exterior. So often, Levinas argues, does an allegedly ineluctable God, once ensconced within theological systems, become objectified; so often is God *posited*, rather than *responded to*. The God of both philosophers and theologians remains most frequently *within*, rather than *outside*, of being. Adumbrations of that which is exterior to being remain just that: mere hints of a truth that would extend beyond the arena in which an appropriative ego reigns supreme. In the end, Levinas contends, Western philosophy is nothing less than an *egology*.

What are the implications of Western philosophy's positing of a sovereign, unconditioned ego for our subject at hand: the role philosophy has played and may yet continue to play with regard to genocide? For philosophy to engage in a fundamental critique of that violation of the other writ large in genocidal acts, that other must exist as someone outside the realm subject to the meaning-giving acts of a sovereign ego. The other to whom I can relate *ethically* must exist as my co-subject, rather than as a being whom I necessarily objectify with my meanings and to whom I am, in turn, so subjected. If philosophy is to engage in an ethical critique worthy of the designation "ethical," it must acknowledge the presence of an other-who-is-truly-other. Indeed, it is only to such an other that I can have properly *ethical* obligations.

If I exist solely within a meaning-giving system to which Levinas gives the name "totality," morality loses all meaning: Relations between human beings are reduced to the play of morally neutral forces. For Jean-Paul Sartre, for example, the other and I are mere alter egos, ciphers who take turns objectifying one another, players in a drama—misnamed "intersubjective" experience—in which there are no genuine subjects and from which there is ultimately "no exit." Alleged "subjects" are condemned to give meaning to one other, to engage, in Sartre's terminology, in "the look," which, in the name of an egoist ambition, serves only to objectify the other. Both parties are thus rendered incapable of exercising moral agency: "Everything which may be said of me in my relations with the Other," claims Sartre, "applies to him as well. While I attempt to free myself from the hold of the Other, the Other is trying to free himself from mine ... ."[4] In this process of "looking" at one another, I and the other constitute a twosome locked in a stalemate, a never-ending contest for power: In Sartre's words, " ... I am referred from transfigurations [of object to subject] to degradation [of subject to object]."[5] My relationship to the other is devoid of anything that can be called moral; I cannot, on principle, see the other as a co-subject, one toward whom I can be morally responsible.

Within the totality of being, Levinas argues, self-interest reigns supreme. Being, in other words, is a realm in which the ego *qua* ego struggles to persist in its appropriative mode. In Levinas's words, "Being is something that is attached to being. That is Darwin's idea. The being of animals is a struggle for life. A struggle without ethics. It is a question of might. ... The aim of being is being itself."[6] Within being, I have no authentic other to whom I must respond; my responsibility is ultimately limited to the work of caring for myself.

Levinas takes his thinking about "being" yet further, moving us into an arena more explicitly political and thus more directly germane to concerns about the relationship between philosophy and genocide. *Being is equated with the realm of war*, a realm which "suspends morality" and "divests the eternal institutions and obligations of their eternity and rescinds ad interim the unconditional imperatives. ... The meaning of the individual ... is derived from the totality."[7] Any significance I have in my being-toward-others, in other words, is fully defined by those ontological schemas that predetermine all intersubjective experience. Once such experience is viewed solely from the perspective of an unexamined whole—in this instance, a schema that reduces interhuman encounters to the struggle of each self to maintain its egoist ambition—we have placed ourselves in danger of succumbing to the reign of the *idea-become-ideology*.

As Levinas suggests, totalizing thought can easily become totalitarian and genocidal. His judgment is supported by the fact that one does not have to exercise much imagination to produce or much memory to recall fixed narratives in which I and the other exist on a continuum of appropriative relationships whose end point is nothing short of genocide. We are all-too-familiar with those ideological schemas of the perpetrators of genocide in which, for example, the other is initially conceptualized as "enemy" or "excess population" and, soon after, as "life unworthy of life," "vermin," "a virus," "a cancer"—to name but a few of the characterizations of the Jewish other in the eyes of Nazi perpetrators of genocide. Once the "imperial" mind comes into play, we can no longer be surprised at a movement that follows a path from thinking the other as outsider and verbally attacking that other to wielding brute physical force against the other—and, in some instances, to committing genocide.

If philosophy remains squarely within the province of being—if the sovereign "I" is posited as one who can never respond to the other-*qua*-subject—philosophy is unable to offer an ethical critique of appropriative acts that I direct toward others. For Levinas, the unfortunate outcome would be that philosophy cannot offer an adequate critique of genocide. Furthermore, by embracing the notion of the sovereign subject who exists *solely* to realize its egoist aims, philosophy does more than remain complacent in the face of genocide. As noted above, philosophy, for Levinas, may well provide fertile ground in which genocide can grow and even *thrive*. With regard to the Holocaust, for example, Nazi Germany defined Jews in terms of racial categories; they could be understood only in terms of the whole, the ideological schema within which each individual Jew was to receive his or her identity. In this instance, totalizing acts of cognition all too easily cleared a path whose end point was genocide. To avoid creating a climate of thought that can serve to nurture our potential to commit genocidal acts, philosophy must do nothing less than radically rethink its essential vocation.

What might constitute an alternative model of philosophizing, one in which a radical critique of the hegemony of the ego, and thus the birth of a genuine ethics, can indeed occur? For Levinas, the response to this query requires that philosophy rethink the traditional relationship between ontology and ethics, a relationship in which primacy has always been accorded to the former. Ethics has most often been seen to constitute a derivative branch of Western thought: What is deemed "good" is understood as good-for-me. The appropriative I remains the primordial atom, the building block of all that exists. Levinas's quarrel with philosophy is thus not a quarrel with any one or more systems of thought competing for primacy *within* the tradition, but rather a critique of the tradition itself, a critique of philosophy-as-ontology. It is not the *adequacy* of any one ontological system as opposed to any other that Levinas questions; such intra-philosophical debates are of mere secondary concern to him. If my ego, the building block of all ontology, is to be subject to a radical critique, such a critique must be directed not toward any measure of the *adequacy* of my powers, but rather toward the *justice* of my exercise of an egoist ambition. I must be called to account not with regard to what I *can* or *cannot* do, but rather with regard to what I, as an ethical agent, *must* not do.

Now who can call me to account in a way that can truly be called "ethical"? This calling-to-account cannot come from the other as he or she is usually understood within traditional (totalizing) philosophical discourse. It must come, Levinas insists, from the other who exists *outside of being*, from one whose existence creates a rupture within being that allows for an ethical relationship to occur. The other-who-is-truly-other must call me from a different plane of existence than ontological totality presents. I am summoned to responsibility for my conduct by a genuine transcendence, one that shines "forth in the face of the other man: an alterity of the nonintegratable, of what cannot be assembled into a totality."[8] The "face," Levinas claims, "puts into question the sufficiency of my identity as an ego; it binds me to an infinite responsibility with regard to the other. ... From the first the other was calling to me, putting into question my resting on myself ... as though ... I had to answer for the other. ... Here is a breakthrough of the Good ... [beyond being]."[9]

Within the realm of being, as we have seen, I am imprisoned by the law of self-interest. As the contemporary philosopher Richard J. Bernstein reminds us, we do indeed exist, *in part*, within being: "Consequently, *qua* beings, this law is also our law. But ... we are not *exclusively* beings. ... We are *human* beings."[10] What this realization means, according to Levinas, is that "with the appearance of the human—*and this is my entire philosophy*—there is something more important than my life, and that is the life of the other."[11] It is beside the point to assess, quantitatively, just how much of our life is spent valuing our own importance as against the importance of the other; what is crucial for Levinas is that I am *able* to escape being, to go beyond it in responding to the call of an other. When the call of the other ruptures being, calling me to account as a moral agent, the fear of death—an essential law of ego-based existence—is inverted into a fear of committing murder.[12]

What is there about the encounter with the face that shatters the sameness of being? It cannot be a play of power, since, as we have seen, the exercise of power is simply an intensified form of that desire to persist in an appropriative existence that comprises the law of being. Although the relationship with the other is asymmetrical—he or she, Levinas argues, comes from "on high"—I do not meet force, at least not in the typical senses of that term. Rather, our encounter takes the form of summons and response. The other contests me by his or her *appeal*, rather than by any show of power which would attempt to surpass my own. Rather than presenting arms against arms, the other disarms me. Thus the other-as-truly-other is both Master (in the sense of occupying a dimension or plane above being) and "poor one," "orphan," or "widow," in the sense of soliciting, rather than coercing, my break with being. What resists me is what Levinas calls "non-resistance," an "ethical resistance."

In the course of my meeting with the face of the truly-other, I am required to justify all my behaviors. Thus, what is contested by the other is not any power I may possess, but rather my "power for power"—my *right* to exercise whatever power I possess. This recognition is the inaugural moment of my existence as a moral agent: "Morality," Levinas asserts, "begins when freedom, instead of being justified by itself, feels itself to be arbitrary and violent."[13] For the first time, I become cognizant of just how arbitrary is my egoist ambition. In the course of my acknowledgment that I can act in an unethical manner toward the other, I am now empowered (in an ethical sense) to refuse this possibility. In particular, what I hear and feel from the other is nothing short of the words "Thou shalt not kill," which means for Levinas that one must reject and resist *any* form of the violation of the other.

Although I am summoned to genuine responsibility by this injunction, it is all too clear that I *need not*—in the sense that I can choose not to—obey it. As genocidal acts most clearly demonstrate, we are free to kill others, even whole peoples, just because of their race, religion, or ethnicity. What cannot be killed, however, is the face of the other, calling me, incessantly, to responsibility. For Levinas, then, "responsibility is the essential, primary and fundamental structure of subjectivity. ... Responsibility in fact is not a simple attribute of subjectivity, as if the latter already existed in itself, before the ethical relationship."[14] Ethics—now understood not as a series of moral directives but rather as an "optics," a new way of *seeing* (in an expanded sense of that word)—becomes "first philosophy."

If I am free, however, to disobey the summons of the other not to kill, how is philosophy, newly understood, to help undo the work of a tradition in which primacy has been accorded to totalizing thought? How can the Levinasian vision work to help prevent the "imperialist" aims of Western ontology from nurturing a genocidal mindset? Levinas offers no book of instructions for combating our potential to commit genocidal acts. Nevertheless, he does provide a new framework for both thought and action within which what had previously been deemed to constitute morality—clearly, given our genocidal history, a flawed morality—can be radically re-envisioned. How would this reenvisioning come about?

The framework for thought and action to which I allude does not consist of moral postulates. For Levinas, philosophy's core has no *content* in the most ordinary senses of that word. The primordial teaching of philosophy is that teaching in which the learner receives "no-thing": He or she receives solely the desire to be taught. Philosophy, in other words, is more verb than noun. It is the ongoing process of freeing itself—and us—of presumption, freeing itself—and us—from the "the inevitable dogmatism that gathers up and gauges an exposition in pursuit of its theme."[15] Faced with the temptation to embrace ideology, which so often motivates acts of genocide, the philosopher must adopt a new understanding of his or her discipline as that which, at bottom, teaches us the need to be taught.

Unless we embrace the Levinasian framework for thinking and acting or at least some version of it—philosophy as response to the other's call to justify our existence—we may well become vulnerable to the temptation to impose "truths" upon others. In the twentieth century and now in the twenty-first as well, we have been made painfully aware of the trajectory so often followed in the course of the imposition of such alleged truths: The movement from verbal to physical force—and ultimately, at several recent junctures, to genocide.

This analysis is not to say that philosophy, understood as one academic discipline among others, must carry the sole burden of helping to reduce our potential for genocide. Levinasian thought summons us to realize that *all* activity of the mind and body must be carried out before the face of the other. That is to say, thinking—and ultimately acting—must, at its core, be ethical. If ethics is indeed an optics, a way of seeing, then we must "see" in *all* modes of thought and action the imperative: "Thou shalt not kill." Already we have noted that Levinas understands *killing* to refer to *any* form of violation of the other, but he takes that thought still further: In light of the perpetual temptation to engage in bystander behavior, he interprets the Sixth Commandment, "Thou shalt not kill," as "Thou shalt do everything in order that the other live."[16] " 'Thou shalt not kill,' " he exclaims, means nothing less than "you shall defend the life of the other."[17]

If, as Levinas says, the "ethical relationship ... subtends discourse,"[18] then *everything* that we teach our children, both in the home and the classroom, must be taught in the mode of standing before the face of the other. Without being grounded in the ethical relationship, all teachings run the risk of drying up and becoming mere dogma. For Levinas, "doing philosophy" means ever-renewing the fundamental moment of being called to responsibility for what I think and do. Unless it is rooted in the face-to-face relationships to which Levinas points, philosophy and ultimately *all* human discourse run the risk of becoming acts of war: attempts by the mightier of intellect and/or body to impress their dogmas, their "truths," on the weaker. The authentic philosopher continually challenges his or her "presumption to know," not by arguing that there is yet more to learn, but by questioning that very endeavor which is typically called "knowing." Teaching with the face of the other before me, I am rendered unable, in ethical terms, to impose any static truth upon my students in the classroom or my children in the home.

In our genocidal world, philosophy, now understood as bearing witness to the face of the other calling me to account, can serve to ward off the temptation to ignore the injunction "Thou shalt not kill." As that discipline which, perhaps more than others, has modeled an egoist appropriation of the world, philosophy has a special obligation to rethink its fundamental aims. At its core, Levinas's vision of philosophy is a vision of philosophy-as-peacemaking. In its radical movement away from a totalizing—and thus warlike—ambition, Levinas's understanding of philosophy models a way of being which can help thwart genocide's ever-present threats.

Notes

1. See John K. Roth, *Holocaust Politics* (Louisville, KY: Westminster John Knox Press), pp. 27–32, for a discussion of the relative silence of philosophy with regard to one genocide, the Holocaust. In this discussion Roth also names many of those contemporary philosophers who have in fact addressed Holocaust issues. For a supplementary listing of philosophers who have studied the Holocaust, see p. 293, n. 29.
2. Emmanuel Levinas, *Totality and Infinity: An Essay on Exteriority*, trans. Alphonso Lingis (Pittsburgh, PA: Duquesne University Press, 1969), p. 43.
3. Ibid., p. 37.
4. Jean-Paul Sartre, *Being and Nothingness*, trans. Hazel Barnes (New York: Pocket Books, 1956), pp. 474–5.
5. Ibid.
6. Emmanuel Levinas, "The Paradox of Morality: An Interview With Emmanuel Levinas," in Robert Bernasconi and David Wood, eds, *The Provocation of Levinas: Rethinking the Other*, trans. Andrew Benjamin and Tamara Wright (London: Routledge and Kegan, 1988), p. 172.
7. Levinas, *Totality and Infinity*, pp. 21–2.
8. Emmanuel Levinas, "Transcendence and Evil," trans. Alphonso Lingis, in A. T. Tymieniecka, ed., *The Phenomenology of Man and of the Human Condition* (Dordrecht, MA: D. Reidel, 1983), p. 163.
9. Ibid., pp. 163–4.
10. Richard J. Bernstein, *Radical Evil: A Philosophical Interrogation* (Cambridge: Polity Press, 2002), p. 179.
11. Levinas, "The Paradox of Morality," p. 172.
12. Emmanuel Levinas, "The Other, Utopia, and Justice," trans. Michael B. Smith, in Jill Robbins, ed., *Is It Righteous To Be? Interviews with Emmanuel Levinas* (Stanford, CA: Stanford University Press, 2001), p. 204.
13. Levinas, *Totality and Infinity*, p. 84.

14. Emmanuel Levinas, *Ethics and Infinity: Conversations with Philippe Nemo*, trans. Richard A. Cohen (Pittsburgh, PA: Duquesne University Press, 1985), pp. 95–6.
15. Levinas, *Totality and Infinity*, p. 29.
16. Roger Burggraeve, "The Bible Gives To Thought: Levinas on The Possibility and Proper Nature of Biblical Thinking," in Jeffrey Bloechl, ed., *The Face of the Other and the Trace of God* (New York: Fordham University Press, 2003), p. 177.
17. Emmanuel Levinas, "In the Name of the Other," trans. Maureen V. Gedney, in *Is It Righteous to Be?*, p. 192.
18. Levinas, *Totality and Infinity*, p. 195.

12
Why Do the Happy Inhabitants of Tahiti Bother to Exist at All?

Robert Bernasconi

Philosophy's involvement in genocide can be usefully appraised by exploring the fact that neither Immanuel Kant nor G. W. F. Hegel advocated mass killing, but those magisterial figures in the tradition of Western thought unwittingly contributed to the formation of a culture of genocide. They did so by proposing philosophies of history that were designed to give meaning to humanity as a species, while nevertheless embracing an idea of progress from which some races were excluded because they allegedly lacked the talents that would enable them to be full participants in humanity's future. Their findings "answered" the question of why the "white race" existed, but did little to explain the existence of the races whose historical agency had been denied. That is to say, the Kantian and Hegelian philosophies of history left unresolved the problem of finding a meaning, a place in history, for the so-called "backward" races in a world dominated by Europe.

Subsequent generations struggled with this legacy. One way they found of dealing with it was to deny the humanity of members of non-white races. However, they more often thought in terms of the supposedly weaker races disappearing from the face of the earth, no doubt because of their susceptibility to European diseases. After 1850, the dominant scientific view was that race mixing led to a loss of fertility, with the result that many whites thought of the other races as a threat to the integrity of their own race. Subsequently, when Social Darwinism spread the ideas of the struggle for existence and the survival of the fittest, the idea that certain races posed a threat to whites became even more pronounced and the thought prevailed that it would be better to hasten their disappearance. Thus, an existing practice received a legitimating rationale. I hope to make a prima facie case that the framework of these discussions had in large measure been set earlier by the way Kant and Hegel approached the question of the meaning of human existence.

I am not arguing that without Kant and Hegel there would have been fewer genocides. Nor do I draw a direct link between them and the actual perpetrators of these crimes. My claim is that, contrary to the tendency of most white philosophers and intellectual historians to isolate Kant and

Hegel from the worst genocides of the last two hundred years, they contributed to the formation of a culture of genocide that has by no means been eradicated and that we need to understand better if we are to combat it successfully. Furthermore, we need to understand how a noble-sounding idea, like cosmopolitanism, can be subverted when it is taken to mean Europeanization or, for that matter, Americanization.[1]

What is genocide? The word was coined by Raphael Lemkin in 1944 in *Axis Rule in Occupied Europe* from the Greek word *genos* understood as "race" or "tribe" and the Latin suffix *-cide* with its sense of killing represented in related words such as *tyrannicide*, *homicide*, and *infanticide*. Lemkin also toyed with another term for the same idea, *ethnocide*, from the Greek *ethnos* (nation). He explained that "new conceptions require new terms," but his claim about the novelty of genocide has not received sufficient attention.[2] For Lemkin, genocide was new because it was governed by an understanding of biological structures. As opposed to earlier attempts to destroy nations through mass murder, the aim of genocide was to secure superiority over another group in many spheres: the political, the social, the economic, the physical, the religious, the moral, and the biological.[3] In each field, the double task of genocide was to destroy the national pattern of the oppressed group and replace it with that of the oppressors. Lemkin warned against focusing exclusively on the first task. The second task, exemplified by the processes of "Germanization," "Magyarization," and "Italianization," was also crucial. Genocide, in Lemkin's conception, was not confined to mass extermination, nor did it require it. As a result, Lemkin considered Nazi laws promoting the German language and the prohibition of the Cyrillic alphabet to be examples of "genocidal legislation."[4]

In this work, Lemkin focused on laws that the Germans had enacted to enforce their occupations of various European nations, basing many of his arguments on the words of Hitler himself. Although Lemkin was well aware of the massacres in Armenia and those in Germany's colonies, including South-West Africa, he did not dwell on them. Genocide called for extermination only where a population was not deemed biologically worthy of being Germanized: in such cases only the soil would be Germanized.[5] Everything depended on whether a population was considered "racially valuable"; the Nazis used subsidies to encourage Norwegian and Dutch women to have children by members of the German armed forces.[6] In sum, Lemkin already recognized what Michel Foucault has since taught us to call *biopolitics*. As Foucault stated the key point: "If genocide is indeed the dream of modern powers, this is not because of a return of the ancient right to kill; it is because power is situated and exercised at the level of life, the species, the race, and the large-scale phenomena of population."[7]

Owing significantly to Lemkin's hard work, his term *genocide* won recognition: In 1948 the United Nations sponsored a Genocide Convention, which defined *genocide* as acting "with intent to destroy, in whole or in part, a national, ethnical, racial or religious group, as such." However, in its final draft and not entirely in keeping with Lemkin's usage of the term, the Convention introduced the idea that genocides had occurred in all periods of human history. Even the fact that the definition, which refers somewhat problematically to intent, highlights the idea that genocide covers destructive acts directed against a national, ethnical, racial, or religious group "as such,"[8] does not rule out the possibility of going against the wishes of most of those who formulated the definition and thinking of it as a specifically modern phenomenon. This is possible because the modern way of thinking about populations as races has even infected the characterization of members of religious groups—most notably, Jews.

The specifically modern character of genocide emerges in the differences between it and mass killing.[9] Mass killing aims at the immediate future. It seeks to secure a victory over an enemy in order to subjugate, control, or contain it. Its goal is a renewed peace, but one in which one nation has won a new advantage over its neighbors. To fulfill its aim, mass killing may lead to extermination and so may call for as many deaths, or more than genocide, but it is still fundamentally different. Genocide, by contrast, aims beyond the immediate future and seeks to transform the whole of history. It thinks of the enemy as a population where membership is largely regarded as inherited and is usually marked by common characteristics. Hence when the extermination of a population is attempted, the contemporary population is not the only target; perpetrators also aim to destroy all records of the existence of the group and its culture. Furthermore, murdering women and children is seen not merely as an attempt to terrorize a population into submission, but as a necessary component in an attempt to eradicate that population from humanity's future. For these reasons, one cannot commit genocide on one's own people—at least not so long as one continues to understand them in those terms. Western culture has found in biology and a philosophy of history a basis for thinking of genocide as, on occasion, necessary for its prosperity, its survival, and even its belief in the value of humanity. Through Westernization this conceptual scheme has spread across the world.[10]

One should not underestimate the impact on Europeans that resulted from the decimation-by-disease of indigenous populations in colonized territory. That devastation made Europeans accustomed to the idea that it was the destiny of "weak" races or populations to begin to disappear on contact with European ways. For some Europeans, it was a short step from accepting the disappearance of weak races to justifying acts that would hasten the inevitable disappearance of those inferior groups. Diseases could be manipulated or manufactured, as in the case of blankets infected with smallpox that were handed out to Native Americans. Furthermore, genocide could be committed in the name of evolutionary progress. Indeed, within Social Darwinism, "the great law of 'the preservation of favoured races in the struggle of life' " sanctioned "the inevitable extinction of all those low and mentally undeveloped populations with which Europeans came in contact."[11] One could intervene to help it once evolution's direction and implications were grasped, as many Western theorists had claimed to have done. Eventually this task was assigned to eugenics, which began as a directive to breed wisely, but soon resorted to sterilization and subsequently to extermination. In its nineteenth- and twentieth century heydays, Social Darwinism was enthusiastically adopted by many prominent philosophers, but the way for its acceptance had already been prepared earlier within the Western philosophical tradition.

Kant's "Idea for a Universal History with Cosmopolitan Intent" was especially influential in separating the question of the meaning of human existence from theology and referring it to the relatively new idea of a philosophy of history. Kant looked to history in an attempt "to discover a purpose in nature behind this senseless course of human events."[12] The meaning of history lay in progress, but, given his strong conviction that there were four distinct hierarchically organized races, whose capacities were fundamentally unalterable, this immediately created the problem of those races alleged to be naturally less capable than the whites. What was their purpose in the overall plan? To follow? To serve? To occupy parts of the globe too hot or too cold for Northern Europeans? But then what of Native Americans? In "On the Use of Teleological Principles in Philosophy," Kant posed the question of why Native Americans existed: "That their national dispositions have not yet reached a *complete* fitness for any climate provides a test that can hardly explain why this race, too weak for hard labor, too phlegmatic for diligence, and unfit for any culture, still stands ..."[13] On numerous occasions in his anthropological writings, Kant characterized the Native Americans as lacking in drive, talent, and culture.[14] There seemed to be no clear way of reconciling their continued existence with the progress of humanity.

Given this problem, it is no surprise to find that in his private notes Kant entertained the possibility that this race might die out, as indeed it appeared to be doing. To the question of how "the entire species" might progress, he responded: "It appears that all of the Americans will be wiped out, not through the act of murder—that would be cruel—but they will die out ... And private conflict will emerge among them, and they will destroy each other."[15] Kant, it must be remembered, was a defender of Native Americans against their exploitation through colonialism, but it is also clear that when he referred to the progress of the entirety of humanity he did not mean everybody. Indeed, in another note Kant wrote that "All races will be extinguished ... only not that of the Whites."[16] They were the exception because they alone had "all impulses and talents."[17]

Kant had glimpsed, but then turned his back on, the problem of reconciling the idea of allegedly inferior races with the attempt to find within history the meaning of humanity. This ambivalence is what distinguished

Kant's position. Some of his contemporaries advocated mass extermination. For example, Christoph Meiners, professor at Göttingen and one of Kant's opponents, wrote that "regrettably, there exist not only individual persons but whole peoples who, cannot be moved towards the Good, and so will be exterminated (*gezwungen*)."[18] However, Kant highlighted the problem and made it more acute by introducing both the scientific conception of hereditary races with permanent limitations and the cosmopolitan conception of universal history.[19] The fact that Kant was against whites killing Native Americans should not distract us from the fact that he needed the latter to kill each other—or for them to suffer some other disaster—if cosmopolitanism was to embrace all of humanity, that is to say, all that remained of humanity after the constitutionally less talented had been purged in one way or another.

The puzzle was that if the meaning of human existence lay in history, and if certain populations or races seemed not to participate in history fully, then why did they exist? Kant asked precisely this question in an anonymous review of Herder's *Ideen zur Geschichte der Menschheit*.[20] Herder had argued that "each individual has the measure of his happiness within him" and that in this way providence provided for cultures that lacked the means to meet the more complex needs that only large societies could satisfy. In response Kant introduced, but then put to one side, an argument that differentiated between kinds of happiness that would allow little consolation to be derived from Herder's argument. More forcefully, Kant then introduced an historical argument based on the possibility that what providence actually intended was an "ever continuing and growing activity and culture" culminating in the culture that arose as a product of "a political constitution based on concepts of human right." This result would be an achievement of human beings and not of nature. It was only with reference to such a history that one could pursue the question of the value of each human existence. In this context, Kant made an argument that, however unwittingly, gave aid and comfort to genocide. Referring to Herder, Kant wrote as follows:

> Does the author really mean that, if the happy inhabitants of Tahiti, never visited by more civilized nations, were destined to live in their peaceful indolence for thousands of years, it would be possible to give a satisfactory answer to the question of why they should exist at all, and of whether it would not have been just as good if this island had been occupied by happy sheep and cattle as by happy human beings who merely enjoy themselves?[21]

The fact that Kant made this argument against Herder is particularly significant because Herder in his own philosophy of history was an advocate of the idea that each people has something vital to contribute to humanity. Unlike Kant, who believed that Europe would probably legislate for all other continents,

Herder's idea of humanity was such that the loss of one people would damage all.[22] Herder had specifically opposed as "stupid vanity" the idea that "all the inhabitants of the World must be Europeans to live happily."[23] Kant's opposition to Herder on this point is underlined by his insistence elsewhere that the world would not lose anything if Tahiti was destroyed.[24] However, although Kant's rhetorical question seems to imply that the best thing that could happen to the happy inhabitants of Tahiti was that they be visited by more civilized nations, ultimately that would solve nothing. They could not, in Kant's view, take on European civilization and become autonomous rational agents. Although climate might provide a partial answer to the question of *how* the different races came into existence, it did not answer the question of *why* they existed and the question remained unanswered.[25] Hence, given his understanding of progress, Kant could scarcely avoid speculating about the disappearance of the non-white races that he judged to be especially lacking in talents.

Hegel's *Lectures on the Philosophy of World History* answered Kant's call for "a philosophical attempt to work out a universal history of the world in accordance with a plan of nature aimed at a perfect civil union of mankind."[26] Hegel identified a race that was historical, the Caucasian race, and at least two races, the Black race and Native Americans, that he placed outside history.[27] However, to be outside history was to be without justification, without a reason to be, just as to be within history was to be subject to the judgment of history.[28] Hegel defended on world historical terms the form of chattel slavery invented to exploit Africans, claiming that such slavery brought them into history and into contact with (European) culture. Nevertheless, because Hegel judged these slaves to be incapable of making European culture their own, they were introduced within history only to be set aside again. Hegel's philosophy of history can be viewed as a secular response to the theological question about whether a specific race had a soul and was thus available for conversion, for salvation, albeit in Hegel's view there was no secular salvation. He described the extinction of the Native Americans without expressing a clear moral judgment: "For after the Europeans had landed there [in America], the natives were gradually destroyed [*untergegangen*] by the breath of European activity."[29] Hegel did not need to pass a judgment. History had already done so.

The views of Kant and Hegel that I have explored here were to have an immensely destructive outcome, which can be illustrated by pointing to just two of the many thinkers who inherited and advanced them. Ernst Haeckel, who is largely remembered for providing the philosophical filter through which Germany understood Darwin, and who in the 1930s was regarded as a forerunner of National Socialism for his position on eugenics, offers a prime example of how these philosophical ideas were given scientific legitimacy.[30] Echoing Hegel, Haeckel judged that the Caucasians were "the most eminent actors in what is called 'World history,' "[31] and that with the possible exception of the Mongolians, no other human type makes genuine (*eigentlich*) history. Elsewhere, he referred to the "lower races," such as the Australian Negroes, as psychologically nearer to apes or dogs than to civilized Europeans: "we must, therefore, assign a different value to their lives."[32] He believed that Kant would not have formulated the doctrines of the immortality of the soul and the categorical imperative, if he had made a comparative study of the lower soul of the savage and phylogenetically separated the fully human soul from those lower forms. Haeckel thereby acknowledged a resistance on the part of Kant's philosophy to this application of his thought, but Haeckel also recognized his strong debt to Kant and paid tribute to Kant's understanding of biology.[33] In later editions of his *Natürliche Schöpfungsgeschichte*, which was based largely on Fritz Schultze's 1875 work *Kant and Darwin*, Haeckel argued that Kant had already anticipated Darwin's theory of selection and the struggle for existence through which the amelioration of the race takes place.[34]

Houston Stewart Chamberlain, another forerunner of National Socialism, was even more direct. He read Kant within the context, as he saw it, of millions of bestial Blacks preparing for a race war. The alternative facing society was to enter a higher stage of culture or to fall into an unprecedented barbarism in which artificially civilized but still superstitious races—"as dreamless as so many cattle"—prospered.[35] Whether Chamberlain's reference to cattle intentionally recalled "the happy cattle" to which Kant compared the Tahitians, Chamberlain shows where philosophies about the meaning of human existence can lead when they are posed within a context framed by the discordant ideas of permanently unequal races and of a cosmopolitan history. Chamberlain certainly distorted Kant's teaching, but this potentially explosive combination of ideas is authentically Kantian and together they gave rise to the idea that a race war was all but inevitable. It was a widely held view in the early twentieth century.

We need to pursue more vigorously the task of understanding how in the West the philosophy of history lent new legitimacy to the idea that some lives are of more value than others, even to the point of tolerating genocide. To do so means departing from that habit of thought that prevails in most contemporary studies within the history of philosophy: namely, the practice of studiously isolating ideas from their cultural implications and historical effects. To understand history we need to investigate how ideas that may not be in relations of entailment still come to be bound together. It is true that being scrupulous in one's argumentation is a safeguard, but in the world of politics, which is what political philosophy and ethics ultimately must address, other forces—for example, a sense that one's race or nation is engaged in a struggle for existence—impact how ideas are weighted and what options present themselves as attractive. Certainly one can believe in progress without wanting to murder all those who resist it. Nevertheless, after the history of colonialism, who can doubt that, however much our contemporary philosophies may differ from those of white supremacy, it was a short step for philosophy to go from theorizing about progress to identifying those who stood in its way and then to treating them as enemies of humanity and making them disappear from the face of the earth?

Notes

1. My arguments relating to Kant and Hegel draw on my essay "Will the Real Kant Please Stand Up?" in *Radical Philosophy* 117 (January/February 2003): 13–22.
2. Raphael Lemkin, *Axis Rule in Occupied Europe* (Washington, DC: Carnegie Endowment for International Peace, 1944), p. 79.
3. Ibid., pp. 82–90.
4. Ibid., pp. 440 and 626.
5. Ibid., pp. 81–2.
6. Ibid., pp. 213 and 504.
7. Michel Foucault, *La volonté de savoir* (Paris: Gallimard, 1976), p. 180; trans. Robert Hurley, *The History of Sexuality*, Vol. 1 (New York: Vintage Books, 1990), p. 137.
8. Some of the difficulties of this definition are explored by the editors in Robert Gellately and Ben Kiernan, ed., *The Spectre of Genocide: Mass Murder in Historical Perspective* (Cambridge: Cambridge University Press, 2003), pp. 14–19.
9. My treatment of this distinction has been influenced by Jonathan Schell, although it is not identical with his. See *The Unfinished Twentieth Century* (London: Verso, 2001), pp. 21–2.
10. For a survey of definitions, see Frank Chalk and Kurt Jonassohn, *The History and Sociology of Genocide* (New Haven, CT: Yale University Press, 1990), pp. 12–26. One must balance the desire to have a fully inclusive concept of genocide for political reasons with the conceptual need to clarify the ideology that promotes genocide among otherwise civilized peoples.
11. Alfred Russel Wallace, *Natural Selection and Tropical Nature* (London: Macmillan, 1891), p. 177.
12. Immanuel Kant, "Idee zu einer allgemeinen Geschichte," *Gesammelte Schriften*, Akademie Ausgabe VIII (Berlin: de Gruyter, 1968), p. 18; trans. H. B. Nisbet, "Idea for a Universal History," *Kant: Political Writings* (Cambridge: Cambridge University Press, 1995), p. 42.
13. Immanuel Kant, "Über den Gebrauch teleologischer Principien in der Philosophie," *Gesammelte Schriften*, Akademie Ausgabe VIII, pp. 175–6; trans. Jon Mark Mikkelsen, "On the Use of Teleological Principles in Philosophy," in Robert Bernasconi, ed., *Race* (Oxford: Blackwell, 2001), p. 48.
14. See the remarks collected by Robert B. Louden in *Kant's Impure Ethics* (Oxford: Oxford University Press, 2000), pp. 98–100.
15. Immanuel Kant, *Vorlesungen über die Anthropologie*, Akademie Ausgabe, XXV, 2 (Berlin: de Gruyter, 1968), p. 840.
16. Immanuel Kant, *Reflexionen zur Anthropologie*, Akademie Ausgabe XV/2 (Berlin: de Gruyter, 1968), p. 878.
17. Immanuel Kant, Akademie Ausgabe XXV, pp. 1, 187.
18. Christoph Meiners, *Grundriss der Geschichte der Menschheit*, 1793, p. 219. Quoted by Eun-Jueng Lee, *"Anti-Europa": Die Geschichte der Rezeption des Konfuzianismus und der Konfuzianischen Gesellschaft seit den frühen Auflösung* (Münster: Litt, 2003), p. 213.

19. Robert Bernasconi, "Who Invented the Concept of Race?," in Bernasconi, ed., *Race*, pp. 11–36.
20. In his *Critique of Judgment*, Kant raises the question of why people should have to live in Lapland. *Gesammelte Schriften*, Akademie Ausgabe V (Berlin: de Gruyter, 1968), p. 369; trans. Werner Pluhar, *Critique of Judgment* (Indianapolis, IN: Hackett, 1987), p. 247. See also p. 378; trans., p. 258. This question is part of a larger argument and shows how in Kant the question has a level of complexity to which this brief study cannot do justice. However, I believe that ultimately the conclusion would be the same.
21. Kant, *Gesammelte Schriften* VIII, p. 65; trans. *Political Writings*, pp. 219–20. The locution "bother to exist at all," which I have employed in my title, may not be the best translation, but it was employed in Lewis White Beck, ed., *Kant on History* (Indianapolis, IN: Bobbs-Merrill, 1963), p. 50.
22. Kant, *Gesammette Schriften* VIII, pp. 29–30; trans. *Political Writings*, p. 52. On Herder's idea of humanity, see Robert Bernasconi, " 'Ich mag in Keinen Himmel, wo Weisse sind': Herder's Critique of Eurocentrism," *Acta Institutionis Philosophiae et Aestheticae* 13 (1995): 69–81.
23. J. G. Herder, *Ideen zur Philosophie der Geschichte der Menschheit* (Frankfurt: Deutscher Klassiker Verlag, 1989), p. 327; trans. T. Churchill, *Outlines of a Philosophy of the History of Man* (New York: Bergman, nd), p. 219. On Herder, see Sonia Sikka, "Enlightened Relativism: The Case of Herder," in *Philosophy and Social Criticism* (forthcoming).
24. Kant, *Reflexionen zur Anthropologie*, p. 785.
25. See further Robert Bernasconi, "Kant as an Unfamiliar Source of Racism," in Julie K. Ward and Tommy L. Lott, eds, *Philosophers on Race* (Oxford: Blackwell, 2002), pp. 145–66.
26. Kant, *Gesammelte Schriften* VIII, p. 29; trans. *Political Writings*, p. 51.
27. See further Robert Bernasconi, "Hegel at the Court of the Ashanti," in Stuart Barnett, ed., *Hegel after Derrida* (London: Routledge, 1998), pp. 41–63 and "With What Must the Philosophy of World History Begin?" *Nineteenth Century Contexts* 22 (2000): 171–201.
28. G. W. F. Hegel, *Grundlinien der Philosophie des Rechts*, sec. 340; trans. H. B. Nisbet, *Elements of the Philosophy of Right* (Cambridge: Cambridge University Press, 1991), p. 371.
29. G. W. F. Hegel, *Die Vernunft in der Geschichte*, ed., J. Hoffmeister (Hamburg: Felix Meiner, 1980), p. 200; trans. H. B. Nisbet, *Lectures on the Philosophy of World History* (Cambridge: Cambridge University Press, 1975), p. 163. See also Michael H. Hoffheimer, "Hegel, Race, Genocide," *Southern Journal of Philosophy*, 39, Supplement, pp. 37–8.
30. "His proposals are being actualized in the new Reich." Gerhard Heberer, *Ernst Haeckel und seine wissenschaftliche Bedeutung* (Tübingen: Franz F. Heine, 1934), p. 14.
31. Ernst Haeckel, *Natürliche Schöpfungsgeschichte* (Berlin: Georg Reimers, 1870), p. 615.
32. Ernst Haeckel, *Die Lebenswunder* (Stuttgart: Alfred Kröner, 1904), p. 450; trans. Joseph McCabe, *The Wonders of Life* (New York: Harper, 1905), p. 390.
33. Ernst Haeckel, *Natürliche Schöpfungsgeschichte* (Berlin: George Reimers, 1868), pp. 81–3.
34. Ibid., pp. 172–3. Fritz Schultze, *Kant und Darwin: Ein Beitrag zur Geschichte der Entwicklungslehre* (Jena: Hermann Dufft, 1875). Schultze's interpretation of Kant

has since been widely questioned. See Arthur O. Lovejoy, "Kant and Evolution," in Bentley Glass, ed., *Forerunners of Darwin 1745–1859* (Baltimore, MD: Johns Hopkins Press, 1968), pp. 173–206.

35. Houston Stewart Chamberlain, *Immanuel Kant* (Munich: F. Bruckmann, 1938), pp. 715–21; trans. Lord Redesdale, *Immanuel Kant* (London: The Bodley Head, 1914), pp. 332–9.

Part III

Will Genocide Ever End? Genocide's Challenge to Philosophy

John K. Roth

In 1994, the political scientist R. J. Rummel, a demographer of what he calls *democide*, published an important book called *Death by Government*. Writing before he could have taken account of the genocidal atrocities in Bosnia, Rwanda, Kosovo, or Darfur, Rummel estimated that "the human cost of war and democide"—he defined *democide* as "the murder of any person or people by a government, including genocide, politicide, and mass murder"—is more than "203 million people in this [twentieth] century."[1]

"If one were to sit at a table," Rummel went on to say, "and have this many people come in one door, walk at three miles per hour across the room with three feet between them (assume generously that each person is also one foot thick, navel to spine), and exit an opposite door, it would take over *five years and nine months* for them all to pass, 24 hours a day, 365 days a year. If these dead were laid out head to toe, assuming each to be an average of 5 feet tall, they would reach from Honolulu, Hawaii, across the vast Pacific and then the huge continental United States to Washington D.C. on the East coast, *and then back again almost twenty times.*"[2]

While Rummel may have thought that such calculations would make the abstraction of huge numbers more concrete, it is not clear that he even convinced himself, for he placed an endnote number at his calculation's conclusion. Note 14 reads as follows: "Back and forth, over 4,838 miles one way, near twenty times? This is so incredible that I would not believe the calculation and had to redo it several times."[3]

In Rummel's vocabulary, *democide* includes many, but perhaps not all, cases of *genocide*. It all depends on how *genocide* is defined. For Rummel, the key defining issue would be the part that killing plays. Here is how Rummel defines genocide: It is, "among other things, the killing of people by a government because of their indelible group membership (race, ethnicity, religion, language)."[4] His qualification "among other things" is important, for it indicates that the genocidal destruction of a group is not restricted to outright killing. The destruction, Rummel observes, can take place *"by other means,* such as by preventing births in the group or by causing mental harm." In a word, "genocide does *not* necessarily have to include killing."[5] No comfort can be taken from the fact that although genocide involves killing—one-sided killing, it is important to add—it does not entail killing necessarily or always.[6] Far more important are questions such as: What can be done about genocide? Will genocide ever end? How do those questions, rooted in the reality of genocide, challenge philosophy in particular?

Part III opens with Raimond Gaita's argument that one of genocide's challenges to philosophy is for critical thinking to refocus genocide itself. It is important to do this work because the term *genocide* may often be misused. Genocide, moreover, may not involve direct and outright murder, a fact that complicates identification of genocide even when it is happening. "Humankind," writes Gaita, "understands itself, in part, when it gives the right names to the crimes it has committed." Far from being a discussion of definitional quibbles, Gaita's analysis shows how important it is to think as clearly as possible about what genocide involves, how it is a devastating crime against humanity, and why its trauma is so immense.

Norman Geras amplifies themes introduced by Gaita. Genocide is a crime against humanity or nothing could be. But now genocide offers another challenge to philosophy, namely, that of discerning what it means to speak of a crime against *humanity.* The concept of a crime against humanity is immensely important, and for that reason, Geras contends, it deserves careful analysis. He finds it crucial to emphasize that crimes against humanity are inhuman acts that "terrorize us all."

Terror is on Laurence M. Thomas's mind as well, and thus he senses another important challenge that genocide poses for philosophy, one that follows from the widespread agreement—Thomas refers to an "objective and self-evident" moral truth—that genocide is *wrong.* If genocide is wrong, then what follows for other kinds of killing, such as suicide bombings? Thomas argues that "genocide and suicide bombings stand or fall together. Hence, if suicide bombings can be justified, then genocide can be justified." Rising to genocide's challenge to philosophy, Thomas develops a perspective that morally condemns suicide bombing and genocide alike.

Not only do philosophies and philosophers employ different approaches and reflect varied traditions of thought, but they also express different moods. Their writing may be cool and restrained, though neither indifferent nor unfeeling. Or, like James R. Watson's, it may be impassioned and unrestrained, though neither undisciplined nor uncontrolled. Watson *feels* genocide's challenge to philosophy, and thus the critical mood of his chapter bears down on philosophy's affectations, its willingness to get along by going along with the academic and political powers that be, all of which results in avoiding the confrontation with genocide and other social catastrophes that, in his view, ought to characterize philosophy at its best.

Watson shows that philosophers are unlikely to meet the challenge that genocide poses unless they feel very strongly—to the point of anger-inspired action—that genocide, the crime of crimes, indeed is wrong.

Edith Wyschogrod is also concerned about how established power creates a climate in which genocide and ethnic cleansing can do their grisly work. Drawing on the insights of Dominique Janicaud, she analyzes and criticizes what he calls *techno-discourse*. Not only is this discourse "a mode of rationality that governs the economy and technology of postmodernity," but also it tends to reduce human individuals to replicable and indiscernible units. Such a mentality helps to make people prey for genocidal killing. With Emmanuel Levinas as her ally, Wyschogrod argues for a different view, one that meets genocide's challenge to philosophy by defending "an ethics of otherness."

Part III closes with a chapter by Paul C. Santilli that complements Edith Wyschogrod's. When Western philosophy considers wrongdoing, he notes, its emphasis often falls on the perpetrators. As Santilli observes, "Western philosophy has contributed much to the legal theories of intention, agency, culpability, and punishment that now inform modern criminal courts." What philosophy has done far less extensively, and far less well, is to pay attention to the victims of harm-doing, to the suffering and to the dead. Even the term *victim*, Santilli argues, can be an obstacle to thinking about and feeling the humanity of those who have been robbed of respect and life. Santilli helps to show that philosophy will evade genocide's challenge unless philosophers evidence solidarity with those who have been or might yet be genocide's targets. Such solidarity would put philosophy and philosophers in the vanguard of those who resist genocide.

Charlotte Delbo was not Jewish, but her arrest for resisting the Nazi occupation of her native France made her experience the Holocaust when she was deported to Auschwitz in January 1943. Delbo survived the Nazi onslaught. In 1946, she began to write the trilogy that came to be called *Auschwitz and After*. Her work's anguished visual descriptions, profound reflections on memory, and diverse writing styles make it an unrivaled Holocaust testimony. At one point Delbo expresses a challenge to her readers: "I beg you / do something / learn a dance step / something to justify your existence / something that gives you the right / to be dressed in your skin in your body hair / learn to walk and to laugh / because it would be too senseless / after all / for so many to have died / while you live / doing nothing with your life."[7] The chapters in Part III suggest that her words are worth remembering, especially by philosophers in an age of genocide. Such remembering could help to bring genocide to an end.

Notes

1. R. J. Rummel, *Death by Government* (New Brunswick, NJ: Transaction Publishers, 1997), pp. 13, 31. Yehuda Bauer's observations about Rummel's data are worth

noting: "Rummel has been criticized for exaggerating the losses. Even if the criticisms were valid, a figure lower by 10 or 20 or even 30 percent would make absolutely no difference to the general conclusions that Rummel draws." See Yehuda Bauer, *Rethinking the Holocaust* (New Haven, CT: Yale University Press, 2001), pp. 12–13, 277n.17. The discussion of Rummel draws on my contributions to Carol Rittner, John K. Roth, and James M. Smith, eds, *Will Genocide Ever End?* (St. Paul, MN: Paragon House, 2002).

2. Rummel, *Death by Government*, pp. 13, 31.

3. Ibid., p. 28.

4. Ibid., p. 31. Further issues surround Rummel's use of the term *indelible*. Apparently it refers to qualities that are permanent or to characteristics that cannot be removed. It is arguable whether a person's religion or language fits that description, even though Rummel includes religion and language in the examples he lists to illustrate indelible group membership. Even nationality, ethnicity, or "racial" identity might be less than crystal clear in that sense. Of course, much usually hinges on how genocide's perpetrators identify their targets. That fact means that hard and fast lines are hard to draw, if they can be drawn at all, between what potential victims can or cannot do to alter identities that would leave them trapped within or allow them to elude a particular genocidal web.

   Yehuda Bauer argues that only national, ethnic, or racial groups should be considered targets for genocide. He would deny that status to religious or political groups. The difference, he claims, is that in the first three cases a potential target of genocide cannot change those identities; only the decision of a potential perpetrator could do so. On the other hand, he contends, membership in religious and political groups is a matter of choice. Unfortunately, Bauer's analysis is neater than genocide's realities turn out to be. Perpetrators may decide that religious and political identities are not always matters of choice. Likewise, their understandings of ethnicity, nationality, and even race may leave open, at least to some extent, an individual's self-determination of identity. Rather than putting too fine a point on the matter, it may be well to leave open the nature of a potential victim group, taking seriously that genocidal perpetrators will reserve to themselves the dubious prerogative of defining a victim group as they will. On these points see Bauer, *Rethinking the Holocaust*, pp. 10–13 and Frank Chalk and Kurt Jonassohn, *The History and Sociology of Genocide: Analyses and Case Studies* (New Haven, CT: Yale University Press, 1990), pp. 25–6.

5. Rummel, *Death by Government*, p. 33. The italics are Rummel's.

6. Genocide is not about reciprocal killing. It is the perpetrator's aim to wipe out the victim group, but the victim group does not have such plans for the perpetrator, let alone the means to carry them out. See Chalk and Jonassohn, *The History and Sociology of Genocide*, p. 23.

7. Charlotte Delbo, *Auschwitz and After*, trans. Rosette C. Lamont (New Haven, CT: Yale University Press, 1995), p. 230.

13

Refocusing Genocide: A Philosophical Responsibility

Raimond Gaita

In the twentieth century, Geoffrey Robertson said in his book *Crimes against Humanity*, international law became accepted in the international community.[1] The twenty-first century, he suggested, will be the century of its enforcement. Among the political and judicial advocates who fight for the development of international law, many are driven by a passion to ensure that respect for national sovereignty should not prevent the prosecution of political and military leaders who are guilty of war crimes or of crimes against humanity, especially genocide.

Sadly, the passion to bring to account people who have committed crimes against humanity seems not to be matched by a passion to understand the nature of their crimes. A practically driven moral impatience has contributed to the degradation of our understanding of the concept of a crime against humanity generally and of genocide in particular. Genocide challenges philosophy in many ways. One of those challenges is to obtain greater clarity about the concept of genocide itself. Without that clarity, the likelihood of bringing perpetrators to justice, let alone bringing genocide to an end, will be diminished. This chapter shows some of the ways in which philosophy can respond.

The distrust of discursive reason

The degradation noted above has been compounded, I think, by a deepening distrust of discursive reason in favor of storytelling amongst significant sections of the intelligentsia. That happened partly because the latter believe that discursive reason expresses and consolidates a Eurocentric bias in discussions of genocide, and because they suspect that the European tradition of discursive reason was itself part of the cultural condition that made the Holocaust and colonial genocides possible. The passion to prosecute and the suspicion of discursive reason generate impatience with the fine distinctions that need to be drawn if we are to understand the nature of genocide—especially (and here there is irony) if we are to sustain a concept of genocide that reaches legitimately from the Holocaust to some of the crimes against indigenous peoples.

At the end of the nineteenth century in Australia, children of mixed blood were often taken from their aboriginal parents. This practice continued until the late 1960s. These children came to be known as "the stolen generation." Because the practice continued for such a long period, it changed considerably over time. In 1997, some of the children and their parents told their stories to a Commission of Inquiry, which presented its findings to the Australian government. Entitled *Bringing Them Home*, the report concluded that genocide had been committed against the children and their parents, even though it was not claimed that even one person had been murdered because of a genocidal intention.[2] More, of course, needs to be said about why the report's allegation was even plausible. Later in this chapter, I offer a description of why and how the children were taken, which explains why I believe, with qualifications, that the report's conclusions about genocide are plausible.

Neither the stories in the report nor any others could settle the question whether the report stated correctly that genocide had been committed against the Aborigines when some of their children had been forcibly removed from their parents. This claim, of course, does not deny that our knowledge of genocide is enhanced by stories of the kind told in the 1997 report, by narrative history of the kind developed by the Holocaust historian Martin Gilbert, or by memoirs of the kind written by the Auschwitz survivor Primo Levi. The power of such works to disclose the distinctive moral character of their subject matter is inseparable from the style in which they are written. But the power of such narratives to facilitate understanding of genocide depends, I believe, on our capacity to locate them in a conceptual space that is to a significant degree formed by discursive reasoning of the kind that is characteristic of philosophy.

If that conceptual space continues to be constricted by legal and political impatience or by forms of anti-intellectualism that now seem to express themselves in an intoxication with storytelling, then we will be unable to answer seriously when people raise protests in a vein similar to the following one: "We've seen the corpses piled high, we've heard the terrible stories that tell how the victims suffered before they died. That is what matters morally. What difference does it make if you call the evil done to them mass murder, a crime against humanity, or genocide?"

To prevent misunderstanding, however, I must now emphasize that the discursive reason I have in mind does not seek merely to extract cognitive content from what it considers to be an emotive, literary form. To the contrary, discursive reason should often express itself in prose enlivened by the realization that to think of philosophy as a quest for understanding is not therefore to think of such reasoning as ideally free of feeling. Or, to put the point (I hope) less ambiguously: Discursive reasoning should (often) express itself in prose that is informed by the realization that the constitutive concepts of philosophical thought about ethics and politics—the concepts with which we assess whether we are thinking well or badly—cannot be idealized as concepts that define good and bad thinking for any rational being whatsoever, irrespective of whether they are affective beings and irrespective of the particular lives that people lead. Common in the Western philosophical tradition, such an idealization of "Reason" is the conception of reason that people have (rightly or wrongly) suspected of contributing not only to our failure to understand the nature of genocide but also to the causes of genocide.

Murder and genocide

Two discussions about genocide run parallel, seldom engaging with one another. The first is between philosophers, social scientists, historians, and political theorists. These participants take seriously the question whether there must be murder if there is to be genocide. For the key participants in the second discussion—mostly lawyers—that question has lapsed almost entirely. The United Nations 1948 Convention for the Prevention and Punishment of the Crime of Genocide, they say, makes the answer clear: there can be genocide even though no one has been killed. Participants in the first discussion, at least those worth listening to, know what the Convention says on the matter. Nevertheless they wonder whether the conception of genocide expressed in that document is adequate to the experiences that made humankind feel the need for such a concept in the first place.

Confronted by Nazi Germany's attack on the European Jews, Winston Churchill was moved in 1941 to speak of "a crime without a name." By 1944, the jurist Raphael Lemkin had coined the name *genocide* and had given an account of it in his often-cited work *Axis Rule in Occupied Europe*. Discussion about genocide did not spread and deepen, however, until the effects of postwar tribunals at Nuremberg, their European successor trials, and the 1961 trial of Adolf Eichmann in Jerusalem began to drive home the significance of the Holocaust. No other crime is so identified with the twentieth century. Were it not for the Holocaust, other instances of genocide—those in Armenia or Rwanda, for example—might have been seen as no different in kind from the crime of mass murder, whose frequency and scale also marked that century but which is as old as political association itself. After the Holocaust, many people were overwhelmed by a sense that they were confronted with a new crime, one that humanity needed to bring into the space of shared understanding even though, as some suspected, aspects of it would always defeat attempts to do so. Some people took the need for a new concept to mean that the crime it identified had not been committed before the Holocaust. Others believed that, although the crime of genocide was old, our moral response to it was new and required the crime to be identified by a new concept.

Lawyers also have reservations about the adequacy of the UN Convention. In general, however, those reservations refer to the Convention's limited application. Some would like to increase the groups—presently national, ethnical, racial, or religious—that can be identified as possible targets of genocide by adding, for example, political groups, disabled persons, or gay people. Proposals of that kind (or any other) to revise the Convention raise many questions. Of those questions, this one is the most basic: What will set the limit to what can rightly be called genocide?

Almost everyone agrees that the term *genocide* is often misused. When lawyers, philosophers, political theorists, and historians meet to consider that issue, what I find most interesting is the bemused incredulity shown by the lawyers when it is proposed that the concept's application should be constrained by its adequacy for grasping the morally overwhelming political experience of the Holocaust, an event that took place decades ago but which we have not yet understood well enough.

"To take murder out of genocide is to render it vacuous," said Inga Clendinnen, whose book *Reading the Holocaust* has been widely acclaimed.[3] She was trying to explain why she deplored allegations that the forcible removal of children of mixed blood from their Aboriginal parents sometimes constituted genocide. Like George Orwell, Clendinnen went on to say, she believes that "it is essential to keep such words mirror bright because ... we will surely continue to need them."[4]

Reasons to agree with Clendinnen are deeply embedded in our experience of genocide, and they partly explain why we are justified to believe that the Holocaust, Rwanda, and Armenia are paradigmatic for genocide. No course of studies on genocide could flatly declare those reasons to be misguided or even inconclusive. Certainly appeals to the UN Convention could not settle the matter. Any course of study on genocide must consider whether the Convention is more seriously inadequate than can be remedied by extending the list of groups who could justifiably be included among the victims of genocide. Nothing in this domain is finally established. The point, however, cuts both ways. Reflection on the deep disagreement since Nuremberg over what counts as genocide should convince anyone that the concept was never "mirror bright."

Clendinnen and those who agree with her appear to believe that the crimes committed against the Aborigines and the crimes committed against the Jews, the Gypsies, the Armenians, and the Tutsis cannot legitimately be brought under one concept if that concept requires those crimes to be morally commensurable. Argument about this matter is not, for the most part, about the facts. Nor is it, in any narrow sense, about the law. The argument is philosophical and moral, enlivened by the question whether a criminal category, whose paradigm is the Holocaust, could apply to what was done to the children and their parents, even during the worst periods of the absorption programs. How, Clendinnen and others have asked, can the policy of taking Aboriginal children of mixed blood from their parents be compared to the "Final Solution?" In the former case, they point out, not a single person was murdered with genocidal intent. Moreover, benighted and cruel though it often was, the policy was sometimes supported by people with unqualifiedly good intentions. The force of their challenge is strengthened by the fact that even at the time when the policy is most plausibly called genocidal, it was unthinkable to choose murder as means to advancing it.

A thought experiment can take us some way toward meeting that challenge. Should the forcible sterilization of a people for the purpose of eliminating them as a people count as genocide?[5] To someone who answers *yes*, the crime might not seem so different morally from the forcible, often brutal, removal of children from their parents when the purpose of those removals (infected with racist disdain for the Aborigines) was to destroy a people.[6] Like most thought experiments, this one does not deliver conclusive answers, but if one answers *yes* to the question above, one may then go on to judge that genocide was sometimes committed against the Aborigines during periods of the absorption programs. Then one may also conclude, perhaps with shock, that if genocide was sometimes committed against the Aborigines because of the crimes against the stolen generation, then crimes worse than genocide were committed against the Aborigines when they were massacred in large numbers, but not with genocidal intent. Grant that, for the sake of the argument. We should then conclude that when genocide involves murder, the latter compounds the crime, but murder is not essential to genocide.

Some people find that outcome too paradoxical to accept, because they are accustomed to think of genocide as amongst the worst, if not the worst, of the crimes against humanity. Geoffrey Robertson says that a crime against humanity is "a crime with a peculiar horror, deriving from the fact that fellow human beings are capable of committing it, thereby diminishing us all—such crimes are not only unforgettable, they are also unforgivable."[7] Many people, including many jurists, believe that we chose the expression "crimes against humanity" to mark out crimes that are so morally abhorrent that they should outrage every decent human being and that a concern to punish their perpetrators should weigh heavily on the conscience of every human being. Forcibly taking children from their aboriginal mothers is a horrible crime, but it is not the worst of crimes. Yet if such acts of removal can, in circumstances of the kind I described earlier, be genocidal, then genocide is not always one of the worst of the crimes against humanity.

The importance of intention and contempt

In a lecture honoring Raphael Lemkin at the United States Holocaust Memorial Museum, Michael Ignatieff lamented how often the term *genocide* is misused. " 'Genocide,' as a word," he argued, "turns on a genocidal intention. 'Genocide' has no clear meaning whatever unless the word can be connected to a clear intention to exterminate a human group, in whole or in part."[8]

Exterminate carries connotations of contempt that are absent from more neutral terms such as *destroy, kill*, or even *murder*. Connotations of contempt would almost always attach to descriptions that expressed the intention to sterilize a people. But although a people can be *destroyed* as surely when the culture that nourishes their identity is demolished as when they are murdered, that attempt would not naturally be described as *extermination*. Nor, I think, could any of the crimes against the stolen generations be described as an attempt to exterminate the Aborigines. Still, the brutality of those crimes was, as I noted earlier, almost always infected with racist contempt for the Aborigines, and it is contempt that first comes to mind when one thinks of the connotations carried by the word *exterminate*.

The significance of this point become more apparent when we remember that the intentional destruction of a people's culture and the imposition of the culture of the conqueror on them can be an expression of respect for them that goes hand in glove with an expression of contempt for their culture. Such might have been the case if de-Nazification had been imposed on European peoples who had been living under Nazi rule for a hundred years or more. Then the destruction of a culture that had partially formed the identity of conquered peoples, a culture that was evil through and through, would arguably have become a moral and political imperative and an expression of respect for what those European peoples had been before Nazism overtook them and for what they might again become.

The importance of contempt for our understanding of genocide—the importance it gives to our sense of what it means to destroy a group—emerges again if one considers the persecutions of a religious group, which, even when the persecutors intend to eliminate the entire group, can be (morally) different things, all of them crimes but not all of them genocide. Ignatieff includes religious groups as possible victims of genocide, as does the UN Convention, but we should be cautious in our agreement. Al-Quaeda's hatred of Jews, murderous and saturated with contempt, strikes me as genocidal because its natural expression in action would be the elimination of Jews from the face of the earth. Religious persecution, however, can be consistent with, even perhaps an expression of, respect for those who are persecuted. And when part of a religious group or even the whole of it is murdered because it is judged to be a threat to the "true faith," then this action seems closer conceptually to the murder of ideologically dangerous political opponents, as took place in the Soviet Union, than to the Holocaust or Rwanda.

Rightly, in my judgment, the Soviet mass murder was not called genocide, although not, it is true, for reasons that inspire admiration. Fearing that the charge of genocide would be applied to Stalin's devastating crimes against political groups, the Soviets bullied the UN into excluding political groups from its definition of genocide. Problematic though it was, the UN's decision not to include political groups did coincide with the integrity of the concept of genocide. We do not need a new name for a crime that is as old as political association itself, and we should not think of genocide as merely the most extreme offense against political liberalism.[9]

If my analysis is valid, the destruction of a people is not always genocide and not always a crime. When it is a crime, it may not be genocide because— as I believe is the case with most (even forced) assimilations—it may not be within the reach of the moral element in the concept which alone can make the crimes that fall under the concept commensurable with some of its horrific paradigms.[10]

The Holocaust as a paradigm of genocide

Two assumptions often inform the belief that there must be murder if there is to be genocide. The first is that the concept of genocide has an inexpugnable moral dimension. The second is that the Holocaust provides the paradigm for that dimension.

To see what is right and what is wrong in those assumptions, one should disentangle three aspects of the Holocaust. All of them are dramatic; they vie for attention. The first aspect makes the Holocaust a paradigm of genocide. The second aspect haunts our imagination, is distinctive to the Holocaust, but is not, I believe, essential to what makes the Holocaust a paradigm of genocide. The third aspect also haunts our imagination, but only in that it should incline someone to say that the Holocaust is mysterious, that it will forever defeat our attempts to understand it fully. If that inclination is sound, then the third aspect of the Holocaust makes it different from and arguably even worse than what makes it a paradigm of genocide. All three aspects provide reasons for saying that the Holocaust is unique. For that reason, they easily run together. When that happens, the Holocaust becomes a misleading paradigm of genocide.

Never, in my view, has contempt for a people been expressed with such ferocious purity (if "purity" is the word for something so evil) as during Nazi Germany's attempt to destroy the Jewish people. Never before the Holocaust, and thus far never after it, has there been such a relentless determination to wipe a people from the face of the earth. By itself, that is a reason why the Holocaust is unique. By itself, it is a reason why the Holocaust is a paradigm of genocide. This is the first of the aspects that I outlined above.

We come to the second aspect when we realize that reflection on the Holocaust as genocide reveals that there is more—and something that is perhaps even more striking—to be considered than what makes it a paradigm of genocide. The Nazis could have realized their intention to rid the earth of the Jews by sterilizing them, but the ways in which the Nazis thought of the Jews, the *radical* nature of their contempt for them, made exterminating murder the psychologically inevitable expression of that contempt. The Jews were murdered as though they were vermin, pollutants of the earth.

It is natural for one's attention to be caught by that fact. I shall call it the *spirit* in which the Nazis conceived and conducted their genocide against the Jews. It is also natural to take the mass murder inspired by that spirit as an essential feature of the Holocaust's paradigmatic character for genocide rather than as a contingent and particular feature of that instance of genocide. If so, one will be resistant to, perhaps offended by, the suggestion that the murder of the Jews only compounded—however immensely—a crime whose nature and paradigmatic status could have been realized without a single murder. We need to explore these points further to clarify the second aspect of the Holocaust, one that helps to explain why that event haunts imagination so profoundly.

The spirit in which genocidal policies are prosecuted has not been much (if at all) discussed in attempts to disentangle our reason for believing that the Holocaust is a paradigm of genocide. Ignatieff speaks of a genocidal *intention*. The UN Convention speaks of motives and also of intentions. In the case of the Nazi genocide against the Jews, I would make the following distinctions: The Nazis' *intention* was to eliminate the Jews. Racism was their *motive*. The *spirit* in which they implemented their intention, and which gave their racism its character, was shown in their repeated allegation that Jews polluted the earth and in the propaganda—written, oral, and visual— that condemned them accordingly. Such distinctions, I readily acknowledge, may easily create confusion. They invite elaboration into further fine distinctions that can make it difficult to see the forest from the trees.

The concepts of *motive* and *intention* already create headaches for lawyers. Could an even more elusive concept—the *spirit* in which deeds are done—be identified in such a way that law could be formulated with regard to it? I leave that question to the lawyers. A negative answer, however, should not obscure the fact that it is the spirit in which the Nazis murdered the Jews— not just the mass killing itself—that haunts our moral and political imaginations. More often than not, when we have tried to understand why we have been haunted by the Holocaust, we have looked for an answer in what makes that event a paradigm of genocide. For reasons I have been trying to delineate, we did not—and could not—find it there.

There is yet a further dimension to this second aspect of the Holocaust. Much of what I have said about the Holocaust can apply to Rwanda, where the Hutus murdered the Tutsis "like cockroaches," but there is something further about the spirit of the Nazis' genocide against the Jews that distinguishes the Holocaust even from the genocide in Rwanda. The Nazis' "Final Solution" was not a measure—not even a deranged measure—taken to address what could seriously be called a social or political *problem*. When the mere existence of a people, irregardless of actual behavior, is supposed to constitute a problem, then we are dealing with a degenerate application of the concept of a problem. Antisemitic stereotypes did, of course, cast the Jews as a problem—identifying them as Bolsheviks, capitalists, and as threats to the racial purity of the German people. But those stereotypes did not express genuinely mistaken beliefs about the Jews which would explain the hatred of them. The stereotypes rationalized the hatred; they did not cause it.

It was the cool, radical contempt for the very existence of the Jewish people that has made the Holocaust so chilling to many who have studied it. The way in which the genocidal intention formed in the heart of European civilization has made it impossible to think of the Holocaust as merely the project of gangsters who had seized power temporarily and were hell bent on mass murder. For the leaders of the Third Reich, ridding the earth of Jews became a civic ideal. Although that goal was implemented under the cover of the Second World War, by no means was it limited to wartime. The "Final Solution" was a terrible intimation of a postwar world in which the death camps would continue. Had Nazi Germany won the war, the attempt to annihilate the Jews totally would have continued in peace time, not in the spirit of finishing business that had started in wartime and whose nature was essentially shaped by wartime conditions but as a political ideal of the postwar Reich.

To sum up this part of my argument concerning the first two of the three aspects of the Holocaust that I believe should be distinguished from one another: The Holocaust, I argue, is a paradigm of genocide because of the relentless single-mindedness with which the Nazis pursued their intention to rid the world of Jews. That same single-mindedness could have shown itself in a program of sterilization. Such a program would still count as a paradigm of genocide, and if it were conducted with the same determination that the Nazis actually showed in their attempt to rid the earth of the Jews, then it should count as *the* paradigm of genocide for anyone who believes that the Holocaust is *the* paradigm of it. We are tempted to think that murder is essential to genocide, because we mistakenly believe that murder is necessary to anything that counts as one of its paradigms. In the case of the Holocaust, we mistakenly think that murder is essential to its paradigmatic character as genocide because the spirit in which the Nazis pursued their genocidal intention, the radical contempt they had for the Jews as a people, made murder the psychologically inevitable expression of that intention. Because of the spirit with which the Nazis pursued their genocide of the Jews, we mistake the psychological inevitability of contempt-driven mass murder for what is necessary to the sober application of the concept of genocide.

Turning to the third aspect of the Holocaust that is important for my analysis, nothing that I have said thus far gives one a reason to speak of the Holocaust as mysterious, outside of history, and forever destined to defeat our attempts to understand it. Are there such reasons? There are, I believe, but it remains unclear whether they fully justify the claim that the Holocaust is mysterious and beyond understanding. These reasons almost always emerge from reflection on death camps such as Auschwitz-Birkenau and Treblinka and not from the extensive killing done by Nazi squadrons (*Einsatzgruppen*) who shot hundreds of thousand of Jews to death in Eastern Europe. In the death camps, genocide became not only horrifically efficient but also transformed, I believe, into something worse than even the term *genocide* connotes. For this crime or, perhaps better, for this *evil*, there neither are nor can be adequate criminal categories. Not even *genocide* can denote it sufficiently.

Evil and the Holocaust

To understand why people have claimed that the Holocaust is mysterious, and why I have claimed that an aspect can never adequately be captured by criminal categories, it is important to take seriously the claim that *evil* is a term that marks out a distinctive and irreducible moral category, one not restricted simply to actions or events that we take to be especially horrible. Some people doubt that the concept of evil should have a distinctive place among our moral categories, and some are hostile to any suggestion that evil should have that status because they take the concept to express a simpleminded Manichean distinction between "good" and "evil" and a disposition to demonize wrongdoers. It is beyond the scope of this chapter to argue why I believe they are mistaken. Clearly, however, the moral sensitivity about the Holocaust that characterizes many of these skeptics—Clendinnen among them—shows that it is neither want of moral sensibility nor lack of imaginative acquaintance with some of the most terrible deeds human beings have committed that makes them doubt the fact that the concept of evil marks a distinctive form of moral horror.

The concept of evil that I believe is essential for the plausibility of the reasons for thinking that the Holocaust is mysterious depends on a conception of the inalienable preciousness of each human being.[11] In some religious traditions, this idea is expressed in the idea that every human being is sacred. One of the best known secular expressions of the idea comes from Immanuel Kant, who said that one must never treat other persons as means to an end but always as ends in themselves. If one has such a conception of human life, then one will, of course, think of all genocide and much else as evil, but one does not need such a concept to characterize fully the nature of genocide, not even in its paradigmatic manifestation in the Holocaust.

Many people who have focused on the "industrialization of death" as marking out what is distinctive about the death camps have found in that notion a clue to the distinctive moral horror of the Holocaust. My claim is that the Holocaust has many distinctively horrible moral aspects. Considered merely as a horribly efficient method of killing, the "industrialization of death" does not take us to an understanding of the distinctively moral elements of genocide, let alone to what prompts people to speak of the mystery of the Holocaust. From another perspective, however, the horrific bureaucratic efficiency of the death camps looks like an unprecedented assault on the preciousness of human beings. From that perspective, appeals to mystery need not be attempts to block explanations. They may record a kind of incredulous awe. Such awe may be silent on the question of whether the concept of evil characterizes only the assault on the preciousness of human beings or whether it also characterizes the motives or intentions of those who committed those deeds.[12]

Suppose I am right about the death camps and that reflection on them—not the mass shootings carried out by the *Einsatzgruppen*—is the primary reason why people have been inclined to speak of the mystery of the Holocaust. We should then conclude that, while the mass murder perpetrated in the death camps is essential to our sense of one of the most striking and disturbing aspects of the Holocaust, it remains the case that this particular aspect of the Holocaust, which was arguably different from and even worse than genocide, should not enter into an account of what is definitive of genocide.

In *Reading the Holocaust*, Clendinnen asked, "Is the guilt attaching to the intention to destroy a whole people ... different in kind from the intention to kill an equal number of individuals? Does the crime of 'genocide' inhabit a moral category of its own?"[13] Clendinnen did not go on to answer these questions, and they remain important. Many people have asked them as they contemplate the unnerving, even distasteful distance between the abstract nature of the concept of genocide, the many distinctions needed to delineate its structure, and the horrific details of the crimes to which it has been applied.

Although the concept of genocide has an inexpugnable moral element, it would be a mistake to conclude that it is intended to mark out a special moral category. Genocide marks out not a distinctive moral offense but a crime. Like all crimes, it is an offense not only against its victims but also against the legal constituency whose laws it has broken. That is one reason why crimes are prosecuted even when their victims are prepared to forgive.

Why is genocide best understood as a crime against *humanity* and not just as a crime against, for example, the Jews, the Gypsies, the Armenians, or the Tutsis? The reason is not, as many people—including jurists—appear to believe, because genocide is especially inhumane. To my mind, Hannah Arendt gave the most incisive account of why genocide should be a crime against humanity. She amplified a remark by the French prosecutor at the Nuremberg Trials who contended that the crimes of the Nazis against the Jews and Gypsies were crimes against humanity because they offended against "the human status" rather than because they were particularly inhumane. Arendt added that we should think of genocide as "an attack upon human diversity as such, upon a characteristic of the human status, without which the very words 'mankind' or 'humanity' would be devoid of meaning."[14] In their failure, so radical in its nature, to acknowledge a common humanity with their victims, in their arrogant assumption that they were entitled to decide which peoples are fit to inhabit the earth, the perpetrators of genocide offend against their victims as individuals and as members of the targeted group. But their crime is also against the constituency of humankind as that is represented in the community of nations. Admittedly, the sense in which there is such a community is still too thin, and so too is the sense in which something can be a crime against humankind. The idea of the human community, however, is not meaningless. The concept of a crime against humanity expresses the belief that those who commit this crime offend the constitution of humanity itself—humanity as we mean it when we say that justice will only be served when we acknowledge a common humanity with all the peoples of the earth.

The Nuremberg Trials and their aftermath encouraged us to bring together and to show to be consistent things that had often been thought necessarily to be in conflict. In calling genocide a crime against humanity, we acknowledge both our need for roots, for local identity, and the imperative that such a need must be respected and defended in the international law of the community of nations. More strongly, if we accept Arendt's account of genocide and call genocide a crime against humanity, we insist that the need for local identity, which shows itself in the diversity of cultures and nations, is part of the very concept of humanity to which we appeal in speaking about the universal principles of justice embodied in international laws on human rights. When she criticized the Israeli government's insistence that Eichmann should be tried by a Jewish court, by Jewish judges in a Jewish state, Arendt made clear how the principle of universality embodied in the concept of crimes against humanity should be reconciled with the many-faceted acknowledgment that the targeted group was a particular people. Eichmann, she said, should be charged with crimes against humanity perpetrated on the body of the Jewish people and tried in a court representing humankind. [15]

Trauma and understanding

I hope that I have explained why, when we bring evidently repugnant crimes under the concept of genocide and therefore under the concept of a crime against humanity, we can reveal a further and perhaps a deeper dimension of their gravity. Although the paradigms of genocide—the Holocaust, Armenia, and Rwanda—are the gravest of the crimes against humanity, I hope, too, that I have explained why some instances of genocide do not fit that description. Were the concepts of genocide and of a crime against humanity not developed, we would never have dreamt of bringing under the same judicial/moral category the crimes of the Holocaust or Rwanda and the crimes against the stolen generations. But they were developed to record, at least in part, a newly developed belief that crimes—be they murder, rape, kidnapping, or, in certain circumstances, the forcible removal of children from their parents—assume a different kind of gravity when they are committed with racist contempt for their victims and with the intention that they should cease to exist as a people.

Crimes that appear relatively insignificant when measured against morally terrible ones can rightly be made to appear more serious than they would be if they were not seen in the light of the concept of genocide. There are, of course, great moral differences between genocide when it is compounded by mass murder and genocide when there is not a single murder. But crimes that are morally very different may nonetheless be properly placed under the same concept. The seriousness of the allegation that genocide was sometimes committed against the stolen generations resides in the fact that if the allegation is true, then some of the crimes against the Aborigines were offenses against the human status, against humanity itself. Accepting that there can be genocide without mass killing, however, does not demean the Holocaust, as some people have thought. To the contrary, such acceptance will enable us to grasp better what it is about the Holocaust that we try to understand when we call it genocide.

Whenever genocide is committed, other crimes are committed as well. Sometimes there will be murder. In the case of the stolen generations, there was kidnapping, rape, and forced labor. The evil in these serious crimes is visible to anyone who looks on them with the eyes of humanity. Beside them, the aspect of genocide that makes it a crime against humanity may look morally bloodless. Surely, it is natural to protest, there is more to be said morally. There is more to be said, but it does not find expression when one tries to explain why genocide should be a crime against humanity rather than only a crime against a targeted group. Or, perhaps better, it shows itself there only indirectly.

Survivors of genocidal mass murder who know of the genocidal intentions of their persecutors suffer trauma deeper in its nature than the trauma of those who have escaped only mass murder. Survivors of genocide and the contempt intrinsic to it suffer terrible natural harm, such as pain and fear, and terrible evils, such as murder, rape, and torture. In addition, they suffer the distinctive evil of being treated as pollutants of the earth, as vermin, or in other ways as undeserving of a place in the world. They also suffer the knowledge that their dead loved ones were the victims of this same contempt. These conditions show that the survivors of genocide must cope with a distinctive trauma.

Great artistry is needed to express the ways in which this trauma lacerates the soul. Justice and compassion therefore require us to be patient in our efforts to understand the distinctive evil suffered by the victims of genocide, and to be patient in the unraveling of the distinctions that will establish and protect the space in which such understanding may grow. It is a false sense of justice, false compassion, and, in the end, a false sense of the practical that would brush aside such efforts for the sake of quick prosecutions.

Humankind understands itself, in part, when it gives the right names to the crimes it has committed.

Notes

1. Geoffrey Robertson, *Crimes against Humanity: The Struggle for Global Justice* (London: Penguin Books, 2002).
2. See *Bringing Them Home: Report of the National Inquiry into the Separation of Aboriginal and Torres Strait Island Children from Their Families* (Sydney: Human Rights and Equal Opportunity Commission, 1997), p. 275.
3. Inga Clendinnen, *The Australian's Review of Books*, May 2003.
4. Ibid.
5. I first suggested this thought experiment in "Genocide and the Stolen Generation," in Raimond Gaita, *A Common Humanity: Thinking about Love and Truth and Justice* (New York: Routledge, 2000).
6. My description applies only to Western Australia during the 1930s, when it was assumed that the full-blooded Aborigines were destined for extinction and that the Aborigines of mixed blood would disappear by intermarrying with lower class whites.
7. Robertson, *Crimes against Humanity*, p. xxv.
8. Michael Ignatieff, "The Legacy of Raphael Lemkin," a lecture delivered at the United States Holocaust Memorial Museum in Washington, DC, in December 2001. See http://www.ushmm.org/conscience/events/Ignatieff.php
9. Serbian talk of "ethnic cleansing" made people speak in the same breath of Serbian crimes and those of the Nazis. The Serbs, however, were principally concerned to expel those whom they deemed to be foreigners—Croats and Muslims—from territories that they claimed as their own. To be sure, when they drove them from those territories, the Serbs did so with a fury fuelled by a complex history of national hatred, past fighting, and atrocities. Probably many Serbian soldiers killed Croats and Muslims in a spirit of ridding the world of "vermin," but when that thought surfaced, it was a consequence of the war rather than one of its causes and internal to the expression of its aims.
10. *Ethnocide* rather than *cultural genocide* is, I believe, the best name for this action when it is properly identified as a crime.
11. For further development of these points, see Raimond Gaita, *Good and Evil: An Absolute Conception*, 2nd edn (New York: Routledge, 2004) and Gaita, *A Common Humanity*.
12. The concept of evil that I have been sketching is consistent with the belief that evil deeds are always explicable by appeal to the ordinary range of human motives—greed, cruelty, cowardice, jingoism, corrupted sense of duty, to name only a few. For further discussion of these matters, see Gaita, *A Common Humanity*, pp. 40–9.
13. Clendinnen, *Reading the Holocaust*, p. 158.
14. Hannah Arendt, *Eichmann in Jerusalem: A Report on the Banality of Evil* (New York: Viking Press, 1963), pp. 268–99.
15. Ibid., p. 261.

14
Genocide and Crimes against Humanity

Norman Geras

In this chapter I consider in what sense acts characterized as being crimes against humanity can be reckoned to be, indeed, against *humanity*. The term *crimes against humanity* is now part of contemporary usage. Designating a class of offense under international law, it has also entered into moral and political discourse more generally. Its range and content are therefore of some interest. Since the notion of a crime that is against humanity is not transparent, it is worth inquiring whether any clear and useful meaning can be given to it.

In the literature on this topic, there are a dozen or more ideas associated with the thesis that, in harming their immediate and their indirect victims, certain types of offense represent an injury as well to humanity. I review all those ideas that I perceive as sufficiently different from one another to merit separate examination. Some of them I reject as putative candidates for giving us the core of the concept of crimes against humanity. Others I accept as being usefully part of the concept, but regard as secondary all the same. I fix on two ideas as primary in disclosing those features *in virtue of which* an act might be persuasively construed as a crime that is against "humanity."

There is a widely noted distinction I make use of in separating into two broad groups the ideas to be considered here regarding why crimes against humanity are properly thought to be such. "Humanity" might refer to "the human race or mankind as a whole." Or it might refer to "a certain quality of behavior" or "human sentiment"—covering some or all of kindness, benevolence, compassion, philanthropy and, indeed, humaneness.[1] I start with three ideas that strike me as inadequate in giving us a persuasive meaning for the claim that certain types of act constitute crimes against *humanity*.

Preliminary arguments

The first of these is that crimes against humanity might be defined simply by being, in the language of Article 6(c) of the Nuremberg Charter, "inhumane acts"—offenses, in other words, against humaneness. This fails by not setting a high enough threshold. Crimes against humanity will be inhumane, to be sure, but inhumane acts are far from all being serious enough that they could, as a category, be sensibly accounted criminal offenses under international law. For there is a common usage in which not only acts of extreme cruelty or acts that cause devastating harm, but also acts simply of a notable degree of unkindness or mean-spiritedness, are spoken of as inhumane. Hannah Arendt evidently had in mind a weak meaning of the expression "inhumane acts" when she described its use in the Nuremberg Charter as "certainly the understatement of the century"—"as though the Nazis had simply been lacking in human kindness."[2] I return to this issue. If we are to look for a convincing sense of the concept of crimes against humanity on the side of our distinction where such crimes are seen as acts violating a body of sentiment or principle to do with the acceptable treatment of human beings, then we need some threshold of seriousness that the bare word *inhumane* does not supply.

Two other understandings of the concept that fail lie on the side of the distinction in which *humanity* is taken as referring to humankind—the human species or global community. Geoffrey Robertson has suggested the following as an interpretation of why crimes against humanity are that. It is "because the very fact that a fellow human being could conceive and commit them diminishes every member of the human race."[3] There is a parallel difficulty here to the one just discussed with respect to "inhumane acts": namely, that this is an understanding of crimes against humanity that would include too much of an insufficiently serious kind. What counts as diminishing everyone in a certain category is so loose an idea that it is hard to see how diminishing them could be reckoned, merely in itself, to be a criminal act. A person might well claim to be diminished when members of a collectivity she belongs to publicly and maliciously disparage certain other sorts of people, as in racial or ethnic abuse. To classify this as a crime against that person—not, note, against the people disparaged, but against the putatively diminished co-member of the collectivity to which the disparagers belong—would extend the reach of the law to absurd and frightening lengths.

Also problematic is the hypothesis that—assuming *humanity* to refer now to the comity of nations or the international community—what makes the acts we are interested in crimes against humanity is that they represent a threat to "the peace and security of mankind" or the peace of the world.[4] There is a twofold problem with this hypothesis. Let us take as an example of a crime against humanity the crime of genocide. (Doing so, I know, presupposes that we already have a rough and ready notion about at least some of what the concept of crimes against humanity should cover. But any definition of the concept that did not accommodate genocide would not be worth our time.) First, it is not necessarily true that any genocide, just as such, threatens the world's peace and security. Localized within a particular national territory and left to run its course there without intervention by external forces, it might threaten no one beyond the targeted group. Second, in some circumstances it could even be that intervention by outside forces would jeopardize international peace more seriously than nonintervention would.

I move on to two ideas that, as a kind of shorthand, I will call half right, though it might be more accurate to say that they are right but secondary. What I mean is that both ideas can reasonably be seen as forming part of a rounded concept of crimes against humanity, but neither is primary to explaining why some acts are justifiably to be treated as *being* crimes against humanity. I explain in what follows.

The first of these two half-right ideas is that it is humankind that is the relevant sovereignty where such acts are concerned, humankind the authority ruling them to be illegal and, consequently, flouted by them. The idea of humankind-as-sovereign seems to have been implicit in the legal thinking at Nuremberg. Geoffrey Best says of the nations that took it on themselves to bring the leading Nazi figures to trial at Nuremberg that they were "representatives simply of the human race."[5] And the Chief Prosecutor for the United Kingdom at Nuremberg, Sir Hartley Shawcross, gave expression to the same assumption in declaring that if "dictators and tyrants ... debase the sanctity of man in their own country they act at their peril, for they affront the international law of mankind."[6] In another of the postwar trials, the *Einsatzgruppen* case conducted under Control Council Law No. 10, a US military tribunal stated similarly that the defendants were being tried "because they are accused of having offended against society itself, and society, as represented by international law, has summoned them for explanation"; their crimes, it said, were "[n]ot crimes against any specified country, but against humanity. Humanity is the sovereignty which has been offended."[7]

The thesis is clear enough and in its way unobjectionable. Still, the reason I call the humanity-as-sovereign notion secondary and therefore merely half right is that we are in a position to say of any given crime against humanity that humanity is the sovereignty it falls foul of, only once the class of act it applies to has been defined and criminalized as being an offense in this category. That humanity is the sovereignty that such acts fall foul of cannot itself be the reason for so defining and criminalizing them—a claim that would be circular—it is the consequence of so defining and criminalizing them. The prevention and punishment of crimes against humanity are the business of all nations—or at least that is now the regulative ideal. But they are so because they have come to be treated as offenses against humanity *to be* prevented and punished. In virtue of what, though, have they been treated as offenses against humanity?

A similar critical objection applies to the other half-right idea. Crimes against humanity, it is often said, are acts that "shock" the conscience of mankind. Or they "outrage" or "offend" the conscience, or the moral judgment, of mankind. Or they are "repugnant in the public conscience" or

"intolerable from the point of view of the entire international community";
or they represent a challenge to the "imperatives," or the "law," or the
"code" of "universal conscience." I take these usages together with other
themes in the literature that are closely related to them: such as that crimes
against humanity are acts that shame everyone, or that they strike at "the
self-respect of the human race"; or that they violate "all recognized values of
humanity," or "universal moral values," or humankind's "highest values."[8]

Yet, if crimes against humanity do indeed shock the conscience of
humankind, or shame us all, or cut against our most important values, none
of these consequences of them could alone suffice to justify regarding all
human beings as their victims. That we are shocked or shamed or offended
in our conscience or our values by acts done to others, even though these
acts may be crimes, and awful crimes, against *them*, is not a demanding
enough criterion as to what may be accounted a criminal act against *us*. For
shock, shame, and moral offense as such do not establish severity of harm. It
may be that it is not humanity-as-victim that is the operative notion here,
but humanity-as-sovereign once more: as a global community we are
shocked, shamed, or offended by certain kinds of act and, being so, we assert
our authority with regard to them, resolve to treat them as criminal and
subject to punishment. But then the question has to be addressed, in virtue
of what about such acts are human beings so shocked, shamed, or offended?
What is it about such acts that carries them across the threshold to where our
most important values are located? Unless we have an answer to these questions, underpinning the shocked conscience of humanity, conscience could
come to take in—or, rather, rule out—far too much under the heading of
crimes against humanity. It could come to rule out swearing in public or
mere outrages of fashion. Conscience, for present purposes, needs more than
intersubjectivity as its basis.

Inhuman acts

I turn now to trying to identify the core meaning of the concept of crimes
against humanity. This next theme has already been anticipated and it
should be seen, I argue, as one of two fundamental, and linked, components
in the understanding of why crimes against humanity are properly so
described. It is that crimes against humanity are inhumane acts, but inhumane acts of and beyond a certain level of seriousness. Scattered abundantly
through the literature, the terminology in which this level of seriousness is
expressed displays a certain variety, but it is a variety that is familiar. Crimes
against humanity are *grave* crimes. They are "atrocious acts," "the most
atrocious offences," "the worst atrocities imaginable"; acts "of unforgivable
brutality," set apart in their "wickedness," intolerable by their "savagery."
They are acts "so serious," "so cruel or inhuman," "so heinous." They are
"odious," "peculiarly horrific," "abhorrent," "unspeakable."[9] Availing myself

of a nuance I think there is in English between *inhumane* (which can range from unkind or moderately harsh, on one side, to extremely severe and worse than that, on the other) and *inhuman* (which is generally applied only over the more severe segment of this range), I reformulate the idea under consideration to read that crimes against humanity are inhumane acts of and beyond a certain threshold of gravity or seriousness, or they are for short *inhuman acts*.

An obvious problem with the idea so formulated is going to be that of specifying the relevant threshold with any great degree of precision. From one point of view we need not be troubled by this. In matters of social, political, and moral differentiation precision of a mathematical kind is often not attainable, even when it is desirable. The philosophical concept of crimes against humanity may be allowed some rough edges; it may be allowed to provide a merely broad and general guideline, though of course the application of the concept in law will have to operate with definitions of the actual acts forbidden that are as precise as can be. However, the permissibility of some roughness notwithstanding, if a threshold of relative gravity is to yield even such a rough boundary, we will need some way of specifying the nature of this boundary, of explicating at least the type of seriousness involved and also something of the degree. I advert to what I see as the second fundamental component in explaining why crimes against humanity are that.

It is an idea usually traced back to the French Chief Prosecutor at Nuremberg, M. François de Menthon, when he spoke of "crimes against [the] human status (*la condition humaine*)"—or, as he also referred to this, "status as a human being." His suggestion has been widely taken up, even if it is not always articulated in an identical way. In the relevant literature, crimes against humanity are said to be crimes against: the human status or condition; the human person or personality; the nature or the essence of mankind; the essential attributes or essential rights of human beings.

A difficulty in attempting to pin this theme down may be seen in the variant of it according to which crimes against humanity attack the human dignity of their victims. It is the same difficulty as we encountered with the "inhumane acts" (without more ado) characterization. A person's human dignity can be violated by anything from assaults that cause the most abject suffering and degradation to, for example, the ingratitude and pettiness shown toward King Lear by his daughters Goneril and Regan. Richard Vernon generalizes the point to cast doubt on the whole conception of crimes against humanity as acts directed against the human status of their victims. It is, he feels, too indiscriminating: In light of Kant's second formulation of the categorical imperative, it could be applied to wrongdoing in general.[10] However, if we take the notion of an offense against the human status together with the previous point about relative seriousness, I think Vernon's worry can be met. We can hold that for an act to be considered a crime against humanity in the sense of its being a crime against the human status of its victims, it must be harmful to their fundamental interests as human beings. It must be harmful to their interests as human beings *just as such*, causing or threatening severe, or (as frequently) irreversible, damage to their well-being and their lives. Genocide and torture are paradigmatic in this respect. On the other hand, taking some small-scale advantage of an acquaintance without her knowledge— say, by introducing a not too serious kind of contraband into her luggage before she travels abroad, to be retrieved at her destination by someone in cahoots with you—would obviously not make the cut, even though it treats your traveler-acquaintance merely as a means. On this account of things, the specification of the threshold of moral gravity will more or less map on to a definition of basic human rights, conceived according to the interest theory of rights. I commend it as a way of understanding the core meaning of the concept of crimes against humanity. They are crimes against the human status, taking the latter idea together with the requirement of a threshold of seriousness, and interpreting the two ideas, taken together, in the terms just indicated: of the fundamental interests of human beings just as such, across all the cultural and other specificities that make individual human beings as different from one another as they are.

I want, however, to explain why I reject two particular versions of the "crimes against the human status" thesis. There is a view that seeks to limit the scope of "crimes against the human status" to genocidal acts, or at least to acts of genocidal potentiality, inasmuch as they are openly discriminatory, targeting people simply because of their membership in some prejudicially regarded group. This was a view espoused by Hannah Arendt, and it seems also to be common amongst French scholars. According to it, crimes against humanity are acts violating the human status of their victims; but only acts that potentially threaten the diversity of humankind by attacking individuals because of the particular category—ethnic, national, religious, political— they fall into are to be seen as acts violating the human status of their victims. These are acts, in other words, that go beyond "gratuitous brutality" and "atrocities," beyond "cruelty," "degradation," and "torture" (I decline to insert the word "mere" anywhere here), and one escapes the "sentimental dilution of crimes against humanity in 'general inhumanity.' "[11] The view is misconceived. It effectively equates crimes against humanity with genocidal or tendentially genocidal acts. But if such acts do indeed attack the human status of their victims by punishing them for some feature of their social identity—a crucial aspect of what for any human being he or she is— then so does torture, by traumatizing its victims (often, where it does not kill them, traumatizing them permanently) in the sense and security of their personal identity—an equally crucial aspect of what for any human being he or she is. And so can mutilation and other forms of extreme violence; and so can prolonged, arbitrary imprisonment—nondiscriminatory in the pertinent sense here as any of these things may be. Just as an act's inhumaneness (without more ado) may be necessary, but is not sufficient, for including it in the category of crimes against humanity, so an act's potentially genocidal character is sufficient, but not necessary, for doing this; not at any rate according to the conception that crimes against humanity are acts attacking the human status of their victims.

I am also skeptical of the suggestion that crimes against humanity threaten humankind, where this is understood to mean not simply threatening other human beings or human groups, but threatening the very existence of the species. I see the hint of such a meaning in Arendt's claim, with reference to the "extermination of whole ethnic groups," that "mankind in its entirety might have been grievously hurt and endangered." Not only hurt; endangered also. It is suggested more unambiguously by Alain Finkielkraut's reading of the judgment at Nuremberg to signify that "humanity *itself* is mortal," "humanity itself can die."[12] We should not be too short with these intimations of the end. The menace represented to the world by individuals and groups with a genocidal cast of mind, when possessed of state power or wide ideological influence, is not something to be shrugged off lightly. It is certainly possible to envisage circumstances in which potent means of destruction in the hands of such people could lead to a global catastrophe. By and large, however, even in the teeth of the most rampant genocide the heavens do not fall; they do not even darken; in turn, fortunately and unfortunately. Judged on a straightforward empirical basis, it seems that we are able as a species to survive successive genocides, the loss or the huge depletion of entire peoples, and just carry on.

Terrorizing humanity

Now, is humanity as a whole the victim of the crimes we classify as crimes against humanity? This is what is said from time to time, though without anything much in the way of elaboration. It is said that crimes against humanity attack all of humankind;[13] that they "are crimes committed not only against their immediate victims, but also against humanity."[14] The point was articulated in the judgment of the International Criminal Tribunal for the former Yugoslavia (ICTY) in the Erdemovic case:

> Crimes against humanity are serious acts of violence which harm human beings by striking what is most essential to them: their lives, liberty, physical welfare, health, and/or dignity. They are inhumane acts that by their extent and gravity go beyond the limits tolerable to the international community. ... But crimes against humanity also transcend the individual because when the individual is assaulted, humanity comes under attack and is negated. It is therefore the concept of humanity as victim which essentially characterizes crimes against humanity.[15]

In what sense, or in what way, are all human beings the victims of crimes against humanity? I assume that it is not simply by a semantic slippage: Such that humanity in the sense of *all of humankind* is to be accounted the victim of these crimes because humanity in the sense of the *human status of the direct victims* "comes under attack and is negated." Eve Garrard has suggested that everyone is harmed by the crimes against others that we call crimes against humanity. But she does not say what precisely the harm is. Beyond a general reference to our being "implicated" in the suffering of fellow human beings, she says only that the harms done to some "are done in some sense to us all."[16] In what sense? Earlier I have given reasons for rejecting the "shaming" and "diminishing" routes to the conclusion that all of humanity might be seen as victims of crimes against humanity. It is not necessarily that, as members of the same species, we are *not* all shamed and diminished by those crimes. But I doubt that someone's being shamed or diminished by acts committed against others could suffice to render those acts criminal offenses against them.

Can any more persuasive content be given to the notion of a universal harm flowing from the especially egregious offenses that are crimes against humanity—a harm sufficient to support the claim that all of humankind are the victims of them? I believe there is something more persuasive here, though I shall leave the matter open whether it is persuasive enough, explaining why I think it acceptable in the context to do this. The best brief encapsulation of it I can suggest is that crimes against humanity terrorize us all. They terrorize not just those they put under immediate attack, or those closely threatened by or in the vicinity of such attack, but human beings in general. I have not found this claim stated in so many words anywhere in the literature I am familiar with. But there are expressions of something close to it. Thus, there is the following gloss by Geoffrey Robertson on the reference in the Preamble to the Rome Statute to "grave crimes [that] threaten the ... well-being of the world." Robertson says: "this is true, in the sense that our psychological well-being suffers from the sight of atrocities by fellow human beings."[17]

In support of the idea that crimes against humanity terrorize—or intimidate—us all, I offer these few indicative but inconclusive reflections. First, and starting from my own experience, I have personally known several people who were unable to watch fictionalized scenes of great violence or cruelty on film. One of them was unable to remain in the cinema when it merely seemed that such a scene might be in prospect. Second, and generalizing, this is just one manifestation of a much more common human reaction: the reaction of avoidance, and its corresponding mechanisms of psychological denial, displayed by so many in the face of atrocity.[18] People, widely, are not only terrified of being the direct victims of atrocity, but also frightened of being too closely confronted with images of, or detailed information about, it. Third, it is surely the case that age-old religious fears, the visions of hell and damnation in particular, have been nourished by the actual forms of barbarity human beings have practiced on one another throughout recorded history. Fourth, some of the stuff of ordinary nightmares too, of the fear that even people in benign circumstances sometimes wake up from, is probably fed by what they know of extreme violation from their waking lives. To round off on this point, our coming, by whatever means, upon stories of horrific violence is for many of us—even resolutely secular and awake, and far from any obvious danger to ourselves—a searing experience, whether only briefly so or more lingeringly.

These observations may suffice to lend substance to Robertson's claim that our psychological well-being suffers when human beings commit atrocities against one another. If it may be jejune to project a world entirely free of the forms of violation that are under discussion, it seems reasonable to hypothesize the possibility of one in which they had been much reduced, a world to which atrocity had become more marginal; and to speculate on the beneficial effects this might have on the mental and emotional well-being of members of our species. That we are all terrorized or intimidated by crimes against humanity provides a more convincing basis, I contend, for the idea of humanity as the victim of these crimes than do the hypotheses about "shaming" and "diminishing."

It may not be a convincing enough basis even so. An initial objection to it could be that generalizing from the common experience of vicarious fear to an altogether universal conclusion is unwarranted. For it is to be doubted that all human beings *are* in fact terrorized or intimidated by those acts we now treat as crimes against humanity. Whether through being more psychologically robust, or less imaginatively empathetic, or more confident in the sense of their own personal security, some people may not be made fearful for themselves at all by learning of such crimes. We could try to meet this objection by just taking the generalization to apply widely enough. That is to say, it might be true of enough people that they are terrorized or intimidated by learning of such crimes, to justify regarding humanity as a whole as the collective victim of them. It would be comparable to saying that the Jewish people were collectively victims of the Nazi genocide, and so were the Armenian people of the Turkish genocide, and the Tutsis of the Rwandan genocide, even if there were some amongst each of these peoples who as individuals remained unharmed. But there is a further possible objection. Is the harm involved, the harm of people being made afraid on learning of some terrible crime against others, severe enough to justify regarding that crime as also a crime against *them*? Should the psychological effects of it count as a crime against humanity-at-large? Are its effects, even amongst those who are made afraid by it, serious enough to merit being treated as a punishable crime? I am unsure how to arrive at a general answer to this question. Given the variable intensity of different individual reactions, there may not be a general answer. It seems at least arguable that there could be enough of a terrorizing effect across a wide enough section of humanity to justify categorizing the types of violation we are interested in here as crimes against humanity, in the sense that humanity is collectively their victim.

I leave the hypothesis in this merely tentative form. Settling it is not vital to the present exercise. That the acts under consideration cause grave harm to their direct victims has already been established as part of the concept of crimes against humanity being proffered. This suffices for their treatment as crimes. And that the kind of harm they cause is harm to the fundamental interests of the direct victims simply as human beings has also already been established as part of the concept being proffered. This suffices for their treatment as crimes against "humanity" (in the sense of the sentiment or set of values). The two secondary or half-right ideas, as I have called these, then also kick in. For, in consequence of the above primary characteristics of the acts in question, they are shocking to the conscience of humankind, and so humankind forbids them through the instrumentality of international law, and from then on their commission is in breach of its sovereign authority. They become crimes against humanity *qua* global community. If, in addition, humankind may be said persuasively to be the collective victim of these acts, then this too is a consequence of the harm that they cause the direct victims, and the idea of humanity-as-victim can be rolled together with the idea of humanity-as-sovereign and that of humanity-as-morally shocked into the cluster of ideas that are relevantly part of the overall concept, but secondary. On the other hand, if it cannot be said persuasively, never mind. The humanity-as-victim idea may then be treated as no more than loosely suggestive—"The psychological well-being of some significant proportion of human beings is somewhat worsened by crimes against humanity"—and dispensable. The concept of crimes against humanity commands a viable meaning even without it.

Conclusions: the universality of human values

I summarize. On the account of them I have given, crimes against humanity are offenses against the human status or condition, which lie beyond a certain threshold of seriousness. They are inhuman acts. Being so, they shock the conscience of humankind, and humankind asserts itself—through the mediation of states, the socio-political communities across which humankind is distributed, and the law of nations by which these are collectively bound—as the sovereign authority criminalizing such inhuman acts. Humankind may also be said, loosely, to be the victim of crimes against humanity. Or perhaps not. It depends on a judgment about how widespread and severe the terrorizing effects of these crimes are. But nothing decisive here hinges on this judgment.

That an act is inhumane is not sufficient for us to treat it as a crime against humanity, and that it diminishes (all members of) the human race is not sufficient either—though crimes against humanity are inhumane, and it is also plausible to think that they diminish humankind. To be accounted a crime against humanity, an act need not threaten the peace and security of mankind or the world. Nor need it be genocidal or potentially genocidal in character, although if it fits this description it will qualify. Again, to be accounted a crime against humanity an act need not, indeed will not generally, threaten the existence of humankind, although if one day one did, it too would qualify.

I add two things by way of conclusion. First, there is a possibility of misunderstanding I have to forewarn against. In pursuing my purpose in this chapter—to identify the nature of those acts that are now regarded as crimes against humanity under international law—I have spoken of a threshold of seriousness at and beyond which inhumane acts are to be treated as offenses in that category. Anyone familiar with the literature, however, will know that there is a threshold issue of another kind. If the one I have been dealing with up to now concerns the severity of the act-type making up the material element of the offense, the other threshold issue has to do with certain jurisdictional preconditions, or putative preconditions, for assigning this class of offense to the domain of international law and hence of the international community, as being more than just an ordinary municipal crime. This other issue I take up elsewhere.

Second, it is plainly an assumption of what has gone before that there are universal human harms. The assumption is not an eccentric one in this context. It is germane, one way or another, to the very category of a crime that is against "humanity," and consistent with a recurrent emphasis in the international humanitarian law literature. But the universalist standpoint is often challenged. This is a challenge to be found, indeed, even in the international-law prehistory of the offense. It is contained in a dissenting memorandum to the report of the so-called Commission of Fifteen to the Paris Peace Conference in 1919. The two American members of that Commission, Robert Lansing and James Brown Scott, there entered a reservation concerning the report's appeal to "laws and principles of humanity." The laws and principles of humanity, they argued, vary according to time, place, circumstance, and individual conscience, and therefore do not provide a sound basis for criminal prosecution in a court of justice. "There is," they wrote, "no fixed and universal standard of humanity."[19]

Lansing and Scott's view is widely echoed today by moral relativist (including postmodernist) currents of philosophical and social-scientific opinion, given to opposing universalist conceptions of the human in light of the specificities of history, culture, and discourse. However, with respect to the issues under consideration here anti-universalist arguments are simply not credible. Having for my own part twice before, in arguing for the idea of a common human nature, highlighted the self-contradiction and absurdity that the would be denial of a common human nature inevitably produces,[20] I limit myself in the present occasion to rehearsing the most salient points of two counterstatements to the relativist position, both of them apt to the issues at hand.

One is by Michael Perry and in defense of the concept of universal human rights. Perry cites a number of passages describing atrocities in the former Yugoslavia during the early 1990s, and goes on to say one could fill volumes with similar reports from other times and places—"reports of cruelty so calculated that simply to hear of it tears the soul"—but that the passages he has cited are in any case "more than adequate ... to illustrate and clarify the fundamental point: Some things are bad, indeed some things are horrible—conspicuously horrible, undeniably horrible—for *any* human being to whom the thing is done." As Perry also says:

> No one believes that rape, or slicing off breasts, or ripping out wombs, or decapitating a child in front of its mother (who has just been raped), or castrating a prisoner (or forcing another prisoner to do so), or throwing a prisoner into hot oil—no one believes that such acts are or might be good for them on whom the horror is inflicted.

Equally:

> However fashionable this relativism (antiuniversalism, antiessentialism, etc.) might be in some quarters today, some things are bad and some things are good, not just for some human beings, but for every human being.

On this basis, Perry contends that the relativist challenge to the idea of human rights is not plausible, and that we should not "take seriously" the denial that human beings are all alike in some respects and that some things are good, and some things bad, for all of them.[21] He is right, we should not take it seriously. And his basis for saying so is, as he claims, "more than adequate." It chimes in with some earlier observations of Stuart Hampshire's on the moral relativist underestimation of universal human needs and of the constancies of human experience, especially in their negative aspects. According to Hampshire,

> There is nothing mysterious or "subjective" or culture-bound in the great evils of human experience, re-affirmed in every age and in every written history and in every tragedy and fiction: murder and the destruction of life, imprisonment, enslavement, starvation, poverty, physical pain and torture, homelessness, friendlessness. That these great evils are to be averted is the constant presupposition of moral arguments at all times and in all places.

All ways of life, Hampshire says, require protection against these great evils. Without protection against them, "[t]here is no tolerable life, decent and worth living."[22]

If these negative constancies are so evident, though, and their denial is not to be taken seriously, how is it that the relativist challenge to human rights (and related universals) is put forward apparently seriously as often as it is? This is, Perry argues, because "some confuse it [the relativist challenge] with a different position that is not only plausible, but correct." He means "pluralism about the human good." The constancies in human experience do not rule out that there are also important non-constancies: that what serves the flourishing of some human beings within a "concrete way of life" may not do the same for others within other such ways of life; nor that a way of life as a whole beneficial for some may not be beneficial for all.[23]

We should not allow this pluralist truth to obscure the equally important universalist truth forming the basis of the concept of crimes against humanity—genocide prominent among them.[24]

Notes

1. See, for example, Egon Schwelb, "Crimes Against Humanity," *British Year Book of International Law* 23 (1946): 178–226, at p. 195.
2. Hannah Arendt, *Eichmann in Jerusalem: A Report on the Banality of Evil* (London: Penguin Books, 1977), p. 275.
3. Geoffrey Robertson, *Crimes against Humanity: The Struggle for Global Justice* (London: Penguin Books, 2000), p. 220.
4. See ibid., pp. 330–31, 496, in reference to the Rome Statute of the International Criminal Court; and Schwelb, "Crimes Against Humanity," pp. 195–6.
5. Geoffrey Best, *Nuremberg and After: The Continuing History of War Crimes and Crimes against Humanity* (Reading: University of Reading Press, 1984), p. 15.
6. *Trial of the Major War Criminals before the International Military Tribunal. Nuremberg 14 November 1945–1 October 1946* (Nuremberg: International Military Tribunal, 1947), vol. 19, p. 472.
7. Bing Bing Jia, "The Differing Concepts of War Crimes and Crimes Against Humanity in International Criminal Law," in Guy S. Goodwin-Gill and Stefan Talmon, eds, *The Reality of International Law: Essays in Honour of Ian Brownlie* (Oxford: Clarendon Press, 1999), pp. 243–71, at pp. 251–2; Diane F. Orentlicher, "Settling Accounts: The Duty to Prosecute Human Rights Violations of a Prior Regime," *Yale Law Journal* 100 (1991): 2537–615, at p. 2556 n. 75; and Matthew Lippman, "Crimes Against Humanity," *Boston College Third World Law Journal* 17 (1997): 171–273, at pp. 216–17.
8. All the expressions in quotation marks in this paragraph are taken from the legal and other literature. I have precise references for them.
9. See the remark in note 8; it applies here too.
10. Richard Vernon, "What is Crime against Humanity?" *Journal of Political Philosophy* 10 (2002): 231–49, at pp. 239–40.
11. See Arendt, *Eichmann in Jerusalem*, pp. 256–7, 268–9, 275–6; and Alain Finkielkraut, *Remembering in Vain: The Klaus Barbie Trial and Crimes Against Humanity* (New York: Columbia University Press, 1992), pp. 35–6, 47–9.
12. Arendt, *Eichmann in Jerusalem*, pp. 275–6; Finkielkraut, *Remembering in Vain*, pp. 26, 31.
13. Finkielkraut, *Remembering in Vain*, p. 9.

14. Ronald C. Slye, "Apartheid as a Crime Against Humanity: A Submission to the South African Truth and Reconciliation Commission," *Michigan Journal of International Law* 20 (1999): 267–300, at p. 270.

15. Margaret McAuliffe deGuzman, "The Road from Rome: The Developing Law of Crimes Against Humanity," *Human Rights Quarterly* 22 (2000): 335–403, at p. 338.

16. Eve Garrard, "Forgiveness and the Holocaust," *Ethical Theory and Moral Practice* 5 (2002): 147–65, at p. 159; see also p. 149.

17. Robertson, *Crimes against Humanity*, pp. 331, 496.

18. See Norman Geras, *The Contract of Mutual Indifference: Political Philosophy after the Holocaust* (London: Verso, 1998), pp. 1–82.

19. "Commission on the Responsibility of the Authors of the War and on the Enforcement of Penalties. Report Presented to the Preliminary Peace Conference," *American Journal of International Law* 14 (1920): 95–154, at pp. 133–4, 144.

20. See Norman Geras, *Marx and Human Nature: Refutation of a Legend* (London: Verso, 1983) and Norman Geras, *Solidarity in the Conversation of Humankind: The Ungroundable Liberalism of Richard Rorty* (London: Verso, 1995), especially chapters 2 and 3.

21. Michael J. Perry, *The Idea of Human Rights: Four Enquiries* (Oxford: Oxford University Press, 1998), pp. 61–3, 71, 86. The references are to chapter 3, which appeared earlier as "Are Human Rights Universal? The Relativist Challenge and Related Matters," *Human Rights Quarterly* 19 (1997): 461–509.

22. Stuart Hampshire, *Innocence and Experience* (London: Allen Lane, 1989), pp. 90–1, 106.

23. Perry, *The Idea of Human Rights*, pp. 63–5.

24. This chapter is drawn from, and abridges one chapter of, a longer work in progress on the concept of crimes against humanity.

15

Innocence, Genocide, and Suicide Bombings

Laurence M. Thomas

If there are any objective and self-evident moral truths, the claim that genocide is a moral wrong of the most repugnant kind would surely seem to be among them. Nevertheless, it is important, perhaps surprising, to note that it is only in recent history, namely since the Enlightenment, that genocide has had the status of a manifestly self-evident moral wrong. That result is closely connected to the fact that human equality, as we understand it, is a modern idea. That reality, in turn, is one reason why slavery has a very, very long history of which American slavery was the last significant expression. During the Islamic Ottoman Empire, the idea that all human beings are created equal would have simply made no sense.[1] The same holds for the Roman Empire. It took the arguments of Jean Jacques Rousseau and Immanuel Kant, among others, to provide the conceptual framework for a shift in the concept of a human being, according to which all human beings are equal at a most fundamental level. Genocide's status as a moral wrong is the outgrowth of this new conceptual framework.

Presently, one might reasonably ask what more could possibly be said to shore up the view that genocide is wrong. Regrettably, a new challenge to the wrong of genocide has appeared from an unanticipated quarter, namely that of suicide bombings. Without becoming snared in Middle East politics, I use this chapter to draw attention to the significant fact that many people who oppose genocide may also believe that suicide bombings are justified. Indeed, suicide bombings have been defended on religious grounds, which is particularly troubling because religious convictions are generally deemed the ultimate court of appeal. What does one say to those who give a religious justification for suicide bombings? If philosophy is to meet the challenge posed by genocide, this question, which is linked to a sound understanding of genocide as well as to an ethical analysis of suicide bombing, deserves philosophical attention.

I argue that genocide and suicide bombings stand or fall together. Hence, if suicide bombings can be justified, then genocide can be justified. Because religious arguments have been presented to defend suicide bombings, I am particularly concerned to undermine arguments of that sort. I mention straightaway that I do *not* hold that all suicide bombings are the same. I am interested in those suicide bombings that have as their target ordinary civilians who, at the time of the bombing, are not presumed to be engaged in war-related activities. Indeed, for maximum psychological terror, civilians of this sort are the best target.[2] The paradigm case would be civilians riding public transportation to get to work, to attend school, or to go shopping. I refer to such individuals as the manifestly innocent. Thus, I am not interested, for example, in suicide bombings of a hotel known to be housing military personnel. Nor am I interested in what I call a means-to-an-end target, where B is an identifiable target of war and to destroy B it is necessary to destroy A. It is possible that a delivery truck might be a means-to-an-end target; however, this is most unlikely to be true in the typical case of public transportation. Suicide bombers clearly make this distinction themselves so as to achieve maximal psychological terror. If only war targets were the object of suicide bombings, that would diminish drastically the psychological terror that such bombings are intended to produce.

Having introduced the claim that genocide and suicide bombings have links that deserve exploration, my initial strategy is to introduce a moral analysis that defends the reality of moral innocence. On the strength of that analysis, I argue that both genocide and suicide bombings are equally wrong. As one would surmise, I am particularly concerned to develop a moral analysis that ought to be accepted by all religious traditions if they are to have any semblance of validating an ideal of holiness. I also contend that this analysis, or some version of it, should be accepted generally by human beings, religious or not, if they are to make sense of their own lives.

Moral innocence

The idea of moral innocence is at the very center of the three monotheistic traditions: Judaism, Christianity, and Islam. As these traditions conceive things, the Almighty epitomizes such innocence. Necessarily, perfect characterlogical moral innocence is an essential property of the Almighty. No one could have a more innocent moral character. As for human beings, who rapidly lose whatever innocence may have been theirs, it is only through constant striving that they can even hope to approach the innocence of the Almighty. In the end, any rapprochement between human beings and the Almighty is deemed to be owing to divine mercy. Evil, of course, stands in opposition to innocence. Whatever is innocent cannot be evil, and vice versa.

Although Judaism, Christianity, and Islam differ in fundamental ways, all three traditions are univocal in their general acceptance of what has been said thus far. A more controversial claim is the following: Even though each tradition claims a kind of moral superiority over the others, each allows that a non-practitioner may nonetheless exhibit profound innocence. In fact, infants are generally considered the embodiment of innocence, whatever the religious commitments of their parents might be. It is understood that infants, unlike adults, are simply incapable of having the psychological structure in virtue of which their motives and, therefore, their behavior could be deemed evil. Let us say that the innocence of children is non-characterlogical.

There is a category of characterlogical innocence that is akin to non-characterlogical innocence in one respect. Unlike infants, adults possess the psychological wherewithal to do wrong. However, adults may not be at fault for a wrong that has occurred. They may be innocent in either a weak or a strong sense. In the weak sense, the adult simply did not commit the wrong in question; in the strong sense, not only did the adult not commit the wrong in question, the adult's character is such that he would not have committed the wrong even if she or he could have done so with impunity. So in the strong sense, it is not just that a man—call him Landon—did not commit the rape in question, because as it happens he was in a different part of the world when the rape occurred; it could also be true that he would not have committed the rape even if he had the opportunity to do so and, moreover, could have done so with impunity. No follower of any of the three monotheistic traditions can be indifferent to this fact about Landon, even if it is known that he does not follow any religious tradition at all. For to know that Landon would not have raped, although he could have done so with impunity, is to know that he is trustworthy in a fundamentally important way. There is no rationally justified way to be indifferent to this fact about Landon, whatever one's religious convictions might be.

The strong sense of characterlogical innocence portends another kind of innocence, namely the innocence that is characteristic of a person who has performed righteous deeds. Each of the monotheistic religions allows that a non-practitioner may exhibit righteous, and thus innocent, behavior. Jews and Muslims, for instance, would acknowledge that Mother Theresa, the Catholic nun, was a righteous person because she was extraordinary in doing good for others, without ulterior motives, throughout her adult life. Again, Jews refer to Oskar Schindler as a righteous gentile because he gave tirelessly of himself to save the lives of a thousand Jews during the Holocaust. In contrast to Mother Theresa, there is no evidence that Schindler was in general an upstanding moral person. Indeed, given the generally corrupt nature of his character, his valiant efforts on behalf of Jews is all the more surprising. Yet, there can be little doubt that he acted righteously, for it is clear that he acted deliberately to save many lives and he did so without ulterior motives. Nelson Mandela provides a third example. A victim of apartheid, he endured more than two decades of harsh and unjustified imprisonment without bitterness and rancor, emerging from prison with magisterial dignity and integrity. By the majesty of his character alone, he set a moral tone of reconciliation in postapartheid South Africa. It is at least doubtful that any other person could have set this moral tone; one may marvel at his characterlogical innocence. Something would be terribly amiss if Jews, Christians, or Muslims dismissed Mandela's behavior as righteous because he belongs to none of those traditions.

Now, the fact that all three monotheistic traditions recognize the possibility of characterlogical innocence among non-practitioners suggests that, even for them, there is a conception of innocence that transcends theological doctrine as such. If so, that outcome supports my view that there is an idea of innocence that is recognized by human beings generally. As indicated in P. F. Strawson's magnificent essay "Freedom and Resentment," human beings in general cannot make sense of life without a concept of innocence.[3] At one end, there are pure motives; at the other, there are impure motives. And it is not possible to be indifferent to this divide, which is simply the divide between good and evil. Anger, revenge, gratitude, and a wealth of other sentiments are inextricably tied to whether or not we have been the object of innocent motives, on the one hand, or evil motives, on the other. What is more, a motive cannot be considered innocent or evil simply as a matter of an individual's subjective preferences.

Imagine that Rachel saves Opidopo from drowning in the river, makes sure that he has food and shelter at the nearby hotel, and then continues on her way home. There, she takes a relaxing bubble bath and enjoys a peaceful sleep. Opidopo may not characterize Rachel's behavior as evil—at least not in the absence of a very long and unobvious story. Suppose, for instance, that it turns out that Opidopo is to be assassinated in the hotel, as per arrangements made by Rachel. This supposition will seem ludicrous. Are we to suppose that Rachel planned Opidopo's near-drowning experience and then saved him?

To be sure, there are many contexts in which a person's motives are difficult to ascertain. It does not follow, however, that the innocence or evil pertaining to a person's motives is simply a matter of subjective preferences. Indetermination and subjectivity are not identical. Opidopo does not have the option, at least not from a rational point of view, to call Rachel's behavior evil. Her behavior, as I described it, is incompatible with an assessment of evil. Thus, if Opidopo did make such a claim, we would suppose either that he mis-spoke or that he did not tell the complete story or that perhaps he is delusional. Or, finally, if Opidopo insists on calling Rachel's motives evil, then his doing so invites the conclusion that perhaps he himself is an evil person. This is because failure to recognize the good that she did on his behalf can only be attributed to a kind of willfulness that bespeaks an evil person.

Significantly, the other side of the coin is that Rachel herself cannot make sense of her behavior as being evil. Were she to don sackcloth and ashes in a repenting ritual for having saved Opidopo's life, we would surely suppose that either this is a very tasteless joke on her part or that she has gone mad. The idea here is not that people are always clear about their own motives.

That is obviously false. In the case at hand, however, there is no room for her to attribute ulterior self-serving motives to rescuing Opidopo.

To recapitulate, thus far I have been concerned to make three points: First, a transcendent notion of innocence is recognized across religious differences and among human beings generally. Second, human beings cannot make sense of themselves without such a concept of innocence. Third, although we may be unclear about the character of a person's motives, transcendent innocence is not simply a matter of subjective interpretation.

A significant consequence of these three points, especially the first, is that if anyone is judged to be entirely evil by an adherent of one of the monotheistic religions, the adherent cannot rightly base this judgment simply upon the fact that the person in question is not an adherent of that religion, since every religious tradition allows that a person can exhibit characterlogical innocence even though she or he is not an adherent of that tradition. This point is important because it enables us, for example, to respect Christianity while condemning the view, once prevalent in Christian thought, that if Jews reject Christ, that rejection suffices to make them not just evil but irredeemably so.[4] More generally, the point portends the importance of distinguishing between characterlogical innocence, on the one hand, and salvation, on the other. The distinction stands even if each religious tradition holds that the highest level of characterlogical innocence comes only with following its precepts. Perhaps according to Islam, Christianity, or Judaism, Mother Theresa cannot have salvation; yet, a considerable measure of characterlogical innocence on her part cannot be denied. Again, all three monotheistic religions may question whether Nelson Mandela shall receive salvation. Still, his ability to forgive those who so brutally wronged him stands as a paradigm of characterlogical moral innocence.

A most riveting conclusion can be drawn from the preceding analysis: each of the monotheistic religions is formally committed to the view that from the fact that a person is not pursuing the religious path according to which she or he shall earn salvation, it does not follow that the individual is thereby an evil person. To be sure, if a person has salvation, then the individual is not evil. However, it is possible not to have or to merit salvation and at the same time *not* to be evil. Thus, the following holds formally: (1) The incompatibility of salvation and evil stands as an incontrovertible truth. (2) The compatability of not having or meriting salvation and yet *not* being evil remains. However, it would seem that many have mistakenly supposed that if (1) is true, then it must also be true that not having or meriting salvation entails that one cannot be innocent. One reason for this mistake, I suspect, is that many have failed to see the distinction between characterlogical moral innocence and salvation that is implicit in all religious thought. Hence, it was mistakenly supposed that not having or meriting salvation entails non-innocence or guilt because not having or meriting salvation entails evil and evil is incompatible with innocence. But as my analysis shows, it is fallacious to think that a lack of salvation entails non-innocence or guilt.

Genocide and suicide bombings

As this chapter's introduction indicated, people do not typically associate suicide bombings with genocide. After offering some general remarks about that relationship, I argue specifically that moral appraisals of genocide and suicide bombings that target the manifestly innocent stand or fall together.

People may not associate suicide bombings (even of the manifestly innocent) with genocide because it is possible to see suicide bombings as a political response to oppression, whereas it is difficult to understand genocide in that way. Because genocide is the ultimate form of oppression, if you will, it cannot easily be interpreted as a response to oppression. By definition, it seems, any group of people that is committing genocide can scarcely be thought to be oppressed, at least not by the people who are targeted for destruction. By contrast, suicide bombings are held by many to be a legitimate response by those who lack the means to free themselves from the tyranny of others. Certainly, many who support the Palestinian struggle in the Middle East invoke just this understanding of the suicide bombings carried out against the citizens of Israel, for Israel is regarded by them to be a nation with enormous military might (vis à vis Palestinians, at any rate) that can impose its will.

Here two questions should be separated. One pertains to whether Israel is oppressive. The other pertains to what is justified in response to oppression. The latter question is my focal point. My position is that even if a nation is oppressing a people, it does not follow that suicide bombings against the manifestly innocent of that nation are justified. Again, the issue of whether suicide bombings are justified is not to be confused with the quite different issue of whether suicide bombings are enormously effective in bringing about a state of psychological terror. When it comes to bringing about a reign of psychological terror, few methods are more effective. But something can be most effective and yet be woefully unjustified. Corporeal punishment, for example, may be an effective way for parents to insure their children's compliance, but the justification of this practice has been much disputed. Effectiveness does not imply justification.

Further, there is the issue of how the targets of suicide bombings are morally characterized. To be sure, it may be a matter of debate whether this group or that group of people is manifestly innocent. However, it begs the question to argue that, say, "Israelis are Israelis" (or pick one's favorite group), and hence it does not matter which ones are targeted because all are equally non-innocent human beings. Logically, the possibility of moral innocence does not permit this move. Even Jews who were in concentration camps recognized that there could be deep moral differences among

Germans. Indeed, in the case of the Nazi doctor Ernst B., Jews testified on his behalf, thereby winning his acquittal at the Nuremberg trials.[5] That said, Dr. Ernst B. never fully distanced himself from Nazi ideology, and he admired the notorious Dr. Josef Mengele, whom he regarded as a friend. In terms of ideology, Ernst B. was a committed Nazi, albeit far less vicious than many others. So, if distinctions can be made among Nazis, and rightly so, then surely distinctions can be made among Israeli citizens, even given the presupposition (for the sake of the argument) that Israel is an oppressive state.

In a word, moral innocence—possible or real—does not justify indiscrimination and indifference with regard to the targets of suicide bombings. It is a fact about war that, in the effort to subdue non-innocent individuals, the killing of innocent people is sometimes unavoidable. It is not a fact about war that the distinction between the innocent and the non-innocent no longer applies. Even in the midst of the enemy, there can be manifestly innocent individuals to whom one must not be indifferent. Surely, children on a school bus fit this description.

It is unfortunate that religious doctrines have been interpreted in all sorts of morally objectionable ways. In *Mein Kampf*, for example, Hitler wrote: "In standing guard against the Jew, I am defending the handiwork of the Lord." To much of Europe at the time, Hitler's remarks were not only perfectly coherent, from a conceptual point of view, but also they resonated deeply with widespread visceral emotions regarding Jews. Many thought that Hitler had a point and that ridding the earth of Jews was not a bad idea. Many thought this way, although they were not prepared to sully their own hands to achieve that goal. Owing to centuries of Christian teaching, the idea that Jews could be blamed for the death of Christ, and therefore were guilty just for being Jews, was simply a part of the European conceptual framework. In effect, then, Christianity was invoked as a justification for the Holocaust.

Needless to say, it is only by ignoring moral innocence that adherents of a religious tradition can suppose that the principles of that tradition could be a pretext for genocide. By parity of reasoning, the same holds for adherents of a religious tradition who hold that suicide bombings are justified even if manifestly innocent people are the targets. Any view that justifies committing genocide against a people also justifies suicide bombings that target manifestly innocent individuals of that group. The surprise is that the converse is also true, namely that any view that justifies targeting manifestly innocent individuals of a group also justifies the genocide of that group.

If one holds that one can be justified in killing the manifestly innocent members of a group, then one cannot have an in-principle moral reason for *not* killing all the members of the group, since no human being can be more undeserving of being killed than those who are manifestly innocent. More precisely, if one can be justified in killing any manifestly innocent person, then one can be justified in killing any person randomly chosen, since it does not matter whether the person is innocent or not; and if the killing of any person randomly chosen is justified, then one could be justified in killing all. Thus, the moral force of the claim that school children are a paradigm example of a manifestly innocent group of human beings is as follows: if they can be targeted for suicide bombings, then surely anyone else can be as well. In that case, the distinction between genocide and suicide bombings that target the manifestly innocent—at least in terms of key aspects of the logic that governs them both—is more verbal than substantive.

In *Les Nouveaux Martyrs d'Allah*, Farhad Khosrokhavar distinguishes between two categories of martyrs: "*martyre défensif*" and "*martyre offensif*."[6] The former behaves in the way that the term "martyr" has been traditionally understood: an individual puts her life on the line for a cause, but it is not, in fact, her desire to die. Nor is killing someone essential to the good that she seeks to do; she would rather accomplish the good in question without any loss of life. The aim of the *martyre offensif*, however, is ineluctably tied (a) to bringing about his own death in order (b) to bring about the death of the person designated as an enemy of Islam.

The obvious question is by what criteria are individuals declared enemies of Islam. It is equally obvious that the criteria are morally bankrupt if persons count as enemies of Islam simply by virtue of not being Muslim, since that identification would deny the possibility of characterlogical moral innocence to non-Muslims. As for salvation, for all anyone knows it may be the case that all non-Muslims, by virtue of being such, lack salvation. As we have seen, however, from just this supposition it does not follow that all non-Muslims are, by virtue of being such, lacking in characterlogical moral innocence.

In Khosrokhavar's discussion of the *martyre offensif*, there is a poignant and disturbing implication that he seems not to have noticed. For the *martyre offensif*, the language of killing the enemy is not just a way of speaking. In particular, it is not just a way of saying that the enemy should be forcefully subdued, and thus killing the enemy is no more than a means to that end. No, killing the enemy is to be understood quite literally as the end that is to be valorized. As Khosrokhavar indicates, the enemy of Islam can be regarded as a beast the sacrifice of which is sacred.[7] It does not matter whether the enemy is one person or a group of people. What follows, moreover, is that where we have an identifiable group of people designated as the enemy, then the entire group of people is to be killed, and doing so is to be valorized. The "logical" outcome is genocide by another name.

When the idea of an enemy of Islam was formulated initially, technologically efficient genocide was not a possibility. Talk of eliminating an entire people from the face of the earth was more rhetoric than an aim that could be realized. Furthermore, limited resources forced one to make distinctions among the enemy, including distinctions between those who were morally innocent and those who were not. Thus, faced with the choice of killing either 15 women and their children (the morally innocent) or 20 soldiers (the not morally innocent), where doing both was out of the question, the wisdom of fighting the good fight invariably counseled against killing the former and in favor of killing the latter.

Aristotle famously remarked that one cannot intend to do the impossible, although one may wish for it. His example was the moon. One may wish for it, he observed, but one may not intend to obtain it. Little did he know that technological advancement would give us pause with regard to the plausibility of whether or not we can have the moon. The relevance of this point to the discussion at hand is that whether or not centuries ago adherents of Islam or Christianity or Judaism may have wished to destroy entirely—that is, to commit genocide against—a people considered to be an enemy of that religion, practical considerations precluded actually intending to do this. Alas, that is no longer the case. Genocide has become all too real and, tragically, it may continue to threaten humankind.

Nowadays, non-adherents of a religious tradition, especially those whose family and cultural background puts them entirely outside of the tradition, are reluctant to say what can and cannot follow from the sacred texts of that religious tradition. To do so is deemed politically incorrect. In the section that follows, however, I make the bold move of arguing that no religious tradition can be rightly understood as justifying the genocide of a people of another religious tradition. The argument that I put forth applies with equal force, and in exactly the same way, to all three monotheistic religious traditions.

Conceptualizing Holy texts: utterances and meaning

One of the cornerstone beliefs of the monotheistic traditions is that the word of the Almighty is unchanging. I do not intend to take issue with this thesis—at least not directly. Nevertheless, whatever we take the word of Almighty to be, a distinction should be made between an utterance attributed to the Almighty and what that utterance means. Often enough, one can easily know what utterance is attributable to a person without knowing what that utterance means. After all, it is certainly possible to know what a person has said, in the sense of knowing what words the individual uttered, and yet be at a loss as to what the person means by what has been uttered. Invoking the Almighty does not vitiate this distinction. To the contrary, invoking the Almighty may underscore its importance. To this consideration, let us add the simple truth that technology can radically alter how we conceive of what we do and should do, as the following example illustrates.

Three hundred years ago, it was impossible to cross the Atlantic Ocean in a weekend (72 hours). In 1700, one could not have had the intention of doing that, whatever else one might have intended to do, although in the words of Aristotle one could have wished that such a thing were possible. Nowadays, on the other hand, one can cross the Atlantic Ocean several times in 72 hours. Imagine, then, a scriptural commandment that says,

"Thou shall visit one's parents as often as circumstances permit." In addition, suppose that one is wealthy and that one is separated from one's parents by the Atlantic Ocean. In 1700, it was not possible to make the trip more than once every six weeks or so under the best of circumstances. In the twenty-first century, by contrast, it is possible to make the trip every weekend. To be sure, traversing the Atlantic Ocean every weekend would be ever so tiring. But our hypothetical commandment from scripture does not say that one should visit one's parents only when one feels refreshed and relaxed. More importantly, although the commandment has not changed, it is implausible to think that people in the twenty-first century would see the commandment as applying in all respects in exactly the way that people in the eighteenth century saw it. If, these days, wealthy folks were to traverse the Atlantic Ocean every six weeks in order to visit their parents, most of us would be quite impressed. Notice, though, that in the 1700s, crossing the Atlantic every six weeks would effectively rule out having a meaningful life (unless, of course, one's meaningful life consisted in going back and forth across the Atlantic). In the 1700s, making the trip every six weeks was effectively out of the question. Once again, though, it is worth pointing out that there has been no change in the commandment itself.

Let us take it as given that, according to each monotheistic religious tradition, the adherents of that tradition should stand up to those who do not accept that tradition. There are passages in the Hebrew Bible, the Christian New Testament, and the Holy Qur'an of Islam that can be interpreted that way. The monotheistic traditions, moreover, are thought to imply that persons who, for the sake of the Almighty, lose their life in this world will be richly rewarded in the world-to-come. The question that arises, though, is whether such passages warrant simply ignoring characterlogical moral innocence. Unequivocally, the answer is *no*, for an affirmative answer would entail that it is morally irrelevant whether or not a person would be innocent of, for example, murder in the strong sense of characterlogical innocence, meaning that such a person would not so behave even if the individual could do so with impunity. Surely it is not irrelevant that a person would be innocent of murder in the strong sense of characterlogical innocence even if according to any and all religious traditions that person lacks salvation; for it will be remembered that lacking salvation is no barrier to possessing characterlogical moral innocence. No religious tradition is morally defensible if it has no conceptual space for this measure of innocence. Indeed, a defining feature of evil is that it is oblivious to innocence at any level except insofar as that innocence serves its ends. Thus, any religious view becomes the embodiment of evil itself if it lacks the conceptual space to acknowledge and affirm characterlogical innocence.

No doubt there are moral monsters in this world—that is, persons entirely lacking in characterlogical moral innocence or nearly so. No doubt we can find such individuals within every walk of life. However, there is never a good argument to show that an entire people lacks characterlogical moral innocence. Significantly, an argument that showed an entire people to be lacking in salvation would not thereby show that all such individuals are thereby lacking in characterlogical moral innocence. Thus it follows that there can be no sound religious argument for committing genocide, since that would entail ignoring individuals with characterlogical moral innocence. For related reasons, there can be no religious argument for committing suicide bombings that target the manifestly innocent among a people or a nation, since doing so would likewise entail ignoring individuals with characterlogical moral innocence.

What if it could be shown that killing an entire people or nation is necessary for the very survival of a religious tradition? No doubt that would change much but not everything, for as my previous discussion has shown, if in reality a group were in the position to eliminate an entire people from the face of the earth, it seems highly unlikely that the group's survival would turn on a genocidal act.

Notes

1. I am grateful to Laurent Rougemont for helping to frame the general argument of this chapter and to both Christophe-Jacques Imize and Rougemont for their constant encouragement. At this point in the chapter, moreover, I am indebted to the important collection of essays in Shaun E. Marmon, ed., *Slavery in the Islamic Middle East* (Princeton, NJ: Marcus Weiner Publishers, 1999).

   Strictly speaking, Islamic slavery did not privilege one skin color over the other, but religious beliefs instead. However, skin color facilitated things enormously because it made people readily identifiable. Accordingly, being a black African was typically a disadvantage merely owing to skin color. Indeed, the terms *negro* and *slave* were often used interchangeably. See John Hunwick, "Islamic Law and Polemics over Race and Slavery in North and West Africa (16th–19th Century)" in Harmon's volume. A classic text on this subject is by Bernard Lewis, *Race and Slavery in the Middle East: An Historical Enquiry* (New York: Oxford University Press, 1990).

2. See Ehud Sprinzak, "Rational Fanatics," *Foreign Policy* (September/October 2000).

3. See P. F. Strawson, *Freedom and Resentment and Other Essays* (London: Methuen, 1977).

4. For an elaboration of these points, see my *Vessels of Evil: American Slavery and the Holocaust* (Philadelphia, PA: Temple University Press, 1993). One of the most laudable moves of the Roman Catholic Church is its shift away from anti-Jewish teachings. Its referring to Jews as the Church's elder brothers was an ingenious way to acknowledge both kinship and difference. For further discussion of the Church's evolution, see Laurence Thomas, "Forgiving the Unforgivable," in Eve Garrard and Geoffrey Scarre, eds, *Moral Philosophy and the Holocaust* (Burlington, VT: Ashgate Press, 2003).

5. See Robert Jay Lifton, *The Nazi Doctors: Medical Killing and the Psychology of Genocide* (New York: Basic Books, 1986).

6. Farhad Khosrokhavar, *Les Nouveaux Martyrs d'Allah* (Paris: Flammerion, 2002), pp. 15–20.

7. Ibid., p. 113.

16
Beyond the Affectations of Philosophy

James R. Watson

> Reflection, which in a healthy person breaks the power of immediacy, is never as compelling as the illusion which it dispels. As a negative, considered movement which is not directed in a straight line, it lacks the brutality inherent in positive movement.[1]
>
> Max Horkheimer and Theodor W. Adorno,
> *Dialectic of Englightenment*

"Have a nice day."

When conversation provokes the look that says, "We do not talk about that," one is well advised to remember that indirection succeeds better than frontal assaults. On the other hand, if one lacks the stomach for deceit in such situations, it is simply a matter of good taste to rehearse the customary denunciations and regrets, referencing either the regrettable aspects of human nature, the inhuman nature of the perpetrators, and/or the incomprehensibility of such matters. Insistence on pushing past these customary exculpatory fabulations will be met by the "we don't talk about that" of all socially approved discourse. One learns, later more often than sooner, that decorum has its own insistence—leave sleeping dogs lie. How then to handle the knowledge that sleeping dogs and their medicated masters have quite a bit to do with the erosion of public discourse? Is it possible that high society, high culture, and higher education are all major players in the "end" of democracy?

Although academic discourse is only a miniscule part of public discourse in the United States, the administration of academic writing is keenly attuned to high society and its preferences. In a capital-driven society what else could be the primary business function of higher education than raising funds. It has become an intuitive thing: universities must be run as businesses. Attunement to prevailing powers and their pocket books is a job for specially trained people. Any fool can interpret the cheers and the boos from the sports-adept alumni, but specialists with keen ears are needed to decipher the grumbling over what the faculty are doing. Financial support of universities is now much more than a desideratum; it is a prime mover in the great flow of academic capital. Adam Smith's category of unproductive labor loses one membership set as academics now exchange directly with capital for the sake of profit-making. Cheers! At last, even the humanities faculty has become productive: economics rules academia. Cheers! The joyous and playful thinker has been rejected by administered rank and tenure committees, which is to say, by managed faculty proudly donning their garb of dependency. Taken under the administrative wing, professors now chirp *Sapere Aude* to the beat of "It's Money That I Love."[2] The truly astonishing thing about the new effectiveness of this very old technique of cooptation is that many of the co-opted faculty construe their sycophantic compliance as a manifestation of self-management.

Admittedly, it does seem odd to talk about the corporate take over of intellectual labors under the guise of academic administration at a time when more and more scholars—some philosophers among them—are turning their attention to genocide and the problematic of human rights. But it is precisely when academic writing threatens to reveal not only the contradictions of society but also the complicities resulting from the way business is done and money is "made" that we encounter the full charge of academic administration. Calls for a return to the classics and classical education, attacks (from both the right and the left, it should be noted) against the evils of postmodernism (whatever it may be), renewed claims for the necessity of educational foundations and thus the need to return to basics are indicative of profound disturbances in society. These developments are not new, but the nastiness of these calls and charges has an uncultivated quality that can be and has been traced back to the Second World War and the onset of the Cold War. With the angry and threatening charge "You politicize everything!" one hears the shrill tones of a cracking social edifice.

Numerous discussions of genocide—concept or instance—have worked themselves into the current field of refereed academic writing, even into the field of philosophical research. In the merit point system of academic management, authors of these refereed and referenced texts should be doing quite well. And, from the side of management, this is as it must be; that is, as long as these writings do not lead the (paying) public into disconcerting behavior. When developed as subjects under the categories of "things we do" and "how we do them," genocide, mass killing, torture, and humiliation threaten to penetrate and dispel the illusions protecting us from the irrationality and cruelty of everyday life. What we have learned in only a few years concerns the return to and proper use of keeping collective nouns singular and particular in their meaning and extent. So, we have learned that bloody public rituals can be staged and funded but only if they assure "us" of the rightfulness of "our" killings, sanction "our" hatred of invading others, feed "our" revulsion at those who just don't get it, and, above all, nourish "our" relish of the mind-numbing power of violence without complexity and contradiction.

"Our" *Passion of the Christ* is the top-selling diuretic for discharging the discomfiting effects of improper genocide discussions regarding Jews. How many honorary degrees will "our" Mel Gibson receive as universities eye the reaction of "our" powers that be? "Do you share *our* values?"

Given the transmogrification of higher education by corporate forces, it is not surprising that disturbing "matters" such as genocide enter philosophical discourse, receive a certain informing, and depart once again without having had any formative or deformative effects on their informing agents. Indeed, hard headedness is a prerequisite for the maintenance of the properly administered social generality of good-natured academic taste and decorum. As an occupied discipline[3] under the direction of business-type doyens, philosophy has been retrofitted with an immune system capable of detecting and warding off disturbances to the flow of academic capital: when *de nobis res agitur* (the matter in question is ourselves), silence roars. How else can one explain why the traditional affirmative tendencies of philosophy continue unabated? God, ultimate meanings, the end of history-ideology-philosophy are proclaimed, affirmed, and repeated *ad nauseum* despite the fact that almost everything in public life indicates "a meaningful connection can no longer be established between what has happened and the great metaphysical ideas."[4]

As a managed, high-end cultural production of affirmative theses in the face of "the blatant indifference of each individual life that is the direction of history,"[5] philosophy is thus degraded to the level of affectation. Understandably, initial feelings of inadequacy are not uncommon within the community of properly supervised high-enders. Not merely maintaining but pushing the envelope of high culture requires the assumption of awesome responsibilities. Philosophers become heavy hitters when they assume their most awesome responsibility—sharing in the guilt of primal founding acts. This undertaking, however, is precarious. It requires something in the realm of philosophy that its affirmative character cannot accept as belonging to the essence of philosophy. This is philosophy's other, some necessary yet strangely non-essential thing, something that must be cast off again and again because, despite its non-essentiality, it stubbornly returns to unsettle what would otherwise stand as successful affirmations. Only "lite-weights" would stand up, refuse Abu Ghraib as another "other" of philosophy, and call for a public demonstration of our national guilt and shame. This, however, would be patriotism of a different kind, one that does not cast off its failures or weaknesses. Behind the veil of the amended pledge of allegiance to the flag and what it stands for, we are assured that God knows and approves of the fact that real Americans hate losers. Real Americans have no shame when they do what they must to save the world from evil. To shame others does not put us to shame. Why then does Mark Danner report the following response of a young Iraqi to the question why the people of Fallujah were attacking Americans? Bear in mind that this was given prior to the revelations of Abu Ghraib in 2004.

For Fallujans it is a *shame* to have foreigners break down their doors. It is a *shame* for them to have foreigners stop and search their women. It is a *shame* for the foreigners to put a bag over their heads, to make a man lie on the ground with your shoe on his neck. This is a great *shame*, you understand? This is a great *shame* for the whole tribe.[6]

Do we understand what this young man says, *in English*, to *a foreigner* who asks why Iraqis are attacking Americans? Well, the really wonderful and magical thing about finding an "Other" is that all ambiguity departs: "For God's sake, it's WAR!" Thus disappears the judgment at Nuremberg.[7]

In "The Cares of a Family Man," Kafka gave us a name for this abjection. Odradek is the subject of Kafka's tale, a strange subject, wooden in appearance, who trails old, broken-off bits of thread. Odradek never dies, never hurts anyone, and always seeks to collect the tangled remnants haunting our conventions and traditions. Philosophy's "other" collects and preserves what is forgotten and distorted in the distillations of high culture. Meanwhile, in managed, administered philosophy a good accounting amounts to a correction that handles matters by bringing everything back to shibboleths of prevailing powers. The abject, however, continues its work of collecting the inevitable remainders. Returning, the remainders give us a hint of what we are denied access to in the privatized archives of power. Thanks to Odradek, despite what we might call the insistence of the philosophical aesthetic, philosophy's "other" remains, and philosophy's work is unfinished. Odradek persists, but the detritus accumulates, and thus invocations of the "end of philosophy" take on the form of specific ideologies proclaiming the end of ideology. Such are the current affectations of philosophy.

After 1940, a series of official Anglo-American decisions regarding the fate of European Jews repeated, with appropriate alterations, sovereign decisions in Spain at the end of the fifteenth century regarding the fate of the indigenous Caribbean population. To win a world war against the Axis in 1942 required, so thought the Allied sovereign powers, the conventional use of the same cost-benefit analysis tested so many times before in the terrible course of the European civilizing process.[8] The fact that certain peoples do not count as much as others in this politics-as-usual calculus bears witness to the persistence of its racist fundament. Millions of Jews or Native Americans are a terrible price, but not unacceptable, especially in the contemporary sense of "collateral damage," from the higher standpoint of Western Christian civilization. A cultural imperative steers decisions at the highest levels of its administration, then and now.

Philosophy's affectations are most noticeable during its ideological-affirmative periods. In itself, so to speak, philosophy's affirmative tendency and thus its affectation are long-term consequences of philosophy's refusal to acknowledge its link to work and the labor process. The scientific management of academics was prefigured in the centuries-old process of work degradation and its transformation into collective labor processes regulated by "higher" Ideas. Subsequently applied to all realms of cultural production, these higher Ideas brought forth a "perfected" stage character-ized by the rational, bureaucratic, and spiritually administered techniques and instruments for the efficient eradication of superfluous human and non-human populations. Thus, the civilizing process as management became, and here we arrive at a point whose contemporary relevance will be mightily resisted, precisely what fascists in the 1920s understood as their political task. This is, at least in part, an answer to Henry Feingold's question:

> The question is, why did not the witnessing nations and agencies sense that the systematic killing in the death camps by means of production processes developed in the West was at the ideological heart of World War II, and therefore required a response? Why were they unable to fathom that Auschwitz meant more than the mass destruction of European Jewry? It perverted the values at the heart of their own civilization; if allowed to proceed unhampered, it meant that their world would never be the same again.[9]

But, we must ask, did Auschwitz begin or perfect the perversion of values? Auschwitz would constitute a perversion of the values of Western civiliza-tion only if it had been a unique occurrence in the civilizing process. It would be so much easier to deal with if it had been a perversion. Perhaps Auschwitz only appears as a perversion because it was a state-sanctioned genocidal action in the heart of Europe. But we do know that it was also implicitly sanctioned by the non-actions of other less central states. If, how-ever, the Nazi genocide was a continuation of a genocidal civilizing process, perhaps the allied "enlightened" states really did learn from Hitler's "failure" to complete the task. Perhaps the "enlightened" states now manage things in such a way that only "rogue" states do their dirty but necessary, civilizing work of genocide. If so, perhaps it is time to admit frankly that the Nazis were executing one of civilization's imperatives.[10] From this hard-won enlightened perspective, "Never again" has a new and highly affected meaning: "never again in the 'civilized' world." Thus, is prefigured what the recently "enlightened" and divinely elected will proclaim as "The Axis of Evil." The Balkans, Afghanistan, Iraq, Iran, North Korea, and Africa are only a few of the many and ever-multiplying rogue areas. And does not every properly educated person know what to expect from this new power axis?

Genocide today is an exportation business. We can rest assured that what-ever atrocities we commit in rogue areas will be outdone by the terrorist forces we produce and provoke: weapons of mass misery production and weapons of mass destruction are supplements for our brave new version of Oceania. Once again (always already), reason in irrational society affirms universality by excluding those it must sacrifice to preserve itself in its contradictory state. The "reason" for affectation, false pretense, is thus as clear as the contradiction between the unabashed proclamation that God is the greatest of writers and an obedient public's having put aside the scripture that admonishes them to "Beware of practicing your piety before others in order to be seen by them; for then you have no reward from your Father in heaven."[11]

Six hundred kilometers per hour is normal for jet travel these days. In this age of large numbers, the speed of jet planes expressed numerically loses its transhuman character. Jet lag is now part of the human condition, at least for the privileged few who share the luxury of reading, writing, eating well, and jet travel. The entertainment industry services this transhuman domain: dry information configured as cool gaming. Cancer and the masses share a metastasis or two. The wealthy avoid the latter but, as yet, they cannot avoid the former. It seems the human has become not much more than a biological resource for those new mutations within the socio-techno matrix of Empire—the posthumans.[12]

Smart machines and bombs regulate the ever-growing biomass, cycling it indiscriminately in carefully orchestrated theaters of war. Civil wars staged as star war extravaganzas bear testimony to the Sublime, the disguised vested interests and complicity nestled in the transcendental settings of home theater spectators.

Still, I think, reflection persists.

Managers wish otherwise. But Albert Camus was right about the curse of reflection: "Beginning to think is beginning to be undermined."[13] Thinking spoils if not countered by "cool." And, as Stuart Klawans notes in his review of *The Matrix Reloaded*, the cool are always the few winners to whom the multitudes flock.[14] In the face of the thousands being massacred, "cool reflection" created the true perversion that found expression in linguistic atrocities such as "collateral damage." Kant got it wrong. In the face of certain images, reason is not triumphant. Which is why "excellence" always requires sacrifices. Excellence trumps all horizontal movements that enlarge the scope of "us" by reducing the category of "them." But, and on this point the heavy hitters really play hard ball, the field of socially expanded connections is too fragile, too contingent, too ambiguous, too conflictual to compete with the daily stagings of necessary sacrifices.[15] The new feudalism of administered society counters horizontal, "lite-weight" movements by ensuring that poverty, humiliation, rejection, and eventual elimination are the only returns for those who still believe in and strive for human equality. The entire history of genocide might be described as a religious, sacrificial attempt to destroy not only specific groups of people but also the public realms making their worldly appearances possible. Even as a possibility, this thought cuts to the quick of complicity. Dirt, disease, sin, labor—all form a superseded horizon from which arises the blinding radiance and saving power of pure thought.

Managed and administered by "superior" minds, society is maintained in such a way that it simply cannot abide an abundance of genius. Labor already reduced to mindless behavior marks the beginning of behaviorism, which marks the beginning of the transformation of child-raising, an intricate task now delegated to "Kid Ranches" where, like the "yids" of old, our "kids" are prepared for the market ("this little piggy went to market"). Otherness, wherever and whenever encountered, is neutralized by the same of "differences" that don't matter—user-friendly multiculturalism and cheap products from China: Wal-Mart as the new comity of nations under the direction of scientific-corporate management. And, of course, a firm commitment to "human rights." Thus, privatized universities, faith-based organizations as replacements for the shipwrecked social democracy experiment, privatized corporate elementary and secondary schools as the salvation of children trapped in public education—each and all committed to excellence and reborn in the reproduction of the One by the Same, the purity of which does not permit its appearance in the dirty plurality of the public realm (except in the guise of noble lies).[16] When we hear of another assault by private, corporate forces on the near-dead public realm, or the born-again majority rally against the minority powers of the secular, their ugly motivation renders comical the academic disputes still being fought on the stage of discredited oppositions:[17] the idea of human equality will be expunged from human memory.

What so many now accept as "the laws of economics" is nothing more than a current alibi in theoretical drag for the history of genocide, also known as "civilization." In an April 2004 broadcast of *The West Wing* television series, President Bartlett, a one-time professor of economics, tells his staff "we can't act contrary to the laws of economics." No one in Bartlett's inner circle questions this alleged necessity. In this silent complicity lies the truth concerning the "liberalism" of *The West Wing* and its corporate connection to its viewing public, which, as a matter of course, has the virtue of returning "liberalism" to its pedigree. The persistence of Calvinism thus seems as impenetrable as its adamantine doctrine of God's sovereignty in the bestowal of grace. Some of us just don't get it! Which, from the standpoint of the *actus purus*, the pure act, is another reason why the idea of human equality lacks government-minted currency.

Contra President Bartlett's corporate-sponsored proclamation, economics is not one thing. Outside of ideological bubbles there are no economic necessities: metaphysical experience repudiates them. Objective and subjective reason form a dialectical image in which neither the object nor the subject is volatized by the other.[18] The collapse of the infinite possibility contained in each of us into the law of value (market exchangeability) is a reification attempting to foreclose on philosophy by replacing objective with unbound subjective reason. Likewise, if the community of the kingdom of God repudiates any essentiality to real history, transcendental history forecloses on objectivity itself. This is Max Weber's linkage, and into which his thought dissolves. Without a dialectical image, reification is inevitable. What we see portrayed in the character of President Bartlett is lived experience as the never-ending flow of capital—a perpetual advertisement of the entertainment industry for our subjugation. No longer need presidents be leaders, only functionaries of the corporate world: quote the Romans ever more! This is the wisdom proceeding from the great learning of President Jed Bartlett. With this and other "leading images,"[19] the business-as-usual industry presents us with the ideology of reconciliation for a non-reconciled society. In its inexorable manner, realism always traffics in images for reconciling us to what remains irreconcilable in metaphysical experience. All enterprises of this kind are anathema to philosophy after Auschwitz.

Another conspiracy of adjustment hides in the conservative restriction of philosophical activity to passive contemplation. The current fashion of integrating business and philosophy accords with Aristotle's division of the whole of life into these two parts, a division that has always reflected as legitimization the separation of concept formation (thinking) from bodily activity (work).[20] This devaluation of work as a conceptual activity has today culminated in the institutional degradation of work—the bureaucratic administration of teachers, the scientific management of professors (research laborers), and the general pedagogical insistence on passive learning. In a word, memorize! Tell me what you know about the Holocaust. How many crematoria at Auschwitz? What was the average number of Jews given "special treatment" at Auschwitz during the months of May and June of 1944? Typical exam questions, no doubt. Students get "A" grades on their Holocaust exams and return home proud of their excellence. And who can doubt that to talk intelligently about the Holocaust, you must first know the facts of the matter? Of course, but who then really talks about such things? The more you know, the worse it gets. The Holocaust—a terrible thing. What more can be said beyond the skilful, impressive recitation of the facts? Master your subject! But that's an old burned-in lesson. Master-servant—a bad infinite until the servants decide against the all or nothing death wager.

In his splendid essay "Against School," John Taylor Gatto says:

> Once you understand the logic behind modern schooling, its tricks and traps are fairly easy to avoid. School trains children to be employees and consumers; teach your own to be leaders and adventurers. School trains children to obey reflexively; teach your own to think critically and independently. Well-schooled kids have a low threshold for boredom; help your own to develop an inner life so that they'll never be bored. Urge them to take on the serious material, the grown-up material, in history, literature, philosophy, music, art, economics, theology—all the stuff schoolteachers know well enough to avoid. Challenge your kids with plenty of solitude so that they can learn to enjoy their own company, to

conduct inner dialogues. Well-schooled people are conditioned to dread being alone, and they seek constant companionship through the TV, the computer, the cell phone, and through shallow friendships quickly acquired and quickly abandoned. Your children should have a more meaningful life, and they can.[21]

Kids in school face what workers face in factories (and offices): canned objects of knowledge imposed from above and administered in carefully prepared dosages. The supposedly higher life of contemplation constructs nothing but symbolic firewalls against the future, the New.[22] Take heed, the really evil pushers of mind-altering substances are "embedded" in the administration of our schools.

Thinking is impossible without intimations of the future, the new. But the future does not announce itself in the manner of logical or scientific-technological projections of the present state of things. A good deal of science fiction today is gloomy precisely because it portrays a future without the new, as an intensification of the past-present and its trends. Given the prevalence of the contemplative mode, it comes as no surprise when contemporary "apocalypse" writers of "the rapture" employ the science fiction genre for the task of preparing the faithful for the End.[23] If what-has-been is conflated with knowledge and thought, disaster is the only reasonable conclusion concerning what will be: what will be can be nothing more than the logical completion of the "What-Was-Being."[24] This is the ideological version of "realizing" a concept. Thought without openness to novelty is contemplation caught in the ideological reflex of material already completely formed and thus faithful to the hierarchy and authority of the centralized state in its management of scarce resources.[25] Teachers today have a very intuitive grasp (I almost wrote "gasp") of this capture.

Honest confrontations with the terrible effects facing us in the wake of unchecked economism and its rapacious exploitation of labor and nonhuman resources are difficult but still possible. Nor need these confrontations succumb to fatalistic resignations. Examples of such confrontations can be found in a collection of essays called *The Coming Age of Scarcity*. When you begin to understand what has made possible the post Second World War "economic miracle," you get really scared. John Roth begins his foreword to this book by observing that *"The Coming Age of Scarcity* scares me."[26] Why? Because the global industrialization program is unsustainable. If continued, catastrophic results are inevitable. One catastrophic consequence of the current maniacal production of scarcity will be an intensification of genocide and "ethnic cleansing" which, in the field of rationalized production, will be understood as a "rational" solution for increasing numbers of superfluous populations.

In all probability, and in conjunction with the raves of the globalization ideologues, the twenty-first century will outstrip the twentieth in genocides and mass killings. The new feudalism of the many providing personal services for the rich few requires massive extermination programs and a perpetual (preemptive) war against the inevitable escalation of worldwide "terrorism." There can be no doubt about those not committed to the realization of the idea of human equality; they will make their peace with these consequences.[27] We must admit at least this much to confront honestly the fact that today billions of people are being transformed into a new kind of being—the specimen,[28] the being who is "polished off" before being killed.[29] In the new global order how could the commitment to excellence signify anything other than a warning to those in the zone of affluence tempted by the idea of "just getting by." The future is not for the weak. Study and learn from Abu Ghraib because such unmanaged images will be rare public occurrences during the perpetual war on terrorism. That is to say, learn or serve: "Life in the late capitalist era is a constant initiation rite. Everyone must show that he wholly identifies himself with the power which is belaboring him."[30] Will Islam ever learn? Will genocide ever end?

The hold of the so-called laws of economics and the exacerbated tendency of philosophy to affirm the status quo under conditions that in no way intimate the great ideas of truth, beauty, justice, and human equality are both indicative of a general failure in the cultural transmission and dissemination of the crucial idea of mediation. In the shadow of genocide and mass suffering, there has been a collective failing of contemporary philosophy. Where and how do we begin to rectify this failure? Theodor Adorno provides some of the clues:

> [I]f one takes seriously the idea of *mediation*, which is sketched but not fully worked out in Aristotle, the idea that form and matter are really *moments* which can only be conceived in relation to each other, the question as to which of them comes absolutely first or is ranked absolutely higher becomes transparent as a false abstraction. And one will then trace the forms of the concrete mediation of these moments, instead of treating the product of abstraction which keeps them apart as the only rightful source of truth. That, really, is the connecting thread which, in my opinion, leads from Aristotle's metaphysics as a whole to the questions currently occupying the minds of philosophers in this field.[31]

Absolute rankings of metaphysical concepts affirm the imbalances of power sustained by correlative affectations, such as antisemitism and racism, serving to direct us away from the irrationalities of our society. If the work process is not considered in the process of concept formation, the impetus in things will remain unrealized or, worse, distorted by simulations of mastery that deflect us from the home that is our future. Philosophy, like any body of work, is "not a machine which lets itself be taken apart."[32] Absolute rankings foreclose on the possibility at work in philosophical labors. Aristotle's expression "the One in the Many" does not express an absolute ranking of the One over the Many. A teleological orientation expressed affirmatively as an actual state of affairs or as an ontological fundament is the very essence of affectation. What comes from the future can never be affirmed as existing when the labor process whereby it is announced is itself taken over and commanded by so-called higher functions. The unity of the many is never simply given but rather indicated by a gesture, what Aristotle called "a this," or a deed whose indications under conditions of the suppression of labor and its redirection can be revealed only by way of parapraxis. The marginal phenomena of everyday life in managed, hierarchical society, the detritus of the rule of absolute rankings, thus contain, precisely as mistakes, the paths or indications of what is announced, the future, in the composite form of formed things and their formed workers.[33] To form something is to be formed by that, "a this," which is formed. Although Aristotle separated the working from the contemplative life, I believe this reciprocity is the basis for Aristotle's turn to the composite of matter and form, particular mediated things, as the point of departure for metaphysics. Which is not to say that Aristotle remained faithful to this reciprocity.

There is no psychological compensation for futile and hopeless labor. Any philosophy indifferent to the degradation of work will, tacitly or otherwise, affirm the banishment of workers from the transcendental realm. More precisely, such philosophies will recoil from the basis of all significance in the flesh of protest. Turgid formulations of reductive, quantitative measures for every quality giving color to existence will be delivered as products of superior minds for the subjugation of the stupid masses. Yes, philosophy and its "noble lies" serve the masters. But the philosophy of mastery is not all there is to philosophy. Camus's rejection of both the nihilism of formal principles and the nihilism without principles, traditional philosophy and modern anti-philosophy, recognizes that only if we restore "to the worker the dignity of a creator,"[34] can we establish a balance between individuals and history. The force of absolute rankings is the spirit of totality and it is this spirit that resists all balance between the *concept* of the absolute and the requirements of individual power and dignity. The imposition of mastery for the sake of profits and unchecked production, the dominance of the idea of unlimited growth (cancerous economics), the immiseration of the many for the sake of the few, the shameless excessive consumption of the privileged, all conspire against the establishment of a rational society in balance with nature, human requirements, and the individual pursuit of personal fulfillment.

Capital expands and accumulates and with it so do abstraction and impoverished language usage. "It's like, you know, we actually don't know much about, like, what it's really like." Shouting matches and vulgar invective become the standard of public discourse as consumption, debt, and the Gross National Product strive for new levels of excellence. Sports, including eating contests, become new forms of literacy. Matter and form expand their separation as well-managed and disgruntled workers look for something still free to kill. And, of course, racism and genocide persist under the cover of abstractions and the skilful displacements of emphases. What we learned from cultural anthropology concerning the intimate interrelations of ideas and ways of life is now relegated and confined to the characteristics of "primitive" societies.[35] Our advanced ones live by ever-increasing abstraction, by completely arbitrary digital codes—meaning, we do whatever we want to do. A recent commercial for heavy-duty pick-up trucks has its spokesman declare, "I have no limitations, and I never compromise." What we want receives neither reflection nor justification. "I can't help it, that's the way I'm wired"—the new variation on an old racial theme. Inputted and outputted, turned-on and turned-off, wasted and blown-away, with-it and cool, with attitude and extreme prejudice, "No one dare fuck with America. These colors don't run!" Yes, we have learned from centuries of mastery, genocide, and the wonderful, exculpatory fabrications of racism. Even the "geeks" (one of the more ugly appellations of current linguistic degradation) eventually turn to weapons of mass destruction.

Extremism, fanaticism, all the forms of the unmediated Absolute—the Absolute sans concept: philosophy began by liberating the Absolute from its dogmatic encapsulations. Philosophical affectations are unfaithful to this liberating arts tradition, but philosophy can still rediscover its better self. At its best, philosophy refuses to let sleeping dogs lay or lie, including its own and especially the dogs of war and mass killing. Genocide challenges philosophy. When philosophy goes beyond its affectations and becomes informed by worldly matters without succumbing to them, it works in the creative sense of being informed by the future with and against the active forces of irrationality in the present-past. This process of realization against all dogmatisms is its reward. There can be no other genuine administration of philosophy.

Notes

1. Max Horkheimer and Theodor W. Adorno, *Dialectic of Enlightenment*, trans. John Cumming (New York: Seabury Press, 1972), p. 195.
2. Horace's motto "Sapere Aude!" is Kant's "Have courage to use your own understanding!" See Immanuel Kant, *Perpetual Peace and Other Essays*, trans. Ted Humphrey (Indianapolis IN: Hackett, 1983), p. 41.
3. The occupation of the academic discipline of philosophy in the United States began in the late 1940s when McCarthyite forces swept through universities, under the cover of "anti-Communism," purging them of critical malcontents, especially those of the philosophical persuasion who failed to talk like "real Americans." This sordid story is the subject of John McCumber's important text *Time in the Ditch: American Philosophy and the McCarthy Era* (Evanston, IL: Northwestern University Press, 2001). What I would append to McCumber's horizon of America's suspicions of philosophy as a critical inquiry "that can lead anywhere and overturn anything" concerns the way in which the exigencies of the Cold War overrode post-Second

World War matters pertaining to America's complicity in the Holocaust. With the end of the Cold War in 1989, another way had to be found by those adamantly opposed to any inquiry that would put in jeopardy what they held as the revealed, eternal truths of the Republic. I propose that the current corporate takeover of the universities and the adoption of scientific-business management of disciplines is focused, at least in part, on the task of neutralizing philosophical inquiry into the Holocaust and the genocidal practices of the civilizing process in general. In the context of this appended horizon, McCumber's judgments hold all too well: "Under such a regime, philosophy cannot be what most philosophers today think it should be—an ongoing process of critical inquiry that can lead anywhere and overturn anything. Rather, it must present itself publicly, if at all, as a body of established doctrine, like geometry or arithmetic, or as an inquiry that, though critical, has somehow been diverted into nonthreatening fields" (p. 14).

4. Theodor W. Adorno, *Metaphysics: Concept and Problems*, trans. Edmund Jephcott (Stanford, CA: Stanford University Press, 2000), p. 121.

5. Theodor W. Adorno, *Negative Dialectics*, trans. E. B. Ashton (New York: Seabury Press, 1973), p. 362.

6. Mark Danner, "Torture and Truth," *The New York Review* (10 June 2004), p. 46.

7. The popularity of the "It's war!" reaction to our commission of atrocities in Iraq does offer a rather definitive answer to a question posed by Eugene Davidson in his conclusion to *The Trial of the Germans* (New York: Macmillan, 1966), p. 580: "Was the Nazi period, as some Germans say, an aberration of a basically humane and enlightened society, or was it the final expression of the *furor teutonicus* always latent in the German character?"

8. We are here denying the uniqueness of the Nazi genocide against the Jews. For a thought-provoking analysis of "Columbus as Protonazi," see Ward Churchill, *A Little Matter of Genocide: Holocaust and Denial in the Americas 1492 to the Present* (San Francisco, CA: City Lights Books, 1997), pp. 85–8.

9. Henry L. Feingold, *The Politics of Rescue: The Roosevelt Administration and the Holocaust, 1938–1945* (New York: Holocaust Library, 1970), p. 313.

10. This is a stronger claim than the one made by Richard L. Rubenstein, *The Cunning of History: The Holocaust and the American Future* (New York: Harper & Row, 1978), p. 21: "we are more likely to understand the Holocaust if we regard it as the expression of some of the most profound tendencies of Western civilization in the twentieth century."

11. Matthew 6:1 (New Revised Standard Version).

12. The removal of the other within the orbital power of capital and the state by the unicellular politics of reproduction (cloning: from the one to the same) is the ultimate eradication of all otherness and thus of all reflection (imagery): "Inasmuch as the individual no longer confronts the other, he finds himself face to face with himself. On account of an aggressive backlash on the part of his immune system, a dislocation of his own code and the destruction of his own defenses, the individual becomes in a sense an antibody to himself. Our society is entirely dedicated to neutralizing otherness, to destroying the other as a natural point of reference in a vast flood of aseptic communication and interaction, of illusory exchange and contact. By dint of communication, our society develops an allergy to itself. By becoming transparent in its genetic, biological and cybernetic being, the body becomes a specter and returns in the form of a self-destructive process. This, too, is the transparency of evil"—Jean Baudrillard, *The Transparency of Evil*, trans. James Benedict (London: Verso, 1993), pp. 121–2. Insofar as metaphor unites reason and

imagination, the eradication of reflection-image in the "production" of the individual follows upon an ontological quest for the source of the immune activity that identifies the other. For an excellent discussion of the ramifications of this ontological quest, see Alfred I. Tauber, *The Immune Self: Theory or Metaphor?* (Cambridge: Cambridge University Press, 1994).

13. Albert Camus, *The Myth of Sisyphus and Other Essays*, trans. Justin O'Brien (New York: Vintage Books, 1991), p. 4.

14. Stuart Klawans, "Medium Cool," *The Nation* (9 June 2003), p. 45.

15. This is what Richard Rorty calls moral progress in the direction of greater human solidarity—*Contingency, Irony, and Solidarity* (New York: Cambridge University Press, 1989), chap. 9. I also explore this way of moral progress in *Between Auschwitz and Tradition* (Atlanta, GA and Amsterdam: Rodopi, 1994).

16. Earl Shorris, "Ignoble Liars: Leo Strauss, George Bush, and the Philosophy of Mass Deception," *Harper's Magazine* (June 2004), p. 68. "For Strauss, as for Plato," writes Shorris, "the virtue of the lie depends on who is doing the lying. If a poor woman lies on her application for welfare benefits, the lie cannot be countenanced. The woman has committed fraud and must be punished. The woman is not noble, therefore the lie cannot be noble. When the leader of the free world says that 'free nations do not have weapons of mass destruction,' this is but a noble lie, a fable told by the aristocratic president of a country with enough nuclear weapons to leave the earth a desert less welcoming than the surface of the moon."

17. As Irving Greenberg reminds us, when it comes to taking action in cases of genocide, self-definitions in terms of belief in God or atheism are problematic. "Cloud of Smoke, Pillar of Fire: Judaism, Christianity, and Modernity after the Holocaust," in Eva Fleischner, ed., *Auschwitz: Beginning of a New Era?* (New York: KTAV, 1977), pp. 45–8.

18. Adorno, *Metaphysics: Concept and Problems*, pp. 142–3.

19. Theodor W. Adorno, *Critical Models*, trans. Henry W. Pickford (New York: Columbia University Press, 1998), p. 45.

20. Aristotle, *Politics*, 1133a, pp. 29–41.

21. John Taylor Gatto, "Against School: How Public Education Cripples Our Kids, and Why," *Harper's Magazine* (September 2003), p. 38.

22. Ernest Bloch, *The Principle of Hope*, trans. Neville Plaice, Stephen Plaice, and Paul Knight (Cambridge: The MIT Press, 1986), Vol. 1, p. 283.

23. At the time of this writing in 2004, the twelfth volume of the "Left Behind" series authored by Jerry B. Jenkins and Tim La Haye had just gone on sale. More than forty million copies of the first eleven volumes have been sold.

24. Bloch, *The Principle of Hope*, Vol. 1, p. 283: "Even for a thinker of development, Aristotle, essence is the το τι ην ειναι, the 'What-Was-Being', in the sense of enclosed definability, statuary distinctness."

25. Consider, for example, Patrick J. Buchanan's *The Death of the West: How Dying Populations and Immigrant Invasions Imperil Our Country and Civilization* (New York: St. Martin's Press, 2002). The Pill, Feminism, the Cultural Marxists, and Illegal Immigration are responsible for the Death of the West—all anti-ontological ontological forces separating man and nature in what-was the unity and harmony of Western Civilization. And what does Buchanan propose as a "solution" to the imminent disaster being prepared by the Cultural Revolutionaries? Not democracy (Buchanan quotes T. S. Eliot on this weakness) but rather Christian Faith: "Absent a revival of faith or a great awakening, Western men and women may simply live out their lives until they are so few they do not matter" (p. 266).

Buchanan does not opine the Novum, that the "I *am* becomes *we are*" since this would be to entertain the opinion of a Communist thinker, anathema to "true" Christians. No reconciliation is possible for Buchanan. Faith ordains that what is coming from without must never be the material by means of which the inner self comes to know itself. Thus Buchanan correctly frames himself as the antithesis of thinkers such as Bloch.

26. Michael Dobkowski and Isidor Wallimann, eds., *The Coming Age of Scarcity: Preventing Mass Death and Genocide in the Twenty-first Century* (Syracuse, NY: Syracuse University Press, 1998), p. ix.

27. This cruel improvisation gives new meaning, in true revisionist fashion, to the old blues song "I Got It Bad and That Ain't Good."

28. Horkheimer and Adorno, *Dialectic of Enlightenment*, "The Culture Industry: Enlightenment As Mass Deception." Adorno references this 1944 text in Lecture Fourteen of *Metaphysics: Concepts and Problems:* "What meets its end in the camps, therefore, is really no longer the ego or the self, but ... only the *specimen*" (p. 108).

29. George Orwell's version of the specimen, the *Muselmann*, is Winston after his torture. During Winston's torture, O'Brien allows him to envision what he will become: "What happens to you here is forever. Understand that in advance. We shall crush you down to the point from which there is no coming back. Things will happen to you from which you could not recover, if you lived a thousand years. Never again will you be capable of ordinary human feeling. Everything will be dead inside you. Never again will you be capable of love, or friendship, or joy of living, or laughter, or curiosity, or courage, or integrity. You will be hollow. We shall squeeze you empty, and then we shall fill you with ourselves." See George Orwell, *Nineteen Eighty-Four* (New York: Knopf, 1992), pp. 268–9. How many of us have the courage to face what centuries of genocide, cruelty, and mass production of misery have filled us with?

30. Horkheimer and Adorno, *Dialectic of Enlightenment*, p. 153.

31. Adorno, *Metaphysics: Concepts and Problems*, p. 41.

32. Pierre Duhem's words, as quoted by Arthur I. Miller, *Insights of Genius: Imagery and Creativity in Science and Art* (New York: Springer-Verlag, 1996), p. 43.

33. This line of thought takes Freud's brilliant expositions of the *Psychopathology of Everyday Life* in a direction not explicitly developed by Freud. It is, however, closely tied to the erotic interests hidden in the latent dream thoughts of modern subjects in their desperate attempt to achieve a modicum of what modern philosophy calls subjectivity.

34. Albert Camus, *L'homme révolté* (Paris: Éditions Gallimard, 1951), p. 341.

35. See Thomas F. Gossett, *Race: The History of an Idea in America* (New York: Oxford University Press, 1997), p. 416.

17

The Warring Logics of Genocide

Edith Wyschogrod

The very mention of genocide usually elicits a shudder, a *frisson* of horror, psychological revulsion, and moral outrage. Images of mass annihilation, of the dead and dying, evoked by that term are especially troubling since genocidal killing, now endemic in the postmodern world, is grasped as a slaughter of the innocents. It is understood that those earmarked for destruction are selected on the basis of criteria that lie outside the standard rules of conduct in war, even if genocidal events occur in the context of what is designated conventionally as war. Genocidal killing is often justified by its perpetrators not principally on the grounds of what the dead are presumed to have done but rather as required by an ontological flaw, as it were, attributed to the victims.

The significations conveyed in ordinary usage pass into the criteria of what counts as genocide as defined by international law. Imbricated in its juridical phraseology is the visceral aversion to what the term evokes, the destruction wreaked upon countless numbers of individuals because of who they are or who they are alleged to be, individuals whose "crime" is an identity to which negative value is ascribed and that is eliminable only through the extermination of its bearers. The legal definition takes cognizance both of the magnitude of the exterminations and of the fact that the targeted groups are deliberately rather than randomly chosen.

In addition to the parameters established by the legal definition of genocide, I also consider meanings ascribed to the term *ethnic cleansing* as starting points for a discussion of the warring logics intrinsic to events of mass extermination. I then turn to Dominique Janicaud's insightful account of the way in which rationality is currently configured as it bears upon, even if (as I believe) it fails fully to capture, the character of the warring logics at work in genocide. I do not interpret "logic" as referring to rules of inference deployed to determine the status of arguments or to a mode of reasoning invoked to justify moral norms, but rather, as referring to a complex of interpretive indicators or perspectives that arise within the sphere of events. In the case of genocidal acts, these logics are exhibited as their modus operandi.

The first of these warring logics is best described as *the rationality of unencumbered replicability*, the sensed multiplication of individuals so that vast numbers are seen as indistinguishable from one another. This absence of distinctiveness gives rise to a second logic, *the logic of indiscernibles*, so that individuals lacking difference meld into an undifferentiated sameness, a solidary yet formless Being from which individuation is absent. I explicate this second logic in terms of Emmanuel Levinas's concept the *il y a*.

In so doing, I do not wish to offer an account of the psychology of the perpetrators. Instead, I shall proceed somewhat in the phenomenologically minimalist manner attributed to Maurice Merleau-Ponty by Dominique Janicaud: "the visible dimension of invisibility ... a search for source-forms [*formes-meres*], an investigation of bodily encroachments and social rumblings which are [cultural in appearances]."[1]

I take for granted the cultural and political specificity of individual events, but in the present context I cannot undertake an analysis of each. However, I presume that the logics of techno-science are imbricated in widely divergent social and cultural situations even when the means of extermination differ. What is more, I argue that this logic is involved in movements of resistance to it.[2]

Genocide or ethnic cleansing: juridical perspectives

Before turning to the warring logics of genocide, consider first its international legal definition as found in Articles II and III of the United Nations' 1948 Convention on the Prevention and Punishment of Genocide. The document identifies genocide's mental and physical aspects. The mental aspect is the "intent to destroy, in whole or in part, a national, ethnical, racial, or religious group, as such." The physical includes five acts: "killing members of the group, causing serious bodily or mental harm to members of the group, ... deliberately inflicting conditions of life calculated to bring about its destruction in whole or in part, imposing measures intended to prevent births within the group, forcibly transferring children of the group to another group."[3]

Acts constituting part of a policy to destroy a group's existence are seen as genocidal and as warranting punishment. The document goes on to declare that targeted groups fall into categories, those that are national, politically constituted; those that are ethnically and culturally determined; those that are racial as identified by their physical characteristics; and those that are religious as defined by beliefs, doctrines, and practices. Crucial for my subsequent discussion is the claim that "group identity is often imposed by the perpetrators."[4] Equally significant for my account is this document's ascription of the term *genocide* to the prevention of births within a targeted group.

Who, it may be asked, is the referent of the "we" who are incensed by genocide. The aversiveness to genocide, reflected in the legal text that defines it, is grounded in the assumption of a humanity that shares a moral perspective, one that presupposes a sense of outrage. Thus the Preamble to the Rome Statute of the International Criminal Court explicitly affirms that the States who are parties to the statute are *"[m]indful* [italics in original] that during this century millions of children, women and men have been victims of unimaginable atrocities that deeply shock the conscience of humanity" and that "this delicate mosaic of a common humanity may be shattered at any time."[5] Without endorsing the ground upon which this sense of abomination is predicated (i.e., the notion of a universal humanity) I nevertheless concur in the claim that our responses are dependent upon the "vocabulary of our culture and its sustaining archetypes," an agreement that does not preclude critical self-awareness of the ways in which memories are transmitted.[6] With this caveat in mind, I shall accept as a premise the claim that genocide usually engenders this visceral antipathy.

In its difference from genocide, *ethnic cleansing* is alleged to fall under the rubric of "war crimes" or "crimes against humanity." A report from Human Rights Watch notes: " 'Ethnic cleansing' is not formally defined under international law [but] a UN Commission of Experts has defined the term, as a 'purposeful policy designed by one ethnic or religious group to remove by violent and terror-inspiring means the civilian population of another ethnic group or religious group from certain geographical areas [in the interest of occupying the territory] to the exclusion of the purged group or groups.' "[7] Thus, Human Rights Watch categorizes as ethnic cleansing the effort of the Sudanese government "to remove the Masalit and Fur populations from large parts of Darfur [the western region of the Sudan] by violent means," moving them to government-controlled towns.[8] In addition, the document notes that the Janjaweed and other ethnic Arab groups have occupied these areas in ways that fit the Commission's definition of ethnic cleansing.

That the line between genocide and ethnic cleansing cannot easily be drawn is attested by the difficulty reported to be experienced in the American government before statements in the second half of 2004 by the then Secretary of State Colin Powell and President George W. Bush referred to the Darfur situation as genocide. According to a 12 June 2004 account in the *New York Times*, thousands of people in Darfur had been killed and more than a million driven from their homes by invading militias. At the time, Powell commented that he was not prepared to select a defining term: "All I know," he said, "is that there are at least a million people who are desperately in need and many of them will die if we don't get the international community mobilized. ... And it won't make a whole lot of difference after the fact what you've called it."[9] In a follow-up op-ed, Nicholas Kristof maintained that the 320,000 deaths in the Darfur region, in which "the world has acquiesced shamefully" by ignoring the event, more than justified applying the term *genocide*. In describing an attack by the Janjaweed against the local Zaghawa tribes, he wrote that the invaders used ethnic and racial language as they shouted, "We will not let Zaghawa live here." The attack, Kristof claimed, "was part of a deliberate strategy to ensure that the village would be forever uninhabitable, that the Zaghawa would never live there again. The Janjaweed poisoned wells by stuffing them with the corpses of people and donkeys, ... blew up a dam, burned all the homes, ... a school, a clinic and a mosque."[10] In regard to their operative logics, both genocide and ethnic cleansing invite scrutiny in that mass extermination plays a crucial role (whether as means or end) in each.

Yet the question plaguing the interpreter remains: How can s/he ascertain that what is alleged to have happened actually did happen. I assume that, even if understandably cautious theories of truth presume that there is no purely transparent language that could render events just as they transpired, the observer nevertheless works within the parameters of what can and cannot have been. Thus we may say, "It could have been x or y, but it could not have been z" where z constitutes a denial of both x and y.[11] In the Sudanese example at hand, the interpreter may not be sure that events occurred exactly as recounted, but s/he cannot dismiss the claim that extermination has occurred, its significance and the responsibility to make known what is happening in Darfur.

Techno-discourse and genocide

Is there a discernible mode of rationality that governs the economy and technology of postmodernity? Dominique Janicaud describes an all-encompassing global language that he terms *techno-discourse*, a world of rational rules, a metarationality that is the rationality inhering in the rational itself. In its social, political, economic, and cultural manifestations, this rationality is expressed as power. He argues further for the possibility of a self-reversal of this omnipresent rationality, a self-reversal that will not descend into irrationality but will open into an alternative exercise of reason that he calls *partage*. In consonance with Hegel, Janicaud maintains that reason is inescapable: *partage* means reason is our share or allotment. I do not enter into the difficulties bound up with the claims for this reversal but focus on the operation of techno-discourse as a point of departure for understanding one of the logics of genocide.

Techno-discourse, Janicaud argues, transcends the practices of specific operational technical discourses to become the lingua franca of an all-embracing audiovisual information culture that constitutes and disseminates meaning. According to Janicaud,

> Techno-discourse ... is a parasitic language inextricably woven into technology, contributing to its diffusion ... making almost impossible any radical analysis or any questioning of contemporary technological phenomena. Every technology has its vocabulary, its codes ... its operative

scenarios. Such is not the case with techno-discourse; it is neither strictly scientific, nor philosophic, [nor] poetic.[12]

However—and this is Janicaud's point—"the scientific and technological revolution is only the most recent manifestation of a process that is much older, more fundamental: the *potentialization* of knowledge as power."[13] It is crucial not merely to chronicle the history of technical progress and the changes it has effected but "to think techno-science," to confront the "possibilities and the dynamics of a process without precedent."[14]

Janicaud maintains that in successfully realizing predetermined ends within a plurality of specific domains in which they are operative, rationality "runs wild" and becomes the subject of a will to totalize or, as Heidegger would have it, to transform thinking into calculation. For Janicaud, however, a historically penetrating genealogical analysis precludes drawing a sharp boundary between calculative reason and Being. Instead he depicts contemporary rationality as an encounter with the Incalculable. The question of what is presupposed by development, by the "postulates of power," cannot be answered calculatively. The sheer scale and magnitude of what seems calculable, the Gigantic, resists quantitative reduction and morphs into the Incalculable. As the shadow haunting the logic of modernity, "the Incalculable," he concludes, "is nothing other than the unconditioned advancement of power, which is continually remeasured and reevaluated." Respecting only scientific technical success, the Incalculable mobilizes "for unlimited development and expansion without any definitive highest aim." Reason is delivered to its "destiny of power," a destiny mandating that we confront the enigmas of power by considering a phenomenology of its effects.[15] The rationality of development manifested as the Incalculable unleashes "the dark side of total mastery and the terrifying 'logic' of a surplus of power," a logic that expresses itself in the "unbearable scourge" of the mass exterminations endemic to the present age.[16] The language of these catastrophic events is that of number, a language that conceals while revealing the incalculability of their magnitude: "First World War 8.7 million dead; Second World War 40 million, Hitler's camps 7 million, Stalin's camps 30 million. Solzhenitsyn's figures."[17]

What role, it may be asked, does techno-discourse play in racial and ethnic genocides? I argue that the imagined replicability of individuals is intrinsic to the logic of techno-discourse and that the replicability principle is then applied to living peoples, whereas for Janicaud, who does not discuss the role of replicability, the explanation for mass extermination lies elsewhere. For him, initial observations of differences in power harden into the exercise of power as domination so that a mystique of hierarchy is created. To be sure, hierarchy plays a significant role. The postwar testimony of Rudolf Hoess, the ex-commandant of Auschwitz, spoke in hierarchical terms of "strict orders as transmitted by *Reichsführer* SS, Himmler."[18] Ultimately appealing to the *Führerprinzip*, to Hitler as the final authority in all matters, Hoess stated that "being a member of the SS and [obedient to its discipline] all orders issued by its leader and by Hitler were right."[19] Similarly Alfred Speer, who in disdain of traditional bureaucracy developed new, looser lines of organization and was distrusted by old-line Nazi officials, overcame objections to his strategies in that none of his critics could invoke the nimbus of Hitler against him. "The backing of the *Führer*," asserted Speer, "counted for everything."[20]

Janicaud contends that Nazism attempted to justify the manner in which it exercised power by grounding itself in what it saw as biological science and in an alleged instinct of aggression. He argues further that Nazism may "find an unexpected reprieve in techno-scientism ... an appeal to power supported by material ameliorations." Thus the spirit of Nazism was a social mirror of aspects of the power of techno-science.[21] I argue, however, that the "soothing effect" relied upon by the Nazis derived from the efficiency and speed of new technologies and, as such, did not reflect their relation to the deeper logics of techno-discourse. To be sure, when Hoess spoke about using the gas Zyklon B to kill Jews at Auschwitz, he said that this innovation "had a soothing effect on me ... We had shortly to begin a mass killing of the Jews. ... Now we [Hoess and Adolf Eichmann] had discovered the gas and the means."[22] But rather than offering a reprieve from the demands of techno-science, his remark is a response to the deeper threatening aspect of its logic: the power to produce an infinite number of copies of entities as found in a variety of domains. A model was thus in place for coping with one of Nazism's more profound fears, that of the unending replication of the despised Other. The perceived uncontrollable multiplication of those who were the subject of loathing elicited the turn to strategies that would be taken as foolproof, techniques that ensured total extermination of the Other.

The possibility of unending reproduction is anticipated in Hegel's account of the wrong or bad infinite. For Hegel, every "something" others itself to become yet another "something," and this procession is never-ending. Infinity thus understood "is only a negation of the finite; but the finite rises again, the same as ever, and is never got rid of and absorbed."[23] Hegel's wrong infinite can be read as an eerie premonitory expression of a mode of genocidal logic, the fear of number "gone wild." In the light of this logic, consider the following entry in the *Stroop Report*, a collection of thirty-two teletypes prepared by Major General Juergen (nee Josef) Stroop for SS Chief Heinrich Himmler. Written in the idiom of statistics, Stroop reported specifically about the daily operations of the SS in putting down the Warsaw ghetto uprising in April–May 1943. At one point, Stroop writes as follows: "[Having received little training] the men of the *Waffen*-SS ... must be given special recognition for their daring, courage, and devotion to duty. ... *Wehrmacht* engineers also executed their tasks of blowing up bunkers, sewers, and concrete houses with tireless devotion. Only the continuous and tireless commitment of all forces made it possible to apprehend and/or destroy 56,065 Jews."[24]

The Nazi use of technologies, gas chambers to kill and crematoria to dispose of the dead, is by now a matter of common knowledge. What must be noted is that various modes of incineration were seen not only as efficient and as rituals of "purification" but also as preventing further replication. A dispatch from the Central Management of the Building Section in Auschwitz reports that corpses from the gas chambers at Auschwitz-Birkenau were burnt in four crematoria at the rate of 4,416 within twenty-four hours.[25] Fire was also used to terrorize and kill. Stroop reported, for example, that the SS started fires in the Warsaw ghetto, forcing Jews to emerge from their hiding places. Some Jews were burned alive as they attempted to escape. On 16 May 1943, Stroop wrote that "the Jewish quarter of Warsaw is no more."[26] It should also be noted that most of the Jewish women and children deported to Auschwitz were immediately sent to the gas chambers. No doubt they were seen as useless, but it must be added that they could also be perceived as providing links to an interminable future. This fear is also discernible in the Nazi effort to curtail the numbers of the Slavic population, even if that population was not destined for total extermination. To this end, medical experiments were conducted that would enable a surgeon and a properly equipped staff "to sterilize several hundred or even a thousand in one day."[27]

In a memoir concerning an earlier genocidal event—it has been referred to as the Turkish Armenocide of 1915–22—Aram Ardonian cites one Zeki Bey, who does not hesitate to kill a child by dashing it to the ground. "Don't think that I have killed an innocent being," Bey asserts. "Even the newborn babes of this people (Armenians) are criminals for they will carry the seeds of vengeance in themselves. If you wish to spare tomorrow, kill even their children." And they spared none.[28]

Formless being

Is there a genocidal logic other than that of unstoppable proliferation to be found in the context of mass extermination? I have maintained that the vast numbers of those targeted are no longer seen as individuals but, in accordance with the logic of replication, as identical units. In conformity with Leibniz's principle of the identity of indiscernibles, if A has the properties of B and only those of B and B has only the properties of A, then A and B are identical. Thus, in contrast to genocide's innumerable individual victims, this non-difference can also be viewed as the converging of these individuals to constitute a vast formless mass, a mass that is simply there. The absence of discernible difference is anticipated in the pre-Socratic philosopher Anaximander's *apeiron* or Unlimited and in the *khora* depicted in Jacques Derrida's analysis of Plato's *Timaeus*. However, the *apeiron* is an ontological storehouse of that which will come into being, and the *khora* gives place to mythos and logos, whereas the formlessness that arises in the logic of genocide is one of irreparable loss, the disintegration of individuals into a mound of indistinguishable units.

I have suggested elsewhere that "what must be brought to the fore is the indeterminateness of Being that would ensue if one imagined not what is prior to beings but the disappearance of all beings ... an impersonal anonymous residue."[29] This being that wells up in the absence of beings, designated by Emmanuel Levinas as the *il y a* and in his view disclosed through horror, preexists the emergence of individuals. A medium "not reducible to a system of operational references," it is a "nocturnal space" into which things can disappear but which cannot itself withdraw.[30] The *il y a* is not to be identified with Heidegger's nonbeing as that toward which anguish is directed, but rather with Being itself. For Levinas, it is not the coming to an end of one's individual existence that is the ground of anguished care but rather the endless continuity of being.[31] Levinas speaks of insomnia or wakefulness as the inability to suspend the primordial affective encounter with the *il y a* through sleep. However, because one's own being or subjectivity is lost in the formlessness of the *il y a*, insomnia cannot be an existential deportment of the individual but must be attributed to the *il y a* itself.[32]

Nevertheless, the *il y a* should not be interpreted as a despairing retreat from the possibility of ethical existence but rather as a move toward an ethics of otherness. In its doubleness, the *il y a* refers not only to the elemental, a terrain that lies escheat prior to the emergence of individuation and the structures of human existence, but also, as we have seen, to Being as that into which the already existing individual can sink. It is crucial to note that this immersion undoes egoity and denucleates the self, an undoing that "strike[s] with absurdity the active transcendental ego."[33] This surrender of egoity allows for the advent of the Other whose very emergence is to be read as proscribing violence and who is the primal source of the moral life. In confronting the face of the Other, one is in the presence of a proscription against harming the Other who is understood not primordially as a visible phenomenon but as an imperative, as discourse rather than percept, language rather than image.

Is it possible to render the inundation by media images of extermination, of the formless mounds of corpses and vast numbers of the living herded together awaiting death, in terms of the menace and destruction of the *il y a*? An eerie parallel can be discerned in Primo Levi's depiction of arrival at Auschwitz: "The world into which one was precipitated was terrible, yes, but also indecipherable: it did not conform to any model; the enemy was all around but also inside, the 'we' lost its limits ... ."[34] The logic of the *il y a*, moreover, is further attested in efforts to conceal genocide. As that which seemingly was already defined by formless expansion, genocide may beget further genocides. Thus Philip Gourevich speculates that a new war could spark a bloody regional conflict involving multiple African states. It "would be a war *about* the genocide in that Hutu power attempts to see itself as in a continuum with earlier Rwandan violence while depending on genocide to justify its rule."[35] Thus genocides would continue to breed while seeking meta-level justification by appealing to previous genocides.

In sum, the proliferation of individuals whose observable differences have been obliterated has led to an identity of indiscernibles so that individuality disappears. Instead a new logic supervenes, that of individuals melded into a formless mass. Does Primo Levi's *Lager*, an "indecipherable" world that "conforms to no model" not provide an existential referent for the Levinasian *il y a*? Are the logics manifested within a given genocidal event not operative in a universe of expanding genocides?

Explaining the shiver of horror

Neither Janicaud's account of techno-discourse nor Levinas's description of immersion in the formlessness of the *il y a* need be seen as entrapments from which there is no exit. Consider, first, that the *il y a* itself is not an insuperable obstacle to ethics; on the contrary it undermines an egoity that hampers self-giving. What is more, in its conceptual inapprehensibility and ego-destroying character, the *il y a* can be read as the obverse of the infinite, the transcendent locus of Good, and, as such, is locked into a structural pairing, as it were. For Levinas, thought must be penetrated by an infinite transcendence that shatters the thought that thinks it. Like the *il y a*, the infinite is excessive in that it exceeds any idea we can have of it. The infinite is not merely unimaginable magnitude but the object of a desire for a Good beyond being. God who remains transcendent is beyond conceptual grasp yet enters existence by way of the Other.[36] The obligation to the Other is itself infinitized so that one becomes one-for-the-other. In so doing, one does not use signs to communicate this self-abandonment. Instead, one makes oneself into a sign, a process Levinas calls sincerity. The referent of this sincerity is termed glory, the glory of the infinite. Unlike immersion in the *il y a*, the subject that is expelled from itself places itself at another's disposal. If glory is a proclaiming of peace and a proscription of violence, as Levinas claims, glory can be called the dynamism of the infinite that may be contrasted with the insomnia or wakefulness that can be discerned as the dynamism of the *il y a*.

It is clear that resistance to genocide at the risk of one's life can be considered a prime expression of an ethics of otherness. But what requires explanation is the far lesser claim to goodness evinced in the widespread response of revulsion to genocide, the *frisson* of horror that is neither heroic resistance nor the self-serving exculpatory profession of revulsion by perpetrators. Although Levinas does not consider the matter, this common response of horror can be linked to the idea of the infinite in relation to the *il y a*, an infinite that is expressed in and as the revulsion that wells up in confronting the dead others even at a remove from proximity to the event. Neither a psychological law based on observation nor a universal moral law, the *frisson* of horror, I maintain, inhabits a discursive space between the command of alterity to refrain from violence, a command that is a precondition of actual language, and the shudder itself, a gesture that is a sign epitomizing that which seeks but cannot find further articulation.

This revulsion can also be interpreted as arising in Janicaud's resolution of the dilemma posed by the rationality of techno-discourse. Rather than abandoning rationality, he develops, as we have seen, an alternative view of reason. Simply put, "to think is to enter into relation," but there is a limit within the relational, a *partage*, a multivalent term that carries connotations of share, allotment.[37] We need not, as Heidegger does, think that which is unthought, that which is other apart from rationality. Instead we are to acknowledge that rationality is inescapable, that it is our lot. Difference must be inscribed within the rational itself.

To be sure, when rationality is expressed as the will to objectivity, it is to be understood as power, its history as the history of power. However, we must not, Janicaud contends, effect a break with rationality but rather see that the rational can face "its destiny of power." In so doing, rationality need not return to its claims of self-sufficiency. Denying that *partage* is a destiny that, in the manner of Heidegger, has been "plotted in the obscure heart of Being, ... it is enacted *between* us and Being." Our *partage* is not abstract but is played out historically. In what is perhaps the most cogent formulation of this perspective, Janicaud maintains that "one must take possession of the legacy of modern reason such that it ceaselessly analyzes and recovers itself. ... There is no formula offering a conciliatory universality." He goes on to say that "rationality does not guarantee understanding: it ignores or stifles singularities and nuance, life's fragility and changeability. Destiny become *partage* is reason made more reasonable."[38]

In pondering the enigma of rationality, that which it cannot think—and this is the crucial point—"there is released the possibility of and 'examination of the *conscience*' of the rational facing its destiny of power [emphasis mine]." It is this reserve of open possibility that challenges the evil of rationality. We can envisage this *partage* or limiting of power because "the possible is held in reserve at the foundation of the power of the rational."[39] What opens this fissure in rationality is its confrontation with its power, with the evil inherent in it. A totally rational self-enclosed system must implode upon or reverse itself just as production and efficiency, when maximized, may implode and manifest themselves in individual atomization and insecurity. Although there can be no "conciliatory universality," there is a reserve in rationality itself that confronts the evil intrinsic to it and renders possible an examination of the conscience of the rational that opens the way to the shudder of horror, the gesture of repudiation.

Afterthoughts

The response to genocide understood as the extermination of peoples is, I have maintained, most frequently one of revulsion and horror, a reaction that can be attributed to a radical overturning and reversal of the warring logics intrinsic to genocide. As exhibited within a genocidal event itself, the first of these logics is manifested as the rationality of unencumbered replicability. When applied to groups of peoples, they are seen as potentially capable of multiplying endlessly. What is more, in targeted groups individuals are viewed as indistinguishable from one another.

The logic of replicability is embedded in techno-discourse, an all-encompassing global language enacted as a complex of rational rules operative in various domains of contemporary existence: economics, politics, technology, and culture. As depicted by Dominique Janicaud, techno-discourse is expressed as power. When the rule of replicability is applied by the perpetrators of genocide to a despised or feared people, unstoppable multiplication is seen as requiring their total extermination. At the same time, the absence of individual distinctiveness gives rise to a second logic, the logic of indiscernibles. Identical and seemingly isolated monads meld into an undifferentiated sameness, a solidary formlessness that is best described in terms of Emmanuel Levinas's concept of the *il y a*, indeterminate being.

Both the logic of infinite replication as imbricated in techno-discourse and the logic of formless being are subject to movements of reversal. According to Janicaud, as techno-discourse reaches its limits, it undoes itself and thereby liberates the possibility of conscience. When confronted with its nature as power, the rational may repudiate the terrifying logic of the surplus of power that eventuates in genocidal killing and, in this undoing, arrive at a *partage*, an allotment or limiting of power. It is this emergence of conscience as a dislodging of techno-discourse that, I argue, releases the horror of genocide.

The "reversal" of the second mode of genocidal logic, the suppression of individuality in the *il y a*, is brought about by the effort to think that which is unencompassible by thought, the infinite. To be sure, like the *il y a*, the infinite in its excessiveness precludes conceptual grasp. However, not to be confused with the formlessness of being, the infinite is the object of a desire for what is beyond being, for a Good that mandates responsibility for the Other. As the expression of divine transcendence, the infinite releases the moral revulsion that is the common response to genocide.

In a 1991 work that sparked considerable debate in French philosophical circles, Janicaud rejected what he conceived to be a theologizing tendency, a phenomenology of the invisible that he attributed at least in part to the influence of Levinas.[40] Arguing against foundationalist perspectives that "overburden immanence with transcendence," Janicaud insisted that he had resolved the principal issues of the debate in his account of a minimalist phenomenology that would undo its speculative unity. Heretofore seen as an ideal, phenomenology should now be an inspiration that nourishes multiple practices.[41] It has not been my aim to wade into the murky waters of this dispute but rather to exploit the tension between the thought of Levinas and that of Janicaud so as to illuminate the warring logics of genocide and the reversal of these logics that issues in the *frisson* of horror, the visceral response to the mass exterminations of the present age.

Notes

1. Dominique Janicaud, "Towards a Minimalist Phenomenology: The End of Overbidding," p. 100. http://ot.creighton.edu/u/otd521/Readings/Janicaud%202000%20Tpward%20minimalist%20phenomenon.pdf

2. As an example, see a popular exposition of the conflicts within the cultural structures of Muslim countries. Analyzing the work of the Islamic scholar Bernard Lewis, Ian Buruma points to Lewis's claim that there is a simultaneous war on modernity and attraction to its "rock and roll" culture. The conflict with modernity occurs in numerous differing situations "from German Romanticism … that began as a reaction to the French Enlightenment … to nineteenth century Slavophiles in Russia who extolled the Russian soul. …" Despite their divergent perspectives, Buruma and Lewis appear to be in accord on this matter. See Ian Buruma, "Lost in Translation: The Two Minds of Bernard Lewis," in *The New Yorker*, 14 and 21 June 2004, p. 190.

3. See "The Legal International Definition of Genocide," http://www.preventgenocide.org/genocide/officialtext, p. 1.

4. Ibid., p. 2.

5. For an expanded text, see http://www.prevent genocide.org/law/icc/statute/part-a, p. 3.

6. James E. Young, *Writing and Rewriting the Holocaust: Narratives and the Consequences of Interpretation* (Bloomington, IN: Indiana University Press, 1988), p. 192.

7. Human Rights Watch, " 'Ethnic Cleansing' in West Darfur." See http://www.hrw.org/english/docs/2004/05/datur8549, p. 1.

8. Ibid.

9. Marc Lacey, "White House Reconsiders its Policy on Crisis in Sudan" *New York Times*, 12 June 2004, A3.

10. Nicholas D. Kristof, "Dare We Call It Genocide?" *New York Times*, 16 June 2004, A21. These observations are offered in the context of his account of the experiences of a woman who survived the carnage she depicts.

11. See Edith Wyschogrod, *An Ethics of Remembering: History, Heterology and the Nameless Others* (Chicago, IL: University of Chicago Press, 1998), p. 168.

12. Dominique Janicaud, *Powers of the Rational: Science, Technology and the Future of Thought*, trans. Peg Birmingham and Elizabeth Birmingham (Bloomington, IN: Indiana University Press, 1994), p. 65.

13. Ibid., p. 75.

14. Dominique Janicaud, *Rationalities, Historicities*, trans. Nina Belmonte (Atlantic Highlands, NJ: Humanities Press, 1997), p. 53.

15. Ibid., pp. 45–7.

16. Ibid., p. 29.

17. Ibid.

18. See *Commandant of Auschwitz: The Autobiography of Rudolf Hoess* (London: Pan Books Ltd., 1961), p. 162. Cited in *Auschwitz, 1940–1945: Guidebook through the Museum* (Krakow: Panstwowe Museum, 1974), p. 40.

19. See the trial documents as cited in *Auschwitz 1940–1945: Guidebook through the Museum*, p. 41.

20. Albert Speer, *Inside the Third Reich*, trans. Richard and Clara Winston (New York: Macmillan, 1970), p. 282.

21. Janicaud, *Rationalities, Historicities*, p. 37.

22. Hoess, *Commandant of Auschwitz*, p. 165, as cited in *Auschwitz 1940–1945*, p. 32.

23. See *Hegel's Logic*, Part One of *The Encyclopedia of the Social Sciences*, trans. William Wallace (Oxford: The Clarendon Press, 1873, reprinted 1982), paras. 93–94, p. 137.

24. See *The Stroop Report*, facsimile edition and translation of the official Nazi report on the destruction of the Warsaw ghetto, translated and annotated by Sybil Milton, Introduction by Andrzej Wirth (New York: Pantheon Books, 1979), p. 10. The content referred to here is dated 16 May 1943. Preserving the sense of the original, the translated book itself is without page numbers.

25. See *Auschwitz 1940–1945*, p. 109.

26. *The Stroop Report.*

27. See *Auschwitz 1940–1945*, p. 73.

28. Aram Andonian, *The Memoirs of Naim Bey: The Turkish Armenocide* (The Genocide of the Armenians by Turks), Documentary Series, Volume Two, Fiftieth Anniversary Publication, 1965. Reprint by Armenian Historical Research Association, p. 46.

29. See Wyschogrod, *An Ethics of Remembering*, pp. 16–17.

30. Emmanuel Levinas, *Existence and Existents*, trans. Alphonso Lingis (The Hague: Martinus Nijhoff, 1978), p. 58.

31. Ibid., p. 20.

32. Emmanuel Levinas, *Time and the Other*, trans. Richard Cohen (Pittsburgh: Duquesne University Press, 1985), p. 48.

33. Emmanuel Levinas, *Otherwise Than Being and Beyond Essence*, trans. Alphonso Lingis (The Hague: Martinus Nijhoff, 1981), p. 161.

34. Primo Levi, *The Drowned and the Saved*, trans. Raymond Rosenthal (New York: Vintage Books, 1989), p. 38.

35. Philip Gourevich, "Letter from Rwanda: After the Genocide," *The New Yorker*, 18 December 1995, pp. 92–3. In regard to the expansion of violence in the region, see Marc Lacey "Life in Congo: Another Coup, Another Crisis," *New York Times*, 20 June 2004. "At its worst," writes Lacey, "the Civil War in the Congo that appeared to be ended in 1998 drew in Angola, Zimbabwe and Namibia on the side of the government and Uganda and Rwanda as backers of rebel forces. In all an estimated three million people died. ... Congo's relation with Rwanda remains tense."

36. Emmanuel Levinas, "God and Philosophy" in Adriaan T. Peperzak, Simon Critchley, and Robert Bernasconi, eds, *Emmanuel Levinas: Basic Philosophical Writings*, trans. Alphonso Lingis and Richard Cohen as revised (Bloomington, IN: Indiana University Press, 1996), p. 139.

37. Janicaud, *Powers of the Rational*, p. 20.

38. Janicaud, *Rationalities, Historicities*, p. xviii.

39. Janicaud, *Powers of the Rational*, p. 238.

40. See Dominique Janicaud et al., *Phenomenology and the "Theological Turn": The French Debate* (New York: Fordham University Press, 2000).

41. Janicaud, "Towards a Minimalist Phenomenology," p. 103.

18

Philosophy's Obligation to the Human Being in the Aftermath of Genocide

Paul C. Santilli

> We have been entrusted with an awesome legacy, and we are being judged by invisible friends, brothers, teachers, parents and they are all dead. And they all had but one wish, to be remembered.
>
> > Elie Wiesel, at the Opening Session of the United States Holocaust Memorial Commission, 15 February 1979

> I do not know / if you can still / make something of me / If you have the courage to try ...
>
> > Charlotte Delbo, *Auschwitz and After*

When Philip Gourevitch walked among the dead Tutsis massacred by the Hutus at Nyarubuye in the Rwandan genocide of 1994, he saw, one year after the killings, that the dead were still there, left unburied as a memorial to what had happened. He noted that the corpses were strangely *beautiful*: "The randomness of the fallen forms, the strange tranquility of their rude exposure, the skull here, the arm bent in some uninterpretable gesture there—these things were beautiful, and their beauty only added to the affront of the place."[1] After stepping accidentally on a skull, hearing its crunch and feeling its vibration, Gourevitch was unsure of his response, worrying that he, like Leontius in Book IV of Plato's *Republic*, was cursed for having his fill "of the lovely spectacle." He felt unreal. Gourevitch confessed that the dead were to him omnipresent but only as "absences" and "only of interest as evidence" in the impending trials of their killers.[2]

The dead

The suffering and death of approximately 800,000 human beings slaughtered in Rwanda in less than one hundred days must seem to the rest of us not on the scene an unreal, spectral event, unable to touch the skin in which we live our days. We live in a different time and space, "as if on another planet," says George Steiner in reference to another genocide, that of the Holocaust. He asks, "Are there different species of time in the same world, 'good times' and enveloping folds of inhuman time, in which men fall into the slow hands of living damnation?"[3] As the historian David Chandler confesses, apropos of his study of genocidal crimes in Cambodia, "we are insulated from what really happened to the minds and bodies of the victims. ... What happened is awful, but it happened long ago to other people. 'Evil,' we like to think, takes place elsewhere."[4]

We do not need Friedrich Nietzsche to persuade us that there is health in forgetfulness and illusion. To remember too much, to be penetrated by too much trauma can destroy one's capacity for vigorous living. As the Lacanians tell us, a certain amount of fantasy is needed to protect us from the lethal intrusion of the "Real." It has long been the aim of philosophic thinking, however, to assault illusory appearances for the sake of truth. I believe that there is a responsibility on the part of philosophers to strip away some of our protective fantasy frames and to inquire about the meaning of the human being after a ferocious twentieth century in which so many human lives have been violated, wounded, and destroyed by state-sponsored terror.

Thought itself provides a distance from an event that allows a thinker a degree of psychological equilibrium with which genocidal events might be approached. If philosophers are to inquire honestly and truly about the significance of so much suffering stemming from mad attempts to purge humanity of its unclean elements, then we must begin by asking whether, in fact, the dead are interesting "only as evidence"? We should ask about the humanness of the *victims* of genocide in an effort to break with what Emmanuel Levinas has called "a long indifference to the sorrows of an entire world."[5]

From criminal to victim

Reflecting on her mission of prosecuting the Serbian criminals responsible for genocidal acts in Srebrenica and elsewhere in Bosnia, Louise Arbour, the former chief prosecutor for the International Criminal Tribunal for the former Yugoslavia, admitted that while the Tribunal believed that every one of the victims counts, "there is an anonymity in the number of victims that is overwhelming, and in that sense the perpetrators have won." She added that "they took away the lives of their victims, that was the easy part, but they also took their identity, their humanity."[6] After the crime, from the standpoint of law and justice, the evildoers, the perpetrators of genocide become, in a way, more important than those to whom the evil was done. For the prosecutor, suffering and death are given; they are facts or items in a chain of proofs pointed toward the accused. The complex issues addressed by legal tribunals for crimes in the former Yugoslavia as well as in Rwanda revolve around the defendants, their mens rea, their purposes and motivations, and their culpability. Gourevitch asks appropriately, "So what does suffering have to do with anything, when the idea is the crime?"[7]

Western philosophy has contributed much to the legal theories of intention, agency, culpability, and punishment that now inform modern criminal courts. No doubt further innovations in moral and legal concepts will be needed the more we take into account the specific kinds of collective or individual violence that have occurred under genocidal regimes in the past century. But such alterations will not of themselves change what has been historically the basic orientation of moral and legal philosophy, which has been directed toward the *agents* of evil and the "idea" of the crime and consequently has neglected those who have suffered from evil. Ironically and sadly, those who have done the most to destroy vast numbers of human beings have been outfitted by modern philosophy, and then by trial courts, with a wardrobe of human-making categories such as intentionality, free choice, moral agency, and fairness. The criminal becomes the true subject in this conceptual framework.

To cite one paradigmatic thinker, Immanuel Kant says that good or evil "could be only the maxim of the will and consequently the *acting person himself as a good or evil person.*"[8] What, of course, is excluded in this remark on the famous notion of "radical evil" is the suffering and death of the victims.[9] Thus, in philosophy the importance of the doers of evil is marked while those who bore their evil remain—as remains—anonymous and insignificant, except as evidence. Those subjected to evil no longer possess the human-making properties of a subject and so are allowed to disappear.

It is possible to call into question this quasi-obsession with criminal agency that shapes our thinking about the worst crimes of the twentieth century and to imagine ways of justifying obligations to those subjected to murderous, genocidal violence. Our standard textbook packages of utilitarianism, Kantianism, and virtue theory, or agent-centered concepts concerning free will, causality, and blameworthiness, may be adequate to define an ethics of the just and the good in normal circumstances in stable communities, but they fail to articulate moral responsibilities focused on the needs of those who have suffered immensely. Clearly the Tutsi now dead in Rwanda and many of the brutalized and mutilated survivors of the massacre cannot be located on the usual conceptual maps that define human lives in terms of happiness or dignity. If we desire a way of grasping their humanity, then we would need to enlarge our usual moral paradigms.

One way of doing so would be to broaden the concept of justice to include what David Patterson has identified with the Hebrew word, *tsedakah*. According to Patterson, *tsedakah* denotes a kind of justice that is not a "getting even with the *other* but an offering *to* the other."[10] *Tsedakah* cannot claim to rectify evil; it is rather a non-egoistic effort to spare "the widow, the orphan, and the stranger" and attend to the needs of the hurt body, regardless of whether the suffering body can be said to have a *right* or *title* to our assistance. Directing our attention toward suffering itself may generate ideas about justice that, while not directly of service to law or politics, may assist each of us in bearing the burden of suffering humanity.

Antihumanitarianism

Philosophers historically have not been very interested in thinking about the suffering body unless it is also the suffering of a self-consciousness that can act to understand or remove its suffering. There are no strong theories justifying obligations of beneficence and charity, which seem always to be afterthoughts of more robust theories of justice, rights, self-development, and "perfect" duties of non-malfeasance. A clue as to why this is so can be found in the recent work of the French philosopher Alain Badiou.[11]

Taking his cue from Kant, Badiou avers that suffering is beneath good and evil, unworthy of the human subject. He means by this that suffering is simply a part of ordinary biological life processes and the animal's struggle for survival and domination. The true realm of the human transcends this animal life, encompassing sublime moments of love, art, politics, and science. Such moments can have their perverse sides and lead to terror, as they did with the Nazis; but it is also in such moments that we find the resplendent visionary acts of a genuine human being. Suffering itself is banal; it does not belong to the elevated region of the good, the free, and the true that constitutes humanness. Without his transcending capacities, man is just a suffering beast, whose condition can be neither good nor evil. Badiou accepts the striking implications of this position:

> To be sure, humanity is an animal species. It is mortal and predatory. But neither of these attributes can distinguish humanity within the world of the living. In his role as executioner, man is an animal abjection, but we must have the courage to add that in his role as victim, he is generally worth little more.[12]

In his or her suffering, then, the victim is an abject animal, not a human being. Philosophy, Badiou would say, should point us to a kind of self-transcendence and toward exceedingly good lives, not backwards toward the closed world of the suffering beast, which is at best a form of evidence of the malignancy of others.

This distinction between the dignity of a freely acting subject and the banality of subjection also inspires a recent polemic by Alain Finkielkraut against humanitarianism's "universal ethics of hospitality." Less sanguine than Badiou, Finkielkraut points out that in the twentieth century the human subject has used his and her "transcending capacities" to construct an ideal humanity built upon the slaughter of millions of actual human beings. For the sake of historical progress, revolutionaries sought to shape a new type of humanity and would not be deterred or embarrassed by the bloodshed in noble revolutions.[13] In chilling words, Finkielkraut speaks of modern concentration camps as factories of death in which actual human beings are waste products of the fabrication of a pure humanity.[14] The infamous saying of the Pol Pot regime could serve as a motto for all the state-administered massacres of our time: "To keep you is no benefit and to kill you is no loss."

Finkielkraut understands that an ethics wishing to provide succor without discrimination or without judgment for those who suffer and those who have died is a logical and relatively sane response to a worldview that generates cadavers as the waste product of visionary ideals. The humanitarian intervention of the association *Medicins sans Frontieres*, for example, seeks to rescue the human being from its terrifying superfluity in what Finkielkraut calls "the murderous dialectic of means and ends." Nevertheless, Finkielkraut regards humanitarian tendencies to place a higher value on the suffering victim than on progressive ideals as "misanthropic" impulses that shadow the unique dignity and autonomy of man. Like Badiou, he thinks that the humanitarian principle reduces humans to suffering animals by rooting human solidarity in weakness and pain rather than in dignity and freedom. This ethics fosters an ideology of "solicitude" that refuses to see human beings in their individuality and infinite variety, preferring to define man "by the torments that overwhelm him."[15] Motivated by what he regards as Rousseauian impulses of pity, "the rescuer without borders embraces all silent calls of distress, subjecting them to no preliminary cross-examination."[16] But for Finkielkraut this stance is merely another kind of reductionism and antihumanism. For the abstract ideals of the revolutionary, it substitutes a model of man who is wounded by useless suffering. A victim-focused humanitarianism sees the world as a "vast hospital," just as Goethe prophesied and feared. Furthermore, having suppressed the ideals and utopian dreams that have led to so much bloodshed, the new philanthropy has no other energizing stimulus than blood to set it into action. So, Finkielkraut concludes: "The humanitarian generation does not like men—they are too disconcerting—but enjoys taking care of them. Free men scare it. Eager to express tenderness fully while making sure that men do not get away, it prefers handicapped people."[17]

These are harsh words, but Badiou and Finkielkraut are right to be suspicious of a philanthropic ethics, which may command sentimental empathy for the suffering victim but also risks degrading the unique dignity of every person. If our psychological default state is a narcissistic fantasy wherein there are different spaces and times for genocide and crimes against humanity, ones that are not of "our" world, then it may be equally narcissistic to think that we can at will intervene and connect with the suffering masses. Would that not suggest, however, that our task as philosophers is to learn how to "think" about victimhood in a way that is *not* reductionist or mystifying?[18]

In the words of George Steiner, is not the obligation of philosophical reason now "to discover the relations between those done to death and those alive then, and the relations of both to us; to locate, as exactly as record and imagination are able, the measure of unknowing, indifference, complicity, commission which relates the contemporary or survivor to the slain"?[19]

I believe that it is possible to think of a relation to the millions who have died and suffered from genocidal crimes in a manner that is rigorously unsentimental. It would be characterized as what Emmanuel Levinas has called a "relation without relation" and it would have to push the limitations on our usual definition of humanity. In contrast to Badiou and Finkielkraut, it would also admit that an appeal to suffering could indeed be an imperative of ethics. Like Levinas, I would hold that it is attention "to the suffering of the other through the cruelties of our century (despite these cruelties, because of these cruelties) that can be affirmed as the very nexus of human subjectivity, to the point of being raised to the level of supreme ethical principle ..."[20]

From victim to humanity

Thinking about evil in the context of suffering need not require a sentimental effort to empathize with unimaginable horror as a way of relating to the humanness of the dead and the anguish of the living. Such attempts are futile and possibly obscene. The word *victim* is itself already an obstacle to thinking about "victims." The "victim" suggests a "not me" who has been rendered less than human in its passive and conquered state. To characterize someone as a "victim" is already to spin the reality of death and suffering into something that happens to an "other," who, in his or her anonymity, may be ignored or whose degradation may arouse "my" pity and "my" humanitarianism. This victim is not "like me" an active, free moral agent. Victimhood can easily be construed as a matter of "rotten luck" for which one can try to feel compassion from a superior standpoint of health and autonomy, but which can never be identified as an all-embracing condition of humankind. Victimhood is the state of the anti-subject, the object of an active subject who would either kill it or seek to rescue it.

To find an alternative to evil as "victimization," we may appeal again to Steiner. In my citation above, note that he does not describe the inmates of the death camps as victims. He twists language and speaks of them as ones who were "done to death." Suppose we try to describe those wounded and killed by genocide, not as utterly dehumanized victims, but as subject-bearers of evil in whose bodies we recognize the mark of our own humanness. Suppose we stretch the conventions of language and name human beings in this state, as "subject-bearers," "patients," or the "done to." This may make it easier to conceptualize evil, first, as a cruelty that is suffered rather than as an act that is imposed and, second, as a contingency of the human body, which is not alien to the subject but simply the other side of the subject as agent or doer.

The proper orientation toward the suffering "other," I claim, is not pity for a dehumanized victim but is rather what Hannah Arendt called "solidarity." For Arendt, *pity* is a self-indulgent arousal of the heart that feeds on the misfortunes of others (exactly what Finkielkraut regards as the humanitarian impulse), while *solidarity* is a dispassionate "community of interest with the oppressed and exploited."[21] Without pretending that feeling or imagination can encompass the horror of all that has occurred, solidarity with the patient subject-bearers of evil means that one soberly understands that genocide's domain is not simply that of the victimized and unlucky other. Solidarity addresses all of *you*, all of *us*, not just *them*. To acknowledge fully the horrors that have occurred in our times, without the fantasy screens by which we enjoy our time, is to hear a clear and terrifying message of human solidarity: "You also were the ones they were after; you too can at any moment drop 'out of humanity.' "[22] What is enunciated in the dismembered bodies at Nyarubuye, Phnom Penh, and Srebrenica, as well as at Treblinka and Auschwitz, is the vulnerability to evil and the subjection that is at the core of our common humanity. Hence, the reception of suffering is not simply an inhuman occurrence; it is fully human and inextricable from the spontaneity and freedom with which the dignity of the subject has been identified after Kant by contemporary philosophers such as Badiou and Finkielkraut.

To move beyond the idea of victimization as merely the degradation or dehumanization of a subject, we need to reflect on Levinas's idea that attention to suffering is "the very nexus of subjectivity." The subjectivity of human beings is also manifested in their very *subjection* to violence as well as in their capacity for violence or in their capacity to resist violence. A test case for this idea would be the *Muselmänner* of the Auschwitz death camp, who were poignantly described by Primo Levi. The *Muselmänner* were prisoners whose basic cognitive and emotional capacities had shut down to the point where they seemed to be "living cadavers," neither quite alive nor yet dead. Primo Levi says this about them:

> The *Muselmänner*, the drowned, form the backbone of the camp, an anonymous mass, continually renewed and always identical, of non-men who march and labor in silence, the divine spark dead in them. Already too empty to really suffer ... They crowd my memory with their faceless presence, and if I could enclose all the evil in our time in one image, I would choose the image which is familiar to me: an emaciated man, with head dropped and shoulders curved, in whose face and in whose eyes not a trace of thought is to be seen.[23]

To use Giorgio Agamben's words, in the *Muselmänner* one encounters "husks of men," "the shipwreck of dignity" and the "uselessness before absolute degradation."[24]

For those of us who were not there, and even for eyewitnesses, it is importantly true that we really cannot say who the *Muselmänner* were, no more than we can say who any of the millions of patient bearers of death and torture really are. But we can say that if we too readily accept the language of degradation, indignity, dehumanization, and "living cadavers" (which is not exactly the language Levi himself uses) to describe the evil of the death camps, then the killers and tormentors really will have succeeded in reducing human beings into objects toward whom we might feel some pity, but toward whom we could not admit the responsibility we would have before another "subject."

Not only but especially for philosophers, the challenge posed by the *Muselmänner*, and all patient sufferers like them, like *us*, living or dead, invites us to investigate, cautiously and tentatively to be sure, a broader definition of humanness that is drawn not exclusively from autonomous agency, dignity, and rationality but from the side of the passivity and receptivity of the one who suffers in the extreme. To do this we would need to stress humanity's vulnerability and subjection in the world, which is the other side of the sovereign freedom of the subject that has so dominated Western ethics. Is there not an important sense in which the "victim" too is "human" even when other people have so assaulted him or her that this being repulses us with what is left of its mutilated flesh, "human" in the same way that his or her tormentors are human, in the way that we onlookers and students of genocide are human? To avoid seeing others as victims *unlike* us, strange and pitiable *objects* of our attention, is to recognize that in them we see desubjectified *subjects*, not just animals beneath good and evil, as Badiou describes them, but our own in-the-human, wounded, and traumatized being, now tragically open for exhibition.[25]

The dazzling declarations of the supreme value of spontaneous freedom and autonomy in modern philosophy have obscured a truth about our passivity and vulnerability, our "patience" and receptivity. The dignity of angelic figures, no matter how good and free they are, could not be ours. It is in the passivity of the flesh that we also find our humanity. In her poem "Tortures," the Nobel laureate Wisława Szymborska expresses this necessary density of our being, without which we would not be human and without which evil would have no meaning:

> The little soul roams among those landscapes,
> disappears, returns, draws near, moves away,
> evasive and a stranger to itself,
> now sure, now uncertain of its own existence,
> whereas the body is and is and is
> and has nowhere to go.[26]

Acknowledging the density and passivity of our corporeal humanity, the body that "is and is and is" may better prepare us to recognize in solidarity the humanness of the fellow sufferer and to judge that we are bound by a moral imperative weighing upon our daily existence, even if we can do nothing. The susceptibility of the subject or its subjected, passive nature is an ineradicable condition of moral judgment. Without what Levinas called "absolute passivity [that] becomes incarnate, corporeality or susceptibility to pain, outrage, and unhappiness," the sorrows of the world would go by us like a breeze, without trauma, wound, or response.[27]

Therefore, the exposed bones of Nyarubuye, or the map of skulls at the Tuol Sleng museum in Phnom Penh,[28] reveal not only the inhuman aftereffects of genocide but also the *human* inhuman, the humanness of the murdered body as such. We are reminded of a humanness that is deeper than the ego. As Jacob Meskin says, "The powerful, agentic, knowing ego does not exhaust what it means to be a human being."[29] To put it another way, while we know that the in-the-human animality of the flesh is the condition of possibility of an evil that assaults both the flesh and the consciousness of a human *subjectum*, we need not conclude from this that evil simply erases the human being, turning the dead and the wounded into things, dust in the distance.

The bones, the ashes in reliquaries, or the fragments of bodies in a killing field are not utterly inhuman, of value only as *evidence* to convict the "real" human subjects—the killers. To recover or preserve them for the sake of burial or memorial is to acknowledge them as worthy of respect. It is not the whole self that is recovered; it is a broken and beaten self that has been "done to death" by evil men. But the recovery of broken bodies is, nevertheless, the recovery of a human essence. It is a morally responsible and patient act in solidarity with others. We speak of the loss of the human in genocide, but it is, of course, precisely the human being that is exposed in the evil done to it. The *genocidaires* have not quite succeeded in annihilating their patients.

Conclusion

I have argued that our responsibilities to the human being require us to extend our moral categories and the paradigm of justice to include, for example, acts of *tsedakah* toward the remains of the in-the-human dead, who are not quite things. The dead too have their demands for "medicine," seeking from us survivors memorials, acts of retribution, prayers, and other ways to bear witness to their humanity and the inhumanity in their humanness. The as-yet-unfulfilled obligation of philosophy to the humanness of those who have not survived the genocidal massacres of our time calls for a thinking, not an indiscriminate sentimentality, that restores to the human family those who have been *dis-membered* from it. I agree with Martha Minow, who says that "the victimized deserve the acknowledgment of their humanity and the reaffirmation of the utter wrongness of its violation."

The response of bystanders, she continues, "should do more than reiterate the boundaries between groups that helped give rise to the atrocities and instead enlarge a sense of community and membership."[30] One way to hold on to the humanity of the dead is to build memorials to them. To memorialize the dead is symbolically to *re-member* them, connecting fragments of a broken community, joining our time with theirs. In her wonderful essay on memory, Eva Hoffman, a child of Holocaust survivors, has said that remembering is the quintessentially moral act: "The dead do not profit from [memory], and neither do we. But the meaning of being human would be diminished if we could not hold those who have died in our minds, if we could not sustain a symbolic relationship to them. Memory is the act of contemplating others through the significance of their lives rather than through their concrete presence, or the uses we can make of them."[31] Such memory, then, would be one way to extend the meaning of justice or *tsedakah* in a philosophically responsible way.

Observing the testimony of surviving "victims" of the violence of apartheid during hearings undertaken by the South African Truth and Reconciliation Commission, Minow was struck by the variety and modesty of many of their requests: "Survivors differ remarkably in their desires for revenge, for granting forgiveness, for remembering, and for moving on."[32] Sometimes all that was sought was a death certificate or a tombstone, a removal of a bullet or a park named after a victim of torture. These requests may have been symptoms of the dispirited state of victims, a "reflection of lowered expectations." But they may also have been, Minow speculates, "dignified assertions made by individuals who have no illusions about the possibility of external repair for their losses."[33] Even these humble requests have an immense moral power: "They can meet burning needs for acknowledgment, closure, vindication, and connection." Does not this testimony suggest that humanitarian obligations need not be framed in Finkielkraut's terms, as indiscriminate, self-righteous impulses to take care of the handicapped? What is needed, rather, is intelligent attention to the specific needs of survivors of crimes against humanity as well as precise, rational, and detailed understandings of what has happened. As Hannah Arendt understood, human solidarity is an achievement of thoughtfulness and wise *judgment*, not sentimental pity. As characterized by Hanna Pitkin, solidarity with survivors would be "responsive to their needs, but respectful of their capacities, empathetic but without merger, attentive to their perspective without surrendering one's own judgment."[34]

There is no easy way to make sense of genocide or to prescribe a path toward memory and solidarity with those who in their flesh and humanity are both like us and irredeemably other. Perhaps the whole business is beyond the resources of reason. Still, I would like to see more philosophers try to reconceptualize our humanitarian obligations to the inhuman brutalization of the human with the same kind of rigor they have applied to moral agency and legal responsibility. Up until now, when dealing with crimes against humanity, philosophical thinking has for the most part focused on their causes and on agent-centered mechanisms of legal redress. We should rethink ethically and ontologically the ways in which the dead and the tortured remain within our human horizons, how they weigh upon our daily life and accompany us, addressing us, not simply from the standpoint of the "other," not simply as evidential preliminaries to trials and to new politics, but as fellow human beings.

Notes

1. Philip Gourevitch, "Among the Dead," in Michael S. Roth and Charles G. Salas, eds, *Disturbing Remains: Memory, History, and Crisis in the Twentieth Century* (Los Angeles, CA: The Getty Research Institute, 2001), pp. 63–73.
2. Ibid., p. 70.
3. George Steiner, *Language and Silence: Essays on Language, Literature, and the Inhuman* (New York: Atheneum, 1967), p. 156.
4. David Chandler, *Voices from S-21: Terror and History in Pol Pot's Secret Prison*, (Berkeley, CA: University of California Press, 1999), pp. 111–12. Echoing this idea, Herbert Hirsch says, "What does my life mean to the dying in Bosnia and the starving in Africa, and concomitantly, what do their lives mean to me? If we answer honestly, very little." *Genocide and the Politics of Memory: Studying Death to Preserve Life* (Chapel Hill, NC: University of North Carolina Press, 1995), p. 18.
5. Emmanuel Levinas, "Peace and Proximity," in Adriaan T. Peperzak, Simon Critchley, and Robert Bernasconi, eds, *Emmanuel Levinas: Basic Philosophical Writings* (Bloomington, IN: Indiana University Press, 1996), pp. 162–9.
6. Cited by Erna Paris, *Long Shadows: Truth, Lies and History* (New York and London: Bloomsbury Publishing, 2001), pp. 417–18.
7. Gourevitch, "Among the Dead," p. 71. In what follows, I am not concerned with definitional issues faced by international tribunals that must distinguish genocide from war crimes and crimes against humanity. There are important distinctions to be made about the kinds of evil that were intended because they serve to clarify specific obligations to the victims. But not much in my present argument will hinge on whether the mens rea of a defendant included the specific intention to destroy an entire ethnic or religious group or fell under the other criteria for geno-cide listed in Article II in the 1948 United Nations Convention on the Prevention and Punishment of the Crime of Genocide. See William Schabas, *Genocide in International Law: The Crime of Crimes* (Cambridge: Cambridge University Press, 2000).
8. Immanuel Kant, *Religion within the Boundaries of Mere Reason*, trans. George di Giovanni, in Allen Wood and George di Giovanni, eds, *Immanuel Kant: Religion and Rational Theology* (Cambridge: Cambridge University Press, 1996), p. 96 (italics added).
9. In the *Critique of Practical Reason*, Kant explicitly distinguishes between evil (*das Böse*) and suffering or ill being (*das Übel*). "Evil" for Kant is an attribute of the will and of action, and not of a person's state or condition. *Critique of Practical Reason*, trans. and ed., Mary Gregor (Cambridge: Cambridge University Press, 1997). See pp. 50–4. In this chapter, I do not deny the existence of "moral evil" stemming from the will of an evil doer, but I am resurrecting the old idea, rejected by Kant,

that there is in suffering itself a primary kind of "natural evil." However, it is beyond the scope of this chapter to provide the kind of typology or phenomenology of suffering needed to justify what I need to argue, namely that some kinds of suffering will of themselves have moral weight, independently of their causes. I am grateful to my colleague Pablo Muchnik for pointing out this gap in my argument.

10. David Patterson, "G-d, World, Humanity: Jewish Reflections on Justice after Auschwitz," in David Patterson and John K. Roth, eds, *After-Words: Post-Holocaust Struggles with Forgiveness, Reconciliation, Justice* (Seattle, WA: University of Washington Press, 2004), pp. 171–82, p. 173.
11. Alain Badiou, *Ethics: An Essay on the Understanding of Evil*, trans. Peter Hallward (London: Verso, 2001). Originally published as *L'ethique: Essai sur la conscience du Mal* (1998).
12. Ibid., p. 11.
13. Alain Finkielkraut, *In the Name of Humanity: Reflections on the Twentieth Century*, trans. Judith Friedlander (New York: Columbia University Press, 2000), pp. 58–9.
14. Ibid., p. 77.
15. Ibid., p. 85.
16. Ibid., p. 87.
17. Ibid., p. 91.
18. Judith Shklar has said that "we do not know how to think about victimhood." Cited by Chandler, *Voices from S-21*, p. 145. As I suggest below, to preserve the common humanity between "victims" and those who think about "them," it is better not to think about "victims" but about human subjects in their abject and broken conditions.
19. Steiner, *Language and Silence*, p. 157.
20. Immanuel Levinas, *Entre Nous: On Thinking of the Other*, trans. Michael Smith and Barbara Harshav (New York: Columbia University Press, 1998), p. 94.
21. Hannah Arendt, *On Revolution* (London and New York: Viking-Penguin, 1963), p. 88.
22. See Steiner, *Language and Silence*, p. 157. Steiner is speaking of the solidarity among Jews after the Holocaust. I do not mean to suggest that a more generalized human solidarity with suffering could have the same power or pathos for those who were not, as Jews were, historically selected for extermination.
23. Primo Levi, *If This Is a Man*, trans. Stuart Woolf (London: Sphere Books-Penguin, 1987), p. 96.
24. Giorgio Agamben, *Remnants of Auschwitz: The Witness and the Archive* (New York: Zone Books, 1999), p. 62.
25. I regret the hyphenation, but I think it is useful for suggesting that it is not simply the self-conscious mind and will in-the-human being which makes us human, but also our mortal, vulnerable capacity to suffer from atrocities. Genocidal atrocities are inhumanly cruel, of course, but not simply because they are inflicted by cruel minds and wills. They are inhumanly cruel because they assault the humanness of the flesh, bone, blood, and spittle in-the-human. They would be cruel if they were the violence of gods rather than men because of what they have *done to us*.
26. Wisława Szymborska, "Tortures," in *Poems New and Collected*, trans. Stanisław Barańczak and Claire Cavanagh (New York: Harcourt, 1998), pp. 202–3.
27. Levinas, "Substitution," in Peperzak, Critchley, and Bernasconi, eds, *Emmanuel Levinas*, p. 93, n. 42.
28. For details about the significance of the Tuol Sleng museum for Cambodian memories of genocide, see Judy Ledgerwood, "The Cambodian Tuol Sleng Museum of Genocidal Crimes: National Narrative," in David E. Lovey and

William H. Beezley, eds, *Genocide, Collective Violence, and Popular Memory: The Politics of Remembrance in the Twentieth Century* (Wilmington, DE: Scholarly Resources, Inc., 2002), pp. 103–22.

29. Jacob Meskin, "The Jewish Transformation of Modern Thought: Levinas and Philosophy After the Holocaust," *Cross Currents* 47 (Winter 1997–98), p. 505.

30. Martha Minow, *Between Vengeance and Forgiveness: Facing History after Genocide and Mass Violence* (Boston, MA: Beacon Press, 1998), p. 146.

31. Eva Hoffman, *After Such Knowledge: Memory, History, and the Legacy of the Holocaust* (New York: Public Affairs, 2004), pp. 160–1.

32. Minow, *Between Vengeance and Forgiveness*, p. 135.

33. Ibid., p. 106.

34. Hanna Fenichel Pitkin, *The Attack of the Blob: Hannah Arendt's Concept of the Social* (Chicago, IL: University of Chicago Press, 1998), p. 166.

Part IV

Resistance, Responsibility, and Human Rights: Philosophy's Response to Genocide

John K. Roth

Born on 31 October 1912, the only child of a Catholic mother and a Jewish father, more than anything else Hans Maier thought of himself as Austrian, not least because his father's family had lived in that country since the seventeenth century. Maier, however, lived in the twentieth century, and thus it was that in September 1935 he studied a newspaper in a Viennese coffeehouse. The Nuremberg Laws had just been promulgated in Nazi Germany. Maier's reading made him see—unmistakably—the fatal interdependence of all human actions. Even if he did not think of himself as Jewish, the Nazis' definitions meant that the cunning of history had nonetheless given him that identity.

Maier lacked the authority to define social reality in the mid-1930s. Increasingly, however, the Nazi state did possess such power. Its laws made him Jewish even if his consciousness did not. As he confronted that reality, the unavoidability of his being Jewish took on another dimension. By identifying him as a Jew, Maier would write later on, Nazi power made him "a dead man on leave, someone to be murdered, who only by chance was not yet where he properly belonged."[1]

When Nazi Germany occupied Austria in March 1938, Maier drew his conclusions. He fled his native land for Belgium, and joined the Resistance after Belgium was swept into the Third Reich in 1940. Captured by the Gestapo, Maier was sent to a series of camps, including Auschwitz, before he was liberated from Bergen–Belsen in 1945. Eventually he took the name Jean Améry, which is an anagram of his original name and the one by which he is remembered, but this philosopher waited 20 years before breaking his silence about the Holocaust. When Améry did decide to write, the result was a series of remarkable essays about his experience. One is simply entitled, "Torture." Torture drove Améry to the following observation: "The expectation of help, the certainty of help," he wrote, "is indeed one of the fundamental experiences of human beings." Thus, the gravest loss produced by the Holocaust, Améry went on to suggest, was that it destroyed what he called "trust in the world, ... the certainty that by reason of written or unwritten social contracts the other person will spare me—more precisely stated, that he will respect my physical, and with it also my metaphysical, being."[2]

Genocide destroys trust in the world. Thus, survivors of genocide and even those who study it may share feelings akin to those expressed by Améry when he remembered what had happened to him and to millions who never returned from the camps. "Every morning when I get up," he tells his reader, "I can read the Auschwitz number on my forearm. ... Every day anew I lose my trust in the world. ... Declarations of human rights, democratic constitutions, the free world and the free press, nothing," he went on to say, "can again lull me into the slumber of security from which I awoke in 1935."[3]

Far from scorning the human dignity that those institutions emphasize, Améry yearned for the right to live, which he equated with dignity itself. It seemed to him, however, that "it is certainly true that dignity can be bestowed only by society, whether it be the dignity of some office, a professional or, very generally speaking, civil dignity; and the merely individual, subjective claim ('I am a human being and as such I have my dignity, no matter what you may do or say!') is an empty academic game, or madness."[4]

Lucidity, believed Améry, demanded the recognition of this reality, but lucidity did not end there. He thought it also entailed rebellion against power that would make anyone a "dead man on leave." Unfortunately, it must also be acknowledged that Améry's hopes for such protest were less than optimistic. On 17 October 1978, he took leave and became a dead man by his own hand.

Améry knew that the United Nations had a Convention on the Prevention and Punishment of the Crime of Genocide and a Universal Declaration of Human Rights, but he remained skeptical about any trust in the world that they promised. His philosophical response to genocide was to test assumptions, among them optimistic ones about human rights, that might be unwarranted in an age of genocide. Penetrating and insightful though it was, however, Améry's skepticism is not the only response that philosophers need to make in a confrontation with genocide. This book's fourth and final part indicates what some of the other options include as philosophers respond to genocide in ways that emphasize resistance, responsibility, and human rights.

With a focus on women and children, Claudia Card shows that social death is central to genocide's evil. In ways that echo themes in Berel Lang's opening chapter and in Jean Améry's reflections on the Holocaust, Card explores how genocide does more than destroy individual lives. It also wrecks "relationships, contemporary and intergenerational, that create an identity that gives meaning to life." If philosophy is to resist genocide, as Card's chapter does, it must take responsibility to do all that it can to foster forms of social vitality that keep social death at bay.

Maintaining the health of social vitality and keeping social death at bay depend, among other things, on curbing racism. John K. Roth explores those themes as he identifies what he calls the "logic" of racism. More often than not, racism is genocidal, and it is also true that genocide usually has racism as one of its primary causes. Roth not only indicates how those relationships work but also argues that the checking of racism would go far toward the elimination of genocide. One of philosophy's most important responses to genocide, therefore, involves a continuing concern to defang racism and to show the incoherence of the concept of *race*, which has long been one of the most pernicious and destructive ideas constructed by the human mind and even by philosophy itself.

Améry had his doubts about the credibility of human rights talk. Nevertheless, neither racism nor genocide are likely to be checked unless universal human rights are defended in spite of the forces that erode confidence in them. David H. Jones takes up that challenge in two ways. First, he argues that there are abundant good reasons to affirm a universal right to life and that genocide ought not to bully people into disbelief about them. Second, he identifies bystander states as a key problem where the credibility of human rights is concerned. To the extent that states fail to intervene when genocide is threatened or under way, the status of human rights is jeopardized. If bystanders can be converted into what Samantha Power has called "up standers," then human rights will be better defended and genocide's threats will be reduced. Jones's critique of bystander states has pointed relevance for bystanding philosophers as well.

Patrick Hayden expands themes related to Jones's by defending the importance of international tribunals that prosecute human rights atrocities so that what he calls "cosmopolitan justice" can flourish. Such justice depends on a well-developed understanding and defense of rights and duties, plus the establishment and maintenance of credible agencies that enforce international law. Hayden envisions attitudes, policies, and institutions that do not fully exist, but his outlook is neither abstract nor utopian. His analysis rests on a level-headed realism about the needs that face humanity in a world scarred by genocide. It also reflects the fact that one of philosophy's tasks and responses to genocide is to imagine and to articulate ethical ways of life that could be realized if their possibilities were revealed. Hayden shows how philosophical imagination that is grounded in historical realities can help to show the way.

Roger S. Gottlieb's chapter balances Hayden's by raising a crucial question: Are human beings too weak to match up effectively against destructive forces, such as genocide, that lay life low. If genocide had happened once but never again, that condition would be cause enough for discouragement and despair. But genocide has happened much more than once. It was going on in Darfur as this book went to press. Gottlieb takes account of such developments in ways that warn how difficult it will be to advance the cosmopolitan justice that Hayden discussed. But Gottlieb also joins Hayden to affirm that one of philosophy's most important functions is to keep horizons open, to raise humanity's sights in ways that encourage resistance, to show that human beings can be stronger ethically than genocide might lead us and want us to believe.

The strength that Gottlieb wants to encourage is largely strength of character. Appropriately, then, Paul Woodruff directs attention to virtues and vices, to qualities of mind and spirit that do much to determine whether individual acts and public policies are right or wrong, good or evil. Hate, greed, jealousy—these are among the vices of mind and spirit that can lead to mass murder and genocide. They lead that way not through isolated individuals, Woodruff shows, "but in the well-organized actions of a group." What his account means for philosophy, indeed for humankind generally, is that effort must be focused on doing whatever can be done to reduce such vices of mind and spirit. "We are all responsible for the character of our communities," Woodruff contends, and a key part of that responsibility is "to act, in every way possible, for the diminishing of hate."

Woodruff's position implies that if human beings, including philosophers, do not act in that way, that fact and the destructive results that follow from it are causes for shame. Michael L. Morgan turns explicitly to such themes as he considers philosophy's responsibilities in relation to genocide. Commenting on his viewing of *Ghosts of Rwanda*, a documentary about the Rwandan genocide, he says that the watching "provokes shame before what one hears and sees, the images and the interviews, and the admissions, often given, that more should have been done, that the denials were evasions." In unsparing and challenging ways, Morgan shows how and why genocide should make us ashamed, and his understanding of *us* includes especially those who have power to intervene against genocide, a category that includes philosophers. Shame, he goes on to emphasize, can lead to constructive change, because to feel shame is to recognize serious shortcomings and to want to be better. If genocide does not shame us, including philosophers, then our condition may well be dreadful, but if a confrontation with genocide does make us ashamed, the hope that we can do a better job of resisting genocide remains and awaits our responsible willingness to realize that hope. That turning, Morgan affirms, would produce "a living for others that is a more genuine way of living with ourselves."

Jean Améry found that torture and genocide destroyed his trust in the world. The chapters in Part IV do not discount his experience, but they do try to respond to experiences such as his by rebuilding in the ruins of genocide at least some of the trust that Améry lost. If philosophy fails to do its best in that regard, the genocidal impulses that left Améry bereft of trust will be emboldened to strike again and again. Philosophy's integrity depends on its determination to resist that outcome.

Notes

1. Jean Améry, *At the Mind's Limits: Contemplations by a Survivor on Auschwitz and Its Realities*, trans. Sidney Rosenfeld and Stella P. Rosenfeld (New York: Schocken Books, 1986), p. 86. The book was originally published in 1966. The discussion of Améry draws on my *Holocaust Politics* (Louisville, KY: Westminster John Knox Press, 2001).
2. Améry, *At the Mind's Limits*, p. 28.
3. Ibid., pp. 94–5.
4. Ibid., p. 89.

19
Genocide and Social Death

Claudia Card

This chapter develops the hypothesis that social death is utterly central to the evil of genocide, not just when a genocide is primarily cultural but even when it is homicidal on a massive scale.[1] It is social death that enables us to distinguish the peculiar evil of genocide from the evils of other mass murders. Even genocidal murders can be viewed as extreme means to the primary end of social death. Social vitality exists through relationships, contemporary and intergenerational, that create an identity that gives meaning to a life. Major loss of social vitality is a loss of identity and consequently a serious loss of meaning for one's existence. Putting social death at the center takes the focus off individual choice, individual goals, individual careers, and body counts and puts it on relationships that create community and set the context that gives meaning to choices and goals. If my hypothesis is correct, the term "cultural genocide" is probably both redundant and misleading—redundant, if the social death present in all genocide implies cultural death as well, and misleading, if "cultural genocide" suggests that some genocides do not include cultural death.

What is feminist about analyzing genocide?

The question has been asked, what is feminist about this project? The answer is both simple and complex. It is simple in that, it is the history behind the project and the perspective from which it is carried out, rather than a focus on women or gender, that make the project feminist. Some of the complexities are as follows.

The evil of genocide falls not only on men and boys but also on women and girls, typically unarmed, untrained in defense against violence, and often also responsible for care of the wounded, the sick, the disabled, babies, children, and the elderly. Because genocide targets both sexes, rather than being specific to women's experience, there is some risk of its being neglected in feminist thought. It is also the case that with few exceptions, both feminist and nonfeminist philosophical reflections on war and other public violence have tended to neglect the impact on victims.[2] Philosophers have thought mostly about the positions of perpetrators and decision-makers (most of them men), with some feminist speculation on what might change if more women were among the decision-makers and if women were subject to military conscription. The damage of war and terrorism is commonly assessed in terms of its ruin of individual careers, body counts, statistics on casualties, and material costs of rebuilding. Attention goes to preventing such violence and the importance of doing so, but less to the experience and responses of the majority of victims and survivors, who are civilians, not soldiers. In bringing to the fore the responses of victims of both sexes, Holocaust literature stands in sharp contrast to these trends. Central to Holocaust literature is reflection on the meaning of genocide.

Women's Studies, in its engagement with differences among women, has moved from its earlier aim to train a feminist eye on the world and all kinds of issues (such as evil) to the more limited aim of studying women and gender. I return here to the earlier conception that recognizes not only the study of women, feminism, or gender, but feminist approaches to issues of ethics and social theory generally, whether the word "feminist" is used or not. My interests move toward commonalities in our experiences of evil, not only commonalities among women differently situated but commonalities shared with many men as well. Yet my lens is feminist, polished through decades of reflection on women's multifarious experiences of misogyny and oppression. What we notice, through a feminist lens, is influenced by long habits of attending to emotional response, relationships that define who we (not just women and girls) are, and the significance of the concrete particular.

Centering social death accommodates the position, controversial among genocide scholars, that genocidal acts are not always or necessarily homicidal (on which more later). Forcibly sterilizing women or men of a targeted group or forcibly separating their children from them for re-education for assimilation into another group can also be genocidal in aim or effect.[3] Such policies can be aimed at or achieve the eventual destruction of the social identity of those so treated. It may appear that transported children simply undergo change in social identity, not that they lose all social vitality. That may be the intent. Yet, parents' social vitality is a casualty of children's forced re-education, and in reality, transported children may fail to make a satisfying transition.

The Holocaust was not only a program of mass murder but an assault on Jewish social vitality. The assault was experienced by hidden children who survived as well as by those who died. Hitler's sterilization program and Nuremberg laws that left German Jews stateless were parts of the genocide, not just preludes to it. Jews who had converted to Christianity (or whose parents or grandparents had done so) were hunted down and murdered, even though one might think their social identities had already changed.[4] This pursuit makes a certain perverted sense if the idea was to extinguish in them all possibility of social vitality, simply on the grounds of their ancestral roots. Mass murder is the most extreme method of genocide, denying members of targeted groups any degree or form of social vitality whatever. To extinguish all possibility of social vitality, child transportation and re-education are insufficient; it may be necessary to commit mass murder or drive victims mad or rob them of self-respect, all of which were done to Holocaust victims.

Although I approach genocide from a history of feminist habits of research and reflection, I say very little here about the impact of genocide on women and girls as opposed to its impact on men and boys. I would not suggest that women suffer more or worse than the men who are also its victims. Nor am I especially interested in such questions as whether lifelong habits of care-giving offer survival advantages to segregated women. (In fact, the evidence appears to be that no one survives without others' care and help.) My interest here is, rather, in what makes genocide the specific evil that it is, what distinguishes it from other atrocities, and what kinds of atrocities are rightly recognized as genocidal. Feminist habits of noticing are useful for suggesting answers to these questions.

Genocide, war, and justice

Genocide need not be part of a larger war, although it commonly is. But it can be regarded in itself as a kind of one-sided war. Precedents for regarding one-sided attacks as wars are found in the idea of a "war on drugs" and in the title of Lucy Dawidowicz's *The War against the Jews*.[5] If genocide is war, it is a profoundly unjust kind of war, perniciously unjust, an injustice that is also an evil.

John Rawls opened his first book on justice with the observation that justice is the first virtue of institutions as truth is of systems of thought. No matter how efficient and well-arranged, he wrote, laws and institutions must be reformed or abolished if they are unjust.[6] Like critics who found these claims overstated, even Rawls noted that although "these propositions seem to express our intuitive conviction of the primacy of justice, no doubt they are expressed too strongly."[7] Not all injustices, even in society's basic structure, make lives insupportable, intolerable, or indecent. Reforms are not always worth the expense of their implementation. Had Rawls made his claim about abolishing unjust institutions in regard to *pernicious* injustices, however, it should not have been controversial: laws and institutions must be abolished when they are evils.

Not all injustices are evils, as the harms they produce vary greatly in importance. Some injustices are relatively tolerable. They may not impact people's lives in a deep or lasting way, even though they are wrong and should be eliminated—unjust salary discriminations, for example, when the salaries in question are all high. An injustice becomes an evil when it inflicts harms that make victims' lives unbearable, indecent, or impossible, or that make victims' deaths indecent.[8] Injustices of war are apt to fall into this category. Certainly genocide does.

The concept of genocide

"Genocide" combines the Greek *genos* for race or tribe with the Latin *cide* for killing. The term was coined by Raphael Lemkin, an attorney and refugee scholar from Poland who served in the United States War Department.[9] He campaigned as early as the 1930s for an international convention to outlaw genocide, and his persistence resulted in the United Nations Genocide Convention of 1948. Although this convention is widely cited, it was not translated into action in international courts until the 1990s, more than forty years later. The first state to bring a case to the World Court under the convention was Bosnia-Herzegovina in 1993. It was not until 1998 that the first verdict interpreting that convention was rendered, when the Rwanda tribunal found Jean-Paul Akayesu guilty on nine counts for his participation in the genocide in Rwanda in 1994.[10] The United States did not pass legislation implementing ratification of the 1948 genocide convention until 1988 and then only with significant reservations that were somewhat disabling.[11] Such resistance is interesting in view of questions raised during the interim regarding the morality of American conduct in Vietnam. By the time the United States ratified the convention, 97 other UN members had already done so.

The *term* "genocide" is thus relatively new, and the Holocaust is widely agreed to be its paradigmatic instance. Yet Lemkin and many others find the *practice* of genocide ancient. In their sociological survey from ancient times to the present, Frank Chalk and Kurt Jonassohn discuss instances of apparent genocide that range from the Athenians' annihilation of the people of the island of Melos in the fifth century BCE (recorded by Thucydides) and the ravaging of Carthage by Romans in 146 BCE (also listed by Lemkin as the first of his historical examples of wars of extermination) through mass killings in Bangladesh, Cambodia, and East Timor in the second half of the twentieth century.[12] Controversies continue over whether to count as genocidal the annihilation of indigenous peoples in the Americas and Australia (who succumbed in vast numbers to diseases brought by Europeans), Stalin's induced mass starvation of the 1930s (ostensibly an economically motivated measure), and the war conducted by the United States in Vietnam.

The literature of comparative genocide—the historian Peter Novick calls it "comparative atrocitology"—so far includes relatively little published work by philosophers.[13] Here is what I have found. Best-known is probably Jean-Paul Sartre's 1967 essay, *On Genocide*, written for the Sartre–Russell International War Crimes Tribunal, which was convened to consider war crimes by the United States in Vietnam.[14] In 1974 Hugo Adam Bedau published a long and thoughtful essay "Genocide in Vietnam?" responding to Sartre and others who have raised the question of whether the United States was guilty of perpetrating genocide in Vietnam.[15] Bedau argues for a negative answer to that question, relying primarily on intent as an essential factor in genocide. His view is that the intent of the United States in Vietnam was not to exterminate a people, even if that was nearly a consequence. Berel Lang's essay "The Concept of Genocide" and the first chapter of his book *Act and Idea in the Nazi Genocide* are helpful in their explorations of the meanings and roles of intent in defining "genocide."[16]

Other significant philosophical works include Alan S. Rosenbaum's anthology *Is the Holocaust Unique? Perspectives on Comparative Genocide*, which discusses the Nazi assault on Jews and Romani during the Second World War, the Atlantic slave trade, the Turkish slaughter of Armenians in 1915, and Stalin's induced famine.[17] Legal scholar Martha Minow reflects philosophically on measures lying between vengeance and forgiveness taken by states in response to genocide and mass murder.[18] Jonathan Glover's *Humanity: A Moral History of the Twentieth Century*, in some ways the most ambitious recent philosophical discussion of evils, includes reflections on Rwanda, Stalin, and Nazism.[19] The Institute for Genocide Studies and the Association of Genocide Scholars (which holds conventions) attract an interdisciplinary group of scholars, including a small number of philosophers. And the Society for the Philosophic Study of Genocide and the Holocaust sponsors sessions at conventions of the American Philosophical Association.

On the whole, historians, psychologists, sociologists, and political scientists have contributed more than philosophers to genocide scholarship. Naturally, their contributions as social scientists have been empirically oriented, focused on such matters as origins, contributing causes, effects, monitoring, and prevention. Yet, philosophical issues run throughout the literature. They include foundational matters, such as the meaning of "genocide," which appears to be a highly contested concept, and such issues of ethics and political philosophy as whether perpetrators can be punished in a meaningful way that respects moral standards. If adequate retribution is morally impossible, and if deterrence is unlikely for those who are ideologically motivated, then what is the point in punishing perpetrators? If there is nevertheless some point sufficient to justify doing so, then who should be punished, by whom, and how?

Controversies over the meaning of "genocide" lead naturally to the closely related question of whether genocide is ethically different from non-genocidal mass murder. The practical issue here is whether and, if so, why it is important to add the category of genocide to existing crimes against humanity and war crimes. Crimes against humanity were important additions to war crimes in that, unlike war crimes, they need not be perpetrated during wartime or in connection with a war, and they can be inflicted by a country against its own citizens. But given that murder of civilians by soldiers is already a war crime and a human rights violation, one may wonder whether the crime of genocide captures anything that they omit.

If the social death of individual victims is central to genocide, then, arguably, genocide does capture something more. What distinguishes genocide is not that it has a different kind of victim, namely, groups (although it is a convenient shorthand to speak of targeting groups). Rather, the kind of harm suffered by individual victims of genocide, by virtue of their group membership, is not captured by other crimes. To get a sense of what is at stake in the hypothesis that social death is central, let us turn briefly to controversies over the meaning of "genocide."

The definition of "genocide" is currently in such flux that the Association of Genocide Scholars asks members on its information page (which is printed in a members directory) to specify which definition of "genocide" they use in their work. A widely cited definition is that of the 1948 UN Convention on the Prevention and Punishment of the Crime of Genocide:

> Genocide means any of the following acts committed with the intent to destroy, in whole or in part, a national, ethnical, racial, or religious group, as such: (a) killing members of the group; (b) causing serious bodily or mental harm to members of the group; (c) deliberately inflicting on the group conditions of life calculated to bring about its physical destruction in whole or in part; (d) imposing measures intended to prevent births within the group; (e) forcibly transferring children of the group to another group.[20]

Every clause of this definition is controversial.

Israel Charny and others criticize the UN definition for not recognizing political groups, such as the Communist Party, as possible targets of genocide.[21] Political groups had been, in fact, recognized in an earlier draft of the genocide convention, and Chalk and Jonassohn do recognize political groups as targets of genocide in their historical survey.[22] Some scholars, however, prefer the term "politicide" for these cases and reserve the term "genocide" for the annihilation of groups into which one is (ordinarily) born—racial, ethnic, national, or religious groups. Yet, one is not necessarily, of course, born into one's current national or religious group, and either one's current or one's former membership can prove fatal. Further, some people's political identity may be as important to their lives as religious identity is to the lives of others. And so, the distinction between "genocide" and "politicide" has seemed arbitrary to many critics. A difficulty is, of course, where to draw the line if political groups are recognized as possible victims. But line drawing is not a difficulty that is peculiar to political groups.

The last three clauses of the UN definition—conditions of life intended to destroy the group "in whole or in part," preventing births, and transferring children—count as genocidal many acts that are aimed at cultural destruction, even though they are not homicidal. "Preventing births" is not restricted to sterilization but has been interpreted to include segregation of the sexes and bans on marriage. Social vitality is destroyed when the social relations—organizations, practices, institutions—of the members of a group are irreparably damaged or demolished. Such destruction is a commonly intended consequence of war rape, which has aimed at family breakdown. Although Lemkin regarded such deeds as both ethnocidal and genocidal, some scholars prefer simply to call them ethnocides (or "cultural genocides") and reserve the term "genocide" (unqualified) for events that include mass death. The idea is, apparently, that physical death is more extreme and therefore, presumably, worse than social death. That physical death is worse, or even more extreme, is not obvious, however, but deserves scrutiny, and I will return to it.

Even the clauses of the UN definition that specify killing group members or causing them serious bodily or mental harm are vague and can cover a wide range of possible harms. How many people must be killed for a deed to be genocidal? What sort of bodily harm counts? (Must there be lasting disablement?) What counts as "mental harm?" (Is posttraumatic stress sufficient?) If the definition is to have practical consequences in the responses of nations to perpetrators, these questions can become important. They become important with respect to questions of intervention and reparations, for example.

Although most scholars agree on including intention in the definition of genocide, there is no consensus regarding the content of the required intention. Must the relevant intention include destruction of all members of a group as an aim or purpose? Would it be enough that the group was knowingly destroyed, as a foreseeable consequence of the pursuit of some other aim? Must the full extent of the destruction even be foreseeable, if the policy of which it is a consequence is already clearly immoral? Bedau makes much of the content of the relevant intention in his argument that whatever war crimes the United States committed in Vietnam, they were not genocidal, because the intent was not to destroy the people of Vietnam as such, even if that destruction was both likely and foreseeable.[23]

Charny, however, objects to an analogous claim made by some critics who, he reports, held that because Stalin's intent was to obtain enough grain to trade for industrial materials for the Soviet Union, rather than to kill the millions who died from this policy, Stalin's famine was not a genocide.[24] Charny argues that because Stalin foresaw the fatal consequences of his grain policies, those policies should count as genocidal. As in common philosophical criticisms of the "doctrine of the double effect," Charny appears to reject as ethically insignificant a distinction between intending and "merely foreseeing," at least in this kind of a case.

The doctrine of double-effect has been relied on by the Catholic Church to resolve certain ethical questions regarding life and death issues.[25] The doctrine maintains that under certain conditions it is not wrong to do something that has a foreseeable effect (not an aim) which is such that an act *aiming* at that effect would have been wrong. The first condition of its not being wrong is that the act one performs is not wrong in itself, and the second is that the effect at which it would be wrong to aim is not instrumental toward the end at which the act does aim. Thus, the Church has found it wrong to perform an abortion that would kill a fetus in order to save the mother but, at the same time, not wrong to remove a cancerous uterus when doing so would also result in the death of a fetus. The reasoning is that in the case of the cancerous uterus, the fetus's death is not an aim; nor is it a means to removing the uterus but only a consequence of doing so. Many find this distinction troubling and far from obvious. Why is the death of a fetus from abortion not also only a consequence? The aim could be redescribed as "to remove the fetus from the uterus in order to save the mother," rather than "to kill the fetus to save the mother," and at least when the fetus need not be destroyed in the very process of removal, one might argue that death due to extrauterine nonviability is not a means to the fetus' removal, either.

The position of the critics who do not want to count Stalin's starvation of the peasants as a genocide would appear to imply that if the peasants' deaths were not instrumental toward Stalin's goal but only an unfortunate consequence, the foreseeability of those deaths does not make Stalin's policy genocidal, any more than the foreseeability of the death of the fetus in the case of a hysterectomy performed to remove a cancerous uterus makes that surgery murderous. Charny's position appears to imply, on the contrary, that the foreseeability of the peasants' mass death is enough to constitute genocidal intent, even if it was not intended instrumentally toward Stalin's aims.

Some controversies focus on whether the intent was "to destroy a group as such." One might argue with Bedau, drawing on Lang's discussion of the intent issues, that the intent is "to destroy a group as such" when it is not just accidental that the group is destroyed in the process of pursuing a further end.[26] Thus, if it was not just accidental that the peasant class was destroyed in the process of Stalin's pursuit of grain to trade for industrial materials, he could be said to have destroyed the peasants "as such," even if peasant starvation played no more a causal role in making grain available than killing the fetus plays in removing a cancerous uterus. Alternatively, some argue that the words "as such" do not belong in the definition because, ethically, it does not matter whether a group is deliberately destroyed "as such" or simply deliberately destroyed. Chalk and Jonassohn appear to take this view.[27]

Further, one might pursue the question of whether it is really necessary even to be able to foresee the full extent of the consequences in order to be accurately described as having a genocidal intent. Historian Steven Katz argues in *The Holocaust in Historical Context* that the mass deaths of Native Americans and Native Australians were not genocides because they resulted from epidemics, not from murder.[28] The suggestion is that the consequences here were not reasonably foreseeable. David Stannard, American Studies scholar at the University of Hawaii, however, finds the case less simple, for it can be argued that the epidemics were not just accidental.[29] Part of the controversy regards the facts: to what extent were victims deliberately infected, as when the British, and later Americans, distributed blankets infected with small pox virus?[30] And to what extent did victims succumb to unintended infection stemming from ordinary exposure to Europeans with the virus? But, also, part of the controversy is philosophical. If mass deaths from disease result from wrongdoing, and if perpetrators could know that the intolerably destructive consequences had an uncontrollable (and therefore somewhat unpredictable) extent, then, does it matter, ethically, whether the wrongdoers could foresee the full extent of the consequences? One might argue that it does not, on the ground that they already knew enough to appreciate that what they were doing was evil.

What is the importance of success in achieving a genocidal aim? Must genocide succeed in eliminating an entire group? An assault, to be homicide, must succeed in killing. Otherwise, it is a mere attempt, and an unlawful attempted homicide generally carries a less severe penalty than a successful one. Bedau and Lang point out, however, that "genocide" does not appear to be analogous to "homicide" in that way. There may still be room for some distinction between genocide and attempted genocide (although Lang appears not to recognize any such distinction) if we distinguish between partially formed and fully formed intentions, or if we distinguish among stages in carrying out a complex intention. But in paradigmatic instances of genocide, such as the Holocaust, there are always some survivors, even when there is clear evidence that the intention was to eliminate everyone in the group. There is general agreement that at least some mass killing with that wrongful intention is genocidal. The existence of survivors is not sufficient to negate fully formed genocidal intent. There may be survivors even after all stages of a complex genocidal intention have been implemented. Bedau observes, however, that there is a certain analogy between "genocide" and "murder," which enables us to contrast both with homicide. Both genocide and murder include wrongfulness in the very concept, whereas a homicide can be justifiable. Homicide is not necessarily unlawful or even immoral. In contrast, genocide and murder are, in principle, incapable of justification.

On my understanding of what constitutes an evil, there are two basic elements: (1) culpable wrongdoing by one or more perpetrators and (2) reasonably foreseeable intolerable harm to victims.[31] Most often the second element, intolerable harm, is what distinguishes evils from ordinary wrongs. Intentions may be necessary to defining genocide. But they are not always necessary for culpable wrongdoing, as omissions—negligence, recklessness, or carelessness—can be sufficient. When culpable wrongdoing *is* intentional, however, its aim need not be to cause intolerable harm. A seriously culpable deed is evil when the doer is willing to inflict intolerable harm on others even in the course of aiming at some other goal. If what is at stake in controversies regarding the meaning of "genocide" is whether a mass killing is sufficiently evil to merit the opprobrium attaching to the term "genocide," a good case can be made for including assaults on many kinds of groups inflicted through many kinds of culpable wrongdoing. Yet that leaves the question of whether the genocidal nature of a killing has special ethical import, and if so, what that import is and how, if at all, it may restrict the scope of "genocide." I turn to these and related questions next.

The specific evils of genocide

Genocide is not simply unjust (although it certainly is unjust); it is also evil. It characteristically includes the one-sided killing of defenseless civilians—babies, children, the elderly, the sick, the disabled, and the injured of both genders along with their usually female caretakers—simply on the basis of their national, religious, ethnic, racial, or other political identity. It targets people on the basis of who they are rather than on the basis of what they have done, what they might do, even what they are capable of doing. (One commentator says genocide kills people on the basis of *what* they are, not even *who* they are.)

Genocide is a paradigm of what Israeli philosopher Avishai Margalit calls "indecent" in that it not only destroys victims but first humiliates them by deliberately inflicting an "utter loss of freedom and control over one's vital interests."[32] Vital interests can be transgenerational and thus survive one's death. Before death, genocide victims are ordinarily deprived of control over vital transgenerational interests and more immediate vital interests. They may be literally stripped naked, robbed of their last possessions, lied to about the most vital matters, witness to the murder of family, friends, and neighbors, made to participate in their own murder, and if female, they are likely to be also violated sexually.[33] Victims of genocide are commonly killed with no regard for lingering suffering or exposure. They, and their corpses, are routinely treated with utter disrespect. These historical facts, not simply mass murder, account for much of the moral opprobrium attaching to the concept of genocide.

Yet such atrocities, it may be argued, are already war crimes, if conducted during wartime, and they can otherwise or also be prosecuted as crimes against humanity. Why, then, add the specific crime of genocide? What, if anything, is not already captured by laws that prohibit such things as the rape, enslavement, torture, forced deportation, and the degradation of individuals? Is any ethically distinct harm done to members of the targeted group that would not have been done had they been targeted simply as individuals rather than because of their group membership? This is the question that I find central in arguing that genocide is not simply reducible to mass death, to any of the other war crimes, or to the crimes against humanity just enumerated. I believe the answer is affirmative: the harm is ethically distinct, although on the question of whether it is worse, I wish only to question the assumption that it is not.

Specific to genocide is the harm inflicted on its victims' social vitality. It is not just that one's group membership is the occasion for harms that are definable independently of one's identity as a member of the group. When a group with its own cultural identity is destroyed, its survivors lose their cultural heritage and may even lose their intergenerational connections. To use Orlando Patterson's terminology, in that event, they may become "socially dead" and their descendants *"natally alienated,"* no longer able to pass along and build upon the traditions, cultural developments (including languages), and projects of earlier generations.[34] The harm of social death is not necessarily less extreme than that of physical death. Social death can even aggravate physical death by making it indecent, removing all respectful and caring ritual, social connections, and social contexts that are capable of making dying bearable and even of making one's death meaningful. In my view, the special evil of genocide lies in its infliction of not just physical death (when it does that) but social death, producing a consequent meaninglessness of one's life and even of its termination. This view, however, is controversial.

African American and Jewish philosopher Laurence Mordekhai Thomas argues that although American slavery natally alienated slaves—these slaves were born severed from most normal social and cultural ties that connect one with both earlier and later generations—the Holocaust did not natally alienate Jews.[35] He does not explicitly generalize about genocide and natal alienation but makes this judgment in regard to the particular genocide of the Holocaust. Yet, the apparent implication is that a genocide no more successful than the Holocaust (an accepted paradigm of genocide) is not natally alienating, because enough victims survive and enough potential targets escape that they are able to preserve the group's cultural traditions. Thomas's analyses of patterns of evil in American slavery and the Holocaust are philosophically groundbreaking and have been very helpful to me in thinking about these topics. Yet I want to question this conclusion that he draws. I want to consider the Nazi genocide in light of the more fundamental idea of social death, of which natal alienation is one special case, not the only case.

Thomas's conception of natal alienation is more specific and more restricted than Patterson's conception of social death. Thomas seems not to be thinking of lost family connections and lost community connections, the particular connections of individuals to one another, but, rather, of the connections of each individual with a culture in general, with its traditions and practices. He finds members of an ethnic group natally alienated when the cultural practices into which they are born "forcibly prevent most of them from fully participating in, and thus having a secure knowledge of, their historical–cultural traditions."[36] He notes that after seven generations of slavery, the memories of one's culture of origin are totally lost, which is certainly plausible. Patterson used the term "natal alienation" for the extreme case of being *born* to *social death*, with individual social connections, past and future, cut off from all but one's oppressors at the very outset of one's life. Hereditary slavery yields a paradigm of natal alienation in this sense. Slaves who are treated as non-persons have (practically) no socially supported ties not only to a cultural heritage but even to immediate kin (parents, children, siblings) and peers. As a consequence of being cut off from kin and community, they also lose their cultural heritage. But the first step was to destroy existing social ties with family and community, to "ex-communicate them from society," as Patterson puts it.[37] In Rawlsian terms, they were first excluded from the benefits and protections of the basic structure of the society into which they were born and in which they must live out their lives. Loss of cultural heritage follows.

Those who are *natally* alienated are *born* already socially dead. Natal alienation might be a clue to descent from genocide survivors (although not necessarily, insofar as genocide depends also on intent). Thus, the natal alienation of slaves and their descendants, when slavery is hereditary, is one clue to a possible history of genocide committed against their ancestors.

Thomas recognizes that alienation is not "all or nothing." A lost cultural heritage can be rediscovered, or partially recovered, later or in other places. Those who were alienated from some cultures may become somewhat integrated into others. Still, he denies that the Holocaust natally alienated Jews from Judaism "because the central tenets of Judaism—the defining traditions of Judaism—endured in spite of Hitler's every intention to the contrary."[38]

The question, however, should be not simply whether the traditions survived but whether individual Jewish victims were able to sustain their connections to those traditions. Sustaining the connections meaningfully requires a family or community setting for observance. Many Jews, of course, escaped being victimized, because of where they lived (in the United States, for example) and because of how the war turned out (the defeat of the Axis powers), and they were able to maintain Jewish traditions with which survivors might conceivably connect or reconnect. But many survivors were unable to do so. Some found family members after the war or created new families. Many did not. Many lost entire families, their entire villages, and the way of life embodied in the *shtetl* (eastern European village). Some could not produce more children because of medical experiments performed on them in the camps. Many survivors lost access to social memories embodied in such cultural institutions as libraries and synagogues.

Responding to the observation that entire communities of Jews were destroyed and that the Yiddish language is on the way out, Thomas argues that members of those communities were destroyed not "as such" (as *shtetl* Jews, for example) but more simply "as Jews," and that the entire community of Jews was not destroyed.[39] He concludes that "the question must be whether the Holocaust was natally alienating of Jews as such, without regard to any specific community of Jews."[40] In answering negatively, he is apparently thinking of survivors who re-established a Jewish life after the war, rather than of non-European Jews, potential victims whose positions might be regarded as somewhat analogous to those of unhunted and unenslaved Africans at the time of the African slave trade.

Some European Jews survived, however, only by passing as Christians. Some hidden children who were raised by strangers to be Christians only discovered their Jewish heritage later, if at all. If they were full members of the societies in which they survived, Thomas does not consider them natally alienated. Those who pass as members of another religion need not be socially dead, even if they are alienated from their religion of origin. Still, if they were originally connected in a vital way with their inherited religion and if they then experienced no vital connection to the new one, arguably, then they do suffer a degree of social death. More clearly, those who were made stateless before being murdered were certainly treated, socially, as non-persons. National Socialist decrees robbed them of social support for ties to family, peers, and community, stripped their rights to earn a living, own property, attend public schools, even ride public transportation, and on arrival at the camps they were torn from family members. Although they were not *born* to social death, they were nevertheless intentionally deprived of all social vitality before their physical murder.

For those who survive physically, mere knowledge and memory are insufficient to create social vitality, even if they are necessary. Those who cannot participate in the social forms they remember do not actually have social vitality but only the memory of it. Further, from 1933 to 1945 many children were born to a condition that became progressively more *natally* alienating.

Contrary to the apparent implication of Thomas's hypothesis regarding the differences between American slavery and the Holocaust, social death seems to me to be a concept central to the harm of genocide, at least as important to what is evil about the Holocaust as the mass physical murder.

Although social vitality is essential to a decent life for both women and men, the sexes have often played different roles in its creation and maintenance. If men are often cast in the role of the creators of (high?) culture, women have played very central roles in preserving and passing on the traditions, language, and (daily) practices from one generation to the next and in maintaining family and community relationships. Where such generalizations hold, the blocking of opportunities for creativity (being excluded from the professions, for example) would fall very heavily on men. But disruptions of family and community, such as being alienated from one's family by rape or being suddenly deported without adequate provisions (or any means of obtaining them) into a strange environment where one does not even know the language, would also fall very heavily, perhaps especially so, on women.

Most immediate victims of genocide are not born socially dead. But genocides that intentionally strip victims of the ability to participate in social activity, prior to their murders, do aim at their social death, not just their physical death. In some cases it may appear that social death is not an end in itself but simply a consequence of means taken to make mass murder easier (concentrating victims in ghettos and camps, for example). When assailants are moved by hatred, however, social death may become an end in itself. Humiliation before death appears often to have been an end in itself, not just a means. The very idea of selecting victims by social group identity suggests that it is not just the physical life of victims that is targeted but the social vitality behind that identity.

If the aim, or intention, of social death is not accidental to genocide, the survival of Jewish culture does not show that social death was not central to the evil of the Holocaust, any more than the fact of survivors shows that a mass murder was not genocidal. A genocide as successful as the Holocaust achieves the aim of social death both for victims who do not survive and, to a degree and for a time, for many survivors as well. Thomas's point may still hold that descendants of survivors of the African diaspora produced by the slave trade are in general more alienated from their African cultures of origin than Holocaust survivors are from Judaism today. Yet it is true in both cases that survivors make substantial connection with other cultures. If African Americans are totally alienated from their African cultures of origin, it is also true that many Holocaust survivors and their descendants have found it impossible to embrace Judaism or even a Jewish culture after Auschwitz. The survival of a culture does not by itself tell us about the degree of alienation that is experienced by individual survivors. Knowledge of a heritage is not by itself sufficient to produce vital connections to it.

The harm of social death is not, so far as I can see, adequately captured by war crimes and other crimes against humanity. Many of those crimes are defined by what can be done to individuals considered independently of their social connections: rape (when defined simply as a form of physical assault), torture, starvation. Some crimes, such as deportation and enslavement, do begin to get at issues of disrupting social existence. But they lack the comprehensiveness of social death, at least when the enslavement in question is not hereditary and is not necessarily for the rest of a person's life.

Still, it is true that not all victims of the Holocaust underwent social death to the same extent as prisoners in the camps and ghettos. Entire villages on the Eastern front were slaughtered by the *Einsatzgruppen* (mobile killing units) without warning or prior captivity. Yet these villagers were given indecent deaths. They were robbed of control of their vital interests and of opportunities to mourn. Although most did not experience those deprivations for very long, inflicted en masse these murders do appear to have produced sudden social death prior to physical extermination. The murders were also part of a larger plan that included the death of Judaism, not just the deaths of Jews. Implementing that plan included gradually stripping vast numbers of Jews of social vitality, in some places over a period of years, and it entailed that survivors, if there were any, should not survive as Jews. The fact that the plan only partly succeeded does not negate the central role of social death within it or the importance of that concept to genocide.

If social death is central to the harm of genocide, then it really is right not to count as a genocide the annihilation of just any political group, however heinous. Not every political group contributes significantly to its members' cultural identity. Many are fairly specific and short-lived, formed to support particular issues. But then, equally, the annihilation of not just any cultural group should count, either. Cultural groups can also be temporary and specialized, lacking in the continuity and comprehensiveness that are presupposed by the possibility of social death. Some mass murders—perhaps the bombings of 11 September 2001—do not appear to have had as part of their aim, intention, or effect the prior soul murder or social death of those targeted for physical extermination. If so, they are mass murders that are not also genocides. But mass murders and other measures that have as part of their reasonably foreseeable consequence, or as part of their aim, the annihilation of a group that contributes significantly to the social identity of its members are genocidal.

Notes

1. This chapter is adapted from an earlier version of this essay, which appeared in *Hypatia* 18 (1): 63–79. Permission for the reprinting has been granted by *Hypatia* and Indiana University Press, the publisher of the journal.
2. The exceptions include, for example, Robin Schott, "Philosophical Reflections on War Rape," in Claudia Card, ed., *On Feminist Ethics and Politics* (Lawrence, KA: University Press of Kansas, 1999); Claudia Card, "Rape as a Weapon of War," *Hypatia* 11 (4): 5–18; and Claudia Card, "Addendum to Rape as a Weapon of War," *Hypatia* 12 (2): 216–18.
3. Unlike Native American families whose children were forcibly transported for re-education in the United States, many Jewish families during the Holocaust sought to hide their children in gentile households. Loss of Jewish social vitality to the children was hardly the responsibility of their families' decisions to do this but, rather, of those whose oppressive measures drove families to try to save their children in this way.
4. An example well-known to philosophers is Edith Stein, student of and later assistant to Edmund Husserl. Her doctoral dissertation on the topic of empathy was originally published in 1917. (See Edith Stein, *On the Problem of Empathy*, trans. Waltraut Stein [The Hague: Nijhoff, 1964].) She became a Catholic nun but was nevertheless deported to Auschwitz from her convent in the Netherlands.
5. See Lucy W. Davidowicz, *The War against the Jews* (New York: Holt, Rinehart, and Winston, 1975).
6. John Rawls, *A Theory of Justice*, rev. edn (Cambridge: Harvard University Press, 1999), p. 3.
7. Ibid., p. 4.
8. For elaboration, see Claudia Card, *The Atrocity Paradigm: A Theory of Evil* (New York: Oxford University Press, 2002), which includes chapters on war rape and on

terrorism in the home. There is not a chapter on genocide, although genocide figures throughout as paradigmatic of atrocities.

9. See Raphael Lemkin, *Axis Rule in Occupied Europe: Laws of Occupation, Analysis of Government, Proposals for Redress* (Washington, DC: Carnegie Endowment for International Peace, 1944).
10. See Diane F. Orentlicher, "Genocide," in Roy Guttman and David Rieff, eds, *Crimes of War: What the Public Should Know* (New York: Norton, 1999), p. 153.
11. Berel Lang, "Genocide," in Lawrence C. Becker with Charlotte B. Becker, eds, *Encyclopedia of Ethics* (New York: Garland, 1992), Vol. 1, p. 400.
12. See Frank Chalk and Kurt Jonassohn, eds, *The History and Sociology of Genocide: Analyses and Case Studies* (New Haven, CT: Yale University Press, 1990).
13. Peter Novick, *The Holocaust in American Life* (Boston, MA: Houghton Mifflin, 1999).
14. Jean-Paul Sartre, *On Genocide* (Boston, MA: Beacon Press, 1968).
15. Hugo Adam Bedau, "Genocide in Vietnam?," in Virginia Held, Sidney Morgenbesser, and Thomas Nagel, eds, *Philosophy, Morality, and International Affairs* (New York: Oxford University Press, 1974), pp. 5–46.
16. See Berel Lang, "The Concept of Genocide," *Philosophical Forum* 16 (1984–85): 1–18 and Berel Lang, *Act and Idea in the Nazi Genocide* (Chicago, IL: University of Chicago Press, 1990).
17. See Alan S. Rosenbaum, *Is the Holocaust Unique? Perspectives on Comparative Genocide*, 2nd edn (Boulder, CO: Westview Press, 2001).
18. See Martha Minow, *Between Vengeance and Forgiveness: Facing History after Genocide* (Boston, MA: Beacon Press, 1998).
19. See Jonathan Glover, *Humanity: A Moral History of the Twentieth Century* (New Haven, CT: Yale University Press, 2000).
20. See Nehemiah Robinson, *The Genocide Convention: A Commentary* (New York: Institute of Jewish Affairs, World Jewish Congress, 1960), p. 147.
21. Israel Charny, "Toward a Generic Definition of Genocide," in George Andreopoulos, ed., *Genocide: Conceptual and Historical Dimensions* (Philadelphia, PA: University of Pennsylvania Press, 1994), pp. 64–94.
22. See Chalk and Jonassohn, *The History and Sociology of Genocide*.
23. See Bedau, "Genocide in Vietnam?"
24. Charny, "Toward a Generic Definition of Genocide."
25. See William David Solomon, "Double Effect," in Becker and Becker, eds, *Encyclopedia of Ethics*, Vol. 1, pp. 268–9.
26. See Lang, *Act and Idea in the Nazi Genocide*, pp. 3–29.
27. See Chalk and Jonassohn, *The History and Sociology of Genocide*.
28. See Steven Katz, *The Holocaust in Historical Context*, Vol. 1, *Mass Death before the Modern Age* (New York: Oxford University Press, 1994).
29. See David E. Stannard, *American Holocaust: The Conquest of the New World* (New York: Oxford University Press, 1992) and David E. Stannard, "Uniqueness as Denial: The Politics of Genocide Scholarship," in Rosenbaum, ed., *Is the Holocaust Unique?*
30. See Lenore Stiffarm with Phil Lane, Jr., "The Demography of Native North America," in Annette Jaimes, ed., *The State of Native America* (Boston, MA: South End, 1992).
31. See Card, *The Atrocity Paradigm*, chapter 1, for development of this conception of an evil.
32. Avishai Margalit, *The Decent Society*, trans. Naomi Goldblum (Cambridge: Harvard University Press, 1996), p. 115.

33. Men are sometimes also violated sexually (usually by other men), although the overwhelming majority of sex crimes in war, including genocide, are perpetrated by men against female victims of all ages and conditions.

34. Orlando Patterson, *Slavery and Social Death* (Cambridge: Harvard University Press, 1982), pp. 5–9.

35. Laurence Mordekhai Thomas, *Vessels of Evil: American Slavery and the Holocaust* (Philadelphia, PA: Temple University Press, 1993), pp. 150–7.

36. Ibid., p. 150.

37. See Patterson, *Slavery and Social Death*.

38. Thomas, *Vessels of Evil*, p. 153.

39. It is commonly estimated that two-thirds of European Jews died. That leaves not only one-third of European Jews but also Jewish communities in many other parts of the world, such as Israel (to which some European Jews fled), the Far East, Australia, and the Americas.

40. Thomas, *Vessels of Evil*, p. 153.

20
Genocide and the "Logic" of Racism

John K. Roth

> My mother's Singer sewing machine, too, vanished in the confusion
> of war like an orphan ...
>
> Danilo Kiš, *Garden, Ashes*

My students have often heard me say that if I had the chance to remove one word, one concept, from human consciousness, my first choice, arguably, would be *race*. Few ideas, if any, have been more pernicious and destructive than that one. *Race* has sometimes been used more-or-less benignly as a synonym for *species* (as in "the human race") or as a word that refers neutrally or in some historical sense to physical, cultural, or ethnic differences among people (as in "the black race"). Overwhelmingly, however, the term *race* has done far more harm than good. Embedded in what can be called the "logic" of *racism*, the reasons are not hard to find.[1]

Race, racism, and genocide

Uses of the term *race* reflect the interests of human groups. Those interests involve power and control. Racial differentiation, usually traceable ultimately to physical differences such as skin color, has typically entailed distinctions between superiority and inferiority. Attempts to justify such distinctions have often appealed to "nature" or to allegedly empirical corroborations, but deeper inquiry into their origins indicates that such appeals have been rationalizations and legitimations for conceptual frameworks that have been constructed to ensure hegemonies of one kind or another. Far from being neutral, far from being grounded in objective and scientific analysis, racial differentiation has promoted division and advanced the interests of those who want to retain prerogatives and privileges that otherwise might not be theirs. The times when racial distinctions have been benign pale in comparison to those when they have fueled abuse, enslavement, injustice, violence, war, and genocide. Whenever the concept of *race* originated, whatever its forms may have been, seeds of destruction were sown with that concept and the schemes that evolved from it. The harvest has been as bloody and lethal as it has been long.

The crops of that harvest include *racism* among the most prominent and fecund. The term *racism* can be variously defined, but in common and minimalist usage it refers to prejudice, discrimination, and institutions, including law, based on beliefs about superiority and inferiority that pertain to groups of people who are thought to share lines of descent ("blood"), physical characteristics (such as skin color), and/or cultural features and identities ("civilization" of one kind or another). Separating groups of people into those that are superior and inferior, splitting groups of people into *us* and *them*, and doing so in ways that find the differences to be *essential* and usually *biological*, racism entails that difference among racially defined groups is threatening. Such threats have often been interpreted in ways that are genocidal.

Ruins and absences

The factors noted above remind me that the Serbian novelist Danilo Kiš (1935–89) was the son of a Montenegrin mother and a Jewish father. Subotica, Kiš's Yugoslavian home town, stood near the Hungarian border. When the Germans attacked Yugoslavia in April 1941, Subotica came under Hungary's control. Not until March 1944, when the Germans occupied the territory of their faltering Hungarian allies, did the Jews of Hungary face the Holocaust's full onslaught. When it came, that disaster took Kiš's father to an Auschwitz death.

Narrated from the perspective of a boy named Andi Scham, *Garden, Ashes* is a poignant, semiautobiographical novel about the Holocaust. In ways unconventional for that genre, Kiš does not take his readers inside a ghetto, a deportation cattle-car, or a death camp. Instead, as the story's title suggests, one is led to consider the Holocaust as an absence, an irredeemed emptiness and irredeemable ruin—ashes—where once there had been life that flowed and flowered like a rich, green garden. The absence is personified by Andi's Jewish father, Eduard, who was taken away and presumably killed at Auschwitz, although his son was never quite sure of that and kept hoping and looking for his father's return, which never came.

Eccentric, difficult, but in his own ways loving and lovable, Eduard Scham was a writer whose masterpiece remained unfinished. The lack of closure, however, was not due entirely to the murder of its author. Scham's project was to be the third edition of his previously published *Bus, Ship, Rail, and Air Travel Guide*. In its revised and enlarged form, this book became a mystical, metaphysical exploration that included not only "all cities, all land areas and all the seas, all the skies, all climates, all meridians" but also spiraling roads and forking paths that carried him "afield in both breadth and depth" so that "abbreviations became subchapters, subchapters became chapters" with no end to their multiplying enigmas.[2]

Like Eduard Scham's travel guide, which led in so many directions without arriving at a certain destination, *Garden, Ashes* lacks closure too. One of the reasons involves the Singer sewing machine that belonged to Andi's mother. The novel's early pages describe it; a sketch of the machine in one of the novel's pages adds to the specificity that Kiš conveys. Andi's mother created beauty with that machine, and thus the sewing machine itself was beautiful, for it signified home and a world in which one could be at home. It is even possible that the destination sought by Eduard Scham's travel guide might have been the place where that sewing machine belonged and where it could be found. The sewing machine, however, was not to be found. Apparently it belonged nowhere, for it "vanished in the confusion of war," writes Kiš.[3] The garden it had helped to create was turned to ashes by the Holocaust.

Consistency and inconsistency

For three reasons, I have referred to Kiš's *Garden, Ashes* in these reflections on "Genocide and the 'Logic' of Racism." First, the detail of this narrative is a reminder of the particularity that is often hidden by terms such as *genocide* or *racism*, which are concepts in ways that fathers, gardens, and sewing machines are not. Second, the destruction of such particularities—and many more—is what racism implies, and that implication also means that, at its core, racism tends to be genocidal. Third, whether there will be, even can be, any closure with regard to this connection, particularly in the sense of dissolving the connection and destablizing the ideas that comprise it, is something that remains to be seen. At least in part the outcomes depend on what philosophy and philosophers turn out be.

What happened to Eduard Kiš helps to make these points clear. He was deported to Auschwitz because he was a Jew. Antisemitism was at the heart of Nazi ideology. Within that ideology, Nazi antisemitism meant that race—specifically the "purity" of German blood and culture—counted for everything. Nothing could be tolerated that might pollute the racial strength on which the Third Reich depended. According to Nazi theory—practice, too, as events unfolded—Jewish life posed this threat to a degree that surpassed all others. Germans, the Nazis argued persuasively, could not afford to let Jews remain in their midst.

As the history of Nazi Germany so emphatically shows, racism's "logic" leads tellingly, if not inevitably, to genocide. For if you take seriously the idea that one race endangers the well-being of another, the only way to remove that menace completely is to do away, once and for all, with everyone and everything that embodies it. Thus, the Holocaust took the lives of approximately 1.5 million Jewish children who were under fifteen. If most forms of racism shy away from such extreme measures, Nazi Germany's antisemitism was more consistent. It followed the path that racism's "logic" mapped out.

Genocides are never identical, but all of them share features in common. The goals of genocide can be diverse, including acquiring wealth or territory, or advancing a belief or ideology, but all cases of genocide entail one or more targeted groups that the perpetrators seek to eliminate in one way or another. Although not the same in each case, steps to isolate and separate people take place. The means and duration of murder are not uniform, but most genocides, if not all, involve mass killing. The perpetrators are always particular people; so are the victims. Nevertheless, whatever their ethnicity or group identity may be, there are perpetrators and victims in all genocides. There are also bystanders. Without them, neither the causes nor the mechanisms of genocide would have their way so easily.

How does racism fit with this pattern of similarity and difference among genocides? In response, two main points loom the largest. First, *the "logic" that operates in and between racism and genocide indicates that racism can exist without genocide, and yet racism tends to be genocidal nonetheless.* Racism can exist at lower or higher levels of intensity. It may express itself in various policies and institutions. Racial discrimination need not be as overt or visible as segregation, de jure or de facto, makes it; racial prejudice need not be as extreme or violent as lynchings or pogroms. Nevertheless, insofar as racism is not self-contradictory but true to its fundamental impulses, it has to take seriously the idea that racial difference is fundamentally at odds with what one deeply values.

Much racial thinking and racism in particular is self-contradictory. One's racial group is thought to be better than another, but the idea is not taken seriously enough to produce sustained or systematic action based on racial discrimination, perhaps because cultural values make it politically incorrect to do so. Racism's impulses can be muted, but such pressures do not eliminate the "logic" of racism, which entails that a perceived racial threat to one's own racial group cannot be ignored with impunity. Furthermore, a savvy racism will include the understanding that in the case of racial threats to one's own racial group, there are many ways—sexual, cultural, political, religious—in which there can be incursions that pollute what is valued and weaken what allegedly should be authoritative. It follows for the "logic" of racism that racial threats to the purity and hegemony of a privileged racial group must be dealt with in a thoroughgoing manner.

Insofar as one harbors racism, whether in full consciousness or only dimly, a person or even a group can be dishonest and inauthentic in failing to acknowledge (1) that a consistent racism will want to rid itself of the threat that racial difference poses, and (2) that this goal can be achieved fully, once and for all, only through genocide. The "logic" of racism calls for an "honest" racist to be genocidal—not necessarily to agitate for genocide *now* but to be prepared to incite and implement genocide if and when the times for it are opportune. Ironically, such a realization might produce a fortunate step that could reduce racism, for it may be that those who practice racial discrimination (however inadvertently), and are racists to that extent, do not want to be murderous and would even resist pressures in that direction. Nevertheless, it would be unwise to take much comfort from the fact that racism may often be of a lukewarm and inconsistent variety. An inconsistent racism may not be overtly genocidal, but inconsistency does not defang racism, at least not completely. One can be inconsistent today and consistent tomorrow. The history of genocide bears witness to that.

Continuing the exploration about how racism fits within patterns of similarity and difference among genocides, the second point that looms largest goes as follows: *Although genocide can be incited and committed, at least in principle, without explicit appeals to racial difference, superiority and inferiority, few genocides, if any, are devoid of racism in one form or another.* To justify this claim, note, first, that racism involves more than dislike of behavior, disagreement with political or religious views held by others, or even disputes about national identities. Behavior can shift so that the provocation for dislike is removed. A person's or a group's political perspectives or religious beliefs can be altered so that the grounds for disagreement are taken away. Even citizenship is negotiable and changeable; the irritations that activate disputes about differences in those areas can also be dissolved.

With racism, however, more is at stake than behavior, belief, and even citizenship. To have the dubious distinction of being worthy of the name, racism is about *essential* and usually *biological* differences. Racism trades in the allegedly unchangeable. What is taken to be unchangeable may be masked by what is changeable and changing, but claims about what is *essential* remain at the heart of racism nonetheless. The "logic" of these considerations works in two related ways.

First, racism's "logic" encourages one to think that when a racial threat is perceived, there is something that must be preserved and protected against that threat. What is valued, racism's "logic" understands, could be harmed, compromised, polluted, ruined—the unfortunate verbs multiply their invidious distinctions. Racist feeling is often aroused because it is sensed that such polluting actions have taken place and that they have weakened the privileged racial identity that deserves hegemony. The remedy is to restore health to the privileged race and to purge the forces that are contaminating threats. Within this "logic" is the idea that the privileged race is essentially what it is. Even if compromised and contaminated, it remains and requires vindication lest it be lost, which could happen if vigilance diminishes. Such vigilance, if it is thoroughly and consistently focused on the perceived threats, will tend to have genocidal inclinations.

Second, where either genocidal inclinations or actual implementations of genocide are concerned, racism is likely to be an accompanying and energizing factor. At first glance, that claim might seem at odds with the formal definition of genocide, which in the United Nations'formulation speaks of potentially targeted groups as "national, ethnical, racial or religious" and identifies a variety of acts that can be carried out with intent to destroy such groups "in whole or in part."[4] At second glance, however, far from eliminating racism, those identifying marks clarify how racism works in genocide and how it is even required for some genocides to take place.

Where the intent is genocidal, the "logic" of that intention means that destruction "in part" is always second-best. The optimal realization of genocidal intent is to destroy a targeted group "in whole." There are practical and philosophical reasons that back such "logic." The Nazi SS leader Heinrich Himmler captured both dimensions of this "logic" in a speech about the destruction of Jewry that he delivered to his men in October 1943. "We had to answer the question: What about the women and children?" Himmler observed. "Here, too, I had made up my mind. ... I did not feel that I had the right to exterminate the men and then allow their children to grow into avengers, threatening our sons and grandchildren. A fateful decision had to be made: This people had to vanish from the earth."[5]

Destruction of a group "in part" rightly qualifies as an instance of the crime of genocide, but Himmler's reasoning cogently underscores that the "logic" involved here would find it imprudent not to finish the job once the tasks of genocide have begun and the opportunity to continue to the end is available. Most genocides do not go "all the way," but that outcome takes place either because pressure or force from the outside intervenes, which happens mostly too late and too little, or because exhaustion of one kind or another sets in, or because of some combination of the two. But the "logic" of genocide says that the destruction, once started, should continue to the end. Not to achieve that outcome is to come up short.

The UN Convention indicates that there can be an intention to commit genocide halfway—"intent to destroy ... in part," as the wording might be read. One need not deny that such intent could be and even has been real, but in those cases a kind of inconsistency has entered into the intentionality. In the case of the Nazis, for instance, it was not understood that 50 percent of the European Jews were a threat or even that only the destruction of the European Jews was the optimal goal to be achieved. Better still and even necessary, as Himmler put it, was action that made the Jewish people disappear from the earth. Nor, according to the Hutu leadership in Rwanda, was it merely 100,000 Tutsi who had to be destroyed. Better still and even necessary, the "logic" of genocide in Rwanda meant that it would be desirable, if possible, for all the Tutsi in Rwanda and, arguably, elsewhere to disappear from the face of the earth.

An objection to this line of reasoning might invoke the possibility that genocide can simply be instrumental and thus its perpetrators might not want or intend to go "all the way" because doing so would be contrary to their interests. The latter, for example, might involve decimating a population but also sparing some portion of it for enslavement or other forms of exploitation. Such theory and practice can certainly be genocidal, but in such cases one would still have to ask: Why must so many, if not all, of these people be decimated?

That question brings back into view the fact that genocide does more than envision instrumental opportunities. Its deepest impulse is to remove a threat. The threat, in turn, will scarcely be describable as such unless the targeted population is portrayed as endangering the prerogatives, the hegemony, and superiority of the perpetrator group. From the perspective of the "logic" of genocide, these threats, moreover, are rooted in what are taken to be, at least by implication, characteristics or qualities that cannot be assimilated into the perpetrator group. If one's group thinks with a genocidal "logic," then that group cannot embrace the national, ethnic, or religious other, even though in principle and over time, all of those identities could change. It cannot embrace them because at the bottom line an essentialist mind-set is typically embedded in genocidal "logic," and in the context of genocidal mentalities that essentialist mind-set is closely related to racism, if not virtually synonymous with it.

Not all essentialist ways of thinking are racist, but racism is a form of essentialism, and genocidal mentalities typically reflect forms of essentialism that are racist. At the end of the day, racism and genocide inflame each other. The "logic" of the one often entails the "logic" of the other. If there are exceptions, they prove the rule: Usually genocide includes racism of one kind or another, and racism tends to be genocidal.

Paradigmatic genocide that it was, the Holocaust emerged from a deeply racist Nazi ideology. The Rwandan genocide, the clearest case of post-Holocaust genocide, was also rooted in racism. Linda Melvern, a discerning scholar of the Rwandan genocide has documented the following points:

> The Hutu extremists believed that the Tutsi were a different race and that they had come from elsewhere to invade Rwanda. Hutu Power taught that the Tutsi were different, that they were lazy; that they did not want to work the land, that they were outside human existence—vermin and subhuman. The effect of the Hutu Power radio, with its catchy nationalistic theme tunes and its racist jingles must never be underestimated. The broadcasts of *Radio-Télévision Libre des Milles Collines* (RTLM) were an integral part of the genocide plot and it was thanks to the propaganda that spewed over the airways that by April 1994 a large number of people in Rwanda had come to believe that the elimination of the Tutsi, or "cockroaches" as they were called, was a civic duty and that it was necessary work to rid the country of them.[6]

Raising voices in abysses of horror

In late June 1994, as the killing incited by the RTLM was still going on, Pope John Paul II sent Cardinal Roger Etchegaray as his envoy to Rwanda.

Addressing the Rwandan people after his arrival, Etchegaray spoke of "the abyss of horror" created by the mass murder that sundered them. Lest that phrase be taken merely as a rhetorical flourish, consider it in more detail.

The word *abyss* has at least three meanings. It denotes, first, a gulf or pit that is bottomless. This meaning suggests that anything or anyone entering an abyss is utterly lost. Second, *abyss* means chaos or even hell; it refers to disorder in which secure existence for anything or anyone would be impossible until order is created or restored. Third, *abyss* has not only spatial, geographical, or cosmological connotations. The term also refers to the ways in which the human mind and spirit as well as its physical condition can be overwhelmed and left bereft by events that apparently elude rational comprehension. In such cases, the human condition itself becomes abysmal.

Events that elude rational comprehension are often riddled with *horror*, another term that should not be spoken or taken lightly. *Horror* refers to intense feelings of a particular kind and to the actions or conditions that cause them. The feelings, which run deep because they are intense and primal, are those of fear, terror, shock, abhorrence, and loathing. Genocide is a primary instance of *horror* or nothing could be. An *abyss of horror*, then, would be a reality so grim, so devastating, so full of useless pain, suffering, death, and despair that it fractures the world—perhaps forever. Genocide is an *abyss of horror* or, again, nothing could be. Racism is not the only force that opens that abyss, but if racism were absent, it would be possible to have at least a cautious optimism about responses to the question "Will genocide ever end?"

A genocidal abyss of horror cannot be closed, at least not completely. Nor can the questions that it raises be answered with confidence and finality. What can be done is to recognize that abysses of horror remain and that the questions they raise deserve to be confronted as we human beings assess and take up our responsibility for both—the abysses and our responses to the questions they leave before us. As one pursues those points, it is well to remember that every form of power includes, even depends upon, raising voices. Leaders have to raise their voices to state their principles, express their visions, and rally their supporters. Governments have to raise their voices to define policies, defend interests, and justify decisions. Supporters of leaders and governments have to raise their voices to back visions and policies; otherwise the power of principles and interests declines and even disappears.

To be effective, the "logic" of racism and genocide also depends on raising voices. That "logic" can have little force unless divisions between people are constructed by speech, fears are expressed in ideology and propaganda, and killing is unleashed by voices that proclaim it to be necessary. The "logic" of racism and genocide also depends on "unraising" voices; it counts on the silencing of dissent and on the acquiescence of bystanders. Every voice unraised against that "logic" gives aid and comfort to those who call for and support genocide, that crime of crimes. Genocide can be prevented before it happens, and it can be stopped after it is under way. Neither prevention nor successful intervention, however, can happen without power. Rwanda's genocidal tragedy resulted from the fact that raising voices against it came too late and too little.

Here an objection may be raised: Raising voices may not count for much, because actions speak louder than words, and attention should be directed much more on what people do than on what they say. That point has validity, but it underestimates the relationship between raising voices and taking action. Racism and genocide do not appear out of the blue. Intentions, plans, and many people are necessary to make them operational. Absent raising voices, the coordination of thought and action required by racism and genocide will not and cannot be in place. The same can be said of resistance to the "logic" of racism and genocide.

Philosophy and philosophers have important contributions to make when it comes to raising voices. Where genocide prevention is concerned, one of those contributions can and should be the continuing deconstruction of racial thinking. For if such thinking is curtailed, especially in contexts where philosophers equally emphasize the idea and ideals of universal human rights, then racism may be neutralized. With that outcome, one of the most potent causes of genocide would be kept in check. Philosophy is by no means the only discipline that emphasizes logical analysis. Nor are philosophers by any means the sole experts in the critical analysis of reasoning. But philosophy and philosophers are in the vanguard of those who value and practice thinking that questions assumptions, asks for evidence, and tracks the connections and implications of ideas. They can do much to criticize, expose, and demystify the ways of thinking that lead to genocide, including the powerful inducement that racism has provided for it. Philosophy and philosophers ignore this task at the risk of leaving humankind in further abysses of horror.

In closing, my thoughts move from Rwanda and back to the Europe of Danilo Kiš and the Holocaust. His novel *Garden, Ashes* ends on somber notes.[7] "We are witnesses to a great breakdown in values," Kiš writes, and Andi Scham observes that his vanished world has left him in a house with a kitchen stove that cannot "generate a real flame: we lacked a real blaze, there was no glow." The novel's last words belong to Andi's mother, who has no husband and no Singer sewing machine: "Lord," she says, "how quickly it gets dark here." The "logic" of racism remains, and with it the specter of genocide shadows our twenty-first century world. None of us alone can remove that shadow, but each of us can do something. For philosophers, that responsibility includes raising voices to unmask and deconstruct the "logic" of racism, raising voices to reveal and undermine that logic's murderous, genocidal impulses. High on philosophy's priorities should be the task of diminishing, if not eliminating, the destructively influential parts that the concept of *race* has played in human history and the work of advancing views of universal human rights that can be as persuasive and credible as possible in a world that remains profoundly wounded by and vulnerable to the threats of genocide.

Notes

1. My use of the term *"logic"* requires some explanation. In this chapter, I use it primarily to signify a conceptual web or configuration, not a series of deductions from principles or a set of inferences from empirical data. The "logic" of racism—and the "logic" of genocide too—may include elements of both kinds, but as used here *"logic"* connotes pattern of thinking and planning, a mapping of relationships among ideas and policies that associate congenially with each other. There are entailments and implications in these patterns and relationships. One idea, one policy, does lead to another, but the relationships are more organic and dialectical than linear and one-directional. My use of scare quotes around the term *"logic"* is not intended to minimize the power or authority that these patterns of thought can have. They both can be immense. But I use the scare quotes to make clear that the "logic" of racism and genocide is less than fully rational, disguised as rational though it may be.

   With regard to my claim that the term *race* has done far more harm than good, I find significant support in the instructive series of articles on race that appeared in *Daedalus* 134, 1 (Winter 2005): 5–116. Especially pertinent are the contributions by Kenneth Prewitt, Jennifer L. Hochschild, George M. Fredrickson, and the philosopher Ian Hacking. Harmful though the very concept of race has been, one cannot—as my own chapter shows—be rid of it altogether, because the idea has to be invoked to deconstruct and subvert it and to resist the harm it has done. Hacking's essay "Why Race Still Matters" (pp. 102–16) is especially important. Noting recent research that seems to link certain diseases and some medical treatments with racially indentifiable populations, Hacking warns that such statistical correlations, helpful though they may prove to be, are neither equivalent to nor sufficient for claims that "races are real kinds, denoting essentially different kinds of people." Nevertheless, he adds, the recent scientific and medical findings may provide opportunities in which "racists will try to exploit the racial difference" (p. 109). Thus, race still matters because the concept must continue to be very carefully watched and examined as inquiry proceeds.
2. Danilo Kiš, *Garden, Ashes*, trans. William J. Hannaker (Chicago, IL: Dalkey Archive Press, 2003), pp. 34, 37, 39. The discussion of *Garden, Ashes* draws on my contributions to David Patterson and John K. Roth, eds, *Fire in the Ashes: God, Evil, and the Holocaust* (Seattle, WA: University of Washington Press, 2005).
3. Kiš, *Garden, Ashes*, p. 169.
4. The United Nations Convention on the Prevention and Punishment of the Crime of Genocide is reprinted in Carol Rittner, John K. Roth, and James M. Smith, eds, *Will Genocide Ever End?* (St. Paul, MN: Paragon House, 2002), pp. 209–11.
5. Major excerpts from Himmler's speech are reprinted in Paul Mendes-Flohr and Yehuda Reinharz, eds, *The Jew in the Modern World: A Documentary History*, 2nd edn (New York: Oxford University Press, 1995). See especially, p. 685.
6. Linda Melvern, "Identifying Genocide," in Rittner, Roth, and Smith, eds, *Will Genocide Ever End?*, p. 101.
7. For the quotations that follow, see Kiš, *Garden, Ashes*, 168–70.

21

The Right to Life, Genocide, and the Problem of Bystander States

David H. Jones

There is a glaring inconsistency between the professed commitment by the international community to protect and promote the universal right to life (RTL), and its abysmal failure to prevent genocide and crimes against humanity, the most flagrant violations of that right. Despite the promise of the Nuremberg Principles, the Universal Declaration of Human Rights, the United Nations Convention on Genocide, and a host of other international agreements and precedents, at least 15 million largely defenseless civilians have been murdered by governments and revolutionary armies since the Second World War. As Leo Kuper pointed out some years ago, a salient feature of this massive failure of international law is the inaction of bystander states, most notably the United States.[1] In this chapter I defend Kuper's view that ending, or at least reducing, the phenomenon of bystander states is the most urgent problem facing the human rights community, since for the foreseeable future, the only feasible means of preventing, or at least mitigating, imminent or ongoing genocides and other kinds of mass murder, is the timely and effective intervention by the international community.[2]

Although philosophers have proposed various long-term strategies for the prevention of genocide (e.g., the general improvement of individual moral character, the development of deeper understanding of our responsibility for "the Other," and the spread of liberal democratic institutions and culture throughout the world), none of them offers a solution to the immediate problem of imminent and ongoing mass killings.[3] Unlike some of my colleagues in philosophy and other writers in the humanities, I do not think that philosophy's main task in this genocidal age is to find a new grounding for human rights such as the RTL or to work out the details of a "post-Holocaust ethics."[4] We already have adequate (though imperfect) *philosophical* understanding of the nature, content, and justification of the RTL.[5] More importantly, we have in place at least the beginnings of the institutions that will be needed for a truly effective international system of law enforcement for the RTL.

What is most needed right now is greater understanding and practical implementation of new and improved international institutions that have the potential to solve or reduce the problem of bystander states. Thus, I think that philosophers interested in human rights should be much more heavily engaged in applied ethics of the kind found in medical ethics, for example. However, a new focus on the practical application of human rights would require that we become far more familiar with the empirical and scientific work of genocide scholars outside the humanities.

The status of the universal right to life as a legal norm in international law

Richard Rubenstein and other skeptics deserve some credit for forcing philosophers to give a clearer account of what it means to say that the RTL still exists even when it is flagrantly violated time and time again.[6] The first thing to emphasize is the distinction between the RTL as an ethical norm and the RTL as a legal norm. The existence of the RTL as an ethical norm consists in the set of reasons that can be given to justify it.[7] These reasons include: (1) the fundamental equality of human beings as shown in their shared genetic endowment, which ensures shared basic capacities such as consciousness, feelings and emotions, the ability to develop a sense of personal identity, to use language, to perform intentional action, to make choices and carry out life plans, all of which constitute the potential to lead a life as a person; (2) the principle of equal consideration and respect, that is, the strong presumption that every human being should have his or her fundamental interests taken into account by both domestic and international institutions; and (3) that staying alive is among the fundamental interests of each human being, because without it no other good, including living a life as a person, is possible. The inference from these reasons to the RTL is not a logically valid deduction; the aim is not to construct some unassailable proof. Rather, each of these reasons provides a consideration in support of the idea that every human being has a prima facie moral claim or entitlement to stay alive, and this is, in effect, the RTL as an ethical norm.

A complete (or more adequate) justification for the RTL would include a second level of reasons to show that (1), (2), and (3) are indeed good reasons that will hold up under critical scrutiny. The defense of (1) would be primarily scientific in nature, drawing on genetics, psychology, and anthropology. By contrast, the defense of (2) would consist largely of drawing out a particularly significant implication of (1) in conjunction with the precept "equal treatment of equals," namely, that any theoretical claim that there are basic and inherent inequalities among human beings is almost certain to be either false or unsubstantiated and, hence, *arbitrary*. The defense of (3) would involve critical reflection on what may seem to be a tautology: one must stay alive in order to have a life as a person. Even if it is a tautology, it is not an "empty" tautology, since in conjunction with (1) and (2) it supplies a very powerful consideration in support of the RTL as an ethical norm. Due to limitations of space, this sketch of a fuller justification will have to suffice here.[8] The justification of the RTL based on the mundane fact of human equality admittedly lacks the metaphysical gravitas and emotional appeal of traditional views based on God or nature, but it has the inestimable advantage of being strongly supported by objective scientific evidence.

The existence of the RTL as a legal norm consists in (1) the institutionalization of the RTL in particular legal systems by means of constitutional provisions, legislation, judicial opinions, and the like, and (2) the activities of the officials and civil servants who occupy roles defined by the legal system (police, prosecuting attorney, judges, wardens, guards, to name a few) and who interpret, enforce, and administer the norm. The most salient instance of the (partial) legal institutionalization of the RTL is, of course, the fact that virtually every legal system contains a prohibition against homicide. However, only the ethical norm version of the RTL is truly *universal* in scope; it applies to every human being who possesses a threshold level of the relevant capacities. (There is, of course, a small minority of distressing exceptions such as congenital idiots, acephalic individuals, and the like, that present difficulties for almost any ethical theory.) Moreover, only the ethical RTL is *independent* (it exists whether or not it is accepted by particular legal systems or conventional moralities). However, the RTL as an ethical norm is a prima facie right; because there are bound to be occasional conflicts with other weightier considerations that override it, its weight is *not absolute*.

It is easy to see why repeated, flagrant, and unpunished violations of the RTL as a legal norm call into question whether it truly exists as a legal "norm," that is, as a standard of conduct that is enforced. Indeed, this seems to be what Rubenstein means when he complains that the supposed laws of God or laws of nature are not really laws at all, since they can be broken with impunity.[9] However, it should be equally clear why repeated and flagrant violation of the RTL does *not* make the ethical norm cease to exist. The reasons that justify the ethical norm remain relevant, valid, and available for us to use in responding to violations by condemning perpetrators, appealing to the humanity that victims share with the rest of us, criticizing bystander governments, demanding more effective enforcement, and the like. Thus, I think Rubenstein is mistaken when he seems to dismiss the RTL as an ethical norm altogether as "either false or meaningless."[10]

The formal recognition of the RTL in international law was significantly advanced when the Nuremberg Principles were officially codified and adopted by the General Assembly of the United Nations in 1946.[11] The incorporation of the Nuremberg Principles into international law was a truly revolutionary event, because they not only made criminal various categories of killing by a state, they also greatly expanded the reach of international law by explicitly renouncing some traditional defenses (e.g., sovereign immunity and superior orders) designed to make sovereign states and their agents immune to criminal prosecution.

The next significant expansion of the RTL in international law came in 1948 with the adoption of the United Nations Convention on the Prevention and Punishment of the Crime of Genocide (UNCG). The UNCG not only defined the crime of genocide as acts that are intended to destroy, or calculated to bring about the destruction of, "a national, ethnical, racial, or religious group," but it also made conspiracy, incitement, and complicity to commit genocide punishable crimes as well. These acts would be crimes whether committed in peace or in war.[12] Moreover, Article I of the UNCG commits the contracting parties to prevent and to punish genocide, thus creating a prima facie legal obligation.[13]

Although the Nuremberg Principles and the UNCG represent a good start on the legislative task of making the RTL a legal norm in international law, they are almost totally lacking in explicit provisions for the executive and judicial functions needed for enforcement, prevention, and deterrence. Since the UNCG leaves open most of the crucial questions of exactly how the law prohibiting genocide was supposed to be enforced and violators punished, it was almost inevitable that it would function largely as an unenforced declaration. The phenomenon of bystander states shows that it has proved all too easy for most states to avoid doing anything at all to prevent or punish the genocides and mass murders that have taken place since 1945. However, the fact that the UNCG is a defective piece of legislation is only part of the explanation for the phenomenon of bystander states. The other part has to do with the serious defects in the political structure of the United Nations.

Flaws that hamper law enforcement at the international level

A brief review of how the Security Council is structured and of the way in which it operates clearly reveals the main flaw that hampers law enforcement at the international level: there is no executive authority that can take timely and effective action. To begin with, only the Security Council has the power to authorize the use of military force against a sovereign nation. With the exception of the rarely used "Uniting for Peace" resolutions, the General Assembly's actions in this area are strictly advisory.[14] The office of the Secretary General has no authority to initiate substantive actions on its own, and so it is confined to executing decisions of the Security Council. Moreover, no military intervention can be approved by the Security Council without the unanimous agreement of the five permanent members (currently Great Britain, France, Russia, China, and the United States). In practice, it is usually extremely difficult, if not impossible, to get the Security Council to approve a resolution calling for armed intervention.

Even when the Security Council does agree to authorize military intervention, it is usually unable to carry out the intervention in a timely and effective manner, because each proposed intervention must be justified on its own merits and an ad hoc coalition of states created through laborious and time-consuming debate, negotiation, and persuasion. Since the United Nations has no standing military forces or weapons of its own, all military personnel, weapons, and logistical support must be supplied by member nations on a voluntary basis. Member nations are usually reluctant to risk their own troops to stop aggression or genocide alone unless it is also in their own national interest. (This was the case in 1971 when Indira Gandhi ordered the Indian army to stop the Pakistani genocide against the Bengalis.)[15] For all these reasons, getting troops on the ground and fully prepared to take military action can take weeks, even months (as was the case in Rwanda).[16]

In addition, during most of its existence since 1945, the United Nations has had no criminal tribunal of its own to try and punish perpetrators of genocide. In recent years this situation has begun to improve with the creation of ad hoc tribunals for the former Yugoslavia (1993) and for Rwanda (1994), and the ratification of a permanent International Criminal Court (ICC) in August 2002. However, it will take years for the ICC to create significant deterrence to genocide; first it will have to become fully operational and then establish a credible threat of criminal punishment by successfully convicting perpetrators, especially political and military leaders responsible for planning, authorizing, and directing genocidal projects.

This brief review shows that the legislative weaknesses in the UNCG and the structural flaws in the United Nations enable and facilitate bystander states, including the United States, to avoid active involvement in the prevention of genocide. The fact that there has been no serious attempt to remedy these weaknesses shows that the major powers, at any rate, prefer things just the way they are. Indeed, recent research shows how skillfully the political leaders of the United States have time and again actively followed a policy of noninvolvement in genocide, exploiting the weaknesses and flaws of the UNCG and the Security Council to do so.

The United States: a paradigmatic bystander state

The United States is far from being the only bystander state, since nearly all nations belong in this category. However, I call the United States a paradigmatic bystander because its failure to prevent genocide is particularly egregious, given its overwhelming military power and wealth, and its self-proclaimed role as the strongest defender of human rights. Peter Ronayne and Samantha Power, both of whom have written in-depth studies of the failure of the United States to prevent genocide, reach almost identical conclusions.

This book has illustrated how the United States has failed on many levels to capitalize on those opportunities both to save tens of thousands of lives and to advance the cause of the United Nations Convention on the Prevention and Punishment of the Crime of Genocide. The failure to act or even at times to speak out against perpetrators of genocide was not inevitable or necessary but the product of choices. As a result of those choices, the pledge "never again" has had a hollow ring, and unfulfilled potential sums up the American record on preventing genocide.[17]

Before I began exploring America's relationship with genocide, I used to refer to U.S. policy toward Bosnia as a "failure." I have changed my mind. ... this country's consistent policy of nonintervention in the face of genocide offers sad testimony not to a broken American political system but to one that is ruthlessly effective. The system, as it now stands, *is working*. No U.S. president has ever made genocide prevention a priority, and no U.S. president has ever suffered politically for his indifference to its occurrence. It is thus no coincidence that genocide rages on.[18]

Limitations of space make it impossible to present the full range of evidence that these authors offer to justify these harsh judgments. However, a summary of their accounts of the way in which the United States conducted itself in response to the 1994 genocide in Rwanda provides a good sample.[19]

After several decades of intercommunal violence between Hutus and Tutsis that claimed hundreds of thousands of lives, the United Nations brought the two sides together to negotiate an end to the civil war in Rwanda and establish a multiethnic democracy. Signed in August 1993, the Arusha Accords set up a system of power sharing and reform whose implementation was supposed to be overseen by a peacekeeping force, the United Nations Assistance Mission in Rwanda (UNAMIR), and a few outside observers. However, a group of militant nationalists in the Hutu majority in Rwanda were obsessed with an almost paranoid fear that the Tutsis would take unfair advantage of the cease-fire to attack and destroy the Hutus, thus gaining political control of Rwanda. The Hutu radicals, convinced that their very survival was at stake, began in late 1993 to plan a systematic preemptive genocide against all Tutsis and moderate Hutus. Lists of victims were drawn up using official records, local Hutu "militias" were secretly recruited and trained, and arms were stockpiled.

The event that triggered the preplanned genocide was an airplane crash that killed the presidents of both Rwanda and Burundi on 6 April 1994. Using this event as a pretext, the Rwandan Hutu extremists almost immediately began to assassinate Tutsis and moderate Hutu officials and political activists in the capital city. A small Belgian contingent of UNAMIR troops guarding the Rwandan prime minister was deliberately provoked into using force, then tortured and killed. Reacting swiftly, Belgium unilaterally withdrew its remaining 420 troops, thus playing right into the hands of the Hutu extremists who hoped for a complete withdrawal of UNAMIR forces. In the Security Council, the United States pressed for a complete withdrawal of all

UNAMIR forces, but it had to settle for leaving a small contingent of 250. There was no support at all in the Security Council for Secretary-General Kofi Annan's plan to send a much stronger force to stop the killing. The only positive action taken by the United States when the genocide began in Rwanda was to send troops to remove its own citizens to safety. With the government-controlled radio spewing hate-filled propaganda against the Tutsis, the ferocious "low tech" genocide spread across Rwanda for 100 days, taking more than 800,000 lives. In mid-May, the Security Council, under enormous worldwide pressure, reversed its decision and mandated a build up of UNAMIR to 5500 troops. But this gesture came too late to do any good; the genocide had wound down by the end of July, several weeks before the new troops arrived in early August.

There can be little doubt that the United States and other members of the Security Council knew beforehand about the Hutu plans and preparations for genocide. In December 1993, a Hutu military officer sent an anonymous letter to UNAMIR detailing plans for the massacre, weapons stockpiles, and targeting of Belgian troops. After investigating and confirming these charges, UNAMIR commander General Roméo Dallaire reported his findings to the Security Council in January 1994, three months before the genocide began. Moreover, a US Central Intelligence Agency study completed that month predicted that if open violence broke out in Rwanda, it could lead to an estimated 500,000 deaths. Yet the United States vetoed any troop increase for UNAMIR.

Not only did the United States know that genocide was imminent before it started, but also it pursued an active policy of nonintervention after the killing had actually begun and the toll of victims mounted. First, the United States engaged in an aggressive public relations campaign of denial and disinformation about the genocidal nature of the killing. Since the United States had very belatedly ratified the UNCG in 1988, it now had a prima facie legal obligation to prevent and punish genocide. The easiest way to avoid this obligation in Rwanda was just to deny that genocide was occurring. Thus, State Department spokespersons would refer to "ethnic violence" or "civil war," but not to "genocide." Second, when the genocidal nature of the killing could no longer be completely denied, the United States still refused to send its own troops to stop the genocide, confining itself to helping with the removal of UNAMIR troops and sending humanitarian aid to refugees. In a final irony, the United States pressed vigorously for the establishment of an International Criminal Tribunal for Rwanda to bring to justice the perpetrators of the very genocide it had done nothing to stop.

One reason often given by US officials for a policy of nonintervention is the supposedly much higher cost of intervention and peace enforcement. However, it is not at all clear that nonintervention ends up being more economical, because genocide has enormous indirect costs such as humanitarian relief for survivors and refugees, aid to surrounding countries, and criminal prosecution. Helen Fein has conducted a study of the comparative costs of early intervention and nonintervention and concludes that there are cost ratios ranging from 4 : 1 to 20 : 1 in favor of early prevention. For example, the actual cost for the United States in Rwanda from April to November 1994 was up to eight times the estimated cost of early intervention (which it rejected because of the costs). By 1999, the United States had spent close to $900 million on Rwanda and its refugees alone.[20]

Some institutional remedies for the problem of bystander states

The main flaw in the political structure of the United Nations is the lack of an executive authority capable of responding to genocide quickly and with sufficient force to stop or reduce the killing. Genocide researchers have identified a number of reforms that could greatly improve the executive efficiency of the Security Council. Three of these proposals seem especially promising.

(1) The Security Council could delegate limited executive authority to the Secretary-General to use military force to respond to human rights emergencies such as genocide and crimes against humanity. We know that there have been clear cases such as Bosnia and Rwanda when immediate action is necessary. The criteria for what constitutes a clear case would be formulated in a standing procedure drawn up by the Security Council, thus providing advance authorization. The Secretary-General would draw up a specific mandate governing each particular intervention. Permanent members would still have a veto which they could only exercise after some specified time (for example, 90 days). Alternatively, re-authorization might be required at the end of a specified period.[21]

(2) As the name implies, a Crime Watch Advisory Board's function would be purely advisory to the Secretary-General who would have the final authority for ordering the intervention. The Board's main functions would be (a) developing an early warning system to identify advance signs of imminent genocide or crimes against humanity, (b) monitoring conflict situations where threats of these crimes are present, (c) keeping the Secretary-General well-informed about potential or emerging crises, and (d) making timely recommendations to the Secretary-General on whether or not to intervene with force in a particular situation using the Security Council's criteria for clear cases. Although the Board would be established by the Security Council, its membership should consist of respected members of the world diplomatic community and others with high moral authority, thus helping to ensure that the Board's judgments would not merely reflect the interests of the permanent members of the Security Council. The Advisory Board

would use as many sources of available information as possible, and work closely with nongovernmental organizations such as Human Rights Watch and Amnesty International.[22]

(3) Creating a permanent United Nations Rapid Response Force (RRF) is the most important structural reform needed. Currently, the Security Council is like a frontier sheriff who must depend on a posse of vigilantes each time robbing and killing gunslingers come to town. Even when the Security Council agrees that military intervention is required to stop an emerging or ongoing massacre, it must still get member nations to volunteer their own forces. All too often, no nation is willing to offer its troops or else the number of troops volunteered is woefully insufficient. Even when sufficient forces are volunteered, they must still be assembled, provided with weapons and supplies, and transported to the area of military operations. The obstacles to achieving these goals are formidable; past experience shows that most of the time it has been impossible to overcome them. By contrast, if the Security Council had a standing RRF, especially trained and equipped to respond to imminent or ongoing massacres, and capable of being deployed in a few days (instead of weeks or months), many (perhaps even most) of the genocides and crimes against humanity could be prevented altogether, or at least reduced in scale and duration. This seems especially true of genocidal outbreaks such as those in Bosnia and Rwanda.

Despite the many competing conceptions of what a permanent RRF would involve, there is a fair degree of consensus on some of the features that would be essential.[23] First, the RRF would need to be large enough to be militarily effective, but not so large that it could not be quickly mobilized and transported. Most proposals fall within the range of 5000 to 15,000 members. Second, the members of the RRF would be volunteer international civil servants who are individually recruited and paid by the United Nations (much like UN weapons inspectors). Recruitment should be highly selective, since volunteers would have to undergo training not only in combat skills, but also in policing and human rights enforcement. The volunteers should also be recruited from as wide a sample of member states as possible to make the RRF truly international. Third, when it is engaged in military operations, the command structure of the RRF should be insulated from micromanagement by the Security Council so that there can be quick response to events as they emerge. The commander in the field should have the power to order the use of coercive force when he or she feels it is necessary, without having to get further authorization from the Secretary-General or the Security Council. Fourth, the principal functions of the RRF would be to keep the peace and prevent killing, create effective safety zones, apprehend alleged perpetrators and gather forensic evidence, help bring in relief agencies, and initiate basic processes of competent and humane government, if necessary.

The political and financial feasibility of
a Rapid Response Force

An important observation with which to begin is that very little of what is contained in proposals for the RRF would be unprecedented for the United Nations. Peacekeeping, peace enforcement, protecting noncombatants from harm, and deploying forces in a crisis—all of these are familiar UN tasks. As John Heidenrich has argued:

> Even the overseas deployment of UN guards directly subordinate to the Secretary-General is not new. It happened in 1991, after the Gulf War, when ordinary UN security guards were deployed into northern Iraq to symbolically guard and help monitor the new Iraq–Kurdish safe zone there. ... The only thing unprecedented ... is that most of these already existing precedents would be combined into a single standing unit, available to the Security Council for relatively small scale but still risky missions of importance.[24]

These observations are not meant to deny that it will be difficult to achieve what is genuinely new, namely, a real (albeit limited) loss of authority by the Security Council, especially the permanent members who have so far jealously guarded their veto power. There is general agreement, however, that the Security Council and/or the General Assembly already possesses the legal power in the UN Charter to enact these reforms, including the RRF.[25] So the main question will be, as always, whether the member states can muster the political will to do what is necessary.

Historical precedents suggest that outside pressure groups will be needed to lobby, to keep the press and television informed, and to engage in moral persuasion in a long-term campaign to change minds and build a political consensus in favor of these reforms. This is what happened in the 40-year campaign by a small but determined group to get the UNCG ratified by the US Senate.[26] A more pertinent example of reform of the United Nations is the coalition of so-called "like-minded states" that, in cooperation with a large contingent of nongovernmental organizations, worked for nearly a decade to achieve the establishment of the ICC, which is now in the process of being organized and made operational.[27] This step was taken in spite of the strong opposition of the United States, which, at the time of this writing, has not ratified the ICC.

The financial feasibility of the RRF may seem doubtful if the estimates of the costs are taken out of context. For example, a 1995 study estimates the start-up costs at between $550 million and $1.65 billion, with a subsequent annual cost of $300 million. However, these amounts must be compared with the annual cost of all UN peacekeeping without the RRF, which in 1995 amounted to about $3 billion.[28] It must also be kept in mind that a large portion of that $3 billion represents the indirect costs of genocides and other mass killings that were not stopped in time, such as refugee camps, food, and other humanitarian aid. There is every reason to think that the RRF would reduce these costs dramatically. Financing the RRF could be handled by a system of assessments, based on the GNP of each member country, which would be similar to the system currently used to finance other UN activities.[29]

Philosophers and other humanists can help to bring about these reforms by raising awareness of the vital need for them in their writing and teaching. Unfortunately, very few philosophers and humanists write about or teach courses on genocide, and those who do tend to ignore the topic of prevention.[30] There are some reasons for thinking that these reforms might eventually happen with or without the help of philosophers. After all, it has been only about two hundred years since we human beings began to feel any compunction about genocide and mass slaughter. For millennia prior to that, massacre of one's enemies was celebrated and memorialized. It is only recently that we have developed a feeling of guilt about committing mass slaughter, often killing in secret or denying it after the fact. Now we call genocide a crime, have trials, and punish some perpetrators. This is progress of sorts. Still, genocides continue.[31] Philosophers have an opportunity to make an important contribution in bringing genocide to an end by paying much greater attention in their research and teaching to the many political, institutional, and economic problems involved in reaching that goal. Only in this way can they avoid being part of the problem of bystander states.

Notes

1. Leo Kuper, *The Prevention of Genocide* (New Haven, CT: Yale University Press, 1985); Roger W. Smith, ed., *Genocide: Essays Toward Understanding, Early-Warning, and Prevention* (Williamsburg, VA: Association of Genocide Scholars, 1999); Neal Riemer, ed., *Protection Against Genocide: Mission Impossible?* (Westport, CT: Praeger, 2000).
2. For convenience I shall use genocide to mean both genocide and crimes against humanity.
3. Samuel P. Oliner and Pearl M. Oliner, *The Altruistic Personality: Rescuers of Jews in Nazi Germany* (New York: The Free Press, 1988); Ervin Staub, *The Roots of Evil: The Origins of Genocide and Other Group Violence* (New York: Cambridge University Press, 1989); Emmanuel Levinas, *Totality and Infinity*, trans. Alphonso Lingis (Pittsburgh: Duquesne University, 1969); Rudolph J. Rummel, *Death By Government* (New Brunswick, NJ: Transaction Publishers, 1994).
4. John K. Roth, ed., *Ethics after Auschwitz: Perspectives, Critiques, and Responses* (St. Paul, MN: Paragon House, 1999), p. xii.
5. James W. Nickel, *Making Sense of Human Rights: Philosophical Reflections on the Universal Declaration of Human Rights* (Berkeley, CA: University of California Press, 1987).
6. Richard L. Rubenstein, *The Cunning of History: The Holocaust and the American Future* (New York: Harper, 1987); see also Roth, ed., *Ethics after Auschwitz*.
7. Nickel, *Making Sense of Human Rights*, pp. 38–41.

8. Brian Barry, "Equality," in Lawrence C. Becker and Charlotte B. Becker, eds, *Encyclopedia of Ethics*, 2nd edn (New York: Routledge, 2001); David H. Jones, *Moral Responsibility in the Holocaust: A Study in the Ethics of Character* (Lanham, MD: Rowman and Littlefield, 1999), pp. 34–8, for a summary account.

9. Rubenstein, *The Cunning of History*, pp. 90–2.

10. Ibid.

11. Howard Ball, *Prosecuting War Crimes and Genocide: The Twentieth Century Experience* (Lawrence, KS: University Press of Kansas, 1999), pp. 86–7.

12. Ibid., 87–90.

13. Riemer, ed., *Protection Against Genocide*, p. 161.

14. John G. Heidenrich, *How to Prevent Genocide: A Guide for Policymakers, Scholars, and the Concerned Citizen* (Westport, CT: Praeger, 2001), p. 57.

15. Rummel, *Death by Government*, pp. 329–30.

16. Peter Ronayne, *Never Again?: The United States and the Prevention and Punishment of Genocide since the Holocaust* (Lanham, MD: Rowman and Littlefield, 2001), pp. 167–71.

17. Ibid., p. 198.

18. Samantha Power, *"A Problem from Hell": America and the Age of Genocide* (New York: Basic Books, 2002), p. xxi.

19. Ibid., pp. 329–89; Ronayne, *Never Again?*, pp. 151–96.

20. Helen Fein, "The Three P's of Genocide Prevention: With Application to a Genocide Foretold – Rwanda," in Riemer, ed., *Protection Against Genocide*, p. 59.

21. Saul Mendlovitz and John Fousek, "A UN Constabulary to Enforce the Law on Genocide and Crimes Against Humanity," in Riemer, ed., *Protection Against Genocide*, pp. 113–14.

22. Ibid.

23. Mendlovitz and Fousek, "A UN Constabulary," pp. 115–18; Heidenrich, *How to Prevent Genocide*, pp. 233–50.

24. Heidenrich, *How to Prevent Genocide*, pp. 233–4.

25. Mendlovitz and Fousek, "A UN Constabulary," p. 112; Heidenrich, *How to Prevent Genocide*, pp. 218–20.

26. Ronayne, *Never Again?*, pp. 13–48; Power, *"A Problem from Hell,"* pp. 155–69.

27. David Wippman, "Can an International Criminal Court Prevent and Punish Genocide?," in Riemer, ed., *Protection Against Genocide*, pp. 85–104.

28. Heidenrich, *How to Prevent Genocide*, pp. 243–4.

29. Mendlovitz and Fousek, "A UN Constabulary," pp. 117–20.

30. David H. Jones, "On the Prevention of Genocide: The Gap between Research and Education," *War Crimes, Genocide, & Crimes Against Humanity* 1 (January 2005): 4–37. Available on line: www.aa.psu.edu/journals/war-crimes

31. Roger W. Smith, "Human Destructiveness and Politics: The Twentieth Century as an Age of Genocide," in Isidor Walliman and Michael N. Dobkowski, eds, *Genocide and the Modern Age: Etiology and Case Studies of Mass Death* (New York: Greenwood Press, 1987), pp. 21–39.

22

Repudiating Inhumanity: Cosmopolitan Justice and the Obligation to Prosecute Human Rights Atrocities

Patrick Hayden

This chapter's departure point is the moral justification for the claim that all persons, and by extension our political societies, have an obligation to contest the impunity that historically has protected perpetrators of genocide and crimes against humanity. Prominent recent examples of gross injustice in the forms of genocide and crimes against humanity include the former Yugoslavia and Rwanda. Between 1991 and 1999, civil war, ethnic cleansing, and other human rights abuses tore apart the republics of the former Yugoslavia. Brutal fighting and repression—including violent expulsion, group rape, and mass murder—resulted in the deaths of more than 250,000 people.[1] In Rwanda, approximately 800,000 people were systematically slaughtered over a 100-day period between April and July 1994. The genocide was carried out by state security forces and armed militias, most notoriously the *Interhamwe* ("those who attack together") and *Impuzamugambi* ("the single-minded ones"). Most of the victims belonged to the minority Tutsi population, but Hutu moderates were targeted as well.[2]

What is to be done when such injustice is unleashed upon our fellow human beings? Clearly it would be best if these terrible events were prevented from occurring in the first place. There are many questions to be asked and debated about how genocide can be prevented, how vulnerable populations can be protected, and how virulent forms of racism can be countered. Yet in the following pages I simply try to reason why a strong case for criminal prosecution of perpetrators of human rights atrocities in the name of humanity is so imperative. Therefore, what follows can be read as an elaboration of the moral vision implied by these lines from the Preamble of the 1998 Rome Statute of the International Criminal Court (ICC): "Conscious that all peoples are united by common bonds ... Mindful that during this century millions of children, women, and men have been victims of unimaginable atrocities that deeply shock the conscience of humanity [the Parties to this Statute affirm] that the most serious crimes of concern to the international community as a whole must not go unpunished."

The need for a permanent international criminal court

Writing in the aftermath of Adolf Eichmann's dramatic prosecution in 1961 for his role in the Holocaust, Hannah Arendt suggested that "the need for a permanent international criminal court" was "imperative."[3] For Arendt, Eichmann's trial in Jerusalem symbolized, in part, the unfortunate triumph of national interests over the demands of universal justice. In Arendt's analysis, the Eichmann trial was flawed for a number of reasons, most notably because the Israeli government rejected the possibility of establishing an international criminal tribunal. In Arendt's view, the shortcoming of the Israeli court consisted of the fact that it represented "one nation only" and laid too much emphasis on Eichmann's crimes as violations against the Jewish people only rather than against humanity itself, that is, against "the human status" of Jews *qua* human beings.[4] As the subsequent occurrence of genocide in countries as diverse as Cambodia, Rwanda, the former Yugoslavia, and East Timor starkly testifies, the relevance of a permanent international criminal court remains undiminished more than forty years after the Eichmann trial.

In the cases of the former Yugoslavia and Rwanda, ad hoc criminal tribunals were formed. The International Criminal Tribunal for the former Yugoslavia (ICTY) was established by United Nations Security Council Resolution 827 of 25 May 1993, making it the first international tribunal of its kind.[5] The International Criminal Tribunal for Rwanda (ICTR) was established the following year by UN Security Council Resolution 955 of 8 November 1994.[6] The ICTR is the first international court charged specifically with prosecuting crimes of genocide, although both tribunals are mandated to prosecute crimes against humanity and war crimes as well. While the efforts of the two tribunals have contributed greatly to the cause of international justice, numerous limitations exist with the ad hoc approach to holding accountable those responsible for grave violations of the human status. Both the ICTY and ICTR, for instance, have been able to indict only a very limited number of perpetrators and have apprehended even fewer. Financial restrictions, lack of cooperation by national authorities, and the absence of political will to apprehend and hand over suspects contribute to this problem. As creations of the UN Security Council, the tribunals are dependent upon the particular political interests of the states on the Council, especially the permanent veto-holding members. For this same reason, there is no guarantee that future tribunals will be established when the need arises. The ICTY and ICTR also are constrained in terms of reach and scope, as their mandates empower them to investigate and prosecute crimes committed in one region only and in a narrowly defined time period. Furthermore, since they are established after the events in question, ad hoc tribunals are unable to act in advance to address suspected human rights violations. That shortcoming also undermines the deterrent effect of such tribunals. Given these limitations, it seems clear that the ad hoc system is not sufficient for adequately addressing the needs of universal justice. It seems equally clear that what is needed is a permanent international forum that is better able to contribute to a global system of justice and individual accountability for genocide and similar international crimes.

Cosmopolitan justice and human rights

On 17 July 1998, 120 states voted in favor of the Rome Statute of the International Criminal Court (ICC), establishing the world's first permanent international criminal tribunal.[7] The creation of the ICC is perhaps the most significant development in international justice since the formation of the United Nations in 1945. For all its potential practical relevance, however, what I am interested in here is identifying the most inclusive account of the scope of ethical concern that allows us to conceive *why* we ought to support the ICC. Put in another way, how can we make sense of the claim that *we*, exactly, have an obligation to prosecute those who have committed or assisted brutal acts that have outraged "the conscience of humankind"?

I believe the most suitable ethical perspective to adopt is that of cosmopolitanism, which recognizes the highly interdependent nature of human life across political and territorial boundaries. Most simply, cosmopolitanism can be described as the view that all human beings have equal moral standing within a single world community. Cosmopolitanism is often distinguished according to the two interconnected strands of moral and legal cosmopolitanism. Moral cosmopolitanism holds that moral commitments transcend political borders by virtue of the fact that all human beings belong to a universal community. Legal cosmopolitanism contends that a global political order ought to be constructed, grounded on the equal rights and duties of all individuals. Moral and legal cosmopolitanism share a commitment to at least three fundamental tenets: (1) individualism, in that individual human beings are the ultimate units of concern; (2) universality, in that all human beings possess equal moral status; and (3) generality, in that persons are subjects of concern for everyone, that is, responsibility for protecting human status has global scope.[8] Taken together, cosmopolitanism seeks to create or transform institutional schemes so as to provide concrete procedural and organizational mechanisms dedicated to securing the human rights of all persons.

Cosmopolitan ideas have a long history, reaching back to the Stoic notion of a global human community or "cosmopolis" based upon the equal worth of each human being. This core idea of classical cosmopolitanism contains the concept that each person is a "citizen of the world" and owes allegiance, first and foremost, "to the worldwide community of human beings."[9] Classical ideas about world citizenship were later taken up by a number of Enlightenment philosophers, most notably Kant. He was convinced of the necessity of establishing a cosmopolitan world order because political violence undermines freedom, equality, and justice. A cosmopolitan association was, for Kant, a "universal community ... where a violation of rights in *one* part of the world is felt *everywhere*."[10] Contemporary cosmopolitanism draws its inspiration from both the classical and Kantian traditions.[11] The fundamental insight that animates contemporary cosmopolitanism is that "justice is owed to all regardless of location or origin, race or gender, class or citizenship."[12] Contemporary cosmopolitanism, then, continues to advance the tradition's persisting concern to be morally inclusive of all individuals, including those who reside beyond our own states.

I believe the case for cosmopolitan justice is best articulated through the concept of human rights. Human rights are to be understood fundamentally as moral claims that provide the basis for a global institutional or legal order (not to be confused with the idea of a world government). Universal human rights are premised on the cosmopolitan ideal that all persons are free and equal, regardless of the society into which they happen to be born, and the purpose of human rights is to respect, protect, and promote the freedom and equality of all persons everywhere. Human rights are general moral claims that every person has to a basic minimum level of treatment—including various freedoms, protections, and benefits—needed for the viability of human life and to which all human beings are entitled. The claims of right-holders impose correlative duties, such that human rights are violated when duty-bearers fail to fulfill their correlative duties without good cause. The duties correlative to human rights are both negative and positive. Human rights should be understood both as positive principles invoked by moral agents to aid and cooperate with other individuals in securing, protecting, and promoting the full realization of their rights claims, and as negative principles not to impede or coerce other individuals from participating in securing, protecting, and promoting the conditions in which individuals will be enabled fully to realize their rights claims.

Henry Shue has argued that the duties correlative to human rights are actually of three kinds, although each kind manifests negative or positive duties that attach to different duty-bearers in varying circumstances: (1) negative duties to avoid depriving right-holders of the objects of their rights; (2) positive duties to protect right-holders from being deprived of the objects of their rights; and (3) positive duties to aid right-holders when avoidance and protection have failed.[13] The prescriptive force of the idea of human rights therefore arises from the assertion that all human beings are moral equals, whose claims to be entitled to decent treatment generate universal obligations to act morally toward others. The discourse of human rights affirms that all persons have equal moral status, that each person is obligated to respect that status, and that entitlement to what is due to humans is universally shared. This last point captures clearly the awareness that all of us belong simultaneously to interdependent local, regional, and global associations and have basic human interests that share common ground.

The view of human rights articulated here allows for commitment to the basic tenets of cosmopolitanism coupled with recognition that our obligations to other human beings include both compatriots and non-compatriots. And the effective satisfaction of those obligations requires that we carefully analyze and explore the mutually reinforcing connections between duties of different kinds. I now add another distinction to the account of duties presented here, namely, that between perfect and imperfect obligations.[14] As suggested above, the human rights core of cosmopolitanism generates both negative and positive duties—and both to compatriots and non-compatriots— to desist from conduct violating human rights and to assist in actions that protect and secure human rights. What the normatively positive duties specify, then, is that we act to establish those social conditions and institutions— currently they may be either nonfunctioning or non-existent—that are able to provide for the acquisition and secure possession of at least the most vitally important human rights entitlements. These obligations are of particular importance in regard to institutions designed to ensure the rule of law, to rectify through judicial means those injustices that violate the rights of individuals, and to punish those responsible for such injustices.

One way to characterize this situation is to say that, when right-holders already possess the objects of their rights, those rights are attended by *perfect* obligations on the part of duty-bearers to refrain from action that compromises or violates those rights and to contribute positively to their continued secure possession. In such cases there are identifiable agents—including specific individuals and institutions—that bear explicit obligations toward right-holders. When right-holders are not yet in possession of the objects of their rights, then *imperfect* obligations of assistance are generated. It is important to note that the quality of imperfection derives from the *absence* of suitable social and political conditions as well as specific agents and institutions with explicit responsibility toward particular right-holders. Imperfection thus reveals the presence of some form of injustice. Nevertheless the obligation still exists to assist in developing the appropriate social and political conditions and effective institutions capable of satisfying unfulfilled claims of justice. In other words, the difference between perfect and imperfect obligations is merely a matter of degree, and the duty here is to act so as to perfect what are otherwise imperfect obligations.

A crucial point that follows is that, owing to the absence of determinate duty-bearers, responsibility for perfecting imperfect obligations falls upon all of us, that is, upon humanity as a whole. Each of us, as members of the moral community of humanity, bears some kind of positive responsibility to act to help develop the specific social practices and institutions through which the requirements of cosmopolitan justice can be met. The current lack of those practices and institutions cannot justify apathy, indifference, or some other failure to act. To the contrary, it is this very absence that triggers our duties to transform the circumstances that render imperfect obligations imperfect. Failure to do so implies that humanity as a whole shares general culpability for the continued presence of grave injustice.[15]

Perfecting cosmopolitan duties

The preceding argument intends to show that the challenge to humanity posed by cosmopolitan morality is to convert imperfect obligations into perfect obligations, that is, to convert our moral obligations under the terms of global justice into actual political practice. Perhaps the best way to characterize this process of conversion is that of institutionalizing imperfect obligations. In essence, such a process translates cosmopolitan *morality* into cosmopolitan *law*. Whereas perfect obligations can be conceived as those that have been institutionalized to the degree that definite duty-bearers and lines of responsibility to correlative right-holders exist, imperfect obligations are those that are still lacking proper institutionalization. Under such conditions, right-holders can be said to exist, but the proper policies and agencies capable of and responsible for ensuring the acquisition and secure possession of the objects of right-holders' claims do not. For the obligations of justice to be met, those obligations must be institutionalized along with their corresponding rights. For this reason, the rights and duties of cosmopolitan morality need to be formally instituted in a juridical system of cosmopolitan law. A system of legal rights and duties will impose binding negative and positive obligations upon pertinent agents, and establish conditions for redress and punishment in the event those obligations go unfulfilled without good cause. Insofar as they can be enforced by law, imperfect obligations begin to lose some of their imperfection and gain a greater degree of perfection.[16]

The historical record provides grim testimony of humanity's moral and political failure to perfect its duties in response to genocide and crimes against humanity. All too often the imperative "never again" has fallen on deaf ears at critical moments. Nevertheless some positive steps have been taken in recent years. The emergence of the system of international human rights (and humanitarian) law, for example, can be viewed as a gradual conversion of imperfect into perfect obligations, of constructing cosmopolitan law out of cosmopolitan morality. Cosmopolitan tendencies are evident, for instance, in the Universal Declaration of Human Rights (UDHR), which asserts that "all humans are born free and equal in dignity and rights. They are endowed with reason and conscience and should act towards one another in a spirit of brotherhood." International human rights law aims not only to help establish the legal, political, and economic climates in which individual freedom and dignity can flourish, but also to help protect the individual against governmental excesses everywhere. Human rights therefore are "part of what is involved in being a member of the moral community" and include "forms of inviolability in the status of every member of the moral community."[17]

According to the Preamble of the UDHR and the discussions of the Third Committee of the UN General Assembly in 1948, the atrocities of genocide and war are additional justifications for prescribing the international system of human rights and generating a global consensus on human rights norms. Moreover, the Nuremberg and Tokyo International Military Tribunals broke new ground in humanitarian law by prosecuting Nazi and Japanese officials not only for war crimes but also for the new category of "crimes against humanity."[18] The novelty and significance of the identification of this "new" crime was due to the fact that a universal moral concept—that of humanity as a collective moral and legal entity against which crimes can be committed and through such acts is degraded and violated—was incorporated into positive international law.[19] The idea of crimes against humanity was further entrenched in international law with the 1948 UN Convention on the Prevention and Punishment of the Crime of Genocide.

Given these developments, I suggest that we characterize the emergent sense of humanity's responsibility for the prosecution of genocide in terms of what Mary Kaldor calls "cosmopolitan law-enforcement."[20] The basic insight underlying the idea of cosmopolitan law-enforcement is that the growth of international humanitarian and human rights norms has coincided with the recognition that intervention into the internal affairs of states is justified for the purpose of ending or preventing large-scale human rights violations and human suffering. In short, the traditional claims to sovereignty and nonintervention on the part of states are being supplanted in international relations by humanitarian practices driven by the human rights and security interests of individuals. Such humanitarian practices can include not only military intervention, food relief, and medical aid, but also post-conflict social reconstruction, police protection, and the capture and prosecution of those responsible for mass atrocities. One significant aspect of cosmopolitan law-enforcement is that it arguably represents not merely a formal response to threats to (inter)national security, but a deepening human response to the suffering of other persons, despite their status as distant strangers beyond our borders.[21]

The most recent step taken in the continued perfection of our humanitarian obligations and in the development of cosmopolitan law-enforcement is the creation of the permanent International Criminal Court. On 11 April 2002, the sixtieth country ratified the Rome Statute. It entered into force on 1 July 2002. Elections of the ICC's first bench, comprised of 18 judges, were held from 3 to 7 February 2003, the inaugural meeting of the Court was held in The Hague on 11 March 2003, and the Court's first Prosecutor, Luis Moreno Ocampo, was elected on 21 April 2003. Several features of the ICC offer hope that it will function as an effective institution that embodies some of the important principles and norms of cosmopolitan justice.

First, the ICC is a treaty-based institution formally independent from the UN system, including the Security Council. As an independent Court, the ICC will be less susceptible to the political machinations of Security Council members, and its ability to prosecute will not be compromised by Security Council vetoes. Second, the ICC has an extensive reach and scope. As stated in Article 5 of the Rome Statute, the Court—effective 1 July 2002—has jurisdiction over the crime of genocide, crimes against humanity, war crimes, and the crime of aggression.[22] While no crimes committed before that date are within the Court's jurisdiction, from the time it entered into force the Court is no longer temporally bound with respect to its operations, as are the ICTY and ICTR. Thus, the ICC possesses inherent jurisdiction within state parties over the essential core crimes of international humanitarian and human rights law, and it will be prepared to investigate and prosecute individuals at all times.[23] Third, while the scope and exercise of the Court was, and still remains, a matter of some controversy, the Court can exercise jurisdiction under any of the following conditions: (1) a state party refers to the Prosecutor a situation in which it is suspected a crime has taken place (in accordance with Article 14 of the Rome Statute); (2) the UN Security Council refers to the Prosecutor a situation in which it is suspected a crime has taken place (in accordance with Chapter VII of the UN Charter); and (3) the Prosecutor initiates proceedings on the basis of reliable information received from states, UN organs, international and nongovernmental organizations (in accordance with Article 15 of the Rome Statute).

Finally, while there are many more pertinent details about the ICC than can be discussed here, it should be noted that the ICC will gain greater moral, political, and legal legitimacy in two additional ways. First, as a permanent treaty-based institution that retains independence from both state parties and the Security Council, the ICC can avoid the charge directed occasionally (and perhaps cynically) at the ICTY and ICTR that those ad hoc tribunals were established merely to carry out a form of "victor's justice." This charge will have little credibility since the Court's investigations and prosecutions will be neither contingent upon prior approval by the Security Council nor merely retrospective in their reach. This should allow the Court to apply fair and impartial justice and cultivate trust in its proceedings. Second, the permanent nature of the Court may enable it to act as a more effective deterrent to future wrongdoing. Given the fact that the Court will be in continuous operation, it is reasonable to conclude that it may serve as a greater deterrent to those who might otherwise be tempted to commit genocide and other egregious human rights abuses. Knowledge that the ICC is constantly empowered to prosecute and punish such crimes may deter individuals from acting with a sense of impunity and thereby decrease the occurrence of future atrocities.

Conclusion

It is clear that contemporary humanitarian and human rights law is not, strictly speaking, a system of cosmopolitan law. Within the current international order and the structure of international law, states are still regarded as the primary political and legal agents. Nevertheless, the convergence of humanitarian and human rights law has injected a strong cosmopolitan ethic into the processes and rules of world politics. Obviously the practical realization of international humanitarian and human rights laws is far from perfect. But the significance of this system's evolution is that it supports cautious optimism that previously imperfect obligations are in the process of being perfected. We must continue vigorous reform of the current international system to develop the institutions and implement the policies that will bring about the type of global protection of human beings that cosmopolitan justice requires. I have suggested, therefore, that establishing and supporting a permanent ICC is morally and politically necessary as one means to satisfy our cosmopolitan obligations. The reform of international law to accommodate the norms and practices of the ICC as a global institution is obligatory as part of the process of securing and protecting the human rights of all. By introducing new rules, standards, and mechanisms of accountability into the global political system and by prosecuting— on behalf of humanity—those responsible for genocide, the ICC represents the constructive pursuit of a form of cosmopolitan law-enforcement that does justice to the imperative rightly expressed by Hannah Arendt more than forty years ago.

Notes

1. See Samantha Power, *"A Problem From Hell": America and the Age of Genocide* (New York: Basic Books, 2002), ch. 12.
2. Ibid., pp. 329–90.
3. Hannah Arendt, *Eichmann in Jerusalem: A Report on the Banality of Evil*, rev. edn (New York: Penguin Books, 1965), p. 270.
4. Ibid., pp. 268–70.
5. UN Document S/Res/827 (1993); <http://www.un.org/icty/basic/statut/stat11–2004.htm>
6. UN Document S/Res/955 (1994); <http://www.ictr.org/ENGLISH/basicdocs/statute.html>
7. China, Iran, Iraq, Israel, Libya, Sudan, and the United States voted against the treaty.
8. Thomas Pogge, "Cosmopolitanism and Sovereignty," *World Poverty and Human Rights* (Cambridge: Polity Press, 2002), pp. 168–95.

9. Martha Nussbaum, "Patriotism and Cosmopolitanism," in Joshua Cohen, ed., *For Love of Country* (Boston, MA: Beacon Press, 1996), p. 4.

10. Immanuel Kant, "Perpetual Peace," in Hans Reiss, ed., *Political Writings* (Cambridge: Cambridge University Press, 1991), pp. 107–8.

11. See, for example, Charles Jones, *Global Justice: Defending Cosmopolitanism* (Oxford: Oxford University Press, 1999), and Darrel Moellendorf, *Cosmopolitan Justice* (Boulder, CO: Westview Press, 2002).

12. Onora O'Neill, "Bounded and Cosmopolitan Justice," *Review of International Studies* 26 (2000): 45–60, at p. 45.

13. Henry Shue, *Basic Rights*, 2nd edn (Princeton, NJ: Princeton University Press, 1996), pp. 51–64.

14. Discussions of imperfect obligations or duties in the context of rights reach back at least to Kant and Mill. There are, however, variations in how perfect and imperfect obligations are conceived.

15. On the idea of collective responsibility extending to all of humanity, see Hannah Arendt, "Organized Guilt and Universal Responsibility," in Peter Baehr, ed., *The Portable Hannah Arendt* (New York: Penguin, 2003), pp. 146–55.

16. This is not to say that fulfilling duties of cosmopolitan justice will ever be *perfect* as such, merely *perfected*.

17. Thomas Nagel, "Personal Rights and Public Space," *Philosophy and Public Affairs* 24 (1995): 83–107, at p. 85.

18. The 1945 *Agreement for the Prosecution and Punishment of the Major War Criminals of the European Axis and Charter of the International Military Tribunal* defined crimes against humanity in Article 6 (c) as follows: "[M]urder, extermination, enslavement, deportation, and other inhumane acts committed against civilian populations, before or during the war; or persecutions on political, racial or religious grounds in execution of or in connection with any crime within the jurisdiction of the Tribunal, whether or not in violation of the domestic law of the country where perpetrated." Available online at http://www1.umn.edu/humanrts/instree/1945a.htm

19. As Arendt noted (*Eichmann in Jerusalem*, p. 272), this concept refers to "an altogether different community" than that of the nation-state and is, properly speaking, the community violated by the crime of genocide.

20. Mary Kaldor, *New and Old Wars: Organized Violence in a Global Era* (Cambridge: Polity, 1999), pp. 124–31.

21. See Nicholas Wheeler, *Saving Strangers: Humanitarian Intervention in International Society* (Oxford: Oxford University Press, 2000).

22. The crime of aggression, which was not included within the jurisdiction of the ICTY and ICTR, suffered definitional problems and will be revisited at a future review conference.

23. Article 6 of the Rome Statute follows the 1948 Genocide Convention in defining the crime of genocide, and authorizes prosecution for the act of genocide as well as conspiracy to commit genocide, attempted genocide, public incitement to commit genocide, and complicity in genocide. Article 7 covers a broad range of crimes against humanity that expands upon violations recognized by the Nuremburg Charter and the ICTY and ICTR, including acts of murder, extermination, forcible deportation and transfer of a population, enslavement, torture, rape, forced disappearance of persons, and apartheid.

23

"The Human Material is Too Weak"

Roger S. Gottlieb

My father-in-law Jacob Greenspan (of blessed memory) was a diminutive, energetic Polish Jew who survived the Holocaust by fleeing into Soviet Russia, along with his wife and approximately 800,000 other Jews, after Germany invaded Poland in 1939. After the war, all Jews who indicated that they wanted to return to Poland were considered potential enemies of the state and sent to labor camps near the Arctic Circle to cut trees. After two and half years in such a camp, the Greenspans were freed; they made their way to Uzbekistan, where they managed to eek out a living for two years. Eventually they returned to Poland and then went to a Displaced Persons camp in Germany, their departure point for immigration to the United States in 1951.

Over the years, Jacob told me this story in bits and pieces, always reminding me that before the war he had been a Communist. "But after I saw Soviet Russia," he told me, "that was the end for me. We used to say, 'Stalin is the Father of the World.' And you know what? They were terrible in that Soviet Russia, just terrible." Then he would put his hand on my arm, his son-in-law, whom he knew quite well as a leftist, a self-proclaimed Marxist, and say: "Roger, socialism is a great ideal, but the human material is too weak."

It was, I am sure, the particular combination of the Holocaust and what he saw of the Soviet Union that made Jacob doubt our collective human strength. For, after all, the Soviet system had been proclaimed as the antidote to fascism, the hope of humanity's future. With the fascists on one side and the communists on the other, where would there be hope? One need not have a particularly ideological bent to be struck by Jacob's words, for in his mind "socialism" was less about some particular economic and political arrangement than about a society of justice and care where people, including but not only Jews, would be respected and allowed to live. Jacob's conclusion was that such a society was not possible. We could try to be decent as individuals, care for our families and our restricted communities, but the dreams of full-scale change in social life were not going to come true.

Though very intelligent, Jacob had practically no formal education, having stopped school at fourth grade to work and to help support his family. Yet his piercing blue eyes, his passionate conviction, and above all his experience of life meant more to me than piles of academic books about the possibility or impossibility of social change. He had lost his grandparents, parents, and seven of his ten siblings to the Nazis, and he had lost his faith in socialism to Stalin. He had been a believer, as I was, in the dream of a truly better world. Now he no longer was. I could not ignore what he said, because it was *he* who was saying it.

Is the human material too weak for a decent society? Certainly there is not a great deal of recent history that would contradict Jacob's truth. If you are not depressed about the state of the world, a friend of mine is fond of saying, you haven't been listening to NPR (National Public Radio). Or, as Elie Wiesel put it, "Has mankind learned the lessons of Auschwitz? No. For details consult your daily newspaper."[1]

Genocide and the environmental crisis

A classic response to Jacob's truth, offered by social theorists as disparate as Max Weber, Karl Popper, and George W. Bush, is to invoke the virtues of capitalist democracy as opposed to both fascism and communism.[2] At least, these theorists tell us, capitalist democracy is structured around competing social powers: the state is checked by the corporations, and both can at times be confronted by quasi-popular movements. At best, eschewing unrealistic and therefore necessarily totalitarian systems, capitalist democracy allows for the unfolding of the individual and community in a way that is particularly fitting to human nature and to objective moral truth. Social problems can be rationally assessed and remedied one by one, an ultimately much more rational and feasible method than trying to impose, all at once and at gunpoint, some self-proclaimed elite's vision of social perfection.

Still the unregenerate socialist despite Jacob's cautionary tales of the Soviet Union, I cannot be a believer in the saving powers of the current system. For one thing, we could (at length) ask whether "capitalist democracy" is a coherent social reality, bringing to mind the ways in which capitalist democracy can give way to totalitarianism (as in Germany) or provide extensive support for it (the United States's past record of giving aid to fascist Chile, or Sadaam Hussein, or Al-Queda). Alternatively, we might focus on the mass destruction perpetrated directly by the United States in Vietnam and Cambodia, which indicates that capitalist democracy is fully capable of mass murder in pursuit of its national interests.

Rather than pursue those lines of argument, however, I wish to bring to mind another form of contemporary mass murder. If it does not stem exclusively from capitalist democracy, I regard the latter as its leading cause.

I refer to the environmental crisis. This crisis—which has become more like a long slow decline than a single apocalyptic event—is in some ways a

Holocaust writ large, a slow tightening of a human-made noose around all of humanity.[3] Climate change, suddenly more dangerous sunlight, poisoned water, fertile soil turning to desert, a cancer epidemic as much as 80 percent of which is shaped by environmental factors—these and other aspects of the crisis are responsible for untold deaths, illnesses, social dislocations, and cultural devastations.[4] While environmental destruction is not new in human history, nothing remotely like this scale of devastation has occurred before. Many critics have rightly identified capitalism as central to this process. The relevant factors include: capitalism's built-in necessity for endless expansion, the commodification of all aspects of life, the push to develop technology, the externalization of pollution from the costs of production, an ideology in which competitive individualism trumps community concerns, and the development of mass consumerism.[5]

Why invoke the environmental crisis in a book on philosophy and genocide? After all, the differences between the environmental crisis and genocide are numerous.[6] The Holocaust and other genocides, for instance, typically involve the centralized, strategically planned annihilation of a particular group, but *ecocide* stems from a myriad of sources and is not anyone's self-proclaimed goal. Rather, it happens because corporations pursue profit, governments develop military power, ordinary citizens seek a "better lifestyle," and peasants deforest hillsides so they can cook dinner. Nevertheless, it is these varying strategies for profit, power, pleasure, or simple survival— and not the grand plan of a 1000-year Reich—that will ruin the world.[7]

Yet if the environmental crisis is not "like" the Holocaust and other genocides, those latter catastrophes have important lessons to teach us about the former. For a start, genocide reveals just how devastating modern states, bureaucracies, and technologies can be; it shows how careful "ordinary men and women" must be about what they take for granted, how they fit in, and what they accept in their social order.[8] This lesson carries into the present, teaching us that while environmentalists' direst predictions must always be evaluated in detail, they cannot be dismissed out of hand due to a mistaken confidence that governments and corporations would not commit mass murder or that intelligent citizens might not just sit back and let it all happen. After Auschwitz, such confidence makes little sense. In a way, the Holocaust "prepares" us to take in the fact of ecocide, teaching that there is virtually no limit to human folly, lust for power, and bureaucratic complicity in mass murder. The slaughter of six million Jews and millions of other victims, carried out coldly and "rationally" by civil servants and professionals as well as politicians and soldiers, by a "legitimate" government and with the sanction or passive acceptance of much of the rest of the world, is an omen for the environmental ruin we are creating now. This time, however, the catastrophe spreads far beyond the borders of any particular community, region, or nation.

As the Jews, Gypsies, homosexuals, and communists were singled out by the Nazis, so we now hear about the countless indigenous peoples with monstrous cancer rates because of uranium mining on their land, or victims engulfed by cultural genocide because their forest homes were turned into so many board feet of lumber, their villages dispossessed in the name of yet another "development" scheme. Also, when we see the full force of our own denial of the ecological dangers surrounding us, we may remember that it was thought impossible—especially by the victims!—that a modern, industrialized state could, let alone would, systematically slaughter millions of unarmed civilians.

Finally, and of great importance, we must remember the sheer irrationality of part of the Nazi enterprise. Alongside the ideological and financial benefits of the Holocaust, there was a kind of madness when the German government made transporting the Jews to the death camps their first priority, even when that priority interfered with their own military goals. Does this not remind us of how the assault on the rainforest eliminates dozens of species of trees that have been evaluated as having potential for cancer treatment (even for the cancers that may afflict those who direct the assault)?

If the evils of fascism and communism taught Jacob the weakness of the human material, industrialized capitalism (democratic or non-democratic) and its consequences (intended and unintended) now convey that message. Their banners and emblems include pesticide-spraying airplanes, dioxin-spewing industrial chimneys, chemical food contaminants, and leaking landfills.

Philosophy's responsibility and response

Does philosophy have anything to say in response to Jacob's truth, a truth that we keep learning—and also forgetting—from generation to generation? An initial answer might well be that philosophy is an academic discipline conducted by professionally trained scholars whose goal is the analysis of concepts and the study of worldviews. If some of its practitioners wrestle with the problem of evil, the validity of norms guiding social systems, or the relation between personal and institutional responsibility, others are legitimately engaged in asking questions about the semantics of "truth" or the mind–body problem. Some philosophers, just like some historians, sociologists, or social psychologists, will concern themselves with Jacob's problem, but others will not.

On the other hand, there are at least some thinkers among us who believe that philosophy is deeply affected, perhaps to the point of impossibility, by Jacob's truth. If the rise of science had unavoidable consequences for epistemology, and the French Revolution taught Hegel (and through him Marx) that human communities and norms always exist in history, then the Holocaust, other genocides, and ecocide teach us of the collective human capacity for madness and evil of such magnitude that the very purpose, the very raison d'etre of philosophy gets called into question.

To explain this point, we could adapt Theodor Adorno's bitter quip that "After Auschwitz it is barbaric to write poetry" (Although he did later acknowledge that "perennial suffering has as much right to expression as a tortured man has to scream.")[9] and say that after the Holocaust it is barbaric to write philosophy.

What would we mean by that? For one thing, that it is barbaric to write philosophy *as if the Holocaust had never happened.* It would be barbaric to think philosophically, that is, without taking—even giving priority to—the human capacity for this kind of horrific action as a permanent possibility and without asking whether one's own philosophical activity contributes in any way to understanding how such an event could take place and how its repetition could be prevented. Why would philosophy that ignored such issues be "barbaric"? For a start, it would be (or is) purely academic in the worst sense of the term, for it would be concerning itself with rationality, truth, moral norms, and philosophical anthropology without ever asking if any of its conclusions could ever have any practical effect. If philosophical practice unfolds in a world shaped by the Holocaust, other forms of geno-cide, and our actual practice of ecocide—if, that is, "the human material is too weak"—then of what possible value are the general principles, from epistemology to ethics, that we philosophers seek to analyze, criticize, and create? If the human material is too weak, then for the most part truth will be obscured by error, rationality by madness, virtue and morality by folly, greed, and violence. Why work to find out what rational norms are if science is to be practiced by experimenters in Auschwitz, or to be bought and paid for by corporations, or controlled by an American political administration that can forbid its own scientists from saying what they know to be the case?[10] If human moral weakness means that cruelty will only continue and grow (given our increased technological and bureaucratic power), what is the point of arguing, as Richard Rorty does, that the goal of public philoso-phy is to find ways for us to be less cruel to each other?[11] We cannot do philosophy as if the Holocaust, genocide, and ecocide are not primary realities, but if they are, then perhaps much philosophy has no point.

To put this view another way: philosophy, no matter how abstruse its subject matter, takes as a kind of transcendental horizon the idea that the truths it produces can be used by human beings. When philosophy is not practiced under that horizon, it becomes no more relevant to the human condition than chess or stamp collecting: interesting or amusing to a certain type of person, but of no use to anyone else. In the face of a Holocaust, or of ecocide, it is barbaric—or perhaps immorally decadent might be a better way to put it—to spend one's life in socially irrelevant pastimes. And this is especially true of philosophy, an activity with pretensions to universal truth and human significance.

The alternative to this kind of barbaric decadence is a discipline for which certain historical truths, rather than simply a certain method or tradition of texts, is essential. One cannot, after all, do philosophy without the presuppositions that humans are rational, live in societies, and engage in action guided by norms. Similarly, philosophy in the present needs to take for granted the knowledge that human beings can commit genocide and are now engaged in ecocide. In this last process "the whole world will become Jewish,"[12] as ecological damage comes to define the final phase of our existence as a species. The Holocaust and ecocide, (along with many other events that could be added to the list) cast doubt on the value of philosophy's entire enterprise. To ignore them is to surrender in advance to their implication that philosophy is pointless.

Please note that I am not arguing that philosophers should stop philosophizing and simply engage in political action: go to demonstrations, support the Green Party, or picket the local polluting factory. I do not think that we have answered all the questions philosophers should ask. The Holocaust and other genocides prompt authentic philosophical inquiry, I believe, because to some extent human beings function philosophically. Philosophers—if we have any social value at all—make critically conscious what others take for granted without questioning. It is philosophy's task to ask, for example, if the instrumental concept of rationality that emerged from the Enlightenment made it harder for Germans to distinguish between efficiency (killing the most Jews at the least cost) and morality. Or if the widespread notion of the fit between modernity and progress is undermined by Germany's all too fatal technologically powered moral regression. Or to what extent "ordinary" Germans, who perhaps were not themselves particularly antisemitic but did nothing to oppose Nazism, bear responsibility for the genocide. These and many other philosophical questions have been asked already.[13] My point is that if philosophy wishes not to be barbaric or immoral it is no longer free *not* to raise them and others like them.

In contemporary terms, the environmental crisis raises its own philosophical questions. For instance, how is it possible that humanity is engaged in an industrial, economic, and cultural system that undermines its very conditions of survival? (If this question seems in some ways sociological or psychological as much as philosophical, that should tell us that not only philosophy's subject matter but also the very idea of disciplinary boundaries can be called into question by history.) Theoreticians of ecocide must also ask what the history of pesticides, the moral structure of consumerism, and the marriage of empirical research and large profits tell us about our conceptions of and norms concerning science, technology, selfhood, and justice. After the twentieth century, they must inquire whether "nature" still exists; and, if it does not, on what we will be able to base norms to guide us toward a rational and sustainable society?

The morally compelling character of the Holocaust and the environmental crisis, the fact that as academics or intellectuals we are not morally free to think as though genocide and ecocide are unreal, can be explained in yet another important way. After the Holocaust we cannot responsibly or morally "do" philosophy (or law, or science) without asking whether we are practicing the contemporary, and in particular the environmental analogue, of *Nazi* ethics, science, or law. Each of these disciplines, after all, contributed to the Nazi effort. Professors of law designed ways to distinguish degrees of Aryanness or Jewishness; philosophers justified the superiority of the so-called Aryan nation; scientists presented antisemitism as rational and did research experiments on concentration camp inmates. If we are not to repeat these patterns in our own time, we cannot turn aside the kinds of questions I have been raising here by saying, "This isn't my area. I'm more interested in the relation between epistemology and philosophy of mind."

The question of complicity

Facing the question of complicity is never easy. The dominant institutions of Germany—universities, churches, corporations, professional associations—went along with the policies of the Third Reich. Germany's philosophers were no exception. In their professional roles, they tended to support or ignore Nazism. And for the most part other individuals in Nazi Germany did not resist in their personal lives.[14] What they did and failed to do is therefore a source of enduring shame for them as individuals and of deep questioning about professional life in general.

The same holds true, I believe, in the present. Therefore, we may not avoid thinking about the Holocaust and ecocide because we may now be reproducing a version of what was done then. Since the dominant institutions of our culture are contributing, each in their own way, to ecocide (just as the dominant institutions of Nazi Germany each had their role in the Holocaust), examining our lives in this respect will not be easy. Especially, it will be difficult because many of our society's dominant institutions—*including the ones in which philosophers are employed*—are engaged in a kind of systematic and lunatic denial of what is actually happening. It is as if passengers on the *Titanic*, when there might have been some hope of saving the ship, were to say: "We cannot interrupt our usual pursuits—dressing for dinner, dancing the night away—for any reason." Thus, most universities hold to the same old distribution requirements, the tried and true disciplinary arrangements, the familiar rules that English Composition is necessary but ecological literacy, God help us, is an "elective." Many philosophy departments, and to a great extent the American Philosophical Association, treat genocide and environmental issues as peripheral at best: an intriguing, but certainly a minor, sub-field.

To go against this grain requires courage. We risk alienating our employers, compromising our standing in the profession, affronting people who think we are overstating the case in an overly emotional way and—the ultimate threat for young academic philosophers—not getting tenure. Resisting the mass, lemming-like movement of modern industrial society requires us to put our energy against a seemingly unstoppable mass going in the opposite—and mistaken—direction. Further, like the Holocaust, the environmental crisis evokes overwhelming emotions: fear, anger, guilt, and despair. But unlike the Holocaust, the environmental crisis is happening *now*. Ironically, there is all the more reason for avoidance and denial, all the more reason to isolate by emotional distance, ridicule, or passive aggressive silence the colleague who stands up at a department or faculty meeting and says: "Something is happening that will not allow us to continue as usual. We need to make some changes."

Here, paradoxically, study of the Holocaust offers a resource of support, encouragement, and even inspiration. Here the Holocaust, certainly a confirmation of Jacob's truth, is *also* a challenge to it.

I have in mind the amazing story of Jewish resistance. From smuggling food into ghettos to resist starvation to an uprising that closed the Sobibor death camp, from organizing (against widespread local antisemitism) armed partisan groups in the forests to sabotage in the slave labor camps, Jews fought back.[15] While the historical information about the extent of this resistance activity is well known, its reality (apart from the Warsaw ghetto uprising) is still largely hidden in the public presentation of the Holocaust, as well as in philosophical assessments of that event's meaning. (I remember hearing on the car radio an NPR special on the anniversary of the closing of Auschwitz, and helplessly yelling at the reporters for not mentioning the revolt that took place in the camp. More seriously, for many years comparable omissions marred the Holocaust Memorial Museum in Washington, DC.)

For the Holocaust, while it *is* the story of the piles of Jewish bodies in horrific pictures that are viewed over and over again, is not *only* that story. It is also a story of Jews with guns, Jews making birthday cakes of crumbs in concentration camps to keep their spirits up, Jews retaining dignity against more than overwhelming odds. It is the story of suffering and victimization but also of courage and even occasional victory. If we fail to recognize the complexity of this story, we will not have confronted the event in its moral fullness.

What is philosophy?

If it is anything at all, philosophy is an attempt to answer the question of what things mean: for instance, what does it mean that humans speak, respond to reasoned argument, believe (or do not believe) in a God, or pursue scientific knowledge? Such as it is, philosophy's importance resides in the fact that what we think things mean shapes what we think is right and how we act. Jacob's truth is above all a philosophical truth, for in the wisdom of his years, he stated it as a reasoned assessment of the meaning of human existence. But Jacob, who spent the war in a labor camp and returned to find his family and community decimated, did not experience Jewish resistance first hand. Although the struggle to survive formed the core of his experience, resistance did not.

That more people killed Jews than Jews resisted, that many times more Jews died than fought back, is surely a terrible truth. But it is not absolutely clear that this numerical difference should obscure what the resisters accomplished and what their resistance signifies for our lives. Quantifying human behavior as the meaning of human existence reveals a particular theoretical commitment that must be argued for. As much as what the perpetrators did, the resisters' remarkable courage and perseverance, even if they are only a small fraction of Holocaust history, represent a human possibility that defines what our species can become. The same partiality affects any attempt to make sense out of the environmental crisis. The main engine of modern industrial civilization may be hell bent on self-destruction, but there are many people who are trying to stop the machine, or at least slow it down so that the drivers can come to their senses.

The significance of human resistance for our assessment of the "human material" is in part up to us to determine. Are resisters a tiny and insignificant minority, or are they an indication that the human material can be much stronger than it usually is? Are they a footnote to an otherwise bleak history or an inspiration for the rest of us, so that we expend our strength to prove that human material is better than Jacob thought? Can we reverse the forces that now govern the world? If Jacob's truth stands, I have been suggesting, philosophy as an enterprise simply loses all but the most minimal of value. But if Jacob's truth must be squared somehow with the truth of resistance, then it is at least possible that philosophy can become part of the resistance movement that Jacob's truth does not include. Since the transcendental horizon under which philosophy functions also requires that Jacob be wrong, it is up to us who claim to be philosophers to prove him so—or to give up philosophy. Our resistance to ecocide signals our belief that humans are capable of a decent society. To sustain ourselves in that effort, we need to remember that as dark as things seem now, they are certainly no darker than they were for the Jews who resisted during the Holocaust. If they could fight back, so can we.

Rejecting the traditional Marxist notion that socialism was inevitable, Leon Trotsky said that humanity had a choice "between socialism and barbarism."[16] We who come after Jacob, living in the midst of humanity's self-caused plagues, have a choice as well: between confirming Jacob's truth or trying, with or without rational hope, to show that the human material is stronger than he thought. To do so we must believe that resistance, since it has been practiced by others, is possible again and again. Then we must make that belief the basis of our philosophy and our lives.

Notes

1. Elie Wiesel, *A Jew Today*, trans. Marion Wiesel (New York: Vintage, 1979), p. 12.
2. Max Weber, *From Max Weber: Essays in Sociology*, eds, H. H. Gerth and C. Wright Mills (New York: Oxford University Press, 1958); Karl Popper, *The Open Society and its Enemies* (Princeton, NJ: Princeton University Press, 1971).
3. Frederic Buell, *From Apocalypse to Way of Life* (New York: Routledge, 2003).
4. Along with Buell's painfully effective summary of recent material, see also Sandra Steingraber, *Living Downstream: An Ecologist Looks at Cancer and the Environment* (Reading, MA: Addison-Wesley, 1997) and Mark Jerome Walters, *Six Modern Plagues and How We Are Causing Them* (Washington, DC: Island Press, 2004). Updates can be found in a variety of environmental magazines and websites, including those of the Sierra Club, Greenpeace, National Resource Defense Council, and Worldwatch.
5. See, for example, Martin O'Connor, ed., *Is Capitalism Sustainable? Political Economy and the Politics of Ecology* (New York: Guildford, 1994) as well as the journal *Capitalism, Nature, Socialism: A Journal of Socialist Ecology*.
6. The historical claims about the Holocaust that follow here are based on a variety of sources, including: Francois Furet, ed., *Unanswered Questions: Nazi Germany and the Genocide of the Jews* (New York: Schocken: 1989); Daniel Goldhagen, *Hitler's Willing Executioners: Ordinary Germans and the Holocaust* (New York: Knopf, 1996); Raul Hilberg, *The Destruction of the European Jews*, 3rd edn, 3 vols. (New Haven, CT: Yale University Press, 2003); Leni Yahil, *The Holocaust: The Fate of European Jewry* (New York: Oxford, 1990).
7. I have developed this comparison in much greater length in *A Spirituality of Resistance: Finding a Peaceful Heart and Protecting the Earth* (Lanham, MD: Rowman and Littlefield, 2003).
8. Christopher R. Browning, "Bureaucracy and Mass Murder: The German Administrator's Comprehension of the Final Solution," in Asher Cohen, Jav Gelver, and Charlotte Wardi, eds, *Comprehending the Holocaust: Historical and Literary Research* (Frankfurt: Verlag Peter Lang, 1988).
9. Theodor W. Adorno, "Cultural Criticism and Society," in *Prisms* 34, 1981; and *Negative Dialectics* (New York: Continuum, 1973), pp. 362–3: "Perennial suffering has as much right to expression as a tortured man has to scream, hence it may have been wrong to say that after Auschwitz you could no longer write poems. But it is not wrong to raise the less cultural question whether after Auschwitz you can go on living." See also Irving Howe's contribution to Berel Lang, ed., *Writing and the Holocaust* (New York: Holmes & Meier, 1988), pp. 178–82.
10. For these claims in the current context, see Jed Greer and Kenny Bruno, *GREEN-WASH: The Reality Behind Corporate Environmentalism* (New York: The Apex Press and Third World Network, 1999). There have been numerous reports of the politicization of science in the George W. Bush administration. See, for example: "Ranking Scientists Warn Bush Science Policy Lacks Integrity," Environment News Service, 20 February 2004, http://www.oneworld.net/article/view/79763/1/
11. Richard Rorty, *Contingency, Irony, Solidarity* (New York: Cambridge University Press, 1989).
12. In response to a television series on the effects of nuclear war, Elie Wiesel said that it seemed "the whole world has become Jewish."
13. See, for example, the other contributions to this volume.

14. The most conspicuous collective exception to this point was the response of some German churches, which was instrumental in curtailing the Nazis' so-called euthanasia program.
15. There is an enormous literature on resistance. Beyond the accounts provided in the works mentioned above in note 6, one might begin with Lucien Steinberg, *Jews Against Hitler* (Glasgow: University Press, 1974), pp. 457–98, and Hermann Langbein, *Against All Hope: Resistance in the Nazi Concentration Camps 1938–1945* (New York: Paragon House, 1994). I have offered a philosophical analysis of the concept of resistance in "The Concept of Resistance: Jewish Resistance to the Holocaust," *Social Theory and Practice* 9 (April 1983), reprinted in Roger S. Gottlieb, ed., *Thinking the Unthinkable: Meanings of the Holocaust* (Totowa, NJ: Paulist Press, 1990).
16. Leon Trotsky as quoted in Jim Higgins, "The Ideas of Leon Trotsky," *Revolutionary History* 6 (Summer 1996).

24
Virtue Ethics, Mass Killing, and Hatred

Paul Woodruff

Thinking about genocide is a challenge by itself; so much anger, horror, dread, and disgust flood the mind. People rather like us, who are not criminals in other ways, kill innocents because of the group to which they belong. Not to be horrified, not to be angry would be a failure of character, and yet horror and anger may drown out the thinking that the subject calls for. To be calm about it is to betray the many who have been killed; so how can I be clear enough about this terrible subject, and not betray its victims? How not betray the victims, while looking to explain what happened to their destroyers? The horror has two edges, one for those who are killed and one for those who, in a devastating moral catastrophe, become killers.

The first challenge for moral philosophy is to be clear about what is especially wrong about genocide—more wrong than killing the same number of persons for different reasons. What is especially wrong about genocide seems to be a moral defect in thinking—the moral equivalent of a thought crime that accompanies the physical crime. But the idea of thought crimes is anathema to anyone who cares about the freedom of belief. People must be free to believe what they will, and no one should ever be blamed or punished for a thought—or so we often think. But we cannot condemn genocide as a special wrong without condemning the thought that comes with it, the thought that a certain group is baneful and must be wiped out. So we need to see how to declare that a certain kind of thinking is wrong in itself.

The second challenge to moral philosophy is to assign blame for a crime that cannot be explained in terms of personal responsibility alone. Shared vices of the mind mark genocide as what it is, and those vices belong to communities, not to individuals alone. So the challenge is to understand how there can be communal responsibility for great crimes. And if responsibility for genocide is communal, how is this crime to be prevented? What punishments could serve as deterrents or correctives?

Vices of the mind

We speak of hate crimes as if murder were especially heinous when it is conceived in hatred. And yet what difference does hatred make? A murder is a murder, and this is a crime that is well defined in legal and moral tradition. Hatred, on the other hand, is not a crime. So why should a killing motivated by hatred be considered more heinous than a killing motivated by greed, when both are premeditated? Murder in the course of armed robbery, and murder in the cause of hatred, would seem to be equally fatal, equally to be prevented, equally to be punished. The same goes for the species of anger we feel as jealousy. Killing in jealous anger is just as deadly as killing from greed or from hatred. If so, hate crimes should not constitute a special category in law. But we are right to want to make a special case for hatred in the realm of ethics, because hatred is bad in itself, and bad in a different way from greed and jealousy.

Greed is a vice that leads to specific crimes, such as theft, exploitation, and fraud. Such crimes can be deterred. Jealousy is an experience that leads to isolated acts of violence, and these probably cannot be deterred. Both kinds of crime leave wounds in society that are raw, but which will eventually heal (although the victims may lose life, or property, or the ability to trust on which social life depends). Hatred, by contrast, tears into the fabric of society. A hate crime is an outer manifestation of a refusal within a community to accept its own members. And this refusal is a crime in itself. So we have two crimes—one, which occurs on the surface, and can be solved and punished simply by identifying a perpetrator and bringing him or her to justice. But the other crime, which is deep within the mind of the community, cannot be so easily solved. Who is to blame for the hatred of hate crimes? And how are they to be punished? The authors of hatred may be everywhere—on the radio, in locker-room whispers, in films and novels, in the pulpits of churches, in sacred texts, in liturgy, in a mother's warnings to her children. And in all these places, where are the people to punish? And if we could find them, could any punishment cure them of hatred or deter others from the same crime? Such are the difficulties we face when we try to construe hatred as a crime of the mind. And yet it seems to be just that.

I will take hatred to be not a crime of the mind but a moral disaster which it is our duty to try to prevent, or, when we cannot prevent it, to heal. This is a matter not of law, but of the ethics of a community. The challenge to philosophers is to work out a way of understanding ethical issues that pertain not to individuals but to communities.

Defining genocide

Analogous questions arise for genocide, which I initially take to be the mass version of hate crimes—mass killing motivated by mass hatred. Genocide is generally considered to be a far more serious crime against humanity than the mass killing of civilians as an act of war, when this is motivated by what is called military "necessity." In most cases, what is called "military necessity" is a mask for a kind of economy in military action: we claim necessity, as in the case of Hiroshima, if we think we can win an easier victory, less costly for us in lives and supplies, by taking the lives of masses of civilians behind enemy lines. "Military necessity" in such a case represents a moral shortcut to victory; it is based on the same kind of calculation as armed robbery, which is a shortcut to wealth. The only difference is that military necessity may be pled in a war on behalf of a just cause, while armed robbery (except perhaps in the case of a Robin Hood) may not.

Mass killing for military necessity has many defenders. I am not one of them; I believe that such dishonest uses of "necessity" as in the military case are deeply corrupting. To plead "necessity" is in bad faith unless it stands for an explanation of this hypothetical form: *If we are to achieve goal G at cost X, with means Y, we must do so in the following way. But of course, we chose to pursue goal G (the goal of unconditional surrender was not forced upon us), we chose to refuse costs greater than X, and we chose not to seek means other than Y.*

So mass killing of civilians is almost always dishonest even in wartime, and it is usually a crime under international law. But genocide seems to be even worse; I contrast genocide against such actions as Hiroshima to bring out what is particularly disturbing about genocide. Suppose that our commanders find it easier to drop bombs, on a plea of military necessity, when they can appeal to racist hatred of the enemy's people. This then borders on genocide, and it seems to be worse than the emotion-free calculation of costs and benefits—the economic model for wartime killing—that I first described. What is the difference that hatred makes?

Hatred is not the only form that racism takes. Indifference may also contribute to genocide; we may disarm our moral scruples in regard to a group if we simply do not allow ourselves to see members of the group as human beings. The six-legged house pests we exterminate we do not hate; we simply set them outside the circle of our moral concern. So it has been in some cases of genocide, carried out not in hatred but in a kind of moral indifference.

My initial account of genocide as mass murder motivated by hatred is flawed. Slavery as practiced in the western hemisphere was motivated mainly by economic concerns, and it resulted in the deaths of millions of people—deaths that could have been foreseen and prevented. The loss of life on slaving ships should count as premeditated murder, because the traders accepted it as part of the cost of their business. Many of us would want to call slavery a form of genocide. Racial hatred was a contributing cause, but it was not THE cause of these killings, which followed from an economic calculation. I would like to amend my initial account of genocide; let it also include mass killing in which racial or ethnic considerations disarm moral scruples that would otherwise deter the killers. By this definition, the deaths of

African slaves, and the deaths of Japanese civilians at Hiroshima, could be counted as belonging to genocide. Let this then be my definition of genocide—mass killing either motivated by mass hatred or facilitated by moral indifference to a category of human beings.

Character and hatred

Consider again the case of hate crimes. In one way, they do not seem to be as bad as other crimes. The people who commit them are not sociopaths or maniacs. They do not make a habit of dragging people behind vehicles, or of clubbing people and leaving them to die in the rain. Their mean streak may surface only in their dealings with people in the group they despise. In such cases, their hatred serves as a kind of excuse, allowing them to suspend the moral rules they follow in cases outside of the hated group. Here the analogy sometimes used by hate killers is self-defense: In self-defense I would be permitted to take human life. So why not in this case, in which the very existence of this person feels like an assault against me?

Hatred of this kind is not a crime in itself, but it is a moral disaster nonetheless, a disaster for both the hate killers and their victims. It opens a space in which an agent who is not otherwise a sociopath acts like one.

Virtue ethics on an Aristotelian model (which I use) aims at fostering the development of character. A virtuous character is pleased by doing what is right and ashamed of doing what is wrong. In hate crimes, the virtue of the agents has broken down in a spectacularly horrible way. These agents, when operating in a cloud of hatred, are pleased by doing what is wrong, and they would be ashamed of doing what is right. Their hatred has reversed their moral polarity; that is what is so disturbing about the doers of hate crimes. In hate crimes, we see how fragile virtues may be when subjected to powerful emotions.

Hatred is a kind of excuse; by "excuse" I mean any consideration that blocks an inference from action to character. If we know that Robert acted violently out of hatred, then we do not infer from his action that Robert has a violent character, because we know how hatred warps the expression of character in those contexts which it clouds. Hatred is like extreme fear; we might say, "He is not himself when his mind is clouded with hatred or with panic. Yes, he did a terrible thing, but he is not the sort of person who regularly does that kind of thing."

The truly virtuous agent has no excuses to give; her virtue guides her always, so long as she is truly virtuous. A virtuous mind, while it is virtuous, is never clouded by the conditions that would allow us to separate character from action. Of course, there are no such people. Virtue is an ideal at which we aim. Part of the goal of the virtuous life is to turn aside from all such excuses; and hatred is one of them.

Besides, the hatred in hate crimes is not found in isolated individuals, but in groups, in communities of thought, where the hatred festers quietly in most cases, erupting only in violence only in individuals who have not learned the self-control that holds their group, largely, in check. But hatred in genocide erupts not in the actions of aberrant individuals, but in the well-organized actions of a group. Hatred in genocide, unlike the hatred behind hate crimes, has swept away the dams of normal self-restraint. In both cases, however, the ethical problem is primarily hatred, and this is what ethical thinkers must address.

To cultivate virtue in yourself, you must weed hatred out of your mind, and the same goes for excessive anger and fear. That is why courage and a balanced emotional life are necessary elements in virtue. Now, if you believe that you should seek for others the virtues you seek for yourself, then you, as a seeker of virtue, should, as a matter of ethics, do what you can to reduce the level of hatred in others.

Can this be done by punishment? In addition to punishing for murder in hate crimes, we feel we should also do something about the hatred that lies behind them. This hatred is shared widely, and shared hatred is setting up more people—who may in other ways be decent folk—for committing hate crimes at all levels of criminality, from slight insults to brazen murders. So why shouldn't hatred be punished, if it is the cause of crime and suffering—if washing it away would leave a healthier society for all of us? But punishment for hate crimes does not seem to reduce levels of hatred. If anything, it raises them.

I am tempted to say that hate-reduction is best done by example, but even that can fail. Gandhi's example did not prevent an outpouring of bloody hatred as British India came apart. Knowledge is more powerful than saintly example; the more you know about people, about whom they love and who loves them and where they want to go, the harder it is to hate them for the group to which they belong. Add to that the weaving together of people in community, and group hatred becomes even harder. Still, a challenge not merely to philosophy, but to us all, is to work out remedies for hatred.

Now we can see why hate crimes have a special place in ethics that they could not deserve in law. Hatred is bad for character; or, rather, hatred can come in-between good character and its expression in action. It follows that in hate crimes there are two things to deplore, the crime and the hate; and these call for separate remedies.

Virtue and community

Classical virtue ethics recognizes that each of us is embedded in a community that supports the development of certain kinds of character. All the way from customs of child-rearing to higher education, the way we treat a developing person affects the character that develops. Child-rearing and education are not the only factors that moderate character. Peer pressure and the wider culture are factors as well. And we must not discount inheritance;

each person's genetic legacy seems to set some limits to development. And then, of course, there are choices. Choosing to drink or take drugs can make me an addict, for example, and other choices can lead to weakening or strengthening virtues. But no one can choose to be brought up in a non-abusive family—that is a matter of luck. And so it is for most of the other factors that are beyond choice.

No individual is wholly responsible for the character that he or she has. I say this not to lighten the load of guilt that criminals must carry, but to emphasize the heavy responsibility of the community in preventing hate crimes and genocide. I am not aware of any hate crimes committed by solitary killers with unique hatreds. Men who kill gay men, for example, always seem to belong to a subculture that hates homosexuality.

The practical question about genocide, then, is about the character of a whole community. We have seen that the virtue of individuals depends to an important extent on the virtue of their community. This leads to another challenge to ethical philosophy—to recast ethical discussions in such a way that they give a different scope to individual responsibility. We are not entirely responsible for our individual characters. But we are all responsible for the character of our communities, because we are all examples to those around us. Any one of us can be imitated, whether we look to be imitated or not. None of us is free from the ethical burden of community, and part of that burden is the responsibility to act, in every way possible, for the diminishing of hate.

25
Shame, the Holocaust, and Dark Times

Michael L. Morgan

Ten years after the Third Reich was defeated and the Nazi death camps were liberated, Alain Resnais was persuaded to create a film about their horrors and atrocities. *Night and Fog* was the result of his subsequent collaboration with Jean Cayrol, who wrote the narration, and Hanns Eisler, who composed the film's musical score.[1] The central theme of this remarkable film is that, appearances notwithstanding, the evil of the death camps and of Nazi fascism remained alive in France in 1955. It might have seemed to the film's audiences that the evil and the horror had been destroyed with the liberation of the camps and with the end of the ruthless empire of death, but Resnais's and Cayrol's message was that they had not. Time might have deposited layers of debris over the past; life might have continued and grown, hiding not only that past but also the forces and agencies of evil that existed in the present, in 1955. The lesson of *Night and Fog*, however, is that while time may make forgetfulness easy and memory difficult, this means that memory becomes a challenge and a task.[2] Forgetfulness goes hand in hand with a terrifying threat, that today and tomorrow, again and again, we will be made to live once more as agents, victims, or bystanders of such atrocities. If those alive in 1955 did not remember the past, then the forces of degradation and inhumanity would continue to win their victories, and we will all be their victims.

I was led to think about *Night and Fog* in 2004 when I watched *Ghosts of Rwanda*, a television documentary broadcast by PBS on the tenth anniversary of the Rwandan genocide, which essentially took place in a 100 days from April to July in 1994. I do not mean to compare the latter film, a historical and educational documentary, to *Night and Fog*, which many regard as perhaps the greatest non-fiction film ever made. Cinematically there is no comparison. Nonetheless, watching the new film brought the older one to mind. As I watched *Ghosts of Rwanda* and listened to the people interviewed, many of whom I had read about—victims, politicians, doctors, United Nations officials, and others—I recalled how often, in the books on the Rwandan genocide, the Nazi Holocaust was invoked as a standard and a warning, as the origin for the agreements and promises to each other that Rwanda—and not it alone—showed us and the world to be breaking. In reflecting on the juxtaposition of the two events, I thought about the juxtaposition of living ten years after the one event and then after the other. I considered what I feel now, what Resnais felt then, what he hoped his audience would feel, then and thereafter, and where history leaves me and us, where we have come and where we have failed, and how and where we stand today.

When I speak of *we* and *us*, how should those terms be understood? First and most generally, *we* may refer to humankind. Second and more specifically, I have in mind people in Western nations whose lives have coincided with the Holocaust and subsequent genocides, those of us who have lived through these catastrophes or have learned about them through reading, film, and more, those of us who are bewildered and deeply upset at where we and Western civilization stand. Third, since I am a philosopher, *we* and *us* also refer to the community of philosophers and thus to philosophy itself. In this respect, I ask where philosophy stands today in a world in which the Holocaust and subsequent genocides have taken place and in which genocidal acts continue to occur. What I say here applies to all three of these understandings of *we* and *us*, and in the context of this book I believe that its relevance for philosophers and philosophy is of special importance.

The cost of forgetfulness

Night and Fog is not an account of the rise of Nazis and the creation of the death camps. Resnais and Cayrol use images, narration, and music to raise questions, to expose evidence to the viewer and to provoke reflection, to elicit our responses and then to unsettle them, to get us to think about how we see and understand what took place. A central theme of this process is the ease of missing what is placed before us, of failing to recognize what we see, of being blinded or having our senses dulled, so that the past is taken as settled, dead, gone, and irrelevant. In the film, the use of color along with black and white, the simplicity of Cayrol's comments and questions and the almost monotonous quality of the narrator's voice, and the gentle lyricism of much of Eisler's music—all tempt us to let the evidence flow by, to glide over the threatening nature of Nazi fascism and the atrocities it produced as they are depicted in the film's photographs and archival footage. But at the same time, the dissonance of what we see and how it is presented is intended to unsettle us about our responses to those temptations. We should leave our viewing disturbed and warned.

In the literature about the Rwandan genocide, references to the Nazis and to the Holocaust regularly call attention to the warning "Never again" as the paradigmatic response to the death camps and Nazi terror.[3] In 1955, in France, Resnais and Cayrol realized that it would be easy not to appreciate the importance of such a warning, of committing ourselves to it and remembering it. In a sense, the primary intention of *Night and Fog* is to restore the past and register the importance of the warning against forgetfulness. It is not that we, who live after Auschwitz, would not want to avoid a repetition of such horrors. Surely, once we realized what had happened at Auschwitz, we would want to prevent anything like it from occurring again. The issue was that one might not see that such a commitment was necessary because it would seem to be irrelevant. One might deny that the conditions for such atrocities are still present or fail to read the signs correctly or ignore the signs when they are there. Or, even more sadly and more terribly, one might have the signs pointed out or even have the occurrence identified and still refuse to accept that what was happening was a repetition of what happened under Nazism. There are many ways, Resnais seems to be saying, in which we might be tempted to avoid our commitments—to humanity and to particular human beings and to the victims of the death camps.

Ghosts of Rwanda is a different sort of film. It is not artful but informational and educational, conventional in its use of interviews and reportage. Nevertheless, its point is similar to *Night and Fog*'s. The film about Rwanda reminds the viewer that what took place in 1994 was a genocide, that after the Holocaust the UN in 1948 passed a convention committing the nations of the world to intervene to prevent genocides from occurring, and that Rwanda marks a failure of that commitment. The film reminds the viewer that the genocide in Rwanda may have occurred during a civil war, but it was a genocide nonetheless, that it included acts of extraordinary brutality and cruelty, and that it was methodically planned and implemented rigorously and efficiently through a mobilization of common people and neighbors under the direction of politicians, government officials, the military, and the media.[4] Moreover, the film documents a failure or a host of failures by individuals, powerful Western nations, and the UN. In this regard, *Ghosts of Rwanda* follows the direction of much of the literature on the genocide. Criticisms have been regularly directed toward a number of individuals, in addition to those who organized and directed the genocide from within the Rwandan political and military institutions, but the most important targets are the leaders of nations—in particular those of Belgium, France, Great Britain, and the United States—and the leadership of the UN.

In the cases of the UN and the United States, whose role on the Security Council and in the UN is so central, the explanations of why they acted as they did, opposing and avoiding military intervention and obstructing effective assistance for vital periods of time, normally focus on the catastrophe in Somalia and the battle of Mogadishu in the fall of 1993, as well as on the problems that were ongoing in Bosnia and Serbia.[5] But whatever the best explanation of their actions, especially the actions of the United States executive (the State Department, the White House, and the military) and the actions of the UN Secretariat, the fact is that when it was known that a genocide was occurring—organized and executed by the government and under government supervision, with lists of victims having been prepared based on racial considerations, with trained militia to support the military and eventually to take over from them, with the use of radio broadcasting of hate propaganda, and more—everything was done to avoid intervention and even to prevent others from intervening.[6]

The message of *Ghosts of Rwanda*, like that of the literature on the Rwandan genocide, is that when some 800,000 Tutsis were slaughtered in a matter of weeks—the killing's intensity surpassed the Nazis' attack on the Jews in that regard—the leadership of the UN and the United States stood by, watched, permitted the brutality to go on, refused to intervene, and even prevented others from doing so. Because of their historical relationships with Rwanda, the governments of France and Belgium responded, in some ways, even more culpably. The television film wants its viewers to appreciate that we are haunted by the "ghosts" of Rwanda—together with those of Cambodia, Bosnia, Kosovo, and, at the time of this writing, by the genocide that is under way in Darfur—and by the warning about what may lie ahead for us if we do not honor the promises we have made to one another.

If *Night and Fog* is about forgetting, then *Ghosts of Rwanda* is about a forgetting mediated by denial. The denial was that of the UN, of the United States government, and of many more; it was a denial that the events occurring in Rwanda after 6 April 1994 were genocide. There were those who denied that genocide was going on, some for weeks, others for months. Why? To avoid the obligations and the responsibilities that would accompany this admission, responsibilities and moral demands tied to the UN's Convention on Genocide. Watching *Ghosts of Rwanda*, then, provokes shame about what one hears and sees, the images, the interviews, and the admissions, often given, that more should have been done, that the denials were evasions.[7] One feels shame before these confessions, which are often themselves expressions of guilt and shame, but the viewer's shame echoes against the commitments after the Holocaust that led to the United Nations Genocide Convention and then, later, to the UN's problematic role in intervention against genocide. Our shame is shame for these denials too; we are ashamed—or should be ashamed, if we are not—of being ones who forget, of being bystanders who did not act on behalf of those in need, and of being deniers or beneficiaries of deniers, even as we today, so many of us, criticize and judge deniers of the Holocaust.

The significance of shame

One cannot, I think, watch the *Ghosts of Rwanda* without a profound sense of sympathy for all those who suffered and who then continued to suffer and for those who suffer to this day, for the victims and survivors of the genocide. We also are horrified by what we see, the brutality of the slaughter, and we are afraid.[8] But beyond the sympathy, horror, and fear, there is something else. At the same time, one cannot but also feel the shame that I have just mentioned.[9] Sympathy is directed toward the victims; shame is directed toward ourselves. Sympathy wants to relieve the suffering and pain of others; shame reflects something about how we feel about ourselves and who we are.[10] But what is the character of this shame? And does it tell us anything about how we should live or about what we ought to do in living, now, ten years after Rwanda and sixty years after Auschwitz?

Shame is a complex state, emotional and evaluative and hence psychological and ethical at once. It is reflexive and yet social, requiring that we look at ourselves and at the way others view us, at once and dialectically.[11] And while shame is akin to guilt, the two are not identical.[12] We can be ashamed about what we have done, just as we can feel guilty for what we have done, but shame is about who we are for having done what we did; we are ashamed for having been the one who did what we did.[13] Guilt is related but different. We feel guilty for having done what we did but not for being who we are.

Shame, moreover, involves losing face and caring that we have done so. We lose face before others. It matters to us how others see us, and so we care about how we present ourselves to them. When we are ashamed in this way, we are focused not on what we have done but rather on how our actions show us to be to others, and we are focused on how they will see us in virtue of that "face" and the way that our action presents us to them. Furthermore, shame may not be about how others actually see us; rather it is about how we think they do or would, as a result of seeing us or looking at us as the ones who acted as we did. What shames us is our own estimate of ourselves, made not from our own perspective, but as our projection based on how others might look at us, given what we know about ourselves as the way they might see us.[14] In short, shame is our own way of seeing ourselves, not through the prism of our actions, but through the prism of how others would see us in terms of our actions. Hence, shame involves a judgment of value about what we think others should think about who we are, given how we have conducted ourselves. But this means that shame requires of us that we have some notion of how we should be or ought to be, the kind of person we ought to be, and the kind of person others ought to expect us to be, in terms of which our actions show us to have failed, to be deficient, to be diminished. When we are ashamed, we have lost face because the face we value and hope to have has been displaced or defaced by another face, which is one that we regret having, one that disgraces or embarrasses us.[15]

All of this depth and complexity is to say that shame reaches far into who we take ourselves to be, who we hope to be, and into how we feel about how we are viewed.[16] Shame is a very revealing emotional state, even if it is one that we do not seek to feel. In an important chapter of his book *The Drowned and the Saved*, Primo Levi reflects on the shame of one who survived Auschwitz.[17] Levi's account is not analytical or systematic. What he seeks to disclose are different modes of shame that occurred for him and for other survivors of Auschwitz and what they mean. His thoughts, written in the shadow of Auschwitz, may begin to help us to understand further what our own shame today might mean.

Primo Levi's sense of shame and its implications for us

Levi's chapter on shame was first published in 1986. Its beginning includes a recollection from his novel *The Reawakening*, which was published in 1963 but written, he says, early in 1947, not long after his return to Turin, Italy. The chapter might be read as a gloss on the passage from the novel, which describes, he says, "the first Russian soldiers facing our Lager packed with corpses and dying prisoners":

> They did not greet us, nor smile; they seemed oppressed, not only by pity but also by a confused restraint which sealed their mouths, and kept their eyes fastened on the funereal scene. It was the same shame which we knew so well, which submerged us after the selections, and every time we had to witness or undergo an outrage: the shame that the Germans never knew, the shame which the just man experiences when confronted by a crime committed by another, and he feels remorse because of its existence, because of its having been irrevocably introduced into the world of existing things, and because his will has proven nonexistent or feeble and was incapable of putting up a good defense.[18]

Levi's chapter on shame goes on to say that it may sound strange to hear that he and other inmates of the camps felt shame and that he wants to interpret that feeling. As victims themselves, what did they have to be ashamed about? But the passage harbors a dialectical turn. His reflection about shame begins with the observation about his Russian liberators and their expressions, their actions or omissions, and their feelings. He sees in them an emotion that he and other inmates have also felt, which he calls "shame" and goes on to characterize it. While Levi, for his own reasons, intended to clarify the dimensions or modes of that shame as he and other prisoners felt it, I want to ask a different but related question: what can his account, itself a response to the fact of Auschwitz, tell us about our own shame, the shame we feel as we recall Rwanda—and Cambodia, Bosnia, Kosovo, and Darfur—against the background of Auschwitz? Is our shame like that of the Russian liberators insofar as it is the response of outsiders who seem "oppressed ... by a confused restraint which seal[s] our mouths" and yet keeps our eyes fastened on the "funereal scene"?

Before we look at Levi's elaboration, we should notice that in the passage about the Russians noted above he points out that the shame he is focusing on is the shame of a particular type of person in a particular type of situation, "the shame which the just man experiences when confronted by a crime committed by another." This is the shame of the bystander, who, instead of doing something to prevent a crime or to interrupt it, allows the crime to occur and, Levi says, "feels remorse because of its existence." Here is a person who is himself just, who knows what is right and is the kind of person disposed to do it, and yet who allows a crime to occur, who, that is, fails to be himself, and in so doing allows something to be done, to exist, that is an affront to the just life and hence to his. Levi calls this feeling of shame "remorse" and "guilt," but it is neither exactly. What is it?

Levi says that this shame as a kind of suffering was felt by the released prisoner "because of a reacquired consciousness of having been diminished." As he goes on to point out, the prisoner had "lived for months and years at an animal level"; his time had been filled with hunger, fear, and fatigue without "any space for reflection [or] reasoning." He had stolen, even from other inmates. At the time, there may have been little opportunity to see oneself in this light, as living this way, but once he was released, there was time and opportunity to look at oneself as one had lived and become. Now clearly this is not true in the same way for the Russian liberator or for us today; what is relevant for us are the crimes or actions of others and our omissions or the omissions of those with whom we identify or who represent us. If the prisoner was diminished as a human being by having lived a certain way, then we, bystanders or heirs of bystanders, are diminished by having failed to act or by being the heirs and perhaps beneficiaries of such omissions. What is similar here is that shame requires a kind of detachment and the opportunity and capacity to enact it; it also involves the employment of that detached attention to look at the self and to see how its actions (or omissions) disclose a deficiency or inadequacy so that the self appears to itself as less than it expects itself to be.

The one ashamed feels under a kind of judgment, but for what?[19] For having done what one should not have done or for not having done what one should.[20] In Levi's case and for others who were in Auschwitz with him, he takes shame to have arisen, for some, precisely because they had not resisted; they had not done anything, or at least not all that they might have done, to oppose that which oppressed them.[21] Even if there was little reason to expect such resistance or little reason to think it could have been effective or even beneficial, there is the feeling that not resisting was inadequate and hence a judgment, one that the prisoner, afterwards, might recognize, is being made of him. He might think that he was not courageous enough, too weak, somehow too willing to sacrifice his dignity or self-esteem. Moreover, this judgment or accusation, as Levi calls it, might come from two directions, either from others or from oneself. And it is worse, he thinks, when it is self-accusation. But what does this mean?

One dimension of shame can be associated with the way others might look at us, and in this way the judgment upon us comes from outside. In the case of resistance, Levi remembers his account in *Survival in Auschwitz* of the hanging of a resistor before the assembled prisoners. As a survivor, he says, he believes that he sees a judgment "in the eyes of those (especially the young) who listen to his stories and judge with facile hindsight, or who perhaps feel cruelly repelled." The judgment is "you too could have [resisted], you too certainly should have [resisted]," and the survivor "feels accused and judged."[22] In such a way, the prisoner may feel shame in view of how others seem to be responding to his omission, but the shame can be mitigated, even if it is felt, by the thought that the judgment or accusation is misplaced, made "with facile hindsight" about how possible and reasonable resistance was. Levi sees here a shame that may be felt but that is unnecessary, in a sense, to the degree that the accusation is itself inappropriate.

But, he continues, "more realistic is self-accusation, or the accusation of having failed in terms of human solidarity." What Levi means is that "almost everybody feels guilty of having omitted to offer help" to another, of failing in basic human solidarity, failing to listen, to speak to another, to give even a "momentary attention" to the other's entreaty. Hence, the shame of self-accusation in such cases is the feeling of having failed to respond or reach out. It is not a sense of having failed to be what others expect us to be; it is a sense of having failed to be what we expect of ourselves. Such shame is despair over who we are when we see ourselves as having omitted to do what we expect of ourselves. It does not require the "eyes" of the other judging us, real or imagined. The accusation comes from ourselves.

With these insights in mind, Levi tells a story of having found a small amount of water in Auschwitz at a time when thirst tortured the prisoners. Levi shared the water with his friend Alberto, but he was seen by Daniele, another prisoner, who later reminded Levi of his failure to share the water with him as well. Levi speaks of his shame at having failed to share the water with Daniele; while he is not sure whether that shame is justified, it does exist, he says, "concrete, heavy, perennial." There is, then, shame before another and shame before oneself; shame is a feeling of failure and inadequacy and having been diminished, but in one case it responds to the other's judgment, while in the other it is a response to one's own accusation. Whether some particular other person does or could judge our omission, or whether we judge ourselves, the shame we feel about ourselves marks our failure of human solidarity if what we omitted to do is to reach out when addressed by the other's entreaty, the other's imploring face.[23]

Levi recalls the incident of his failing to share the water with Daniele, and whether his self-accusation is justified or not, he admits to feeling ashamed. At the end of the chapter, he returns to this sense of having failed in human solidarity. "There is another, vaster shame," he says, "the shame of the world." Citing John Donne, he notes that we live together and are responsible one for another—"every bell tolls for everyone." Each of us is called to do what we can to care for the suffering and the hungry. Levi and his compatriots were swallowed by an "ocean of pain." Having lived in it together, they could not live as if alone. The just, he says, "felt remorse, shame, and pain for the misdeeds that others and not they had committed, and in which they felt involved." On the one hand, as we have seen, that shame was shame about themselves and their omissions. It was a sense of failure and of being diminished. But it was another kind of shame too, and this is the vaster shame that Levi has in mind here. He says it was grounded in the realization that "what had happened around them and in their presence, and in them, was irrevocable." That is, it was done and could not be undone; it could not be eradicated or washed away. Having been done, it was always a potential for humankind. Hence, Levi suggests, one feels ashamed at being human in such a human world. This, I take it, is what Levi means by the vaster shame, "the shame of the world." It is not a shame grounded in what one has done or in what one has omitted to do; it is a shame about being in a world in which such evil, pain, and suffering—such atrocities—exist and are a part of human potential.

In *The Drowned and the Saved*, Levi's reflections are largely about shame for what one has done or omitted to do, or, in the case of shame about the world, for what has been done in the world in which one lives. As I emphasized, Levi comments that shame may be more or less justified, more or less reasonable and grounded. We might say that some shame, based on what we have done or failed to do, is fitting and appropriate to who we are, while some shame is inappropriate, excessive, and perhaps even misplaced. I have in mind Levi's narrative of his own failure to share the water with Daniele and his comments about resistance. Levi seems to have been willing to say that shame about not striking a blow against one's oppressor is wholly misplaced, whereas shame about not listening to a fellow inmate, not acknowledging a look, or not speaking to another prisoner may well be justified even if it is not required.

Something analogous is the case with regard to shame that arises in a different way, and it is something that Levi refers to on several occasions in *Survival in Auschwitz*. Often we are ashamed of ourselves for looking the way we do, for having certain properties or features. It is often the case, for example, that in societies permeated with racial or ethnic bias, members of a group that is oppressed and belittled are ashamed of looking the way they do and of having certain features—hair of a specific texture or color, noses or eyes or lips of a certain shape—or of wearing certain clothes, of not having certain tastes or skills or abilities. In *Anti-Semite and Jew*, Jean-Paul Sartre argues that both the antisemite and the Jew can be inauthentic by measuring themselves by standards that are imposed by others and then by feeling ashamed or diminished precisely because they fail to meet those standards. Levi notices that the death camp inmate could feel such shame by looking a certain way and having certain features. When his training as a chemist gave him the opportunity to work in the camp laboratory, he was presented to the German doctors before he was selected to work there. Three young German girls also worked in the laboratory. Levi reflects on how they looked at the inmates:

> Faced with the girls of the laboratory, we three feel ourselves sink into the ground from shame and embarrassment. We know what we look like: we see each other and sometimes we happen to see our reflection in a clean window. We are ridiculous and repugnant. Our cranium is bald on Monday, and covered by a short brownish mould by Saturday. We have a swollen and yellow face ... our neck is long and knobbly. ... Our clothes are incredibly dirty, stained by mud, grease, and blood. ...[24]

Earlier in *Survival in Auschwitz*, Levi spoke about his first experience in the laboratory, when he was interrogated by Doktor Pannwitz. Levi describes their encounter and especially Pannwitz's look: "that look was not between two men; and if I had known how completely to explain the nature of that look, which came as if across the glass window of an aquarium between two beings who live in different worlds, I would also have explained the essence of the great insanity of the third Germany." The laboratory girls looked at Levi and his compatriots with repulsion, disdain, and humor; Pannwitz looked at him with utter detachment and an impression of carelessness. Levi remembers that he felt a "mad desire to disappear, not to take the test." This experience, I take it, is also one of shame. Whether it is shame before the look of revulsion or shame before the look of lack of concern or solidarity or relatedness, it is shame, a sense of one's own unworthiness, of one's own repulsiveness, stench, and offensiveness. Levi took himself to be someone or something upon which no one should have to gaze, at which no one should have to look. One could serve others best by disappearing, by not being present. Shame is about self-negation.

But while there may be cases when such shame is warranted, when one is responsible for having put oneself in such a shameful—offensive or repulsive—state, there are times when one ought to be "ashamed" at being ashamed, when one's shame is itself mistaken and inappropriate.[25] The Jew's sense of shame when confronting antisemitic attitudes or practices, akin to what is known as Jewish self-hatred, is such a state. That shame is itself offensive, for it is an unwarranted, misplaced, and distorted feeling about oneself, and one about which one ought to be ashamed. Feeling ill about oneself for having features that one should not be ashamed of having, whether one has them or not, is itself worthy of shame. If shame is an emotional form of self-criticism about who one is, then it, like any criticism, can be well taken or poorly formed and developed. Just as one can be unjustified in feeling shame about having failed to resist the Nazis, so can one be unjustified in feeling shame about how one looks to one's oppressors or to others or about how one feels about being taken by others as repulsive or inadequate, as cowardly or arrogant, as too shy or unassuming. And if one is unjustified and is persuaded by that fact, then one can feel ashamed at being ashamed or, alternatively, proud about—or at least accepting of—one's sense of shame.[26]

Were the three girls in the laboratory justified in treating the Auschwitz inmates as repulsive and disgusting? Did it make sense for Levi and the others to feel ashamed at how they looked and were taken to be? Levi's account uses two devices to suggest that the prisoners do look the way the girls view them and hence that their shame at looking that way is appropriate: they look at one another and even see themselves reflected in clean windows. Even if the prisoners can no longer smell the difference that their odor carries, they can look at others from a distance, in a detached way, and they can even see themselves as if in a mirror, reflected and facing them. When they do so, they can see how alien and repulsive they look, not by the girls' standards alone but even by their own. In the camp, they are normal and ordinary, but when measured against standards of everyday life, they are awful to look at, to smell, to be with. The girls' disdain makes sense and is justified, and hence their sense of shame about themselves makes sense. Or does it? After all, what are these standards? Why do they not apply in the camp? How is it that Levi looks and smells as he does? Is it shame he should feel or something else, perhaps anger, bitterness, or even pride?

Responses to shame about and for the world

For Levi, there is something shameful about going on at all, after having been an inmate in Auschwitz along with so many others who were slaughtered or who died. He discusses the shame of having acted in certain ways, of having failed to act, of being degraded, and of now being alive at all as a privileged survivor—an undeserved privilege. He also points to the shame one feels as a survivor, or as a bystander, or as a German, as a Jew, as a human being alive in the world. One can feel shame, then, for those groups or on behalf of them, for Germans or for survivors or for all human beings. This last could be what he means when he talks about the vaster shame, the shame of the world; this might be a shame at being human at all in a world in which there was an Auschwitz and in which there seem to be no reliable obstacles to its repetitions.[27]

It might have been this kind of shame that I felt as I watched *Ghosts of Rwanda*, as I read the memoirs of Roméo Dallaire, the field commander of the UN peacekeeping force in Rwanda in 1994, and studied the books that recount the events of those months and years with vivid and precise details about the genocidal massacres, the brutality and precision of the slaughter— books such as those by Gérard Prunier, Linda Melvern, Alain Destexhe, Michael Barnett, Philip Gourevitch, and Samantha Power. Dallaire may have felt guilt about not having completed his mission satisfactorily. American leaders such as Madeleine Albright and Bill Clinton may have expressed guilt at not having argued for intervention or acting to intervene when they had the power and authority to do so. Perhaps we inhabitants of the first world, who lived through those years and who live now in a world in which the lessons of Auschwitz have not been learned and indeed in which they have been ignored or rejected, cannot feel guilt in the way that powerful leaders may do. But we can and should, I believe, feel shame—about being citizens of nations that did nothing or acted insufficiently to prevent recent genocides, about the collective inhumanity of all peoples and nations as expressed in the actions, inactions, and procedures of the UN, and perhaps most of all at being alive in a world containing Auschwitz and then the crimes in Cambodia, Bosnia, Rwanda, and Darfur. We can and should, I believe, feel shame about living in a world where genocide is always possible and where its prevention is continually negotiable, where genocide is only one matter among many, very much capable of being ignored or permitted, where Auschwitz can be forgotten and where it can be denied that what happened in Rwanda, for example, was genocide.[28]

When thinking about such shame, remorse about oneself and one's world, an image comes to mind. In *Shoah*, Claude Lanzmann's epic film about the Holocaust, there is a powerful sequence when he interviews the barber, Abraham Bomba, in an Israeli barbershop. Years before, in Treblinka, Bomba had been made to cut the hair of Jewish women just prior to their being sent to their death in that camp's gas chambers.[29] Lanzmann's questions urge Bomba to recall details—where did the barbers cut the women's hair, how many barbers were there, how long did this go on, how did you cut their hair, what did you cut with, were there mirrors, how did you feel when you saw the women naked, when you saw them with children? There is a very dramatic, painful moment, when Bomba recalls that he had no feeling, he felt dead, and then he tells Lanzmann that one day women from his home town of Czestochowa were led in, many of whom he knew, some of whom were neighbors and close friends. As he continues to cut the hair of the man in his Tel Aviv barber chair, Bomba goes on to say,[30] "When they saw me, they started asking me, Abe this and Abe that—'What's going to happen to us?' What could you tell them? What could you tell?" Bomba's voice begins to crack; he begins to weep, as he says, "A friend of mine worked as a barber— he was a good barber in my hometown—when his wife and his sister came into the gas chamber. ... I can't. It's too horrible. Please." Lanzmann prods him to go on, he resists, but eventually he continues:

> They tried to talk to [my friend] and the husband of his sister. They could not tell them this was the last time they stay alive, because behind them was the German Nazis, SS men, and they knew that if they said a word, not only the wife and the woman, who were dead already, but also they would share the same thing with them. In a way, they tried to do the best for them, with a second longer, a minute longer, just to hug them and kiss them, because they knew they would never see them again.[31]

Bomba's tears are driven by the memory of that episode, of what he had done and not done, of the women who asked him what was to happen to them, of his friend—was it a friend or Abe Bomba himself?—being confronted by his wife and sister in Treblinka, seeking to give them a last hug and kiss, yet going on cutting the hair. He remembers Abe Bomba and the others then, in Treblinka, and now, in Tel Aviv. Are they tears of guilt? Of loss? Of shame? Perhaps they are tears of all these, but at least shame seems prominent, at having done what he did and now of saying it out loud, of describing it and admitting it, before Lanzmann and before all the movie's viewers, before all of us. They are tears of shame about how to go on, while one does go on, about who one is and what the world is. Bomba's tears grip us and call out to us, summon us to remember, not to forget, and to feel our shame along with his.

Abe Bomba's tears of shame come in remembering. Mine too—shame for what has been done in our world and shame that comes with remembering a past that has been forgotten. The shame we feel in reading about Cambodia, Bosnia, Rwanda, and Darfur bears on our failure to act, to intervene, to take note, but our failure bears both on the victims of these genocides and on the forgetting of the past that itself bears on our—the world's and philosophy's—failure.

Levi's shame is recalled and yet, one can see, it is also present in the recollection itself. For Levi, there is shame in testifying to the past, the shame that comes with his recognition of having been spared, of having survived, and of not being in a position to testify accurately, of not being the one who should be testifying, the one who cannot remember.[32] The text that Levi recalls from his own book *The Reawakening*, cited earlier, tells of how the shame that Levi remembered and that the prisoners had felt was mirrored in the shame they saw in the eyes and the faces of their liberators. The Russian liberators of the camps were struck dumb; they did not speak, nor did they smile or greet the prisoners. They did not, could not face them, and Levi saw in their stares, their expressionlessness, the shame he had known in the presence of others in the camps.

But that shame, the shame of the liberators, did come with liberation; it was part of a process of opening the camps to view, clearing them, releasing and recovering the prisoners, and eventually obliterating the camps themselves. Shame then brought with it obliteration, for by obliterating the camps, one was also trying to obliterate the shame that came with witnessing them and their victims. In fact, it is true that shame seeks to nullify itself by negating what gives rise to it.[33] For us, Resnais says, that too easily means forgetting. We may seek to avoid shame or dispose of it by forgetting, by treating the past as dead and gone, by closing off the past from the present or, as *Night and Fog* shows us, by allowing the present to cover over, bury, or isolate it as though the past is in its own world and separate from ours.

In reality, however, the prisoners, the survivors of the camps, can really be liberated only if they are remembered; if not and if the past, their lives in the camps, is dead and gone, forgotten, then they are not free. As William Rothman points out, there is a moment in *Night and Fog* when the camera captures prisoners standing behind a barbed-wire fence, staring at their liberators and at the camera of the liberators. The narrator asks, "Are they free? Will life know them again?" These questions, Rothman comments, are not for the prisoners alone; "they are no less questions about the world, questions for the world. They are questions about, questions for, us."[34]

As viewers of Resnais's film, as viewers of the ghosts of Rwanda and readers of accounts of Cambodia, Bosnia, and Darfur, as philosophers, has that shame compelled us to remember these pasts, to restore them to reality, and to make "life know them again?" And what does that phrase mean? What is it for life to know the past again, the past of horror and atrocity, of brutality and genocide? What is it to "know" such pasts? If Rothman is right, part of such knowing is realizing that the fences of *Night and Fog* and the separation between image and reality, between past and present, are not real boundaries and barriers. To restore the reality of the past, to overcome forgetfulness, a failure to see and to understand, is to "acknowledge that—like the Kapo and the Nazi officer—this [prisoner who stares out at us in the film] belongs to our world, that we belong to his" and "the world of the film is our world." Realizing this, we come to realize too that "responsibility for liberating the camps—condemning the executioners, laying the dead to rest, welcoming the survivors into our midst, freeing ourselves and our world—is in our hands, the hands of all us survivors."[35]

What can we expect of ourselves and of our world? What might shame lead us to do? How might it lead us to live?[36] Levi comments that survivors are often asked whether Auschwitz could occur again, and while refusing to make judgments, he registers a few remarks. One is that Cambodia did occur, and he might have mentioned, had he lived today, Bosnia and Rwanda and Kosovo and now the Sudan. Another comment he makes is that mass slaughter is unlikely to occur in the Western world, Japan, and what was once the Soviet Union. Why not? Because, he says, "a sort of immunizational defense is at work which amply coincides with the shame of which I have spoken."[37] The ethnic cleansing in Bosnia and Kosovo belies Levi's hopes, but let me set aside that issue and ask what he meant when he spoke of shame coinciding with a sort of "immunizational defense." What did he have in mind?

Shame is about feeling unworthiness, for ourselves individually, for members of groups (including philosophers) or nations of which we are members, and for humanity as a whole, for our world, as a place which does not measure up. Measure up to what? Charles Taylor has argued that shame is one of those emotions that requires a sense of import, of mattering, about certain properties or ways of life or actions. Such a sense of import is what I have tried to bring to attention in this chapter while commenting on Levi and his notion of judgment or accusation and when I used the word *standards*. Shame is how we feel about ourselves, our groups, and our world when they do not meet standards of worth and value. But what are the standards that figure into our shame of living in a world in which Auschwitz and subsequent genocides exist?

Just as the shame we feel has several dimensions, so too are there many standards against which our failures are measured. Levi refers to our sense of human solidarity. Others, such as the Holocaust survivor-philosopher Jean Améry, speak of our sense of solidarity with all those whose human dignity is under assault.[38] Some religious thinkers refer to a defense of the notion of being created in the divine image.[39] Perhaps no one has captured more profoundly than Emmanuel Levinas the preeminence of this sense of human sociability as fundamentally valuable for all human life and hence as that sense of human mutual responsibility which ought to determine how we live and all that we do. Genocide, the slaughter of human communities, massacres, and all the brutality and cruelty that are part of these acts are dramatic and momentous rejections of this value. Levinas saw this and frequently spoke out about it. In Resnais's terms, sociability calls for our responsibility to make a world in which life will know the victims and survivors of genocides again, in which life knows the past. It calls for us to be the liberators of the prisoners and victims of the past and in this way to liberate ourselves from shame and from the artifice of pretending, forgetting, and evasion. One standard of our failure, in our own eyes, is the standard of responsibility for the life and well-being of others, responsibility to care for the needy and to aid the suffering. Shame at failing to meet such a standard is what Levi saw in the speechless eyes of the Russian liberators.

But for us, watching reports about the Sudan today, reading accounts of the massacres in Rwanda and Srebrenica and Kosovo, the shame is also about the failure of forgetting, of allowing the past to be dead. It is the shame about denial, specifically the denials of the leaders of the UN, of my country, the United States, and of other countries—for example, Great Britain, France, Belgium—that what has occurred is genocide. Hence it is also shame about our having avoided an obligation to others, to ourselves, to all humankind. It is about carrying out a liberation of the victims of the past that is in effect a false liberation, a way of avoiding who we ought to be by cutting off the present from the past.

Shame, then, can accompany the failure of the wrong kind of liberation, but it can also lead to true liberation, to overcoming the forgetting, the avoidance, and the failure. Shame can lead to recovery of who we want ourselves to be, to a truer self.[40] Responding to shame in this way, however, is no easy task; the shame itself, an iteration of Levi's shame and that of the Russian liberators, shows how deep and broad it can be, how resistant we are to an honest recovery of our selves and to an honest confrontation with the demons of Auschwitz and genocide. Responsibility is not a speechless, immobilized response to the face of horror and atrocity but rather the word of kindness itself and the touch of care and concern, a living for others that is a more genuine way of living with ourselves. When shame gives rise to remembering, it breaks down barriers, and when the barriers come down, what stands before us, reaching out, is another person.[41]

Notes

1. There are several discussions of *Night and Fog* that I have found helpful, among them: William Rothman, *Documentary Film Classics* (Cambridge: Cambridge University Press, 1997), pp. 39–68; Jay Cantor, "Death and the Image," in his *On Giving Birth to One's Own Mother: Essays on Art and Society* (New York: Alfred A. Knopf, 1991), pp. 143–77; Ilan Avisar, *Screening the Holocaust: Cinema's Images of the Unimaginable* (Bloomington, IN: Indiana University Press, 1988), pp. 6–18; André Pierre Colombat, *The Holocaust in French Film* (Metuchen, NJ: Scarecrow Press, 1993), pp. 121–66.

2. In his discussion of *Night and Fog*, Rothman says that the task Resnais sets for the film is "to restore the reality" of the camps, as if they had been destroyed by their liberation and evacuation and by time itself. He says that "the film undertakes this task so that we may no longer 'pretend to know nothing about' the 'endless, uninterrupted fear' that was—is—the 'true dimension'" of those camps (Rothman, *Documentary Film Classics*, p. 45; see also pp. 48, 53, 60). By restoring the reality of the world of the past, the film also restores the reality of the present (pp. 48–9).

3. See, for example, Samantha Power, *"A Problem from Hell": America and the Age of Genocide* (New York: HarperCollins, 2002), p. 357; Alain Destexhe, *Rwanda and Genocide in the Twentieth Century* (New York: New York University Press, 1995), p. 32; Michael Barnett, *Eyewitness to a Genocide: The United Nations and Rwanda* (Ithaca, NY: Cornell University Press, 2002), pp. 1, 8, 21, 169–70; Gérard Prunier, *The Rwanda Crisis: History of a Genocide* (New York: Columbia University Press, 1997); Philip Gourevitch, *We wish to inform you that tomorrow we will be killed with our families* (New York: Farrar, Straus and Giroux, 1998), p. 170 ("Rwanda has presented the world with the most unambiguous case of genocide since Hitler's war against the Jews. ... The West's post-Holocaust pledge that genocide would never again be tolerated proved to be hollow, and for all the fine sentiments inspired by the memory of Auschwitz, the problem remains that denouncing evil is a far cry from doing good") and p. 316. Commenting on radio about the 1963 killings in Rwanda, Bertrand Russell said that it was the most horrible and systematic extermination of a people since the Nazi extermination of the Jews; see the article, "L'Extermination des Tutsi," *Le Monde* (4 February 1964). Russell's comment is frequently cited, for example by Linda Melvern, *Conspiracy to Murder: The Rwandan Genocide* (London: Verso, 2004), p. 9, and also in her book *A People Betrayed: The Role of the West in Rwanda's Genocide* (London: Zed Books, 2000), p. 17. See also Gourevitch, *We wish to inform you*, p. 65.

4. The numerous books on the Rwandan genocide discuss its history and the precise ways in which it was prepared for—the racial system of classification that became a pervasive feature of Rwandan life but that was mobilized and utilized for social and political purposes by the Belgian colonial administration, the system of identity cards, the preparation of lists of Tutsi and Hutu accomplices or supporters of democratization of the Rwandan Patriotic Front (RPF), and so on—but particularly

noteworthy accounts are provided by Prunier, *The Rwanda Crisis* and Melvern, *Conspiracy to Murder*. According to Melvern, the first time the word *genocide* was applied to what was occurring in Rwanda was on 9 April 1993, in response to the slaughter of 10,000 people, in two days, in Gikondo, many of whom were seeking shelter in a Catholic church and were massacred by the militia, the *Interahamwe*, "slashing with their machetes and clubs, hacking arms, legs, genitals, and the faces of terrified people who tried to protect the children under the pews. ... Not even babies were spared" (p. 182). Only two people seem to have survived the slaughter. For a further description, based on the report of Major Brent Beardsley, assistant to the UN front commander Roméo Dallaire, see Dallaire's *Shake Hands with the Devil: The Failure of Humanity in Rwanda* (Toronto: Random House Canada, 2003), pp. 278–81. Beardsley and a team of observers came upon the Polish church shortly after the massacre. Dallaire's description of the "unbelievable horror," of mutilations, the disemboweling of a pregnant woman and the severing of her fetus, is grisly and shocking. Dallaire concludes his account as follows: "The massacre was not a spontaneous act. It was a well-executed operation involving the army, Gendarmerie, Interahamwe and civil service" (p. 281).

5. See, for example, Melvern, *A People Betrayed*, pp. 77–80; Barnett, *Eyewitness to a Genocide*, pp. 34–48; Melvern, *Conspiracy to Murder*, pp. 68–71. For a discussion of the crisis in Bosnia, see Melvern, *A People Betrayed*, p. 174 and, more comprehensively, Power, "*A Problem from Hell*," chap. 9.

6. For excellent, detailed, and persuasive accounts, see the books cited above in notes 3 and 4, especially Dallaire's disturbing memoir, *Shake Hands with the Devil*. Dallaire, who is widely cited in all the books on the Rwandan genocide, was the Canadian Lieutenant General appointed as the field commander of the United Nations Assistance Mission for Rwanda (UNAMIR).

7. I am thinking particularly of the admissions made by those who were, in their own ways, major players in the international political activity that permitted the genocide to go on, among them Kofi Annan, Madeleine Albright, and even Bill Clinton.

8. In his important essay on the films *Night and Fog, Hotel Terminus*, and *Shoah*, Jay Cantor calls attention to the horror and the fear: if death were really present in the images and pictures, then "one would feel, as the narrator of Alain Resnais's documentary *Night and Fog* reminds us, 'endless, uninterrupted fear' " ("Death and the Image," p. 145). In fact, Cantor notes, Resnais accomplishes something remarkable: "He makes the horrible ordinary, so we might believe it; and then he makes the ordinary horrible, so that we might fear it" ("Death and the Image," p. 148). In the film, the ordinary is represented by train tracks, fields, fences, old buildings—in short, the remains of the past that today appear benign and almost lyrical. By exposing what lies "beneath" them, so to speak, Resnais makes them "terrifying," "horrifying." Memory leads to fear. My attention is not on this fear or terror but rather on the shame we feel when we realize that we have forgotten, repressed the memory, even when what we are looking at tells us that what we have forgotten is that the past is, in fact, present today, perhaps far from view, like Darfur, but present nonetheless.

9. About one-third into the film, there is an interview with a Rwandan woman in her early twenties, I would say. With a gentle face and eyes, she recalls a massacre at a church in Nyarbuye. Later in the film, we hear about a visit to that church by the British journalist Fergal Keane, who covered Rwanda for the *Sunday Times* and wrote a book about the genocide, *Season of Blood*. We see his visit, the remains of slaughtered victims piled outside the church and in the church, scattered under

and around pews. He then mentions stopping at the local mayor's office, where he sees a mother and two children, survivors, one of the children, a young girl, emaciated, her hand black, fingers chopped off, and with a wound on the back of her head. We realize that this skeletal, suffering child, then thirteen years old, had survived and become the young woman we met earlier, Valentina Iribagiza. It is a moving moment. In a *Times* article, Keane writes: "I left Rwanda shortly afterwards vowing never to go back. In a few weeks I had witnessed brutality and evil on a terrifying scale. ... However, Rwanda did not go away, nor did the memory of Valentina and other survivors of genocide. I found myself endlessly questioning: how could this have happened? How could people butcher children? What kind of man can kill a child?" What did Keane feel then? Was it horror? Anguish? Shame? No doubt all of this and more. Later in the film, when we hear apologies and expressions of shame from former US national security advisor Anthony Lake, the UN's Kofi Annan, and former US Secretary of State Madeleine Albright, we are shown too their visits to the church at Nyarubuye, with its skeletons, a moving testimony to a horrific past.

10. In *Pride, Shame, and Guilt* (Oxford: Oxford University Press, 1985), Gabriel Taylor describes these three emotions as emotions of "self-assessment." She writes: "In experiencing any one of these emotions the person concerned believes of herself that she has deviated from some norm and that in doing so she has altered her standing in the world" (p. 1).

11. Shame does not require that others actually see us; it can arise as a feeling about how others might see us. It occurs at a moment of "social consciousness" in this broad sense. See Philip Fisher, *The Vehement Passions* (Princeton, NJ: Princeton University Press, 2002), pp. 65–8: "The feeling of shame occurs in the moment of becoming aware of others, the moment of a return to social consciousness ..." (p. 67). Fisher emphasizes that shame, like an apology or embarrassment, comes after other feelings.

12. The relationship between shame and guilt is widely discussed in psychological and philosophical literature on shame. A recent, if brief, discussion can be found in Martha C. Nussbaum, *Hiding from Humanity: Disgust, Shame, and the Law* (Princeton, NJ: Princeton University Press, 2004), pp. 207–9, where she says: "Guilt is a type of self-punishing anger, reacting to the perception that one has done a wrong or a harm. Thus, whereas shame focuses on defect or imperfection, and thus on some aspect of the very being of the person who feels it, guilt focuses on an action (or a wish to act), but need not extend to the entirety of the agent, seeing the agent as utterly inadequate" (p. 207). This view does not mean that actions cannot give rise to feelings of shame. Nussbaum points out that there is a good deal of psychological literature about how guilt and shame "trigger" one another; see pp. 376–7, n. 99.

13. Shame is originally about nakedness and exposure, about looking to others as we do, when it is inappropriate or wrong to do so. For us, however, there are many ways in which shame can arise. We can be ashamed of ourselves for looking the way we do, for saying what we have said at the wrong place or time, for having done what we should not have done, and on and on. Moreover, we can be ashamed of ourselves personally, our group, our country, or all of humankind. To feel ashamed is to feel negatively about ourselves and others because we recognize that we have failed or are diminished by how we are or by what we have done. We seek to relieve that sense of being diminished by changing our character or by doing what we should. See Robert C. Roberts, *Emotions: An Essay in Aid of Moral*

Psychology (Cambridge: Cambridge University Press, 2003), pp. 227–34: "Shame's consequent concern is to restore one's respectability or reduce one's disgrace" through self-justification, rationalization, or efforts to avoid similar situations in the future (p. 229).

14. The taking up on this external point of view is the result of a kind of moral imagination, of projection and construction. For discussion of the role of imagination or what he calls "phantasy" in complex emotions such as shame, see Richard Wollheim, *On the Emotions* (New Haven, CT: Yale University Press, 1999), pp. 148–224.

15. For an important account of shame, in all its richness and complexity, see Bernard Williams, *Shame and Necessity* (Berkeley, CA: University of California Press, 1993), pp. 77–102 and 219–23. One of Williams's aims is to show how the Kantian view of human psychology, action, and morality inadequately appreciates shame, the distinction between shame and guilt, and the notion of the moral self. As Williams points out, shame is connected with nakedness and exposure or with "being seen, inappropriately, by the wrong people, in the wrong condition. ... The reaction is to cover oneself or to hide. ... From this there is a spread of applications through various kinds of shyness or embarrassment" (p. 78). But shame is not just the being seen as naked, it is the feeling that we have about being seen; it is a "reaction of the subject to the consciousness of [a loss of power]" or, in Williams's citation of Gabriele Taylor, it is "the emotion of self-protection" (p. 220). See Taylor, *Pride, Shame, and Guilt.*

16. Nussbaum, *Hiding from Humanity*, especially chap. 4, provides a wide-ranging discussion, philosophical but based on psychological evidence, about related themes. She writes, for example, that shame "is a painful emotion responding to a sense of failure to attain some ideal state. ... In shame, one feels inadequate, lacking some desired type of completeness or perfection" (p. 184).

17. Primo Levi, *The Drowned and the Saved*, trans. Raymond Rosenthal (New York: Summit Books, 1988), chap. 3, "Shame," pp. 70–87. Levi is cited by several authors who have written about the Rwandan genocide. See, for example, Gourevitch, *We wish to inform you*, p. 275.

18. Levi, *The Drowned and the Saved*, pp. 72–3. For the quotation, see Primo Levi, *The Reawakening*, trans. Stuart Woolf (New York: Collier-Macmillan, 1965), p. 2.

19. For discussion of the standard of judgment or the import that the property or feature has about which we are ashamed, see Charles Taylor, "Self-interpreting Animals," *Human Agency and Language: Philosophical Papers I* (Cambridge: Cambridge University Press, 1985), pp. 53–5. See also Charles Taylor, "The Concept of a Person," *Human Agency and Language* (Cambridge: Cambridge University Press, 1985), pp. 109–12.

20. Also, of course, for how one looks, for features or characteristics one has, in general, that is, for perceived imperfections, deficiencies, or inadequacies. Since I am particularly interested in the shame I felt—and others feel—about our world and the omissions of the United States, other governments, and the UN with regard to intervening in genocides and failing to deal with the conditions that give rise to genocide, I focus here on shame that arises from actions or failures to act.

21. Levi, *The Drowned and the Saved*, pp. 76–8.

22. Ibid., pp. 77–8.

23. In such cases of failure, as Bernard Williams points out, we can feel both guilt and shame: "In a moment of cowardice, we let someone down; we feel guilty because we have let them down, ashamed because we have contemptibly fallen short of

what we might have hoped of ourselves" (*Shame and Necessity*, p. 92). Williams notes that John Rawls discusses such a case in *A Theory of Justice* (Cambridge: Harvard University Press, 1971), p. 445.

24. Primo Levi, *Survival in Auschwitz*, trans. Stuart Woolf (New York: Collier Books, 1961), pp. 128–9. The passage is quoted and discussed by Robert S. G. Gordon, *Primo Levi's Ordinary Virtues: From Testimony to Ethics* (Oxford: Oxford University Press, 2001), pp. 51–2. Gordon is primarily concerned with the role that looking and the look play for Levi.

25. Commenting on Levi's discussion of shame in *The Drowned and the Saved*, Richard Wollheim remarks that what Levi and the other prisoners were ashamed about, their wretched condition, was not something they did to themselves, whether we are talking about their attitude of self-interest or their horrible physical condition. Still, the shame was felt and was somehow appropriate. "For we know," says Wollheim, "that lack of responsibility, or, for that matter, lack of intention, are fully compatible with deep, burning shame about what we have become" (*On the Emotions*, p. 199).

26. Charles Taylor discusses whether shame can be justified or not and that it can be more or less rational. See "Self-interpreting Animals," pp. 49–50.

27. One feels this shame about the world, I believe (at least I feel it), when reading books such as Imre Kertész's *Fateless*, Christopher Browning's *Ordinary Men*, and Jan Gross's *Neighbors* as well as Levi's *Survival in Auschwitz*. Wollheim discusses Levi's indication that there is such a shame "on behalf of humanity, of the whole human species" (*On the Emotions*, p. 200). He describes this deep feeling of shame as arising from a situation that brings into question one's very sense of self as an "ongoing creature, related to his past, to his present, and to his future, in the ways in which we persons necessarily are. ... Levi is further telling us, and out of his own experience, that life in the Lager, life as it was made, not, of course, by the prisoners, but for the prisoners by their captors, was of such an abject nature that merely to survive it and to go on existing, thinking of oneself as a person as life requires, was a permanent occasion for shame" (pp. 200–1). So it was that "for many innocent men and women, the very broadest way they had of looking at themselves, that is, as persons, became so shot through with mistrust that they mistrusted everything that involved it" (p. 201).

28. The strategy to avoid using the term *genocide* to avoid the implications of such an admission, in view of the 1948 Genocide Convention, has been widely discussed. A clear and telling account can be found in Power, *"A Problem from Hell,"* especially pp. 358–64. In *Ghosts of Rwanda* and excerpted in Power's book (pp. 363–4), there is a now famous State Department briefing, conducted by Christine Shelly on 10 June 1994, during which she is asked how she would describe the events taking place in Rwanda. Shelly answers that "we have every reason to believe that acts of genocide have occurred in Rwanda." She is then asked what the difference is between "acts of genocide" and "genocide," and after equivocating, she is asked, "How many acts of genocide does it take to make a genocide?" Shelly answers: "Alan, that's just not a question that I'm in a position to answer."

29. Jay Cantor discusses the interview with Bomba in "Death and the Image," pp. 159–62, emphasizing Lanzmann's manipulation of the dialogue, the artifice of it all.

30. Or at least he appears to continue; in fact the scene was staged. Bomba had retired as a barber.

31. Claude Lanzmann, *Shoah: An Oral History of the Holocaust* (New York: Pantheon, 1985), pp. 111–17. This book contains the text of the film. The interview with

Bomba was done in a Tel Aviv barbershop. During a visit to Indiana University, Lanzmann answered questions from members of my class on the Holocaust. I recall his saying that the interview with Bomba had to be done several times, until Bomba broke down and wept.

32. Levi, *The Drowned and the Saved*, pp. 81–5.
33. As Bernard Williams points out, "Gabriele Taylor has well said that 'shame is the emotion of self-protection', and in the experience of shame, one's whole being seems diminished or lessened. … The expression of shame … is not just the desire to hide, or to hide my face, but the desire to disappear, not to be there" (*Shame and Necessity*, p. 89). Shame, that is, seeks our non-existence, our total negation. And then, as Roberts says, it seeks to restore one's respectability or one's worthiness, either honestly or dishonestly; see earlier, note 13.
34. Rothman, *Documentary Film Classics*, pp. 58–9.
35. Ibid., pp. 61–2. Rothman associates these challenges with the fate of art and of our artfulness, so to speak: "If we fail to look around us—fail to punish the guilty, fail to free the survivors, fail to lay the dead to rest, fail to recognize the executioners and victims that are everywhere in our world, fail to recognize the executioners and victims that, we, ourselves, are—that does not mean we are unaware of the horror, that our unawareness is the horror. It means that we are masters of the art of pretending not to know what we cannot help knowing. If we remain deaf to the 'endless cry,' it means we are pretending not to hear" (p. 63); see also pp. 65, 67–8.
36. As an emotion or feeling, shame is a way we are oriented to what we have done, to our features and character and the way we look, in terms of how others do or might see us. But it is also or can also be a motivation to act. Feeling shame leads us to explain ourselves, to avoid being seen in a certain way, to apologize and ask for forgiveness. There is a moment in the film *Now, Voyager* when Jill, Charlotte Vale's niece, recalling how mean she had been to Charlotte (Betty Davis), hugs her and asks her for forgiveness—motivated by the shame she feels for having acted that way in the past. Or is guilt the motivation? Or both?
37. Levi, *The Drowned and the Saved*, pp. 86–7.
38. See Jean Améry, *At the Mind's Limits: Contemplations by a Survivor on Auschwitz and Its Realities*, trans. Sidney Rosenfeld and Stella P. Rosenfeld (Bloomington, IN: Indiana University Press, 1980).
39. See Irving Greenberg, "Cloud of Smoke, Pillar of Fire: Judaism, Christianity, and Modernity after the Holocaust," in Eva Fleischner, ed., *Auschwitz: Beginning of a New Era?* (New York: Ktav Publishing, 1977), pp. 7–55, and Emil L. Fackenheim, "On the Life, Death, and Transfiguration of Martyrdom: The Jewish Testimony to the Divine Image in Our Time," *The Jewish Return into History* (New York: Schocken, 1978), pp. 234–51.
40. As Bernard Williams suggests, shame can motivate positive responses as well as negative ones. The one who is ashamed of himself can "wish to hide or disappear" or "more positively, shame may be expressed in attempts to reconstruct or improve oneself" (*Shame and Necessity*, p. 90). Since shame arises from an act of omission or from some failing or defect (perceived by the agent as a defect, of course), and since it "elicits from others contempt or derision or avoidance," Williams adds that one's responses to shame seek reconciliation with others and with oneself, a sense of wholeness, communal and personal.
41. During the Rwandan genocide, Philippe Gaillard headed the delegation of the International Committee of the Red Cross in that country. He is one of the heroes

of Linda Melvern's account in *A People Betrayed*, and he is interviewed extensively in *Ghosts of Rwanda*. At the end of the PBS film, Gaillard comments that he and his wife had not had children (nor seemed to want to have them), but upon their return, after the atrocities, they both felt the strong desire to have children and to produce life. The film ends with Gaillard's remark that he has never explained to his son that the boy's life is a response to genocide.

Epilogue: "After? ... Meaning What?"

John K. Roth

> ... I promise you that after ...
>
> Elie Wiesel, *One Generation After*

When American voters went to the polls on Tuesday, 2 November 2004, a brief article in the *New York Times* reported that the Sudanese army had not only surrounded the camps of internally displaced people in Sudan's western region of Darfur but also was likely to relocate them forcibly, which it subsequently proceeded to do. At that time, the number of the homeless in Darfur numbered more than 1.5 million. The United Nations indicated that 70,000 people had died from disease and malnutrition in the seven preceding months. Another 200,000 refugees had fled to Chad, where they were in dire straits.

A month earlier and very briefly—for no more than four minutes, to be precise—the situation in Sudan was addressed by John Kerry and George W. Bush in the first of their three debates in the 2004 American presidential campaign. Jim Lehrer, the debate's moderator, initially asked Kerry whether American troops should be sent to Sudan. Following the lead taken in early September 2004, when the US Secretary of State Colin L. Powell called the situation in Sudan a genocide, Kerry too applied the "G word" to Darfur. In the two minutes he was given to address Lehrer's question, the Democrat's nominee urged "logistical" as well as humanitarian support. "If it took American forces to some degree to coalesce the African Union," he added, "I'd be prepared to do it because we could never allow another Rwanda. It's a moral responsibility for us in the world."

Lehrer gave Bush, the Republican incumbent, ninety seconds to respond and to express his position on Darfur. The American president, too, called the Darfur situation genocide. He mentioned that $200 million in aid had been committed by the United States. He noted US support for the UN in Darfur. He also stated that the United States "shouldn't be committing troops," and he expressed the hope that "the African Union moves rapidly to save lives."[1]

To the best of my knowledge, those four minutes represented the sum total of attention that genocide received during the 2004 presidential campaign in the United States. There and elsewhere, the record of philosophers has been considerably better, but not so much better as to be a cause for congratulation. Even as this volume of reflection on philosophy, genocide, and human rights went into production for publication, the situation in Darfur had deteriorated further. If the UN was reluctant to identify Sudan as a site of genocide, it did not hesitate to call the conditions in Darfur the world's worst humanitarian crisis at the time. An early December 2004 report by UN Secretary-General Kofi Annan went on to say that "in Darfur, chaos is looming as order is collapsing."[2] Annan indicated that 2.3 million people, more than a third of Darfur's population of about 6 million, were in desperate conditions as the Sudanese government and its proxies, the Arab militias known as Janjaweed, continued their decimating assaults against the Fur, Zaghawa, and Masaalit, the key African population groups in western Sudan. The genocidal methods employed in the onslaught included lethal dehydration as wells and water supplies in the arid environment were ruined, rape, starvation (partly produced by hijacking of relief goods or by preventing relief agencies from gaining access to those in need), forced relocation, and outright killing by shootings and bombings.

The writings of Elie Wiesel, a survivor of Nazi Germany's genocide against the Jews, sometimes include Holocaust-related dialogues.[3] Spare and lean, they often consist of just a few hundred words or less. These dialogues are distinctive not only for their minimalist qualities but also because their apparent simplicity, their unidentified settings, unnamed characters, abrupt and open endings, raise fundamental questions in moving ways.

In Wiesel's *One Generation After*, for example, one partner in a dialogue tries to rescue the other from a downward-spiraling sadness. "Look around you," says the upbeat voice. "The trees in bloom. The shop windows. The pretty girls. What the hell, let yourself go. I promise you that after ..."

After—but not allusions to spring's new life—that's the word, the problem, that gets the other's attention. "After?" asks the downcast voice. "Did you say: after? Meaning what?"[4] The dialogue ends with that question, but far from being over, it has only begun.

After—that word is ordinary because human life is thick with time. Encountering what is present, anticipating what lies ahead, our living is always *after*, whose meanings denote a subsequent or later time and a seeking or questing for something one does not have. In those senses, philosophy is an after-word. When Plato contended that philosophy begins in wonder, he understood that philosophy does not come first but comes to life in the aftermath of preceding experience. Once it comes to life, philosophy takes on life of its own, which can be life-giving or life-threatening or many other things in between.

As history has unfolded, philosophy now lives after genocide, a fact that makes, or should make, philosophers wonder about what philosophy's promise is to be. The chapters in this book have tried to take stock of that situation, but they are only a beginning. What comes after them in philosophy will do much to determine whether the answers to the questions "After? Meaning what?" are ones that support the hope that genocide will end.

Sadly, there is a sense in which those who perpetrate genocide tend to have a crucial advantage. Those who intervene or prosecute or philosophize after the fact usually arrive too late. The horror unleashed by human hands makes it unclear that justice can be achieved. The repetition of genocide since the Holocaust makes it hard to glimpse how prevention can happen. My friend, Hank Knight, a Holocaust scholar at the University of Tulsa in Oklahoma, is a fine song writer, and his lyrics in a song called "Hardly Ever Again" capture moods and concerns that should make people, including philosophers, think long and hard:

> In '45, remember when
> The world said, "Never, never again!
> Never again: six million lost;
> Never again: The Holocaust."
> "Never," we said, "Never again,"
> But this is now and that was then.

> "Hardly ever again."
> Is that what we meant to say?
> "Hardly ever again."
> Will we turn and walk away?
> This is now and that was then;
> And we meant "hardly ever again."...

> But this is now and that was then.
> When will we ever mean "never again?"[5]

The historian and legal scholar Michael Bazyler argues persuasively that the model of monetary restitution in Holocaust-related cases helps to put on notice individuals and institutions that pursue human rights abuses, including genocide. That notice, he contends, indicates that those who commit genocide or violate human rights in other ways will be held responsible for their misdeeds.[6] Like post-genocide trials, such as the one in the International Criminal Court at The Hague, where Slobodan Milosevic is the first head of state to be put on trial for genocidal atrocities—specifically the ones that took place during the 1992–95 Bosnian War—restitution comes *after*. Legal proceedings and acts of restitution that come *after* may help to forestall genocide by putting people on notice, as Bazyler contends, but trials and acts of restitution are only two arrows in the hoped-for quiver of genocide prevention. What about others that are needed as well and how might philosophy and philosophers contribute to them?

"The beast of genocide," says Gregory H. Stanton, director of the International Campaign to End Genocide, "lurks in the dark." Roméo Dallaire, the Canadian general who headed the United Nations Assistance Mission in Rwanda, makes a related point when he urges that "the need is to stop the disconnect between the experiential and the intellectual."[7] To the extent that Stanton's warning is heeded in ways that advance Dallaire's imperative, the answer to the fundamental question, "Will genocide ever end?" can at least be *perhaps*. That realistic conclusion is ever-so-tentative. Yet it is not without hope and substance because international awareness about what it will take to move beyond genocide is becoming clearer. More effectively than they have done so previously, philosophers can raise their voices in this cause.

Consider five overarching themes on these topics. First, genocide prevention is a goal that exceeds any single person's expertise, any discipline's methodology, or any government's reach. Genocide prevention requires working together at every point. Second, no automatic link exists between intellectual analysis of genocide and the action that is needed to prevent it. That connection can be made only through political will. How to muster and sustain that political will is among the most important questions raised by the continuing threat of genocide in our world. Third, governments, even if they are alert and activated, will not—indeed, cannot—do everything that is necessary to prevent, stop, or heal the wounds that genocide inflicts. That fact requires the mobilization of other agencies that may be able to lend a hand in this crucial work. Fourth, at times there is no substitute for military intervention, which is essential to maintain stability and security. Military intervention, however, is not enough to meet the needs that genocidal threats present. Crucial needs include political, economic, and educational aid—somewhat along the lines of a post–Second World War Marshall Plan—to defuse potentially genocidal situations. Fifth, prevention of and intervention in genocide are long-term commitments, otherwise genocide prevention will remain ineffective. The long-term commitments must involve all sorts of institutions, and not least of all the media, which have the power to alert, inform, and urge the need for action. In all of these areas, philosophy and philosophers have much needed contributions to make. They can ask crucial questions, provide conceptual clarity, identify and undermine ideologies that are genocidal, persistently call attention to differences between right and wrong, advance and assess arguments that pertain to those differences, bolster support for human rights, and encourage creative responses to educational needs. Importantly, philosophy and philosophers can do these things not abstractly but with attention focused on the particularities of existing situations, genocide—actual and threatened—among them.

These five overarching themes have a series of good news/bad news implications that identify key areas in which vigilance and hard work, including vigilance and hard work for philosophy and philosophers, remain if the temptations of genocide are to be curbed in the twenty-first century. Here, very compactly, are several of those implication clusters.

1. We have the concept of genocide. It is defined, for example, by the United Nations Convention on Genocide. The concept helps us to identify genocide when it happens and, importantly, when it may be coming. But the bad news is that education about genocide is lacking, and, in addition, the scope and meaning of the concept remains debatable. As a result, there are loopholes in the legal frameworks about genocide. The concept's definition, moreover, is not likely to be universally agreed upon. Even if it were agreed upon, the sense of obligation to prevent genocide may remain ambiguous. Deeper study and better education about genocide are needed if genocide is to end. If they are moved to do so, philosophy and philosophers can provide help in these areas.

2. Prevention and proof of genocide depend on determining perpetrator intent, which is not easily done, especially in pre-genocidal situations. Nevertheless, there is good news about demonstrating intent, because we know that ideologies can show it. Some ideologies are genocidal; philosophy can help to identify them and thus contribute to early warnings against genocide. Yet, even if we can sense genocide's coming by study of ideologies, the control of hate-inflaming communication, education, and media—crucial though it is—remains both problematic and lacking. If genocide is to end, there must be media usage and control in that direction. Here the signal for philosophy and philosophers is that they will need to become more engaged in public life and discourse than their often abstract theorizing and highly specialized academic projects have inclined them to be.

3. The good news includes the fact that we have worthwhile analyses of risk assessment and credible approaches to early warning where genocide is concerned. Nevertheless, too often no one gives the perpetrators—potential or actual—reason to pause. Early warning is an important piece, but still a small one, in a very large and complicated genocide puzzle. If genocide is to end, early warning systems must produce policies and actions that give its agents reason to pause. Philosophy and philosophers have encouraged thinking that is creative, imaginative, and original. Often genocide confronts us with what is unimaginable, or so it seems, but its extremity requires us to stretch our minds and to energize our wills to find ways that can check the advantages that genocide's perpetrators often enjoy. At the very least, philosophy can offer encouragement that helps to keep genocide's perpetrators—potential or actual—at bay.

4. Military intervention can be effective in preventing and stopping genocide. Such intervention is crucial for establishing security in which genocide cannot erupt or prevail. Yet, military power is state-focused; what it can do depends on state authority, and states jealously guard their sovereignty. Where genocidal situations are involved, how states will allow their military power to be used, if at all, for prevention and intervention remains at issue.

Genocide's threats are unlikely to disappear until more effective international military cooperation against genocide becomes operational. Philosophers can do more than they have done before to advance these aims.

5. We know too much for it to be a surprise when genocide happens. Nevertheless, genocide indicators are difficult to operationalize for genocide prevention. Accountability is among the most crucial aspects of this problem. Who, for example, does one call to get preventative action going when genocide is threatened or under way? If genocide is to end, calls of that kind must be placed and answered. Accountability for genocide prevention must be put in place. Philosophers know how to think well about responsibility and accountability. If they put their minds to it, they can lend assistance in these areas too.

6. The good news is that we know a great deal about what to do to check genocide or to keep it from re-erupting after it has happened. Those steps include: establishing security, neutralizing genocidal leaders, engaging in regional planning, ensuring that political moderates have a voice, avoiding ethnically based governments. In spite of such knowledge, however, genocides continue. They reveal either the failure or the inadequacy of basic institutions—political, religious, and humanitarian. Genocide's threat will not end until those institutions perform better than they have thus far done. Philosophers have a part to play in getting those institutions to make the improvements that are needed. That work may properly emphasize the importance of philosophy's self-criticism, which may be needed to move philosophers to give concerns about genocide a higher priority than has typically been the case.

7. National interest is not always a barrier to genocide intervention. The case can be made that prevention and intervention are part of a nation's values and thus of its interests. On the other hand, decisions are often made on the basis of political considerations that override appeals to "higher values." When that happens, value-based appeals for prevention and intervention are muted and unheeded. Genocide is unlikely to end unless the tendency to override ethical considerations is reversed. If philosophy and philosophers do not rise to this challenge, then the quality of human life will be jeopardized far more than necessary.

8. It is good news to know that religion can be a powerful and persuasive force in genocide prevention. The negative example of Rwanda bears witness to this claim, for virtually all analysts of that genocide are convinced that it could have been prevented or stopped if strong religious protests against the genocide had been raised. But that same negative example also shows that religion is a key part of the problem where genocide is concerned. Religion can separate people; it can legitimate violence that is genocidal. If the quality of religious life improves by becoming less exclusive and more inclusive, so will the odds in favor of genocide prevention. Philosophy and philosophers have often worked successfully to help make religion less dogmatic and sectarian, more thoughtful and inclusive. Focused with genocide more consciously in mind, this work needs to continue.

9. Reports, testimonies, acts of memory and memorialization, legal proceedings, restitution settlements—these responses keep attention focused on what happens in genocide. They make it more difficult to perpetrate genocide and to ignore the brutality, the killing, and its aftermath. Unfortunately, reports can be buried. Apologies may ring hollow. The past recedes. Life goes on. Restitution cannot bring back the dead. Justice may not take place. Legal proceedings drag on. Long-term rebuilding falters. Denial gets a hearing. Perpetrators go back to business as usual. Nevertheless, the antidotes for genocide include resistance against the disappearance of what has been seen and felt in genocide's killing fields. Even though they cannot set everything right, restitution and courts of law play crucial parts in the process of preventive memory and policy. Philosophical reflection on genocide has its part to play in these activities, and if it does not take place, memory will be less deep and ethical than it ought to be.

10. Not only are there many nongovernmental organizations (NGOs) that do have deep commitments to humanitarian causes, but those organizations, along with many governmental ones, are staffed by individuals who often display immense courage, persistence, and resilience in battling against genocidal threats. Yet the bad news includes the fact that NGOs may unwittingly aid and abet potentially genocidal regimes by creating or intensifying one set of problems as they respond to another. When to disengage as well as when to engage remain issues that can often be riddled with ambiguity and unintended negative consequences. Such difficulties are among those that never make it possible for us to say with complete assurance that genocide will end, but greater confidence that it can and will end can be legitimately found if philosophy and philosophers bring their critical judgment to bear on these issues of engagement and disengagement.

11. The media possess immense power and sophistication to report accurately, to keep us informed of events in real time, and to cover the globe. Where genocide is concerned, the excuse that "I did not know" or "we were unaware" can no longer have much credibility. But the bad news is that too often the media spin, simplify, and scoop. The spins are multiple, contested, incomplete, more-or-less true, and they reflect "interests"—political, economic, philosophical—that contribute to the ideologies and mistrust in which genocidal dispositions thrive. In no small part, then, the prevention of genocide depends on media committment to that goal. Philosophers also have a part to play in holding the media accountable in this way. The ethical challenges and moral questions of philosophy provide steps that can be taken in these directions.

The chapters in this book illustrate and suggest how philosophy and philosophers can engage in the work of genocide prevention, which hinges first and foremost on establishing institutional accountability—governmental and nongovernmental—aimed in that direction. As a result, the questions that most need answering include the following: How do we best establish, support, and encourage institutions to take responsibility to prevent or check genocide and to keep that goal among the highest priorities? Few, if any, questions are more important than that one. After genocide has taken place, in the age of genocide that is ours, philosophy's promise, the credibility of its future, requires that attention to that question should be high on philosophy's list of priorities.

Giving testimony about his experiences in Bosnia, Kemal Pervanic, a survivor of genocidal ethnic cleansing in the Balkans, said that his story, unfortunately, was "nothing new." Then, as if echoing what Elie Wiesel might have said, he added: "I heard the concept of genocide first *after* it happened."[8]

The beast of genocide does lurk in the dark, as Gregory Stanton said, but the dark is not only the darkness of murderous ignorance, lethal discrimination, and bloodthirsty arrogance. Instead, genocide lurks largely in the darkness of irresponsibility and nonaccountability, which prevents too little and intervenes too late. General Dallaire got it right: the disconnection between the experiential and the intellectual must be stopped. He might have substituted *philosophical* for *intellectual*. If that disconnection is stopped, then perhaps genocide can be stopped as well. Caring persons, especially philosophers, have no right to regard those objectives as hopeless.

Notes

1. See the transcript of the candidates' first debate in the 2004 presidential campaign, which took place in Coral Cables, Florida, on 30 September 2004, *New York Times*, 1 October 2004.
2. See "Annan Warns Chaos Looms in Violent Darfur," *New York Times*, 6 December 2004.
3. The following paragraphs are adapted from my contributions to David Patterson and John K. Roth, eds, *After-Words: Post-Holocaust Struggles with Forgiveness, Reconciliation, Justice* (Seattle, WA: University of Washington Press, 2004) and Carol Rittner, John K. Roth, and James M. Smith, eds, *Will Genocide Ever End?* (St. Paul, MN: Paragon House, 2002).
4. Elie Wiesel, *One Generation After*, trans. Lily Edelman and the author (New York: Avon Books, 1972), pp. 72–3.
5. Reprinted by permission of Hank Knight.
6. See Michael Bazyler, "Using Civil Litigation to Achieve Some Justice," in Carol Rittner, John K. Roth, and James Smith, eds, *Will Genocide Ever End?* (St. Paul, MN: Paragon House, 2002), p. 156.
7. Stanton and Dallaire made these comments at the Aegis Trust–British Foreign and Commonwealth Office (BFCO) Genocide Prevention Conference, an international inquiry that took place at the Beth Shalom Holocaust Centre in England on 22–25 January 2002. This conference included participants from government, the military, nongovernmental organizations, and universities, as well as genocide survivors.
8. Pervanic was one of the genocide survivors who participated in the Aegis–BFCO Genocide Prevention Conference on 22–25 January 2002.

Select Bibliography

As this book's endnotes indicate, many sources have informed the work of its contributors. Listed below are books, many of them recent publications, that figured most prominently in the volume's contents. Their authors are either philosophers, scholars with philosophical interests, or writers whose reflections contain important implications for philosophy.

Adorno, Theodor W. *Metaphysics: Concept and Problem*. Translated by Edmund Jephcott. Stanford, CA: Stanford University Press, 2000.

——. *Negative Dialectics*. Translated by E. B. Ashton. New York: Seabury, 1973.

——. *Prisms*. Translated by Samuel and Shierry Weber. London: Neville Spearman, 1967.

Agamben, Giorgio. *Remnants of Auschwitz: The Witness and the Archive*. Translated by Daniel Heller-Roazen. New York: Zone Books, 1999.

Améry, Jean. *At the Mind's Limits: Contemplations by a Survivor on Auschwitz and Its Realities*. Translated by Sidney Rosenfeld and Stella P. Rosenfeld. Bloomington, IN: Indiana University Press, 1980.

Arendt, Hannah. *Eichmann in Jerusalem: A Report on the Banality of Evil*. Revised edition. New York: Penguin Books, 1965.

——. *The Origins of Totalitarianism*. New York: Harcourt, 1951.

——. *On Revolution*. London and New York: Viking-Penguin, 1963.

Badiou, Alain. *Ethics: An Essay on the Understanding of Evil*. Translated by Peter Hallward. London: Verso, 2001.

Ball, Howard. *Prosecuting War Crimes and Genocide: The Twentieth Century Experience*. Lawrence, KS: University Press of Kansas, 1999.

Barrett, Michael N. *Eyewitness to a Genocide: The United Nations and Rwanda*. Ithaca, NY: Cornell University Press, 2002.

Bartov, Omer. *Mirrors of Destruction: War, Genocide, and Modern Identity*. New York: Oxford University Press, 2000.

——. *Murder in Our Midst: The Holocaust, Industrial Killing, and Representation*. New York: Oxford University Press, 1996.

Bartov, Omer, and Phyllis Mack, eds, *In God's Name: Genocide and Religion in the Twentieth Century*. New York: Berghahn Books, 2001.

Bauman, Zygmunt. *Life in Fragments: Essays in Postmodern Morality*. Oxford: Blackwell, 1995.

——. *Modernity and the Holocaust*. Ithaca, NY: Cornell University Press, 2000.

——. *Postmodern Ethics*. Oxford: Blackwell, 1993.

Becker, Lawrence C., and Charlotte B. Becker, eds, *Encyclopedia of Ethics*. Second edition. New York: Routledge, 2001.

Bernasconi, Robert, ed., *Race*. Oxford: Blackwell, 2001.

Bernstein, Richard J. *Radical Evil: A Philosophical Interrogation*. Cambridge: Polity Press, 2002.

Bodmer, Walter Fred, and Robin McKie. *The Book of Man: The Human Genome Project and the Quest to Discover Our Genetic Inheritance*. New York: Oxford University Press, 1994.

Braiterman, Zachary. *(God) after Auschwitz: Tradition and Change in Post-Holocaust Jewish Thought*. Princeton, NJ: Princeton University Press, 1998.

Buell, Frederic. *From Apocalypse to Way of Life*. New York: Routledge, 2003.

Camus, Albert. *The Myth of Sisyphus and Other Essays*. Translated by Justin O'Brien. New York: Vintage Books, 1955.

——. *The Plague*. London: Penguin, 1965.

Card, Claudia. *The Atrocity Paradigm: A Theory of Evil*. New York: Oxford University Press, 2002.

Chalk, Frank, and Kurt Jonassohn. *The History and Sociology of Genocide*. New Haven, CT: Yale University Press, 1990.

Chandler, David. *Voices from S-21: Terror and History in Pol Pot's Secret Prison*. Berkeley, CA: University of California Press, 1999.

Charny, Israel W., ed., *Encyclopedia of Genocide*. Santa Barbara, CA: ABC-CLIO, 1999.

Clendinnen, Inga. *Reading the Holocaust*. Cambridge: Cambridge University Press, 1999.

Cohen, Joshua, ed., *For Love of Country: Debating the Limits of Patriotism*. Boston, MA: Beacon Press, 1996.

Cohen, Josh. *Interrupting Auschwitz: Art, Religion, Philosophy*. New York: Continuum, 2003.

Collins, Margaret S., Irving W. Wainer, and Theodore A. Bremner, eds, *Science and the Question of Human Equality*. Boulder, CO: Westview Press, 1981.

Dallaire, Roméo. *Shake Hands with the Devil: The Failure of Humanity in Rwanda*. Toronto, Canada: Random House, 2003.

Davis, Stephen T., ed., *Encountering Evil: Live Options in Theodicy*. Second edition. Louisville, KY: Westminster John Knox Press, 2001.

Delbo, Charlotte. *Auschwitz and After*. Translated by Rosette C. Lamont. New Haven, CT: Yale University Press, 1995.

Des Pres, Terrence. *The Survivor*. New York: Oxford University Press, 1976.

Destexhe, Alain. *Rwanda and Genocide in the Twentieth Century*. New York: New York University Press, 1995.

Dobkowski, Michael, and Isidor Wallimann, eds, *The Coming Age of Scarcity: Preventing Mass Death and Genocide in the Twenty-First Century*. Syracuse, NY: Syracuse University Press, 1998.

Eze, Emmanuel. *Achieving Our Humanity: The Idea of the Postracial Future*. New York: Routledge, 2001.

Fackenheim, Emil. *Encounters between Judaism and Modern Philosophy*. New York: Basic Books, 1993.

——. *The Jewish Return into History*. New York: Schocken, 1978.

——. *To Mend the World: Foundations of Post-Holocaust Jewish Thought*. New York: Schocken Books, 1989.

Falk, Richard. *On Human Governance: Toward a New Global Politics*. University Park, PA: Pennsylvania State University Press, 1995.

Finkielkraut, Alain. *The Future of a Negation: Reflections on the Question of Genocide*. Lincoln, NE: University of Nebraska Press, 1998.

——. *In the Name of Humanity: Reflections on the Twentieth Century*. Translated by Judith Friedlander. New York: Columbia University Press, 2000.

——. *Remembering in Vain: The Klaus Barbie Trial and Crimes against Humanity*. New York: Columbia University Press, 1992.

Fleischner, Eva, ed., *Auschwitz: Beginning of a New Era?* New York: KTAV, 1977.

Foucault, Michel. *Discipline and Punish: The Birth of the Prison*. Translated by Ann Sheridan. New York: Vintage, 1995.

——. *The Order of Things: An Archaeology of the Human Sciences*. New York: Vintage, 1994.

Fredrickson, George M. *Racism: A Short History.* Princeton, NJ: Princeton University Press, 2002.

Gaita, Raimond. *A Common Humanity: Thinking about Love and Truth and Justice.* New York: Routledge, 2000.

——. *Good and Evil: An Absolute Conception.* Second edition. New York: Routledge 2004.

Garrard, Eve, and Geoffrey Scarre, eds, *Moral Philosophy and the Holocaust.* Burlington, VT: Ashgate Publishing Company, 2003.

Gellately, Robert, and Ben Kiernan, eds, *The Spectre of Genocide: Mass Murder in Historical Perspective.* Cambridge: Cambridge University Press, 2003.

Geras, Norman. *The Contract of Mutual Indifference: Political Philosophy after the Holocaust.* London: Verso, 1998.

Glover, Jonathan. *Humanity: A Moral History of the Twentieth Century.* New Haven, CT: Yale University Press, 2000.

Golomb, Jacob, and Robert Wistrich, *Nietzsche, Godfather of Fascism?* Princeton, NJ: Princeton University Press, 2002.

Gossett, Thomas F. *Race: The History of an Idea in America.* New York: Oxford University Press, 1997.

Gottlieb, Roger S. *Liberating Faith: Religious Voices for Justice, Peace, and Ecological Wisdom.* Lanham, MD: Rowman and Littlefield, 2003.

——., ed., *Thinking the Unthinkable: Meanings of the Holocaust.* Totowa, NJ: Paulist Press, 1990.

Gould, Stephen Jay. *The Mismeasure of Man.* New York: W. W. Norton, 1996.

Gourevitch, Philip. *We wish to inform you that tomorrow we will be killed with our families.* New York: Farrar, Straus and Giroux, 1998.

Grob, Leonard, and Haim Gordon, eds, *Education for Peace: Testimonies from World Religions.* Maryknoll, NY: Orbis Books, 1987.

Grossman, Dave. *On Killing: The Psychological Cost of Learning to Kill in War and Society.* New York: Little, Brown, 1996.

Gutman, Roy, and David Rieff, eds, *Crimes of War: What the Public Should Know.* W. W. Norton, 1999.

Gurr, Ted Robert. *Peoples Versus States: Minorities at Risk in the New Century.* Washington, DC: United States Institute of Peace, 2000.

Hallie, Philip. *In the Eye of the Hurricane: Tales of Good and Evil, Help and Harm.* Middletown, CT: Wesleyan University Press, 2001.

Hayden, Patrick, ed., *The Philosophy of Human Rights.* St. Paul, MN: Paragon House, 2001.

Hayner, Priscilla B. *Unspeakable Truths: Facing the Challenge of Truth Commissions.* New York: Routledge, 2002.

Heidenrich, John G. *How to Prevent Genocide: A Guide for Policymakers, Scholars, and the Concerned Citizen.* Westport, CT: Praeger, 2001.

Held, David. *Democracy and the Global Order: From the Modern State to Cosmopolitan Governance.* Stanford, CA: Stanford University Press, 1995.

Hilberg, Raul. *The Destruction of the European Jews.* 3 vols, revised edition. New Haven, CT: Yale University Press, 2003.

Hirsch, Herbert. *Genocide and the Politics of Memory: Studying Death to Preserve Life.* Chapel Hill, NC: University of North Carolina Press, 1995.

Hoffman, Eva. *After Such Knowledge: Memory, History, and the Legacy of the Holocaust.* New York: Public Affairs, 2004.

Horkheimer, Max, and Theodor W. Adorno. *Dialectic of Enlightenment.* Translated by John Cumming. New York: Continuum, 1999.

Janicaud, Dominique. *Powers of the Rational: Science, Technology and the Future of Thought.* Translated by Peg Birmingham and Elizabeth Birmingham. Bloomington, IN: Indiana University Press, 1994.

——. *Rationalities, Historicities.* Translated by Nina Belmonte. Atlantic Highlands, NJ: Humanities Press, 1997.

Jok, Madut Jok. *War and Slavery in Sudan.* Philadelphia, PA: University of Pennsylvania Press, 2001.

Jones, Charles. *Global Justice: Defending Cosmopolitanism.* Oxford: Oxford University Press, 1999.

Jones, David H. *Moral Responsibility in the Holocaust: A Study in the Ethics of Character.* Lanham, MD: Rowman and Littlefield, 1999.

Kaldor, Mary. *New and Old Wars: Organized Violence in a Global Era.* Cambridge: Polity, 1999.

Kant, Immanuel. *Critique of Practical Reason.* Translated and edited by Mary Gregor. Cambridge: Cambridge University Press, 1997.

——. "Perpetual Peace." In *Political Writings.* Edited by Hans Reiss. Cambridge: Cambridge University Press, 1991.

——. *Religion within the Boundaries of Mere Reason.* Translated by George di Giovanni. In *Religion and Rational Theology: Immanuel Kant.* Edited by Allen Wood and George di Giovanni. Cambridge: Cambridge University Press, 1996.

Katz, Steven. *The Holocaust in Historical Context.* New York: Oxford University Press, 1994.

Kekes, John. *Facing Evil.* Princeton, NJ: Princeton University Press, 1990.

Kirchheimer, Otto. *Political Justice: The Use of Legal Procedure for Political Ends.* Westport, CT: Greenwood Press, 1980.

Kuntz, Dieter, ed., *Deadly Medicine: Creating the Master Race.* Washington, DC: United States Holocaust Memorial Museum, 2004.

Kuper, Leo. *Genocide: Its Political Use in the Twentieth Century.* New Haven, CT: Yale University Press, 1982.

——. *The Prevention of Genocide.* New Haven, CT: Yale University Press, 1985.

Lang, Berel. *Act and Idea in the Nazi Genocide.* Syracuse, NY: Syracuse University Press, 2003.

——. *Post-Holocaust: Interpretations, Misinterpretations, and the Claims of History.* Bloomington, IN: Indiana University Press, 2005.

Lanzmann, Claude. *Shoah: An Oral History of the Holocaust.* New York: Pantheon, 1985.

Lara, Maria Pia, ed., *Rethinking Evil.* Berkeley, CA: University of California Press, 2001.

Lee, Sander, ed., *Inquiries into Values.* Lewiston, NY: Mellen, 1988.

Lemkin, Raphael. *Axis Rule in Occupied Europe.* Washington, DC: Carnegie Endowment for International Peace, 1944.

Levi, Neil, and Michael Rothberg, eds, *The Holocaust: Theoretical Readings.* New Brunswick, NJ: Rutgers University Press, 2003.

Levi, Primo. *The Drowned and the Saved.* Translated by Raymond Rosenthal. New York: Vintage, 1989.

——. *Survival in Auschwitz: The Nazi Assault on Humanity.* Translated by Stuart Woolf. New York: Touchstone Books, 1996.

Levin, Roger. *The Origin of Modern Humans.* New York: Scientific American Library, 1993.

Levinas, Emmanuel. *Entre Nous: On Thinking of the Other.* Translated by Michael Smith and Barbara Harshav. New York: Columbia University Press, 1998.

——. *Existence and Existents.* Translated by Alphonso Lingis. The Hague: Martinus Nijhoff, 1978.

Levinas, Emmanuel. *Otherwise Than Being and Beyond Essence*. Translated by Alphonso Lingis. The Hague: Martinus Nijhoff, 1981.

———. *Totality and Infinity*. Translated by Alphonso Lingis. Pittsburgh: Duquesne University Press, 1969.

Lifton, Robert J. *The Nazi Doctors: Medical Killing and the Psychology of Genocide*. New York: Basic Books, 1986.

Lifton, Robert J., and Eric Markusen. *The Genocidal Mentality: Nazi Holocaust and Nuclear Threat*. New York: Basic Books, 1990.

Mack, Michael. *German Idealism and the Jew: The Inner Anti-Semitism of Philosophy and German Jewish Responses*. Chicago, IL: University of Chicago Press, 2003.

Mamdani, Mahmood. *When Victims Become Killers: Colonialism, Nativism, and the Genocide in Rwanda*. Princeton, NJ: Princeton University Press, 2000.

Margalit, Avishai. *The Ethics of Memory*. Cambridge: Harvard University Press, 2002.

Melvern, Linda. *Conspiracy to Murder: Planning the Rwanda Genocide*. London: Verso, 2004.

———. *A People Betrayed: The Role of the West in Rwanda's Genocide*. London: Zed, 2000.

Midgley, Mary. *Wickedness: A Philosophical Essay*. New York: Routledge, 1992.

Minow, Martha. *Between Vengeance and Forgiveness: Facing History after Genocide and Mass Violence*. Boston, MA: Beacon Press, 1998.

Mineau, André. *The Making of the Holocaust: Ideology and Ethics in the Systems Perspective*. Amsterdam: Rodopi, 1999.

Moellendorf, Darrel. *Cosmopolitan Justice*. Boulder, CO: Westview Press, 2002

Morgan, Michael. *Beyond Auschwitz: Post-Holocaust Jewish Thought in America*. New York: Oxford University Press, 2001.

Morgan, Michael L., ed., *A Holocaust Reader: Responses to the Nazi Extermination*. New York: Oxford University Press, 2001.

———. *The Jewish Thought of Emil Fackenheim: A Reader*. Detroit, MI: Wayne State University Press, 1987.

Naimark, Norman. *Fires of Hatred: Ethnic Cleansing in Twentieth Century Europe*. Cambridge: Harvard University Press, 2001.

Neiman, Susan. *Evil in Modern Thought: An Alternative History of Philosophy*. Princeton, NJ: Princeton University Press, 2002.

Nickel, James W. *Making Sense of Human Rights: Philosophical Reflections on the Universal Declaration of Human Rights*. Berkeley, CA: University of California Press, 1987.

Noddings, Nel. *Women and Evil*. Berkeley, CA: University of California Press, 1989.

Nussbaum, Martha C. *Hiding from Humanity: Disgust, Shame, and the Law*. Princeton, NJ: Princeton University Press, 2004.

Oliner, Samuel P., and Pearl M. Oliner. *The Altruistic Personality: Rescuers of Jews in Nazi Germany*. New York: The Free Press, 1988.

Paris, Erna. *Long Shadows: Truth, Lies and History*. New York and London: Bloomsbury Publishing, 2001.

Patterson, David. *Along the Edge of Annihilation: The Collapse and Recovery of Life in the Holocaust Diary*. Seattle, WA: University of Washington Press, 1999.

Patterson, David, and John K. Roth, eds, *After-Words: Post-Holocaust Struggles with Forgiveness, Reconciliation, Justice*. Seattle, WA: University of Washington Press, 2004.

Patterson, Orlando. *Slavery and Social Death*. Cambridge: Harvard University Press, 1982.

Peperzak, Adriaan T., Simon Critchley, and Robert Bernasconi, eds, *Emmanuel Levinas: Basic Philosophical Writings*. Bloomington, IN: Indiana University Press, 1996.

Phillips, D. Z. *Interventions in Ethics*. Albany, NY: State University of New York Press, 1992.

——. *Philosophy's Cool Place*. Ithaca, NY: Cornell University Press, 1999.

Pogge, Thomas. *World Poverty and Human Rights*. Cambridge: Polity Press, 2002.

Power, Samantha. *"A Problem from Hell": America and the Age of Genocide*. New York: Basic Books, 2002.

Prunier, Gérard. *The Rwanda Crisis, 1959–1994: History of Genocide*. New York: Columbia University Press, 1997.

Ratner, Steven S. and Jason S. Abrams. *Accountability for Human Rights Atrocities in International Law: Beyond the Nuremburg Legacy*. Second edition. Oxford: Oxford University Press, 2001.

Rawls, John. *A Theory of Justice*. Revised edition. Cambridge: Harvard University Press, 1999.

Riemer, Neal, ed., *Protection from Genocide: Mission Impossible?* Westport, CT: Praeger, 2000.

Rittner, Carol, John K. Roth, and James M. Smith, eds, *Will Genocide Ever End?* St. Paul, MN: Paragon House, 2002.

Rittner, Carol, John K. Roth, and Wendy Whitworth, eds, *Genocide in Rwanda: Complicity of the Churches?* St. Paul, MN: Paragon House, 2004.

Robertson, Geoffrey. *Crimes against Humanity: The Struggle for Global Justice*. London: Penguin, 2002.

Ronayne, Peter. *Never Again?: The United States and the Prevention of Genocide Since the Holocaust*. Lanham, MD: Rowman & Littlefield, 2001.

Rorty, Amelie, ed., *The Many Faces of Evil: Historical Perspectives*. New York: Routledge, 2001.

Rorty, Richard. *Contingency, Irony, Solidarity*. Cambridge: Cambridge University Press, 1989.

Rosenbaum, Alan S. *Is the Holocaust Unique? Perspectives on Comparative Genocide*. Second edition. Boulder, CO: Westview Press, 2001.

Roth, John K. *Holocaust Politics*. Louisville, KY: Westminster John Knox Press, 2001.

Roth, John K., ed., *Ethics after Auschwitz: Perspectives, Critiques, and Responses*. St. Paul, MN: Paragon House, 1999.

Roth, John K., and Michael Berenbaum, eds, *Holocaust: Religious and Philosophical Implications*. St. Paul, MN: Paragon House, 1989.

Roth, John K., and Elisabeth Maxwell, eds, *Remembering for the Future: The Holocaust in an Age of Genocide*. 3 vols. New York: Palgrave, 2001.

Roth, Michael S., and Charles G. Salas, eds, *Disturbing Remains: Memory, History, and Crisis in the Twentieth Century*. Los Angeles, CA: The Getty Research Institute, 2001.

Rothman, William. *Documentary Film Classics*. Cambridge: Cambridge University Press, 1997.

Rubenstein, Richard L. *The Cunning of History: The Holocaust and the American Future*. New York: Harper, 1987.

Rubenstein, Richard L., and John K. Roth. *Approaches to Auschwitz: The Holocaust and Its Legacy*, Second edition. Louisville, KY: Westminster John Knox Press, 2003.

Rummel, Rudolph J. *Death by Government*. New Brunswick, NJ: Transaction Publishers, 1994.

Sartre, Jean-Paul. *On Genocide*. Boston, MA: Beacon Press, 1968.

Schabas, William. *Genocide in International Law: The Crime of Crimes*. Cambridge: Cambridge University Press, 2000.

Shapiro, Ian, and Lea Brilmayer, eds, *Global Justice*. New York: New York University Press, 1999.

Shelton, Dinah L., ed., *The Encyclopedia of Genocide and Crimes against Humanity*. Detroit, MI: Macmillan Reference, 2004.

Shue, Henry. *Basic Rights*. Second edition. Princeton, NJ: Princeton University Press, 1996.

Sluga, Hans. *Heidegger's Crisis: Philosophy and Politics in Nazi Germany*. Cambridge: Harvard University Press, 1993.

Smith, Roger W., ed., *Genocide: Essays Toward Understanding, Early-Warning, and Prevention*. Williamsburg, Virginia: Association of Genocide Scholars, 1999.

Simon, Thomas W. *Democracy and Social Injustice*. Lanham, MD: Rowman and Littlefield, 1995.

Sontag, Frederick. *The God of Evil: An Argument from the Existence of the Devil*. New York: Harper and Row, 1970.

Stannard, David. *American Holocaust: The Conquest of the New World*. New York: Oxford University Press, 1992.

Staub, Ervin. *The Psychology of Good and Evil: Why Children, Adults, and Groups Help and Harm Others*. Cambridge: Cambridge University Press, 2003.

——. *The Roots of Evil: The Origins of Genocide and Other Group Violence*. Cambridge: Cambridge University Press, 1989.

Steiner, George. *Language and Silence: Essays on Language, Literature, and the Inhuman*. New York: Atheneum, 1967.

Tatz, Colin. *With Intent to Destroy: Reflecting on Genocide*. London: Verso, 2003.

Taylor, Gabriele. *Pride, Shame, and Guilt*. Oxford: Oxford University Press, 1985.

Thomas, Laurence M. *Vessels of Evil: American Slavery and the Holocaust*. Philadelphia, PA: Temple University Press, 1993.

Totten, Samuel, William S. Parsons, and Israel W. Charny, eds, *Century of Genocide: Critical Essays and Eyewitness Accounts*. Second edition. New York: Routledge, 2004.

Totten, Samuel, and Steven Jacobs, eds, *Pioneers of Genocide Studies*. New Brunswick, NJ: Transaction Publishers, 2002.

Tuck, Richard. *Natural Rights Theory*. Cambridge: Cambridge University Press, 1976.

Valentino, Benjamin A. *Final Solutions: Mass Killing and Genocide in the Twentieth Century*. Ithaca, NY: Cornell University Press, 2004.

Waller, James. *Becoming Evil: How Ordinary People Commit Genocide and Mass Murder*. New York: Oxford University Press, 2002.

Walliman, Isidor, and Michael N. Dobkowski, eds, *Genocide and the Modern Age: Etiology and Case Studies of Mass Death*. New York: Greenwood Press, 1987.

Watson, James R. *Between Auschwitz and Tradition: Postmodern Reflections on the Task of Thinking*. Amsterdam: Rodopi, 1994.

Weikart, Richard. *From Darwin to Hitler: Evolutionary Ethics, Eugenics, and Racism in Germany*. New York: Palgrave Macmillan, 2004.

Weitz, Eric C. *A Century of Genocide: Utopias of Race and Nation*. Princeton, NJ: Princeton University Press, 2003.

Wheeler, Nicholas. *Saving Strangers: Humanitarian Intervention in International Society*. Oxford: Oxford University Press, 2000.

Wiesel, Elie. *A Jew Today*. Translated by Marion Wiesel. New York: Vintage, 1979.

Williams, Bernard. *Shame and Necessity*. Berkeley, CA: University of California Press, 1993.

Woodruff, Paul, and Harry A. Wilmer, eds, *Facing Evil: Confronting the Dreadful Power behind Genocide, Terrorism, and Cruelty*. Chicago, IL: Open Court, 1988.

Wyschogrod, Edith. *An Ethics of Remembering: History, Heterology and the Nameless Others*. Chicago, IL: University of Chicago Press, 1998.

——. *Spirit in Ashes: Hegel, Heidegger, and Man-Made Mass Death*. New Haven, CT: Yale University Press, 1985.

Index